Indigenous Archaeologies

ARCHAEOLOGY AND INDIGENOUS PEOPLES SERIES

Sponsored by the World Archaeological Congress

Books in this series:

Kennewick Man: Perspectives on the Ancient One, Heather Burke, Claire Smith, Dorothy Lippert, Joe Watkins, and Larry Zimmerman, editors

Indigenous Archaeologies: A Reader on Decolonization, Margaret M. Bruchac, Siobhan M. Hart, and H. Martin Wobst, editors

Being and Becoming Indigenous Archaeologists, George Nicholas, editor

Indigenous Archaeologies

A Reader on Decolonization

Editors

Margaret M. Bruchac, Siobhan M. Hart,
and H. Martin Wobst

Routledge
Taylor & Francis Group
LONDON AND NEW YORK

First published 2010 by Left Coast Press, Inc.

Published 2016 by Routledge
2 Park Square, Milton Park, Abingdon, Oxon OX14 4RN
711 Third Avenue, New York, NY 10017, USA

Routledge is an imprint of the Taylor & Francis Group, an informa business

Library of Congress Cataloging-in-Publication Data:
Indigenous archaeologies: a reader on decolonization / Margaret M. Bruchac, Siobhan M. Hart, H. Martin Wobst, editors.
p. cm—(Archaeology and indigenous peoples series; v. 2)
Includes bibliographical references.
ISBN 978-1-59874-372-2 (hardcover: alk. paper)—ISBN 978-1-59874-373-9 (pbk.: alk. paper)
1. Ethnoarchaeology. 2. Social archaeology. 3. Indigenous peoples—Material culture. 4. Decolonization. I. Bruchac, Margaret M. II. Hart, Siobhan M. III. Wobst, Hans Martin, 1943-
CC79.E85I628 2010
325.3—dc22

2010018893

ISBN 978-1-59874-372-2 hardcover
ISBN 978-1-59874-373-9 paperback

CONTENTS

PREFACE

Decolonizing Disciplines and Indigenizing Archaeologies

Indigenous peoples the world over—Australian Aboriginals, Native Americans, Canadian First Nations, Pacific Islanders, and many others—have a vested interest in the material remains of the past and in the intellectual construction and mapping of their cultures, identities, and territorial relations based on those remains. Over the last few decades, the world's Indigenous populations have become increasingly engaged in the theory and practice of archaeology, and increasingly vocal about issues of sovereignty and cultural patrimony, as part of a concerted effort to gain control over archaeological and political uses of their pasts. Archaeologists, in turn, have become increasingly aware that their practice must concern itself with more than just past things, since past things are integral to Indigenous ancestral relations and are meaningful to Indigenous peoples today.

Colonialist, imperialist, and ethnocentric theories and methods—long central to the interpretation of archaeological remains—are often ill-suited to interpreting the different materialities of precapitalist and contemporary Indigenous societies. Many of these theories emerged from colonial encounters that have had far-reaching global effects. The power relations at play in archaeological research are not always visible and are rarely in balance with Indigenous concerns. Archeological theories grounded in colonial relations can have real-world implications that continue to affect the sovereignty and human rights of contemporary Indigenous populations.

At the intersection of points of conflict and cooperation, a new multi-dimensional field has emerged, under the rubric of "Indigenous Archaeologies." Around the world, Indigenous peoples and archaeological practitioners are working to devise less colonial, more culturally sensitive methods to redress historical wrongs and reorient with Indigenous values. Many Indigenous people are themselves archaeologists. The perspectives of these multivocal, multinational, transcultural participants make this field particularly useful for thinking about the many and important social articulations of archaeology in the present.

We recognize that these categories and boundaries are artificial. There is no single body of Indigenous people, nor is there a unified voice among archaeologists. Each encompasses, embodies, and is situated in a nest of social relations that shapes their actions and reactions in the practice of archaeology. By exposing the international complexities of these relations, we hope to make visible the potential for collaboration and shared power in interpreting, constructing, and interacting with the past.

In this reader, we have attempted to capture the major dimensions of Indigenous Archaeologies: decolonizing methodologies; archaeology as social practice and lived experiences; political dimensions of cultural heritage; intersections among archaeological theories and Indigenous histories; different ways of knowing the past; and complications among local and global concerns. We bring these issues into sharper focus by sampling recent scholarship and discourse shaped by unique local and global geographies and histories.

This book is designed to be used as a stand-alone volume introducing the topic of Indigenous Archaeologies for Indigenous or non-Indigenous readers, in academic or non-academic settings. The reader comprises ten topically and geographically organized sections, appropriate for adoption in a semester length course. Most selections are excerpts from longer works chosen to illustrate the wide range of relevant topics and perspectives, and interested readers are encouraged to consult the original publications. In excerpting and reproducing previously published material, we maintained original spellings, accents, and text emphasis. References to figures not reproduced here were removed, and in most cases, footnotes were removed, unless they referred to references, in which case they were incorporated into the text. In-text citations and references were reformatted using a consistent style.

The first three sections introduce the concept of Indigenous Archaeologies, exploring the complex notion of "Indigeneity" and the historical, philosophical, and intellectual foundations of decolonizing practice. The six sections that follow cover the world, region by region, offering case studies and reflections by Indigenous and non-Indigenous practitioners on the particular challenges, conditions, and transformations that have shaped, and continue to influence, the practice of Indigenous Archaeologies in that region. The concluding section offers thoughts on future directions of this emerging field. The comprehensive reference list, compiled from the sources referenced in each excerpt, provides a valuable resource for further reading and research.

Drawing on our own experiences from a collegial partnership that straddles both sides of the Indigenous/non-Indigenous divide, we believe that the field of Indigenous Archaeologies holds the potential for radically transforming the practice of archaeology. This reader captures a snapshot of recent successes resulting from crosscultural and crossdisciplinary partnerships. Future challenges and unanticipated discoveries await. A far more complex mix of empirical science, traditional knowledge, material analysis, ethnographic study, and creative innovation will result from intentional cooperation and collaboration with Indigenous peoples. This shared production of knowledge will expand the depth of information to be gained from exploring the past, even as it complicates and humanizes our relations in the present.

Margaret M. Bruchac
Siobhan M. Hart
H. Martin Wobst
June 2010

Acknowledgments

Margaret M. Bruchac:
This work is dedicated to my present-day Indigenous and non-Indigenous colleagues, who are so committed to decolonizing the field, to the upcoming generations of Indigenous archaeologists whom we hope to inspire by example, and to the ancestors who came before and to their collective wisdom (including lessons we have not yet learned). I offer particular thanks to my supportive muses Grey and Mkazitok, and to my dear husband Justin. And to all of my Abenaki relatives, *mziwi negwet kamigweso ngonniak*.

Siobhan M. Hart:
This volume is the outcome of many collaborations and relationships among archaeologists and non-archaeologists, Indigenous and non-Indigenous. Much of it has been made possible through the hard work of others, so we offer gratitude to the authors and copyright holders who have granted permission to reproduce their work in this volume and who are, more importantly, reshaping archaeology to serve social justice. We owe Mitch Allen of Left Coast Press thanks for his enthusiasm, support, and patience as this volume developed. Sincere thanks go to Tony Shaw for assistance with transcriptions and bibliographic references and so much more.

H. Martin Wobst:
I would like to thank Marge, Siobhan, and Mitch for their virtually infinite patience and hard work that saw this book finally into print. The idea for it originated with Claire Smith and other Closet Chickens, during one of those intense one-day driving seminars across settler societies. I was excited about it then but am even more so now that the edifice has finally been erected. I want to give thanks to Jude and Kutya, who saw less of me than they or I would have liked while I was at work on the manuscript. This chapter is dedicated to the many Indigenous populations today whose human rights are being trampled on daily. We would like this book and its readers to help stop their suffering!

SECTION I

Decolonizing Globally

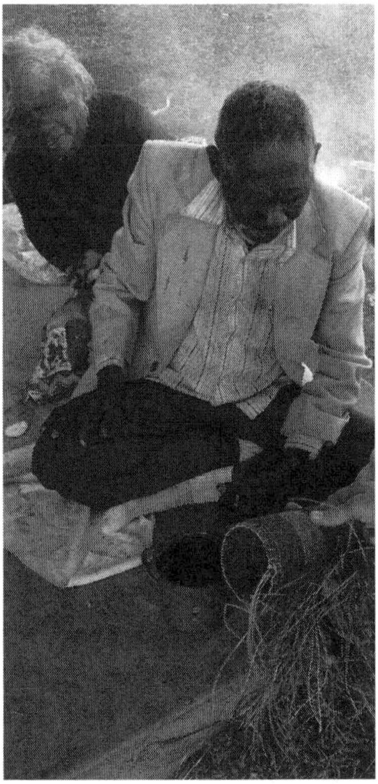

Glen Wesan and Jimmy Wesan, looking at a dabu basket made by Bulainjan, in Beswick community, Northern Territory, Australia (photograph courtesy of H. Martin Wobst)

1

Indigenous Archaeologies: A Worldwide Perspective on Human Materialities and Human Rights

H. Martin Wobst

Archaeology and Materiality

Virtually all aspects of the physical world that humans interact with have been materially affected by human action. There are, of course, the obvious human artifacts (the houses, fields, clothes, hammers, pots, computers, guns, and the like). But there are also more indirect material effects, such as the prevalence, distribution, and extinction histories of animal and plant species, and the levels of pollutants, flood frequencies, and erosion speeds. Human material effects are the domain of archaeologists, in their roles as the social scientists that look at human behavior through the lens of artifacts and other material effects, past and present. Since few other social scientists are working with such data, there is no good reason why archaeologists should confine their study to the past (as they usually have done), particularly since many societies today are so crassly materialist. There needs to be a science that keeps the sum total of human material interactions, past and present, in its (and our) field of vision, and archaeology fills that niche (Holtorf and Piccini 2009; Shanks 2009; Wobst 1983, 2006).

Archaeologists have demonstrated that human material effects on people and on their material surroundings have varied and changed tremendously since human beginnings. Archaeological theory has been evolving to keep up with this increase in archaeological knowledge (for example, Bentley, Maschner, and Chippindale 2008), and archaeological methods have been improving in reliability and precision (compare Brothwell and Higgs 1963 with Maschner and Chippindale 2005). Nevertheless, when it comes to assessing, describing, and explaining the diversity and range of variation in human relations with artifacts, we are only barely scratching the surface. Such knowledge is vital for developing a body of theory for HUMAN material culture in all times and places (rather than for how it works today, at the centers of the industrialized world). Such theory, in turn, is vital if we hope to gain social control over some of the trajectories of change in our present material effects on this world, since they are beginning to threaten our very survival (Parry et al. 2007).

How then can we broaden our understanding of how artifacts and humans relate to each other? This chapter explores this question, with particular attention to "Indigenous Archaeologies." I present my answers in separate lines, twines, or strands. I do this while realizing full well that all these individual strands of human materiality, the human cultural ways of interacting with artifacts, form a weave that is nearly inseparably intertwined with artifacts and the environments they inhabit. Archaeologists want to describe and understand this interconnected whole; they want to understand how it changes from one end to the other, across all its many strands; they want to explain how it got to look that way, and they should be very interested in how different it will look in the future. To improve our understanding requires probing humans in their diversity and range of variation in the past and present, developing a sensitivity to the interconnected or systemic nature of humans and their materiality, and addressing detailed and specific questions about all aspects of human materiality, one question at a time.

Archaeologies—The Word

If the goal of archaeology is to study human materiality, why talk about "archaeologies"? The term is chosen here (and often used in the literature on Indigenous materialities) to make clear from the outset that different people have different ways of and logics for interacting with their material world and the human artifacts around them (cf. Shepherd 2005). Putting "archaeology" into the plural reminds us from the outset that we need to be sensitive to the different ways in which people in a given society relate to their artifacts, and we need to get a much sharper sense of how materiality varies and changes across space, time, and perceived social boundaries. Materiality, like culture, is forever in process, forever undergoing change, contested and contextual, and so, although always changing, it never really reaches any ultimate goal (Miller 2005). To convey this sense, "archaeologies" foregrounds the dynamics, the changes, and the differences and contrasts, as well as our attempts to capture them sensitively in our theories and methods. The plural form acknowledges the fact that different materialities exist around the globe and through time, and all these materialities are important building stones and points of reference toward theories of human materiality. The word also expresses our sense that none of these materialities (or different points along the ranges of variation in materiality) is inherently or essentially better or worse than any other.

Indigenous—The Word

The word "indigenous" is fraught with many meanings (see Watkins 2005: 430–32 for a broad discussion). Few of these meanings are neutral, uncontested, or problem free. For the purposes of this book, the English common sense or dictionary definition is a good point of departure: something in the direction of "having been in a given locality for a long time" or "being (the) home-grown." That is, the word implies a contrast between old-timers and newcomers, and between what is embedded in a locality and what is from elsewhere—in other words, a contrast in time (having been vs. new) and space (here and elsewhere). If we want to expand our sense of how humans vary, such contrasts are a good start, because they remind us that the world is more varied than we (or our archaeological predecessors) thought and that we can learn something from this contrast, about the newcomers, about the old-timers, or about humans in general.

At the same time, though, "indigenous" is a relative term, invoked when there are newcomers in the picture. The same "indigenous" people who obviously differ from recent newcomers may themselves have been newcomers there at some point in the past. History keeps transforming newcomers into indigenous people. For example, when Germans colonized the areas to their east some 800 years ago, they were newcomers there (Higounet 1986). Those same Germans, 800 years later, considered themselves indigenous, compared to the eastern European "newcomers" who were settled on their lands after the end of World War II (de Zayas 2006). Native Americans understand themselves to be the indigenous inhabitants of North America, despite the on-going debate among European newcomers about when, precisely, the aboriginals arrived (see, for example, Burke et al. 2008; Thomas 2000). Thus, one's "indigenousness" is not absolute, but variable, and its characteristics are defined relative to encounters with people newer to a place. Indigeneity is an inextricable element of relationship to the land, particularly when power and politics require one to identify as resident or newcomer, indigenous or other.

"Indigenous People" with a Capital I

There are lots of different circumstances that expose old-timers to newcomers, and people indigenous to a place to people from elsewhere. Most of the "Indigenous People" at the focus of this book have suffered from Western colonialism. Colonialism generated, and lived off, massive contrasts between the colonizer (newcomer) and the colonized (old-timer) and between state citizens (often colonizing far outside their own nation-state) and the colonized people (often far away from the state that colonized them). Under the circumstances, the distance alone between the accustomed home turfs of colonizer and colonized would make for massive and easily observable difference, not to speak of the tremendous contrasts in power that colonialism itself generated and helped to amplify.

The very process of colonialism was underwritten by the assumption of massive difference between colonizer and colonized. "Scientists" then assigned this difference to two opposed points in time (colonizer—present and future; person to be colonized—the past), thus empowering the colonizer to colonize in the interest of the future (Fabian 1983; Wobst 1991).

Colonialism is one of many examples in which observed difference is used to essentialize "the Other" (Wobst and Smith 2003); Others are bestowed with or assumed to possess "natural," "innate," or "essential" characteristics exemplified by their difference from those of the observer and are also assumed to share these characteristics with the members of their group (without any of these assumptions having been demonstrated by actual observations). Many of these characteristics are then taken to be of distinctly lower value than the colonizer's own cultural repertoire. In this way, colonizer and colonized are logically separated by an unbridgeable gap, before they have the opportunity to establish normal social relations, and the process of colonialism is empowered (Memmi 1967, 71; Wolf 1982).

By focusing on the materiality of Indigenous* populations in this volume, we do not intend to construct Indigenous people as humanly different from the people who became their colonizers. Many of the initial encounters between Indigenous populations and their colonizers were rendered disastrous by instances when the power and the difference between Indigenous and newcomer were extreme. The history

---

* In the following text, the term *Indigenous* is spelled with an initial cap, to stress the agency, sovereignty, and right to self-determination and respect of their human rights equivalent to that of nations, ethnic groups, and other named political entities.

of colonialism should put into sharper contrast what can be learned from better understanding of the Indigenous side in interpreting human materiality, wherever that may be, whether the encounter is with colonizers or with other Others.

Such encounters, however, do not reflect or create a worldwide class of people with natural characteristics essentially different from those of any other class of humans. Colonized Indigenous populations are highly varied and diverse. The extreme case of the Indigenous encounter seamlessly grades into contacts between Indigenous populations and state administrators, ethnic groups and nation-states, and descendant populations and other stakeholders, vis-à-vis their rights, archaeological remains, and heritage. In many of these arenas, for many Indigenous populations, the colonial encounter has never ended.

Are Indigenous Populations Non-White?

When people talk about Indigenous populations and their archaeologies, they often talk about populations that are racialized as non-white. This has led some anthropologists and theorists to suspect that "Indigenous Archaeologies" are just an attempt to shore up, with the help of cultural attributes, what may be considered a racialized classification (cf., Echo-Hawk and Zimmerman 2006). This is not our take here. Although colonialism is deeply implicated in the origins and history of racism and racializing, it was practiced on all the world's continents and applied to all the world's stereotypic races, including Europeans. For example, the Irish were once considered to be a separate human race, and the British colonization of Ireland went on before and at the same time as the European colonization of the Americas (Allen 1997; see, for example, Delle 1999 and Smith 1998). The populations in the throes of colonialism share their characteristics as *a result of colonialism*, not as a result of their indigeneity! Every colonized population, in counter-posing old-timers with newcomers, was inherently culturally different from the colonizers. The differences that were characteristic of each context, each history, and each place of colonial encounter made visible different cultural contrasts. The sum total of these differences does not plot onto "us" (white) versus "them" (non-white), but onto the human behavioral range and variation.

Indigenous Archaeologies and Power

In colonial contexts it is easy to fathom who is writing history (and archaeology) for whom. Colonizers, in control and to shore up that control, foreground their own materiality and background that of the colonized, if they don't make it completely invisible. The history and the archaeology of the colonized are engaged to aggrandize the colonizer's modernity and to document the lack thereof among the colonized, to highlight colonial competence against colonized incompetence. In that way, the encountered materiality that would have been superb for broadening our sense of the width and breadth of modern human materiality instead is redirected: It is turned into a tool to retroactively justify colonization, to eradicate Indigenous materiality as a logical alternative to the colonizers' materiality, and to make its most obvious material remains disappear before they could even be considered (Wobst 2005).

Indigenous Archaeologies go the other way. Rather than aiming to aggrandize the colonizers and devalue the colonized, they probe the Indigenous material record, past and/or present, to understand the materiality of particular places, to understand it in terms of the old-timers there, and to learn what that materiality may add to our knowledge of human materiality in general. In highlighting Indigenous materialities, both similarities and differences encountered in cultural contact situations are treasured: They give voice to the previously colonized, they make it easier for others to understand that given place and time, and they broaden our sense of the vitality of the human species in general, in all its diversity and variation.

Indigenous Archaeologies as Decolonization

If one were to plot the places of residence of all people who call themselves archaeologists on a world map, that map would show extreme clusters. Most of the clusters would represent the original colonizing powers and their outliers, and/or the centers of nation-states and imperial powers. It is these experts who have interpreted the materiality of everybody else. Not surprisingly, the literature on "Others" is pervaded with the biases of the colonizers or of the administrators of nation-states. A very important function that Indigenous Archaeologies fulfill is to make archaeologists and others aware of this bias and thereby to encourage them to replace obviously biased representations with accounts that more sensitively report what is there and how it got to be that way, rather than filtering one's observations through the colonizers'/administrators' lens. This is a decolonizing process that, in many areas of the world, has only barely begun (Smith and Wobst 2005a).

Much of the financial benefit of archaeology presently ends up in archaeologists' salaries, and in the infrastructure of the institutions located in the centers of the former colonial powers and present nation-states, and much archaeology is regulated or mandated by nation-state administrators. Since only a very few archaeologists today are members of Indigenous groups, decolonization also needs to include training more Indigenous people to become archaeologists, and to see them placed into positions where they can shape interpretations of Indigenous materiality. In parallel, Indigenous populations need to be empowered to develop an ever more pervasive institutional infrastructure, so that they can directly engage in and benefit from the administration, stewardship, analysis, and presentation of their archaeological and historical heritage. This requires reallocation of resources in their direction and redistribution of power away from the former colonial powers and/or present administrative centers (see, for example, Smith and Jackson 2006, excerpted in Chapter 14 this volume).

In an ideal world, there would be at least as many members of Indigenous societies who work as archaeologists and stewards of their archaeological record as there are others, and the majority of the material heritage unearthed already would be in what the Indigenous custodians considered to be appropriate museums and repositories in, or as close as possible to, their traditional homelands. On a worldwide basis, progress in this direction has been glacial. There are still vastly too few archaeologists of Indigenous heritage (see, for example, Nicholas 2010), and most Indigenous polities lack the resources to underwrite any sort of archaeological infrastructure. Overcoming this imbalance requires proactive measures in the field of archaeology, such as, among others, in scholarship programs for members of underrepresented groups, salary support for Indigenous archaeological practitioners, subvention for publication curation and safeguarding, and pro bono work by non-group members of other populations as needed (see Smith 1999 for methods of decolonizing science, excerpted in Chapter 5 this volume).

Indigenous Archaeologies—The Social Dimension

In many parts of the industrialized world, archaeology is the most popular social science. People read about it in their spare time, they flock to institutions that house archaeological remains or that re-enact the past, and many movies about archaeology have become blockbusters (Holtorf and Drew 2007). In contrast, for many Indigenous populations, the past is known and understood and thus is not a source of great interest in the same way. Archaeology virtually never is part of their traditional cultural practice. Indigenous people are exposed to archaeology when outsiders, often as part of the colonizer or state, interact with archaeological remains on their territory and remove them from there, often seriously violating Indigenous cultural sensitivities and leaving site destruction and material loss in their wake.

That kind of interaction is of virtually no benefit to Indigenous populations. The archaeologists remain fully encapsulated in their world, and the Indigenous population, if anything, becomes more alienated from its heritage (because the outsiders who run archaeology give little to the community and take with them what they unearth). Archaeological fieldwork uncovers Indigenous remains that often are laden with deep cultural meaning. Excavation may interrupt or terminate the culturally understood pathway of who and what is unearthed, violate cultural prohibitions and taboos against interacting with them, de-sanctify their sacredness, and devalue the context and the cultural practices associated with them. The very thought of having to excavate something to assure its safekeeping is foreign to most Indigenous populations.

Archaeologists need to realize that in most populations, but particularly in many Indigenous populations, artifacts (including those of the past) are deeply culturally and socially embedded. To do any kind of archaeological fieldwork, thus, requires a fine-grained understanding of the social dynamics of artifacts in the society where one wants to do archaeology. Access to these artifacts requires a framework of negotiation according to the cultural protocols of the society, the establishment of long-term social relations, and the gradual development of shared research goals and benefits for archaeologists and Indigenous people (see, for example, Castañeda and Matthews 2008; Silliman 2008). Given the many problems that Indigenous people face, including habitat destruction, poverty and expropriation, and high rates of infant mortality, suicide, alcoholism, and disease, the rank-order of goals among archaeologists and Indigenous people is bound to be quite different. Archaeologists are well advised that the narrower their definition of archaeology, the harder it will be to generate sympathetic feelings and support for their project. The ultimate goal needs to be to maximize the benefit to the host society, and the ultimate arbiter of the benefits that result from these negotiations should be the Indigenous group, considering its long-term interests.

To realize those goals will require archaeologists to significantly enlarge the box that housed their definition of archaeology. A number of new approaches have been developed to define such a broader archaeological practice including, but not limited to, "community archaeology," "archaeology as participatory action," and "archaeology as community service learning." These dimensions of practice have been developed by archaeologists working with and informed by both Indigenous and non-Indigenous communities. There is lots of room for archaeologists to move in new directions, even in the areas of the world where these approaches were first pioneered.

Archaeology and Human Rights

Given massive cultural differences and huge power differentials, Indigenous populations have been at the receiving end of egregious human rights violations, on all continents, since the very beginning of archaeology and the emergence of research interest in the Other. Often working against explicit vetoes, treasure hunters and professional archaeologists have ransacked treasured material belongings and remains from the past, at the expense of the Indigenous. Their sacred material patrimony is traded to the highest bidders, and their sacred sites are violated. Their bodies are removed from their homeland and pickled for museum display and storage, and their relatives are unearthed from their places of burial to end up on storage shelves in museums, as show and tell in college labs, or for scaring children at Halloween. Sacred images from the past even turn up on T-shirts in souvenir shops. In the United States, such abuse was still common well into the twentieth century.

Rising Indigenous resistance, decolonization, international pressures, and the development of professional ethics for archeologists all have contributed to increasing respect for the human rights of Indigenous people, including rights relating to their heritage, culture, archaeological record, and materiality. In many countries, laws have been passed to make it easier for Indigenous populations to defend themselves against onslaughts of inhumane treatment, to remedy past wrongs, and to retrieve what had been illegally removed. Thus, in the United States, the Native American Graves Protection and Repatriation Act (NAGPRA 1990) and the American Indian Religious Freedom Act (AIRFA 1978) acknowledged some basic Indigenous human rights for federally recognized Native American communities. Yet even where the archaeologists themselves think that they are now doing passably well by the standards of Indigenous populations, the on-the-ground experience of Indigenous people still contrasts markedly with this assessment. And in many parts of the world, Indigenous human rights are still routinely violated as a matter of state law (see, for example, Wobst 2004).

Laws might very well have been passed to defend Indigenous cultural heritage, but sometimes not in recognition of Indigenous human rights. Rather, their aim is to preserve everybody's archaeological record for the nation, or for all humans. With that kind of legal construction, Indigenous artifacts end up in national and international repositories as input for scientific analyses again, with the scientists as judges of what should be done to them, without regard to the interest of the rightful cultural custodians and with little concern for the human rights of the people who originated these artifacts. To the Indigenous person, it does not matter if it is the colonial tyrant, a vocational grave robber, or a professional archaeologist empowered by state law who violates his or her cultural patrimony. They all produce the same pain and suffering, and their actions are felt as violations of human rights. Under these circumstances, the only ethically acceptable practice for professional archaeologists (even with the state law fully behind them) is to respect the Indigenous human rights and back off.

Indigenous people tend to be the farthest removed from the centers of nation-states. Often, these areas also contain valuable natural resources and minerals that are coveted by mining and other multinational corporations. Against the onslaught of the wealthiest multinational corporations, the most well-meaning laws often have no effect. In areas such as the Canadian North, the Australian Outback, the Brazilian tropical forests, and the Argentinean Pampas, the power differential between those who want access to the Indigenous cultural patrimony and the Indigenous cultural custodians is so immense, that the Indigenous people virtually always end up losing in court (if they have enough experience and resources to defend themselves in court). Where they have no access to the court, for lack of resources, they tend to lose out to brute force.

These are not just Indigenous concerns. There is, of course, considerable violence being done to all peoples' archaeological heritage. Indigenous populations, however, because their contrast to newcomers tends to be strongest, clearly are still suffering the worst abuses. Indigenous Archaeologies thus carry out research on the relationships, sensitivities, and practices that link Indigenous populations to their cultural patrimonies, their artifacts, and other aspects of their worlds, so that newcomers can avoid causing pain and suffering. They help to publicize abuses, study the systemic conditions that led up to them, and work on eradicating their causes. They aid Indigenous peoples in their struggles to gain control over their archaeological resources and cultural patrimony, and to become strategic about their archaeological resources. They push for improvements in the human subject controls on, and ethical standards for, archaeologists. And they work on improving the laws and regulations that govern interactions with Indigenous populations and others. In the face of continuing serious human rights violations against Indigenous populations, Indigenous Archaeologies obviously need to be political and pro-active (see, for example, McGuire 2008a). This realization is in stark contrast to the archaeological self-understanding only a few generations ago, when archaeologists proclaimed that archaeology properly needed to stay completely clear of politics. Often, it was (and in many areas of the world it still is) in the name of "apolitical" science that many of the worst abuses against Indigenous populations and other descendant populations have been committed.

Indigenous Archaeologies Worldwide

The practices that link archaeologists and the materiality and cultural patrimony of human populations are very different from one place to another, and through time in a given place. This fact is brought out in sharper detail when one looks at Indigenous Archaeologies in an international or global perspective, as in this volume. In this way, practices that are clear improvements over previous ones show up in clear contrast. Such an international and comparative look at Indigenous Archaeologies underscores that there is nothing natural or ultimate about any particular human or archaeological practice and that all the practices that link Indigenous populations and archaeologists can be improved. It is for this reason that one should avoid the term "best practices" (they can too easily be mistaken for the end product and *the* cook book, instead of being simply the best among the strategies available for comparison). Even the "best" strategies are as worthy of further improvements as the others.

Each region of the world represented in this volume has its own interesting research topics, and its own serious problems, when it comes to righting previous wrongs, improving respect for Indigenous human rights, facilitating Indigenous control over Indigenous cultural resources, and adding Indigenous materialities to our sense of *human* materiality. In worldwide perspective, this volume exposes the tip of the iceberg of all the constructive activity in Indigenous Archaeologies that has been done already. At the same time, it provides a sense of the tremendous amount of work that needs yet to be done, so that archaeologists and Indigenous people may shape and convey better appreciations of the endless variety of human materiality. We hope that the readers of this volume will join us in this worldwide project!

SECTION II

Indigeneity

Who are the "Indigenous"? There is no fixed definition of populations that are identified as Indigenous, by self or others. If the practices of Indigenous Archaeologies are to help in global decolonizing efforts and learn from the material relations of Indigenous peoples, one needs a good sense of how "Indigeneity" enters into modern political, social, and scientific practices and perspectives. The United Nations has developed the following working definition of the concept of "Indigenous peoples":

> Indigenous communities, peoples and nations are those which, having a historical continuity with pre-invasion and pre-colonial societies that developed on their territories, consider themselves distinct from other sectors of the societies now prevailing on those territories, or parts of them. They form at present non-dominant sectors of society and are determined to preserve, develop and transmit to future generations their ancestral territories, and their ethnic identity, as the basis of their continued existence as peoples, in accordance with their own cultural patterns, social institutions and legal system.
>
> This historical continuity may consist of the continuation, for an extended period reaching into the present of one or more of the following factors:

a. Occupation of ancestral lands, or at least of part of them;
b. Common ancestry with the original occupants of these lands;
c. Culture in general, or in specific manifestations (such as religion, living under a tribal system, membership of an indigenous community, dress, means of livelihood, lifestyle, etc.);
d. Language (whether used as the only language, as mother-tongue, as the habitual means of communication at home or in the family, or as the main, preferred, habitual, general or normal language);
e. Residence on certain parts of the country, or in certain regions of the world;
f. Other relevant factors.

On an individual basis, an indigenous person is one who belongs to these indigenous populations through self-identification as indigenous (group consciousness) and is recognized and accepted by these populations as one of its members (acceptance by the group). This preserves for these communities the sovereign right and power to decide who belongs to them, without external interference. (United Nations Secretariat of the Permanent Forum on Indigenous Issues 2004)

Although the particulars of their historical circumstances vary widely, Indigenous peoples share common concerns regarding sovereignty, self-determination, and control over traditional lands and resources. To assist in contextualizing the archaeological theory, method, and practice in the readings that follow, this section includes three approaches to defining and circumscribing Indigeneity that aim to lay open some of the complexities of this concept and the identities it constitutes.

Ronald Niezen identifies three primary means of defining the Indigenous: legal/analytical (the "Other"), practical/strategic (self-definition), and collective (a global in-group). He grapples with political dimensions of Indigenous relations vis-à-vis the state that have been shaped by experiences of loss and resistance over time. Indigenous identities and concerns are most visible, and perhaps most effectively communicated, when Indigenous communities stand up to resist further domination and find common cause with one another against their oppressors. Niezen insists that colonial histories, full of betrayal and bloodshed, must be told before the Indigenous can fully recover their identities.

All categories that construct, define, and position cultural identities represent lived objectivities and subjectivities. Indianicity, indigeneity, and alterity emerged from the historical circumstances we now know as coloniality. Writing from a South American perspective, Alejandro Haber attacks the question by identifying "Indigenous" as a colonial configuration of cultural diversity, formed by the experiences of colonist and colonizer alike. For Haber, postcolonial Indigenous identity is abstract and separate, engaged with non-Indigenous relations. In this sense, the act of resisting colonial processes is not an Indigenous act, since "resistance" was not necessary in the era before colonialism. Haber describes precolonial Indigenous identity, in dramatic contrast, as local and familial; to be *criollo* (raised in this place) is to understand oneself and one's community as part of an intricate, relational web of being within a particular bioscape and landscape. Haber suggests that the question "who is Indigenous?"—which inspires a colonialist politics of the self—should therefore be replaced by the question "who are we?" so as to evoke and restore Indigenous senses of being.

Naming oneself as Indigenous, in the modern world, is a public act of self-representation that signals association with other Indigenous people who are, almost by definition, marginal and oppressed. Political marginalization has inspired Indigenes to craft pan-Indigenous identities that, however expedient they might be, are too easily essentialized, stereotyped, and commodified. Yin Paradies explores the racial dimensions of modern Indigenous identities as social and historical constructs. He argues that political constructions of pan-Indigeneity do not represent authentic precontact Indigeneity, nor do they fully address modern concerns. Paradies defines himself as Aboriginal-Anglo-Asian Australian, a complicated modern identity that does not easily reconcile with romantic notions of indigeneity. He notes that Indigenous groups have uneasy relations with mixed individuals, especially when group cohesion rests on the shared experience of subordination. The "protocols of Indigeneity" that position Indigenes as both racially pure and morally superior to non-Indigenes, according to Paradies, ignore the transcultural realities of postcolonial families and limit the liberating potential of self-definition.

The excerpts in this section are not intended as a comprehensive consideration of Indigenous identity. Rather, these particular definitions of Indigeneity offer a thought-provoking introduction to some of the many ways of approaching Indigenous identity. In subsequent sections of this reader, authors from around the world discuss how they view, construct, or embody distinct regional definitions of Indigeneity through the use of particular theories, methods, practices, and relationships.

2

A New Global Phenomenon?

Ronald Niezen

Who Are the "Indigenous"?

The controversy surrounding the international movement of indigenous peoples includes not just struggles over land, resources, recognition, and sovereignty but also, perhaps as a prelude to all other contests, the complex, delicate issue of defining the term "indigenous." This is becoming all the more pertinent as the term is increasingly associated with new rights and benefits (especially political power) and as the peoples claiming indigenous status emerge with greater frequency and insistence from Africa and Asia—in other words, from hemispheres that differ from the Americas in terms of the complexities of historical settlement, colonialism, and, above all, the development of various authoritarian state systems that resulted from national liberation of former European colonies in the mid- to late twentieth century. How do people from within these diverse social and historical contexts fit into a widening rubric of "indigenous peoples"?

Indigenous delegates to international meetings have often expressed the idea that a precise, legal definition of the term "indigenous" would impose standards or conditions for participation in human rights processes that would be prejudicial to their interests. For one thing, such a definition would be controlled by the very state powers that they see as the principal source of their exploitation, marginalization, and suffering. What is more, Member States of the United Nations do not follow a

---

Excerpted from Niezen, Ronald. 2003. A New Global Phenomenon? In *The Origins of Indigenism: Human Rights and the Politics of Identity*, 1–28. Berkeley and Los Angeles: University of California Press.

formal definition of the nation or the state, so a double standard would be applied to indigenous peoples if the terms that are key to their benefits of belonging were interpreted too inflexibly.

The lack of a rigorous definition of the term "indigenous" also presents a challenge to scholarly analysis. But this state of affairs is in some ways preferable: a rigorous definition, one that in effect tried to close the intellectual borders where they were still porous, would be premature and, ultimately, futile. Debates over the problem of definition are actually more interesting than any definition in and of itself. With this as our starting point, we find that there are multiple approaches to the term "indigenous," each with its own political origins and implications. The ambiguity of the term is perhaps its most significant feature.

"Indigenous peoples" have been provisionally defined in three basic ways: legally/analytically (the "other" definition), practically/strategically (the self-definition), and collectively (the global in-group definition). The analytical approach seeks to isolate those distinctive phenomena among the original inhabitants of given territories that coalesce into a global category. The exercise is frustrating because of the historical and social diversity of those who identify themselves as "indigenous." The question of definition thus has the inherent effect of pitting analysis against identity; there will inevitably be a group, seeing itself as indigenous, that is excluded from the scholarly definition, its pride assaulted, its honor tarnished, and, more to the point, its access to redress obstructed.

There are nevertheless some areas of general consensus among formal attempts at definition. The most commonly recognized features of indigenous peoples are descent from original inhabitants of a region prior to the arrival of settlers who have since become the dominant population; maintenance of cultural differences, distinct from a dominant population; and political marginality resulting in poverty, limited access to services, and absence of protections against unwanted "development." These features can be found in a seminal 1987 U.N. report by José Martínez Cobo (1987, 48):

> Indigenous communities, peoples and nations are those which, having a historical continuity with pre-invasion and pre-colonial societies that developed on their territories, consider themselves distinct from other sectors of the societies now prevailing in those territories, or parts of them. They form at present nondominant sectors of society and are determined to preserve, develop and transmit to future generations their ancestral territories and their ethnic identity, as the basis of their continued existence as peoples, in accordance with their own cultural patterns, social institutions and legal systems.

Comprehensive and durable as Martínez Cobo's definition is, it does not apply unfailingly to all situations in which people claim indigenous status and protections. It does not fit comfortably, for example, with those areas of mainland Southeast Asia in which there have been complex patterns of displacement and movements of peoples across national boundaries. Some analytical approaches to defining Indigenous peoples have attempted to take such complexities into account, principally by noting the possibility that indigenous peoples might not currently occupy their ancestral territories. According to James Anaya (1996, 3), communities and nations are considered indigenous because they have deeper attachments to the lands in which they live (or ancestral lands from which they were removed) than the more powerful sectors of society that have either settled on those same lands or benefited in other ways from their resources. The legal approach to indigenous peoples has also developed the presupposition of their coexistence with another ethnic group, dominant either within a present-day state or within the area traditionally inhabited by the indigenous people. "There must be another ethnic group and a power relationship involved before the descendants of the original inhabitants are understood as indigenous in the legal meaning of the term" (Scheinin 2000, 161).

Martínez Cobo's working definition has also been contested by some states. India, for example, has rejected its self-definitional aspect (included in the words "consider themselves") and has pressed for what I would call a "gatekeeper definition," one used to determine who can and cannot have access to U.N. meetings and the possibility they provide, however remote, of restorative justice. India has presented the view that it represents nearly one billion indigenous people (the entire population of the burgeoning nation) and that there is no need for others to present claims of indigenous ancestry that rival those of the state. This approach received support from Miguel Alfonso Martínez's (1999, para. 88) study of indigenous peoples and treaties for the United Nations: "[I]n post-colonial Africa and Asia autochthonous groups/minorities/ethnic groups/peoples who seek to exercise rights presumed to be or actually infringed by the existing autochthonous authorities in the States in which they live cannot . . . claim for themselves, unilaterally and exclusively, the 'indigenous' status in the United Nations context."

Such reasoning runs squarely into the claims of indigenous peoples themselves, and not just those from Africa or Asia, who argue that only they, as self-determining people, can determine who they are, regardless of what the state may wish of them. It matters little to those who are marginalized whether their oppressor has itself undergone a history of colonialism and passage from freedom into statehood. No one group has a monopoly on the promulgation of stigma and discrimination. It is like the intergenerational nature of family violence: the abused learn to practice abuse with greater refinement.

The disjuncture between analysis and identity has led to the implementation of a practical definition of "indigenous peoples." To avoid such thorny issues as those raised by Alfonso Martínez's report, the Working Group on Indigenous Populations has, since its inception in 1982, maintained an open-door policy toward participation in its annual two-weeklong gathering of indigenous peoples and organizations. One might expect this to be a source of mystification like an Oriental paradox—the definition of no definition, the color of the wind. But the real paradox is that it works: indigenous delegates come to the meetings with little insecurity about their own status as "indigenous," and few open doubts about the claims of others. . . .

This brings us to the third definition of indigenous peoples, one informally developed and acted upon by indigenous delegates themselves. This definition has never been made explicit or committed to writing. It begins with the fact that the leaders of indigenous communities and organizations are always careful to distinguish their identity and experience from those of states. Indigenous peoples are not mere extensions of state policy, so it will not do simply to refer to the "aboriginal peoples of Canada," the "Indians of the United States," the "indigenous peoples of Brazil," and so on. For indigenous representatives, the impulse to seek a wider identity is often regional, sometimes community based, and occasionally individual. It seems to begin with a sense of regional solidarity with those who share similar ways of life and histories of colonial and state domination that then grows into the realization that others around the world share the same experience.

There is thus a global aspect to indigenous identity, rarely expressed overtly, that functions as the basis for bringing people together in international meetings. It is close to a practical implementation of Martínez Cobo's definition, without any of the impediments or rancor of a formal system of membership. There is, nevertheless, a clear awareness among indigenous delegates of who represents an indigenous people or organization and who does not. Entering an indigenous caucus meeting as an observer has some of the same feel to it as being a scarcely tolerated visitor in a remote village. There is little overt unfriendliness, but at the same time there is a palpable sense of bonds uniting others that a mere observer can never fully share.

What is the basis of that connection? A glance around the room shows a striking variety, seemingly the entire range of human appearance and costume (including tattoos and decorative scarification). Within this variety there is an attachment that all participants share to some form of subsistence economy, to a territory or homeland that predates the arrival of settlers and surveyors, to a spiritual system that predates the arrival of missionaries, and to a language that expresses everything that is important and distinct about their place in the universe. Most importantly, they share the destruction and loss of these things. Their cultural markers gain self-conscious significance the more they are diminished by outside forces. They also share the corresponding commitment to find stability and restorative justice—even if it means using the very tools of literacy and law that, in other hands, are responsible for their oppression.

What many seek to achieve, whether realistically or not, is a correction of the historical deficit, an opportunity to present their own experience alongside the exclusionary and incomplete accounts of the founding of states, or what Prasenjit Duara (1995, 4) describes as "the false unity of a self-same, national subject evolving through time". Historical narrowness is inseparable from repression. Possessing, with the blinding clarity of a revealed truth, an original founding story that includes all the mistakes, betrayals, and bloodshed of nations built upon the lives of others is felt to be a first step toward liberation. . . .

3

This Is Not an Answer to the Question "Who Is Indigenous?"

Alejandro F. Haber

The term *Indigenous* in the sense that it is presently used has its origin in colonialism. As colonialism has had different histories in different areas of the colonized world, the categories that designate the colonial identities are also diverse. This does not mean that colonialism is a fragmented and unrelated phenomenon, but that colonialism, as capitalism, is a worldwide process that has local conditions of production and reproduction (Thomas 1994). The poetics and politics of colonial discourses and categories can be read from a global perspective, but the reading has to retain a local scope if it is to disentangle the mechanisms of production and reproduction of present day colonial relations. That an understanding of colonial categories is local is evident in the fact that an academic book published in the city of Catamarca can be read with unanticipated connotations, just on the other side of the Ambato mountains, a couple of hours away. Local resistances always inform the diversity of colonialism and colonialist categories.

It is quite common to hear, both inside or outside the country, that the contemporary Argentinean population is mainly of European descent, and that Indigenous populations were exterminated in early colonial times. More than a description of the history of assumed and ascribed identity categories, such assertions can be read as descriptions of individual and collective self-understanding. In strict historical terms, the only period when the category *Indian* can be said to be non-existent is before colonialism (Bonfil Batalla 1972). Nevertheless, any account of even that period—such as archaeology professes to write—is of necessity

---

Excerpted from Haber, Alejandro F. 2007. This Is Not an Answer to the Question "Who Is Indigenous?" *Archaeologies: Journal of the World Archaeological Congress* 3(3): 213–29.

uttered from inside a matrix of colonial relations. If we are to accept the meaning of *Indigenous* as referring to the people who lived here before the colonizers arrived, a relational consideration of that term is unavoidable (Ingold 2000). This means that there is nothing in itself to be considered Indigenous or non-Indigenous. Instead, these are positions—sometimes quite mobile—that are embedded in networks knitted by colonial relations (Bonfil Batalla 1972; Reissner 1983; Todorov 1987). Moreover, a relational framework is not limited only to the people who could be categorized as Indigenous or Non-Indigenous, as it also encompasses those who categorize.

Each of the characters is caught in the same web of colonial relationships of otherness; it is from that web that to *be or not to be Indigenous* can be assigned or assumed. To ask, or for that matter, to answer, the question "Who is Indigenous?" is not a simple act of inquiry about something that is there to be known, as if it had no relation to the one who is here, wanting to know. I am not implying that identities are simply assumed or assigned as a matter of contextual convenience; I am saying that categories of identity are representations of subjectivities that are built as part of lived experience; subjectivities that are formed in the course of relations to other subjectivities and objectivities in life. . . .

Multicultural Policy and Renewal of Colonialism

In 1994, a Constitutional reform was implemented in Argentina. After 140 years of considering Indian peoples as the object of war and treaties, the new constitution acknowledged the pre-existence of Indigenous communities, and their communal rights to land (National Constitution of the Argentine Republic, reformed in 1994. Article 75, Clause 17). The multiculturalism implied in the new legislation includes notions of respect for cultural difference and affirmative discrimination, but it recapitulates colonialist relations, itself being juxtaposed with former colonial categories.

In the new legal context, hundreds of communities have declared themselves as Indigenous. They are undergoing a process of self-assertion, cultural reconstruction and empowerment, usually presenting themselves to the state under the terms of the law to gain official recognition. In the last decade, to be Indigenous is starting to be an assertive self-ascription and not just a classification for oppression along a vector of discrimination. But unlike the Pampa, Patagonian and Chaco regions where Indigenous populations retained their languages, religions, and ethnic identities as part of the anthropological colonialist categorization used during the 19th century, the former Tucumán and Buenos Aires regions lack the same kind of neat delineation between identities.

Because of the multiple and diverse colonial histories, and the different local effects of general colonial projects (such as Evangelization and State obligatory schooling), the result is a multiplicity of local understandings of related subjective identities that is only partially glossed by multiculturalist policies. There is no general agreement as to what is considered to fall into one or another labeled category. Every categorization is locally contextualized, flexible up to a point, and conditioned on the particular relationship between the author and the object of the categorization. The complex historicity of colonialism in different parts of the country has produced a diversity that cannot be covered by general legal categories but, once again, the self-representation of the authorship of the state is constructed in opposition to Indigenous peoples, as if "whiteness" was a self-evident category.

In that context, the academic representations about "Who is Indigenous?" cannot be understood as a description of the field, but as political statements with direct social consequences. For example, a recent book written by two archaeologists from Buenos Aires is dedicated to ethnic identity on the Atacama plateau (García and Rolandi 2004). The title of the book is "Who are we?", referring not to the authors but to the local people who, by reading this book, can find an answer to their identity written in the first person by others. Thus the content of the book lies along the same line of colonialist politics. Because local people tend to call themselves *criollo* (in the local sense of the word as someone who has been raised in the locality), the authors consider that the local people are not Indigenous but *criollo* (in the elite sense of the word as white).

To ask "Who is Indigenous?" implies a politics of the self, because it is oriented towards the demarcation of the limit between self and other. The present Indigenous political identity of communities and leaders is taking advantage of the legal framework that seems to introduce a new platform after five centuries of colonialism. But it is still a colonialist category. This is why Indigenous leaders have to explain yet again that to be Indigenous is not just a matter of culture or of descent, but of life and territory. . . .

Life, Relationship and Visible Authorship

To ask "who is Indigenous?" implies a colonialist language and a colonialist categorization of people. One asks about the other, and, in the process, describes and determines what the other is. Why not start from the question "who am I?" instead? What are my relationships to the world? A person who feeds the land with coca leaves and alcohol considers that act a Catholic ritual. Rituals conducted in archaeological Indian sites, on the other hand, consisting of offerings and prayers, are seldom conducted during Catholic Easter or identified with the Virgin Mary. Neither Indian nor Indigenous have anything to do with marking this kind of activity, but they are probably attached to local, provincial, or even Kolla identity, none of which are seen as contradictory with Catholic and Argentinean identities. Inside the current of life subjectivities are not labeled in oppositional or directional categories.

Life is not based on essential features understood in reified terms. Everything in the world is alive; everything has intention and acts on other beings. There is no being that can be secluded from its relationships with other beings, without giving way to dramatic consequences. Life is contained in seeds. Everything comes from a seed. Thoughts come from their seed. Seeds should be cared for, treated with love and respect. Good relationships between beings are relations of love, care and respect; the *aymara aruni* term *uywaña* means "to be raised." To raise other beings (children, plants, animals, the house, the dead, antiques, the mountains, the springs) is part of the reciprocal relationship of being raised by those same beings. That explains why being *criollo* is so important to the Indigenous way, perhaps conveying a synonym for Indigenous but only when uttered from the perspective of the self, not the other.

The category of being Indigenous refers to some essence separated from life, and it has the aim and/or the consequence of separating people from their labour force, land and resources. In the last decade of legislation, to be Indigenous has been reconsidered by thousands of communities. From the *criollo* (Indigenous) perspective, to be "Indigenous" is just a category one is forced into by state policy. The legislation states that for a community to be considered Indigenous, it has to declare itself as Indigenous. Thus, "to be Indigenous" means to be part of a self-determined community of people who enunciate their life project in a community of relational beings (including people, land, water, the dead, antiques, animals, etc.). My friend Miguel Ramos, a young member of the recently self-declared Indigenous community of Antofalla, put it in clear and simple words when asked by a middle-class white girl "Why do you say you are Indigenous?" Miguel, in his first experience of a university class to which I had invited him to teach my archaeology students about Indigenous archaeology, answered: "That is what I always asked myself. Now I know that to be Indigenous does not stain, to be kolla does not stain. And now I am happy to be Indigenous." Miguel, himself in the process of learning about Indigenous politics, underlines the importance of being Indigenous as a matter of relational identity in a colonialist world. For Miguel, "to be Indigenous" is to say "I am Indigenous"; to create the authorial fact of self-determination. He himself, having spent his childhood as a peasant boy, knowing how to raise the water in the canals to make the water want to raise the plants in the plot, to make the Mother Maize and the Mother Potato want to raise the family, is the one teaching me to identify the hardly visible 2000-year old irrigation networks on his community lands. He says: "to make a canal one has to make the water want to go to the plot." This sense of life is the one sustained from an Indigenous perspective, and it is in that sense that the term *criollo* (raised in this place) is understood.

The question "Who is Indigenous?" implies that it can be determined by another through the application of some criterion. This draws the understanding of Indigenous into the game of language of classification on the basis of the criteria applied (race, language, religion, culture, ethnicity, etc.): someone who is not Indigenous refers to someone else as Indigenous. From there, "to be Indigenous" can be described without reference to the world of life: knowledge gives way to government; anthropology gives way to the State; discourse on others gives way to colonialism. The question "Who is Indigenous?" implies a colonialist politics of the self. And it is the politics of the self that has to be reworked if a non-colonialist—or better an anti-colonialist—practice is to be developed. From an Indigenous perspective, being consists in raising life. From this perspective, the question "who is Indigenous?" is nonsense. Everyone is already re-defined by colonialism, and to speak the language of colonialism is not a matter of choice, even if one speaks against it. To be Indigenous can be assumed to be a strategy of empowerment resisting the state, but the self is already being raised and raising life, in reciprocal relationships of care, love and respect to other beings in the world.

The question "Who is Indigenous?" is not about the person who answers, but about the person who asks. It cannot be asked from archaeology or any other academic discipline. It is a matter of self-determination in the context of struggle for liberation from oppression. The question "who is Indigenous?" should be replaced by the question "who are we?" Subcomandante Marcos, from the Zapatista Army for National Liberation, answers: "*We are this. The one who grows between fences. The one who sings. The one who cares for the old word. The one who speaks. The one who is of corn. The one who lives in the mountain. The one who walks the earth. The one who shares an idea. The true us. The true person. The ancestor. The person of the web. The one who respects history. The one who dresses humbly. The one who speaks flowers. Who is rain. Who has knowledge to give. Who hunts with arrows. Who is the river. Who is the desert. Who is the sea. The different. The one who is a person. The one who walks faster. Who is the people. Who is the mountain. Who is painted with colour. Who speaks the truth. Who has three hearts. Who is father and elder brother. Who walks the night. Who works. The man who is man. The one who walks among the clouds. The one who has words. The one who shares blood and ideas. The child of the sun. The one who goes one and another way. The one who walks in the mist. The one who is mysterious. The one who works the word. The one who orders in the mountain. The one who is brother, sister*" (words of Subcomandante Marcos from the Ejército Zapatista de Liberación Nacional, March 11th 2001 at the Zócalo of México, D.F.).

4

Beyond Black and White: Essentialism, Hybridity, and Indigeneity

Yin C. Paradies

Although some have expressed understandable distaste at the thought of non-Indigenous people defining their Indigeneity (Huggins 2003, 60), such defining (whether official or popular) unavoidably involves both Indigenous and non-Indigenous people in "a process of dialogue, of imagination, of representation and interpretation" (Langton 1993, 33). It is also clear that the fluid and contextual nature of Indigenous identity

Excerpted from Paradies, Yin C. 2006. Beyond Black and White: Essentialism, Hybridity, and Indigeneity. *Journal of Sociology* 42(4):355–67.

over time and place is not particular to either Australia or the Indigenous context. There are innumerable types of human identity that vary across many aspects of experience, including race, ethnicity, gender, sexuality, age, class, physicality, language, religion and profession, to name only a few. All these identities are complex, multi-faceted socio-historical constructs which are established through public acts of self-representation, private accountings of oneself or through the experience of being named by others (Jenkins 1994), including by prevailing discourses. Although I will focus here on racial identities, it is important to remember that "we do not experience the world only as Indigenous or non-Indigenous" (Cowlishaw 2004b, 70–71) but also through many other facets of our identity that we adopt and/or that are ascribed to us by others.

Indigenous people in Australia have, for some decades, been engaged in debates about Indigenous identity. One element of these debates has been the implicit (or explicit) goal of creating a distinct, coherent and thus relatively homogeneous pan-Indigenous social and political community. It has been suggested that only within this haven of pan-Indigeneity can Indigenous people "resist the seduction of assimilation and confidently work at rebuilding a unique identity" (Ariss 1988, 136). If so, such a pan-Indigenous community may be a necessary element in surviving ongoing colonial imperatives by the Australian nation-state (Dodson 1994; Russell 2001, 76; Werbner and Modood 1997, 249). Also, instrumentality aside, such a communal shared identity is a pleasurable and empowering experience for many (Ang 2001, 11).

However, despite assertions to the contrary (Dodson 1994, 9), Indigenous constructions of (pan-)Indigeneity also involve elements of boundary construction/policing, which seek to construct Indigenous and non-Indigenous identities as "mutually impermeable and incommensurable" (Gilroy 1993, 65). Such policing serves to alienate past and potential future Indigenous people (O'Regan 1999, 194–95), or force those who inhabit Indigeneity into a "prison-house" of identity (Ang 2001, 11; Oxenham et al. 1999, 70; Scott, 1992b, 18), which may isolate them "from contemporary life and full citizenship" (Brydon 1995, 141) and, hence, may even reduce the political power of the Indigenous community. The ambivalence and alienation resulting from such constructions is especially acute for many urban Indigenous people, who live in increasingly anonymous communities in which the need to acquire an imprimatur of Indigeneity is a source of conflict (Cowlishaw 2004a). Moreover, the powerful tropes of Indigeneity mobilized during this boundary construction interpellate every Indigenous person, without regard to their individual characteristics, through a plethora of stereotyped images (Morrissey 2003, 191) that coalesce around specific fantasies of exclusivity, cultural alterity, marginality, physicality and morality.

In order to challenge prevailing stereotypes, Indigenous people are often required to publicly confess our intimate subjectivities (I. Anderson 1997, 5; Nakata 2003, 134–35). Although this requirement may be a manifestation of the colonial gaze, such confessions serve to remind us of the situated and partial nature of knowledge (Russell 2001, 73). As such, I will utilize autobiography as a rhetorical construction (Ang 2001, 24) along with contemporary scholarship on identity both in Australia and abroad to explore the aforementioned fantasies of Indigeneity. In declaring the particularity of my Indigeneity, I recognize that I will inevitably be interpellated by readers in ways that either establish or undermine my authority to speak on the fraught issue of Indigenous identity.

I identify racially as an Aboriginal-Anglo-Asian Australian. Along with scholars such as Ang (2001, viii) and Russell (2001, 98), my personal history compels me to identify as more than just Indigenous and as other than exclusively White, while moving beyond this dichotomy in also recognizing my Asian heritage. Like Russell (2001, 98), I refuse to "surrender my other identities" in order to be Indigenous and, as such, I also identify as "and/or" as well as "not/nor" Aboriginal-Anglo-Asian. Descended from both Indigenous and Euro-Australian ancestors I am both colonizer and colonized, both Black and consummately White (Lehman 2004).

Many Indigenous Australians also share my diverse racial background, with, for instance, 22 percent of Indigenous people reporting "European" ancestry in the 2001 Census (Australian Bureau of Statistics 2003). Furthermore, about half of all Indigenous people in a marriage or de facto relationship have a non-Indigenous partner, with over 80 percent of children from these "mixed" partnerships adopting an Indigenous identity (Ross 1999). Yet, despite this heterogeneity in the Indigenous community, asserting a multi-racial Indigenous identity is neither common nor straightforward because racial loyalty demands that anomalous individuals choose to be either exclusively Indigenous or exclusively non-Indigenous (Boladeras 2002, 131; Cowlishaw 2004a, 114). Those, like me, who refuse this compulsion in the hope of creating a hybrid space of multiplicity (Russell 2002, 141–42), instead find ourselves inhabiting "a strange in-between space" (Russell 2002, 139) where we are frequently not accepted as Black (Cowlishaw 2004a, 116), and where we are subject to the opprobrium directed at "the half-different and the partially familiar" (Gilroy 2000, 106). The prospect of such derision combined with the demands of racial loyalty are evident even in otherwise excellent scholarship on Indigenous identity, which seamlessly reinforces exclusive Indigencity by discussing (in the contributors' biographies)

Indigenous heritage to the exclusion of non-Indigenous heritage (Oxenham et al. 1999, 32–s50).

Due, in large part, to my grandmother being a member of the Stolen Generations, I do not speak an Aboriginal language, I do not have a connection with my ancestral lands or a unique spirituality inherited through my Indigeneity, I have little contact with my extended family, and the majority of my friends are non-Indigenous. Also due to this same history, I am a middle-class, highly educated professional working in the field of Indigenous research. As such I am frequently interpellated as Indigenous and called upon to deploy my Indigeneity in a professional context, while at the same I am labeled by some as an inauthentic "nine-to-five black" or a "coconut" who has stolen the place of a "real Aborigine" (Paradies 2005). Despite assertions by some Indigenous scholars that a unique spirituality (Foley 2000) or relationship to land (Moreton-Robinson 2003) epitomize Indigeneity, the available statistics suggest that many Indigenous Australians fail to conform to the fantasy of cultural alterity: 88 percent of us do not speak an Aboriginal language as the main language spoken at home; only a little over half of us identify with a particular clan, tribal or language group (Australian Bureau of Statistics 2003); and most of us live in single-parent or nuclear households rather than extended family arrangements (Zubrick et al. 2004, 38).

Moreover, there is a growing Indigenous middle class as demonstrated by the fact that between 1994 and 2002 the proportion of Indigenous people with at least a Bachelor degree increased threefold (from 1 percent to 3 percent), the proportion of Indigenous people who were employed rose from 36 percent to 46 percent and mean equivalized gross household income for Indigenous people 15 years and over rose from $345 to $387 per week (Australian Bureau of Statistics 2002). Yet despite (or perhaps because of) the fact that, in absolute terms, our lot as Indigenous people is improving, there is a prevailing misconception that "If you're middle class you can't be Aboriginal" (Boladeras 2002, 135). Being educated, well-remunerated or simply enjoying material assets "can expose one to suspicion of wanting to be white" (Cowlishaw 2004a, 113; see also Grant 2002; Purdie et al. 2000). Although many Indigenous people rightly desire the privileges that, until recently, have been synonymous with Whiteness, such desire is associated with being less Indigenous (Cowlishaw 2004a, 116; Dudgeon and Oxenham 1989).

There is no doubt that Indigenous people have suffered a deplorable history of marginalization, discrimination and exclusion that continues to this day (Dunn et al. 2005; Lattas 2001; Mellor 2003), and that such a history has led to a "solidarity grounded in a common experience of subordination" (Portes 1998, 9). However, it is also evident, from international contexts, that when group cohesion is premised on the impossibility of transcending such subordination, the achievement of individual success endangers this cohesion. As a result, social norms are formed that seek "to keep members of a downtrodden group in place and force the more ambitious to escape from it" (Portes 1998, 9). This emphasis on marginality also risks reinforcing the danger of fatalism which pervades the minds of many Australians (Brough 1999) who, faced with the myth of worsening Indigenous disadvantage, believe there is no solution to this intractable problem and hence no point trying to address it. Furthermore, in our individualistic Western culture it is far too easy to blame such "intractable" disadvantage on Indigenous people themselves (Brough 1999).

Arguably even more prevalent than the fantasy of marginality that adheres to Indigeneity is the pernicious fantasy of the "Indigenous look." Along with many other Indigenous Australians I fail to match the stereotyped physicality of an "Indigene": that is, I have white skin and relatively European features. Despite assertions to the contrary (Perkins 2004, fn 3), it is clear that skin colour and physicality are "exceptionally important in the recognition and validation of Aboriginal identity" (Boladeras 2002, 147; see also Oxenham et al. 1999, 79–82; Schwab 1994, 94), as they are in similar international contexts (J. Cunningham 1997). Fair-skinned Indigenous people experience "racism, scorn and disbelief" from other Indigenous and non-Indigenous people alike, whose perennial interrogation of their identity leads to acute anxiety (Foley 2000; Purdie et al. 2000) as well as "ambivalence, and doubts about themselves as 'real' [Indigenous] people" (Boladeras 2002, 147). This intense questioning of authenticity, which can hit you with the force of a sledgehammer, is due to the profound disruption that white-skinned Indigenes represent for the Black-White racial dichotomy, so fervently clung to in Australia. As one person put it, "sometimes . . . it would be just a lot easier to say I'm not Aboriginal . . ." (Boladeras 2002, 116). Yet many people choose to publicly identify as Indigenous, exposing themselves to "an uneasy pathway through life . . . strewn with doubt, disbelief and confrontation" (Boladeras 2002, 153).

For me, as for many other descendants of the Stolen Generations (both fair-skinned and dark), it "was the choice of others that I be denied the shared experiences . . . that contribute to an [essentialized] Aboriginal identity" (Russell 2002, 137–38). However, unlike Russell (2002, 137–38), I do not accept such an essentialized view of Indigeneity, and I refuse to recognize that, among individuals who have Indigenous ancestry, there is a group of people who "qualify" as Indigenous and a group who don't. Indeed, it is disturbing that Russell is reluctant to identify as Indigenous, in part, from fear of "other people's reactions, especially those of Aboriginal people" (2002, 141–42). Similarly, Kathryn Hay (Tasmanian parliamentarian and former Miss Australia) is ambivalent about identifying as Aboriginal "because of what people would expect if I said I was Aboriginal" (Purcell 2002, 234–35). Clearly, such trepidation at being "caught out" as inauthentic arises from the deleterious notion that "there are protocols and ethics to adhere to when 'becoming Aborigines'" which require "years of hard work, sensitivity and effort" to master (Huggins 2003, 63). Such purported "protocols" lead to the questioning, challenging and doubting of Indigeneity by ourselves and others, and results in academics like Russell (2001, 98) stating that, because she was "raised to be part of the mainstream white community I feel incapable of stating that I am Aboriginal."

A particularly troubling aspect of the "protocols of Indigeneity" is the positioning of Indigenes as inherently morally and epistemologically superior to non-Indigenes (Kowal and Paradies 2005). Although this phenomenon is driven by non-Indigenous attempts to mitigate their privileged position (Land and Vincent 2005) and assuage the guilt of continuing colonization, such a positioning is more often perpetuated than protested against by Indigenous people (see Paradies 2006a, for an example). The idea that Indigeneity is synonymous with suffering (Russell 2002, 141–42) and marginality, together with the misconception that such "victimhood" (Palmer and Groves 2000) bestows privileged access to social truths (Cowlishaw 2004b, 64; Stanley and Wise 1993, 227), leads to uncritical acceptance of the views, opinions and scholarship of Indigenous people about Indigenous issues (Langton 1993, 27). This phenomenon is sometimes also accompanied by a corresponding rejection of non-Indigenous views, which are portrayed as "tainted with racism" (Cowlishaw 2004b, 65). Such moralistic positioning is untenable given the various and contradictory views that Indigenous people hold and, more importantly, such an approach fails to recognize that engaging in debate with Indigenous people is a sign of intellectual respect (Land and Vincent 2005).

This instinctive urge to foist moral rectitude onto those who are oppressed and marginal (Hage 2003, 116) also leads far too many to conclude that repugnant acts such as racism cannot, by definition, be perpetrated by Indigenous people. Of course, this reasoning is fallacious, there being "no reason why those subjected to racism of the worst kind cannot be racist themselves" (Hage 2003, 116–17). Similarly, the view that being Indigenous requires one to resist White hegemony (Cowlishaw 1988, 243) or strive to alleviate the disadvantage of Indigenous people (Huggins 2003, 64), also inappropriately portrays Indigenous people as intrinsically virtuous (Cowlishaw 1988, 243; Russell 2001). These moral qualifications, that some would have us espouse as prerequisites of Indigeneity, evince a profound failure to recognize that "wisdom and virtue are as unevenly distributed among Indigenous people as elsewhere" (Cowlishaw 2004b, 71).

Taken as a whole, these fantasies of Indigeneity raise the question of "who is a 'real indigenous' person" (Smith 1999, 72) and through processes of forced inclusion, which are never completely successful (Ang 2001, 83), protocols of cultural survival end up replacing "one form of tyranny with another" (Appiah 1994, 163). The "border patrol is kept busy erasing and denying whatever does not or will not fit" (Ferguson 1993, 165), repudiating the variety and complexity of contemporary Indigenous Australia (Muecke 1992) and leaving a community fragmented into those who can authentically perform Indigeneity and those who are silenced and/or rendered outside the space of Indigeneity because they cannot, or will not, perform (Griffiths 1995, 238; Smith 1999, 72).

In addition, this community fragmentation cleaves to fault lines of power, with some Indigenous elites, in seeking to preserve the status quo, colluding with neo-colonial governments to coerce Indigenous people into performing an essentialized Indigeneity which compromises their "capacity to be individually—and differently—Aboriginal" (Moore 2005, 188). This phenomenon is of dubious utility, even to these elites, as shown in the application of native title law where the neo-liberal state makes an "impossible demand for authenticity" by recognizing prior sovereignty only for those Indigenous people who can prove that they have "been relatively untouched by history" (Schaap 2005, 19). In doing so, the state denies the existence of actual Indigenous people who, by adapting and changing, have survived colonialism while unavoidably shedding their pristine primeval identity. . . .

SECTION III

Philosophical, Theoretical, and Historical Underpinnings

The practice of "Indigenous archaeologies" compels engagement, not only with Indigenous places and peoples but also with the philosophies and knowledges that emerge from Indigenous thoughtscapes and landscapes. This section examines the synergies among several theoretical approaches, as envisioned by writers who engage with philosophy, knowledge, modernity, ethics, feminist theory, property, and other issues central to Indigenous archaeologies. In sum, these writers argue that Indigenous archaeologies matters, not because it enlarges the anthropological gaze on exotic peoples at the margins of social discourse but because it grapples with theoretical issues that are central to the discipline.

The section opens with "Colonizing Knowledges," an excerpt from Linda Tuhiwai Smith's *Decolonizing Methodologies: Research and Indigenous Peoples* (1999). This Maori scholar critiques Eurocentric scientific approaches and modes of categorization and organization. During the emergence of the modern European state, when science was being positioned as a rational, all-embracing method for gaining understanding of the world's peoples, master discourses cast the Indigenous as non-European (and therefore nonscientific) "Others." Indigenous knowledges were imagined to be ideologically undeveloped and inferior to classical and Enlightenment philosophies. According to Smith, modern perceptions of "research" are thus inextricably linked with domination and loss, as a carry-over from both the colonial era (when European nations claimed Indigenous territories), and the salvage era (when anthropologists labored to "rescue" Indigenous objects and histories). In addition, antiquated Orientalist constructions (Said 1978) have long been used by scientists and theorists to determine who and what qualifies as Indigenous, further legitimating imperialistic control. As a result, Indigenous peoples have historically had difficulty asserting their intellectual authority in the presence of non-Indigenous "experts."

"Indigenous Worldviews and Ways of Knowing as Theoretical and Methodological Foundations behind Archaeological Theory and Method," by Heather Harris, contrasts Indigenous worldviews with Western worldviews. Many Indigenous peoples consider the universe to be alive with power, will, and intelligence. Western thought, she observes, is shaped by dichotomies such as "animate and inanimate, natural and supernatural, man and nature, life and death, past and future, subject and object, observer and observed." Indigenous thought, by contrast, is holistic rather than reductionist, and experiential rather than positivist. Beliefs in the fundamental equality and interconnectedness of all beings (including past ancestors) shape spiritual practices that reflect cyclical movements through space and time. Indigenous observations of the natural world can serve as important sources of information for archaeology, precisely because they reference the experiences of many people in specific locales over long periods of time.

In "Remythologizing the Relationship between Indians and Archaeologists," Larry Zimmerman calls attention to the dynamics of social relations and discourse, in print and in person. He notes that many Indigenous people distance themselves from archaeologists, but increasing numbers recognize that archaeologists can provide expert assistance in land claims and cultural site preservation. He urges that we build new relationships based on trust rather than polemic, since "archaeology need not come to a screeching halt when it accedes to Indian demands." The World Archaeological Congress and other organizations are shaping codes of ethics that encourage "covenantal archaeology" in order to improve both social relations on the ground and interpretations of the Indigenous past. Even so, processes of "remythologizing" are now in play as Indigenous peoples and archaeologists, in their roles as potential allies and opponents, move to claim positions, carve out research territories, and name the issues at stake.

"We are witnessing the emergence of a new form of archaeology . . . informed by Indigenous values and agendas," says H. Martin Wobst, in "Power to the (Indigenous) Past and Present! Or: The Theory and

Method behind Archaeological Theory and Method." Wobst identifies archaeological theory, method, and data as being inherently biased in support of the state as the social model. Archaeological practitioners falsify the records of non-state societies by classifying them as either "incipient states or failures to reach statehood." Wobst calls for a broader archaeological vision that integrates material culture with language, poetry, music, dance, oral traditions, and other forms of nonmaterial or ephemeral cultural expression. By de-emphasizing the supposed differences between artifact and nonartifact, "nature" and "culture," the visualscape can also be expanded to include astronomical observations, geomorphology, flora and fauna, and sensual experiences. If archaeologists broaden their theory, they will experience a closer sense of past Indigenous materialities. They are also likely to become more "grounded in the problems of their Indigenous contemporaries, sensitive to Indigenous needs, and willing to further Indigenous projects and agendas."

Sonya Atalay, in "Indigenous Archaeology as Decolonizing Practice," emphasizes the importance of theoretical location. She suggests moving dominant Western concepts, such as "the linear and departmentalized view of time, systems of production and reproduction of knowledge, and the role of research in society," to the margins of archaeology, while bringing Indigenous concepts to the center. If archaeologists focus on traditional Indigenous teachings concerning history and heritage, and attend to the social responsibilities surrounding the production of research and knowledge, she believes they will naturally come to recognize the importance of ethics and social justice. Archaeologists who shift locations, theoretically if not physically, can also serve a far more diverse audience, expanding the range of human knowledge to be gained while avoiding further damage to Indigenous concerns.

Ian Lilley, author of "Archaeology, Diaspora, and Decolonization," offers insights into the thoughtscapes of Anglo-Celtic and Aboriginal peoples in Australia, two groups that have been uprooted and relocated by colonial circumstances. Despite the largely voluntary nature of their historical relocation, white settlers often imagine themselves as peoples in diaspora, victimized by British colonialism. Indigenous Aboriginals are also diasporic, having been separated from their land, heritage, and identity by white settler societies. Non-Aboriginal Australians are generally supportive of the human rights of Aboriginal and Torres Strait Islanders but are skeptical concerning their claims to land. For Aboriginals, "people literally *are* their history, the latter being read as patterns of interaction among people and relationships between people and place over time" (Clifford 1994, 310). Native peoples will go to "extraordinary lengths to maintain attachments to distant family members and homelands," despite attacks on their sovereignty and survival. Ancestral relations, although frayed by colonial forces, can be reanimated by traditional journeys along Dreaming tracks that reinforce inalienable connections to land (McBryde 1987; Sutton 1994 [1988]). Citing similar circumstances in the Middle East, Lilley calls for a "heritage recovery" approach to "the archaeology of the disenfranchised" (Scham 2001; excerpted in Chapter 40 this volume), as a means of both political and material restoration.

"Dwelling at the Margins, Action at the Intersection? Feminist and Indigenous Archaeologies," is one of the more challenging readings in this section. Writing from the perspective of feminist theory, Margaret Conkey works methodically through complex points of theory, logic, and method, offering insights that can better our understanding of Indigenous theory. She begins by observing that material objects never "speak for themselves." Archaeologists must, therefore, account for the choices and strategies involved in their representations of the past, of their research process, and of themselves. Conkey identifies position, subjectivity, politics, and experience as integral dimensions of one's interpretations and understandings. Feminist theory can inform Indigenous archaeologies by offering a model for analyzing not only the element of experience but also "what counts as experience" and "who gets to make that determination." This kind of intersectional approach positions experience and history within a sociocultural framework (Russo 1991) and appropriately identifies all analytical categories as "contextual, contested, and contingent." Conkey also notes the influence of both white patriarchal values and white feminist values on our understandings of Indigenous gender roles; she suggests that feminist scholars abandon their sense of expertise on womanhood and engage in reciprocal dialogue with Indigenous women to discern what matters most to them (Mihesuah 2003). In closing, she points to the flaws in "archaeologies of difference" that depend on modern liberal notions of pluralism, natural diversities, or static identities, while ignoring issues of appropriation and representation.

George Nicholas and Kelly Bannister address crucial issues of ownership in "Copyrighting the Past? Emerging Intellectual Property Rights Issues in Archaeology." Human societies embody unique systems of knowledge that, together, constitute a compendium of human wisdom over time. Archaeologists have captured a great deal of material from the Indigenous past and have long endeavored to control, through this material, how this past will be interpreted and communicated. Nicholas and Bannister observe that Indigenous archaeological finds are natural repositories of Indigenous cultural identity, containing data and meanings that are highly significant to Indigenous descendants. Archaeological sites and finds thus contain both cultural property and intellectual property.

This section ends with an article that articulates some of the assumptions, principles, and frameworks that undergird archaeological codes of ethics. Claire Smith and Heather Burke, authors of "In the Spirit of the Code," reflect on the values, concerns, and beliefs embedded in codes produced by archaeological professionals. Expressions of concern for shared stewardship, preservation, knowledge, and control are often held up as ethical norms to guide archaeological practice, but these norms are socially constructed by the situational needs of those who script these codes. Stewardship of archaeological finds, for example, privileges a scientific standpoint that does not necessarily equate with Indigenous cultural survival. As a means of articulating ethical values in practice, these authors call for an analysis of the spirit and principles embodied in ethical codes and the use of these codes in working through ethical dilemmas. They insist that archaeology is not apolitical; to the contrary, archaeologists must examine their own biases, assumptions, and inclinations, particularly when they exercise their power to construct identities, in absentia, for the Indigenous people they study.

5

Colonizing Knowledges

Linda Tuhiwai Smith

Establishing the Positional Superiority of Western Knowledge

The project of modernity signaled the end of feudalism and absolutist authority, legitimated by divine rule, and announced the beginning of the modern state. The new state formation had to meet the requirements of an expanding economy based on major improvements in production. The industrial revolution changed and made new demands upon the individual and the political system. The modern state was wrested from the old regime of absolutist monarchs by the articulation of liberal political and economic theories (Jaggar 1983). As a system of ideas, liberalism focuses on the individual, who has the capacity to reason, on a society which promotes individual autonomy and self-interest, and on a state which has a rational rule of law which regulates a public sphere of life, but which allows individuals to pursue their economic self-interest. Once it was accepted that humans had the capacity to reason and to attain this potential through education, through a systematic form of organizing knowledge, then it became possible to debate these ideas in rational and "scientific" ways.

The development of scientific thought, the exploration and "discovery" by Europeans of other worlds, the expansion of trade, the establishment of colonies, and the systematic colonization of indigenous peoples in the eighteenth and nineteenth centuries are all facets of the modernist project. Modernism is more than a re-presentation of fragments from the cultural archive in new contexts. "Discoveries" about

---

Excerpted from Tuhiwai Smith, Linda. 1999. Colonizing Knowledges. In *Decolonizing Methodologies: Research and Indigenous Peoples*, 58–77. London: Zed Books.

and from the "new" world expanded and challenged ideas the West held about itself (Hall 1992). The production of knowledge, new knowledge and transformed "old" knowledge, ideas about the nature of knowledge and the validity of specific forms of knowledge, became as much commodities of colonial exploitation as other natural resources (Goonatilake 1982). Indigenous peoples were classified alongside the flora and fauna; hierarchical typologies of humanity and systems of representation were fuelled by new discoveries; and cultural maps were charted and territories claimed and contested by the major European powers. Hence some indigenous peoples were ranked above others in terms of such things as the belief that they were "nearly human," "almost human" or "sub-human." This often depended on whether it was thought that the peoples concerned possessed a "soul" and could therefore be "offered" salvation and whether or not they were educable and could be offered schooling. These systems for organizing, classifying and storing new knowledge, and for theorizing the meanings of such discoveries, constituted research. In a colonial context, however, this research was undeniably also about power and domination. The instruments or technologies of research were also instruments of knowledge and instruments for legitimating various colonial practices. . . .

Whilst colonialism at an economic level, including its ultimate expression through slavery, opened up new materials for exploitation and new markets for trade, at a cultural level, ideas, images and experiences about the Other helped to shape and delineate the essential differences between Europe and the rest. Notions about the Other, which already existed in the European imagination, were recast within the framework of Enlightenment philosophies, the industrial revolution and the scientific "discoveries" of the eighteenth and nineteenth centuries. When discussing the scientific foundations of Western research, the indigenous contribution to these foundations is rarely mentioned. To have acknowledged their contribution would, in terms of the rules of research practice, be as legitimate as acknowledging the contribution of a variety of plant, a shard of pottery or a "preserved head of a native" to research. Furthermore, according to Bazin (1993, 35–36), "Europeans could not even imagine that other people could ever have done things before or better than themselves." The objects of research do not have a voice and do not contribute to research or science. In fact, the logic of the argument would suggest that it is simply impossible, ridiculous even, to suggest that the object of research can contribute to anything. An object has no life force, no humanity, no spirit of its own, so therefore "it" cannot make an active contribution. This perspective is not deliberately insensitive; it is simply that the rules did not allow such a thought to enter the scene. Thus, indigenous Asian, American, Pacific and African forms of knowledge, systems of classification, technologies and codes of social life, which began to be recorded in some detail by the seventeenth century, were regarded as "new discoveries" by Western science (Goonatilake 1982). These discoveries were commodified as property belonging to the cultural archive and body of knowledge of the West (Adas 1989).

The eighteenth and nineteenth centuries also constituted an era of highly competitive "collecting." Many indigenous people might call this "stealing" rather than "collecting." This included the collecting of territories, of new species of flora and fauna, of mineral resources and of cultures. James Clifford (1988, 231), for example, refers to ethnography as a science which was

> [a] form of culture collecting . . . [which] highlights the ways that diverse experiences and facts are selected, gathered, detached from their original temporal occasions, and given enduring value in a new arrangement. Collecting—at least in the West, where time is generally thought to be linear and irreversible—implies a rescue of phenomena from inevitable historical decay or loss.

The idea that collectors were actually rescuing artefacts from decay and destruction, and from indigenous peoples themselves, legitimated practices which also included commercial trade and plain and simple theft. Clearly, in terms of trade indigenous peoples were often active participants, in some cases delivering "made to order" goods. The different agendas and rivalries of indigenous groups were also known to have been incorporated into the commercial activities of Europeans. Hence, muskets could be traded and then used to pursue traditional enemies or one group of people could be used to capture and assist in the enslavement of another group who were also their traditional rivals. Indigenous property is still said to be housed in "collections," which in turn are housed either in museums or private galleries, and art and artefacts are often grouped and classified in the name of their "collector." These collections have become the focus of indigenous peoples' attempts to reclaim ancestral remains and other cultural items (known in the West as "artifacts") belonging to their people. . . .

The nexus between cultural ways of knowing, scientific discoveries, economic impulses and imperial power enabled the West to make ideological claims to having a superior civilization. The "idea" of the West became a reality when it was re-presented back to indigenous nations through colonialism. By the nineteenth century colonialism not only meant the imposition of Western authority over indigenous lands, indigenous modes of production and indigenous law and government, but the imposition of Western authority over all aspects of indigenous knowledges, languages and cultures. This authority incorporated what Said (1978, 205–6) refers to as alliances between the ideologies, "clichés," general beliefs and understandings held about the Orient and the views of "science" and philosophical theories. . . .

Colonizing the Disciplines

Academic knowledges are organized around the idea of disciplines and fields of knowledge. These are deeply implicated in each other and share genealogical foundations in various classical and Enlightenment philosophies. Most of the "traditional" disciplines are grounded in cultural world views which are either antagonistic to other belief systems or have no methodology for dealing with other knowledge systems. Underpinning all of what is taught at universities is the belief in the concept of science as the all-embracing method for gaining an understanding of the world. Some of these disciplines, however, are more directly implicated in colonialism in that either they have derived their methods and understandings from the colonized world or they have tested their ideas in the colonies. How the colonized were governed, for example, was determined by previous experiences in other colonies and by the prevailing theories about race, gender, climate and other factors generated by "scientific" methods. Classification systems were developed specifically to cope with the mass of new knowledge generated by the discoveries of the "new world." New colonies were the laboratories of Western science. Theories generated from the exploration and exploitation of colonies, and of the people who had prior ownership of these lands, formed the totalizing appropriation of the Other. . . .

Of all the disciplines, anthropology is the one most closely associated with the study of the Other and with the defining of primitivism (Stocking 1987). As Adam Kuper (1988, 5) argued, "The anthropologists took this primitive society as their special subject, but in practice primitive society proved to be their own society (as they understood it) seen in a distorting mirror." The ethnographic "gaze" of anthropology has collected, classified and represented other cultures to the extent that anthropologists are often the academics popularly perceived by the indigenous world as the epitome of all that it is bad with academics. Haunani Kay Trask (1993) accuses anthropologists of being "takers and users" who "exploit the hospitality and generosity of native people." Trinh T. Minh-ha (1989, 59) makes similar references to anthropology and anthropologists, including those whose intent now is to train Third

World anthropologists. "Gone out of date," she says, "then revitalised, the mission of civilizing savages mutates into the imperative of 'making equal'." In writing a history of geography, Livingstone (1992) refers to this discipline as the "science of imperialism par excellence." His comment relates to geographical studies into such things as the mapping of racial difference, the links which were drawn between climate and mental abilities, the use of map makers in French colonies for military intelligence and the development of acclimatization societies (Livingstone 1992, 216). As suggested above in the Introduction, history is also implicated in the construction of totalizing master discourses which control the Other. The history of the colonies, from the perspective of the colonizers, has effectively denied other views of what happened and what the significance of historical "facts" may be to the colonized. "If history is written by the victor," argues Janet Abu-Lughod (1989, 118), "then it must, almost by definition, 'deform' the history of the others." Donna Awatere (1983, 6–7) claims that, "The process of recording what happened automatically favours the white occupiers because they won. In such a way a whole past is 'created' and then given the authority of truth." These comments have been echoed wherever indigenous peoples have had the opportunity to "talk back" to the academic world. . . .

The "Authentic, Essentialist, Deeply Spiritual" Other

At a recent international conference held in New Zealand to discuss issues related to indigenous intellectual and cultural property rights, the local newspapers were informed and invited to interview some of the delegates. One news reporter thought it would be a good idea to have a group photograph, suggesting that it would be a very colourful feature for the newspaper to highlight. When she and the photographer turned up at the local *marae* (cultural centre) they were so visibly disappointed at the motley display of track suits, jeans and other items of "modern" dress, that they chose not to take a photograph. "Oh, I forgot to come as a native," joked one of the delegates. "My feathers got confiscated at the airport when I arrived." "I suppose my eyes are too blue." "Are we supposed to dress naked?" As we have seen, the notion of "authentic" is highly contested when applied to, or by, indigenous peoples. "Authorities" and outside experts are often called in to verify, comment upon, and give judgements about the validity of indigenous claims to cultural beliefs, values, ways of knowing and historical accounts. Such issues are often debated vigorously by the "public," (a category which usually means the dominant group), leading to an endless parading of "nineteenth century" views of race and racial difference. Questions of who is a "real indigenous" person, what counts as a "real indigenous leader," which person displays "real cultural values" and the criteria used to assess the characteristics of authenticity are frequently the topic of conversation and political debate. These debates are designed to fragment and marginalize those who speak for, or in support of, indigenous issues. They frequently have the effect also of silencing and making invisible the presence of other groups within the indigenous society like women, the urban non-status tribal person and those whose ancestry or "blood quantum" is "too white." In Tasmania, where experts had already determined that Aborigines were "extinct," the voices of those who still speak as Aboriginal Tasmanians are interpreted as some political invention of a people who no longer exist and who therefore no longer have claims. . . .

6

Indigenous Worldviews and Ways of Knowing as Theoretical and Methodological Foundations behind Archaeological Theory and Method

Heather Harris

Indigenous Worldview

Although the outward manifestations of Indigenous cultures across North America and beyond vary greatly, there are surprising similarities in worldview, enough so that it is possible to contrast Indigenous worldview with Western worldview. Many Indigenous scholars recognize this. The Hawaiian scholar, Haunani Kay Trask contends that, "Indigenous knowledge is not unique to Hawaiians, but is shared by most Indigenous peoples throughout the world" (1993, 80). Gregory Cajete, a Tewa educator, claims that among American Indian tribes, "there are elemental understandings held in common by all . . . derived from a similar understanding and orientation to life"(1994, 42). "Cosmologies differed from tribe to tribe, but basic beliefs were constant" according to Osage-Cherokee thinker, Strickland (1997). Blood scholar, Leroy Little Bear, makes a clear statement regarding the similarities in worldview among Indigenous peoples, saying, "there is [sic] enough similarities among North American philosophies to apply the concept generally" (2000, 77).

One of the foundations of Indigenous worldview is that the universe is alive, has power, will and intelligence. The dichotomy between animate and inanimate held in the Western worldview usually has little

---

Excerpted from Harris, Heather. 2005. Indigenous Worldviews and Ways of Knowing as Theoretical and Methodological Foundations behind Archaeological Theory and Method. In *Indigenous Archaeologies: Decolonizing Theory and Practice*, ed. H. M. Wobst and C. Smith, 33–41. London: Routledge.

meaning in Indigenous ways of seeing. Nothing is inanimate—even the rocks, mountains, weather phenomena, celestial bodies and the earth itself are alive to most Indigenous peoples. A corollary of this idea that everything is alive is that because everything is animated by the same life force, all have a fundamental equality. This idea is often expressed when Indigenous people say that we are all related, we are all equal, that humans are no more important than the smallest creature, a plant or a stone. This is very different from the Western religious concept of people having dominion over the earth and the Western scientific concept of many evolutionary biologists who place humans at the top of the evolutionary scale.

Another area where there is great divergence between Indigenous and Western thought is in the holistic view of Indigenous peoples versus the dichotomous view of the West. Cowlitz philosopher, Rudolph Ryser, calls the fundamental mode of thought of the Indigenous peoples of the Western Hemisphere Caurto Spiritism and the fundamental Western mode of thought Progressivism (1998, 21). The holism of Indigenous thought, according to Ryser, is characterized by conceptions of the interconnectedness of all life; perpetual movement of all through space and time; connection between the past, present and future; and life and death as aspects of the same thing (1998, 21). Western thought, on the other hand is often organized around dichotomies like animate and inanimate, natural and supernatural, man and nature, life and death, past and future, subject and object, observer and observed. These divergences in fundamental perceptions between archaeologists and Indigenous people can result in serious misunderstandings, some which are illustrated in this paper.

Indigenous and Archaeological Views at Variance

One aspect of the Indigenous view of everything in the universe being alive is the belief that the dead are alive and in communication with the living. To say that the dead are alive is an oxymoron to the Western way of thinking, but is an obvious truth to the Indigenous way of thinking. Indigenous people have very different views about the dead, very different attitudes about their relationships and responsibilities to them, and very different feelings about them from those held by most Westerners. In some aboriginal cultures where reincarnation is a firmly held belief, there is not even a clear separation between self and present loved ones, ancestors and descendants.

In the Indigenous view, those who no longer walk among the living are considered to be still living but usually somewhere else—the spirit world—however that may be conceived in different cultures. I say "usually" because, in many cultures, the spirit world and ordinary reality are not seen to be completely separate. Many native people believe they communicate with the dead at times through their lives in dreams and visions, and even encounter them occasionally in the ordinary world. Deceased loved ones may come to encourage, warn or give advice to the living. They may speak of the future or they may come just to visit. Powerful individuals, such as shamans, may be able to communicate with the dead virtually at will.

In those cultures where there is belief in reincarnation, there is no separation between the living and the dead; self and ancestors (or descendants); or past, present and future. One is alive today, has always been living and always will be living. That kind of belief system generates very long-term considerations. One will, in a very real and immediate sense, reap the future consequences of one's actions. With these kinds of beliefs about the dead, it is impossible to consider human remains or even artefacts which are evidence of past lives in a detached manner as data or archaeological materials. These views of the dead as not really separated from the living result in an appreciation of the past and sense of responsibility to the dead which is so much more personal, emotional and profound than the sense of many Western people of the past as primarily an intellectual curiosity.

From my brief discussion of views of the dead and reincarnation, it becomes obvious that Indigenous people have a concept of time which differs from the Western view. In the Western view, we can only live in the present, the past is over and the future does not yet exist. The present is only a moment, the cusp between the past and present. It is often said that in the Indigenous view, time is cyclical rather than linear. I conceive of it more as overlapping spirals which can intersect at any place, like a small child's scribbled crayon drawing in three dimensions or a tangled Slinky. The concept of a spiral conveys the idea of regular movement in one direction, while in the Indigenous view one can move through time in any direction if one is powerful enough. The dead seem to be able to do this, maintaining ongoing contact between themselves and the living. In such a belief system, it is important not to offend the dead just as it is important not to offend the living. The dead must be treated with respect because they remain a vital part of the living world. Whether an ancestor died recently or long ago, in the Indigenous perspective, they are relatives, and relatives are loved and must be cared for, even though they are also quite feared in some societies. They can never be thought of as specimens.

Those who think from an Indigenous perspective find the objectification in Western thought very hard to understand, dangerous and frightening. A logical outcome of dichotomous thinking which places the researcher in one category and everything studied in the category of object leads, in the Indigenous view, to racism, colonialism, environmental destruction and many other ills which have destroyed the natural balance between all the entities make up the universe. Objectification precludes respect. It precludes considering others, whether they are animals, plants, artefacts, other humans or the earth itself, as innately valuable and, therefore, places them in a category of things available for exploitation. Some Indigenous peoples believe that this objectifying attitude may bring about the end of the world as we know it.

Indigenous Ways of Knowing

Although there is growing recognition among Western scholars of the value of Indigenous knowledge, Western science-generated knowledge is generally seen as the only valid source of knowledge. As Vine Deloria has said, "In America we have an entrenched state religion, and it is called science" (1997, 211). Roberts and Wills support Deloria's contention, saying, "in today's globally dominant Western culture, science is assumed to be not simply *a* way of seeing but *the* way of seeing reality" (1998, 43; emphasis in the original). Knowledge generated by non-Western systems is often dismissed as unfounded because the methods used to collect data, record it and analyze it differ from Western scientific methods.

I would argue that, although Indigenous methods of knowledge production may differ from Western ones, their efficacy has been proven when the bodies of knowledge they have produced have allowed aboriginal societies to survive over long periods of time, sometimes in very difficult environments. Even though Indigenous ways of knowing do not include the Western scientific principles of reductionism, objectivism and positivism they have not only produced knowledge which allowed societies to reproduce themselves, but have even produced knowledge which is, at times, superior to that of Western science, as in the examples of Indigenous knowledge of local animal and plant species, weather prediction and environmental changes over time.

Indigenous ways of knowing may not be valid from the narrowly scientific Western perspective but they are valid from the Indigenous perspective and continue to order Indigenous reality. Indigenous knowledge is holistic, rather than reductionist, seeing the universe as a living entity; it is experiential, rather than positivist, contending that experiences which cannot be measured are no less real than those that can be measured.

The contrast between the Indigenous way of perceiving the world and learning about it and the Western way results in the kinds of differences of opinion which commonly occur between Indigenous people and archaeologists. If archaeologists or scientists of other Western disciplines are to better understand and communicate with Indigenous peoples, they must be open to the idea that Western science is not the only method by which knowledge can be created; other peoples have successfully created knowledge with their own methods. Indigenous peoples do have tested methods for creating knowledge. Observations are made of phenomena by many people over long periods of time and under different conditions. Information is pooled and passed on orally from generation to generation. Mnemonic devices are sometimes used to help remember the information. For especially important knowledge there may be particular devices which are used and specific situations in which the knowledge is transmitted. A fine example of Indigenous methods of preserving and transmitting knowledge, which is particularly relevant to archaeologists, is the oral histories of the Gitxsan and related peoples of northwest British Columbia and southeast Alaska. Correlating archaeological and, particularly, paleoenvironmental evidence, indicates that the Gitxsan and their relatives remember accurately, and in great detail, their history stretching back to the initial peopling of the area in the Pleistocene (Harris 2002).

How Indigenous Knowledge Can Make a Contribution to Archaeology

When archaeologists accept that Indigenous knowledge systems create valid knowledge, they are able to access bodies of information which can be used in correlation with data from archaeological sources advancing archaeological understanding (Anyon et al. 1997; Echo-Hawk 2000; Yellowhorn 1996). Oral history is an obvious source of information that could guide archaeological investigation and assist in interpretation of archaeological data, but it is not the only kind of Indigenous knowledge which can inform archaeological research. Another source is toponyms. The Indigenous landscape is one in which virtually every feature of the land and waters has a name and in which names have meaning. In many Indigenous cultures the names of places tell what the place is or has been used for, who utilized the location, or what historical events may have occurred there. Another source of Indigenous knowledge which could guide archaeological investigation and interpretation is things which may appear to be visual or poetic works of art to the uninitiated observer. Indigenous people's songs often tell stories of historical places and events. Objects which appear to be works of art are often much more than decorative articles and may be mnemonic devices which relate to stories of historical events and places. The so-called totem poles of the Northwest Coast of British Columbia and Alaska are a prime example of such mnemonic devices. Each crest on a pole represents a historical event in the past of the kin group which raised the pole.

The land considered wilderness by Westerners, for many Indigenous peoples, is an open book. The land is full of the very stories of the past that archaeologists seek. Indigenous people are often very interested in their history and many welcome the opportunity to add to their knowledge from other sources such as archaeology. Two sources of knowledge with different methodologies are likely to increase the understanding of a subject, a time period, a geographical area or a people.

Accepting Indigenous methods of creating and preserving knowledge and adding that knowledge to that obtained by archaeological methods is bound to expand archaeological horizons. Ideas gleaned from Indigenous knowledge and thought are likely to expand and transform archaeological theory and indicate new directions for archaeological investigation and new ideas for archaeological interpretation. An example of this, again from the Northwest Coast, is the oral histories which indicate either that people lived in the area during the last glaciation in refugia or that deglaciation must have been much earlier than previously believed. The paleontological evidence for such a proposition is expanding yearly (Dixon et al. 1997; Fedje and Christiansen 1999; Heaton and Grady 1993; Heaton et al. 1996; Hetherington et al. 2001) and the search for the correlating archaeological data is on (Fedje and Josenhans 1999; Hetherington et al. 2001). . . .

7

Remythologizing the Relationship between Indians and Archaeologists

Larry J. Zimmerman

Remythologizing Relationships between Indians and Archaeologists

As is important in syncretism, both sides are in the process of *remythologizing*, that is, making their belief systems seem as if they were not exactly what they earlier seemed to be. This is an important and *positive* process that is generally neither intentional, nor conspiratorial, nor planned. It is a necessary step toward reconciliation. Although some will see this paper as a criticism of archaeology, that is not my intent. Rather, my interest is in exploring how people process the past and trying to understand what seem to be ironical and sometimes paradoxical actions and statements of archaeologists.

For example, to maintain the notion that the discipline was speaking with one voice, no views from archaeologists favoring reburial appeared in mainstream literature, that is, in the key journals or major series, until very recently, but the remythologizing process was nonetheless operating to make the profession seem more reasonable. The best example of this is a sequence of commentaries appearing early in the 1990s in *American Antiquity*, the flagship journal of the Society for American Archaeology, where the important, mainstream theoretical, methodological, and ethical issues are presented and discussed.

Although the controversy had raged since the early 1980s, little of significance about repatriation had appeared in the journal except for

---

Excerpted from: Zimmerman, Larry. 1997. Remythologizing the Relationship between Indians and Archaeologists. In *Native Americans and Archaeologists: Stepping Stones to Common Ground*, ed. N. Swidler, K. E. Dongoske, R. Anyon, and A. S. Downer, 55–56. Walnut Creek, CA: AltaMira Press.

the "fine print" appearance of the SAA's reburial policy in business meeting minutes. Finally, *American Antiquity* published a commentary by Goldstein and Kintigh (1990) on "Ethics and the Reburial Controversy." The authors took a "middle-of-the-road" position suggesting that while archaeologists must be more attentive to Indian concerns, they also must "address our various constituencies, educate all of the publics about the past, and make certain that we don't alienate or disenfranchise past, present, or future generations" (Goldstein and Kintigh 1990, 590).

The authors were writing as individuals, but many took this to be a softening of the SAA position, given that Goldstein had been SAA secretary and that Kintigh had been head of the SAA ad hoc Committee on Reburial, involved in negotiations on NAGPRA. Klesert and Powell, two archaeologists who had worked closely with Indians, submitted a critique of this commentary to the journal but were rejected. Soon thereafter, the journal editor, J. Jefferson Reid, noted that his attendance at the Third Southwest Symposium included a plenary session of Native Americans commenting on archaeology and archaeologists where he was astounded by "new and rather startling" realizations that Indians didn't trust archaeology or its accounts of the Indian past and that the latter were seen as a threat. He concluded that "[a] North American prehistory irrelevant to North American Indians would seem to be in jeopardy or, minimally, in serious need of epistemological adjustment" (Reid 1992, 195). Two issues later, J. Reid published a very negative critique of Goldstein and Kintigh by Clement Meighan (1992), one of the more "vocal" archaeologists against reburial. Meighan's critique clearly put archaeologists against reburial on the radical conservative fringe while bolstering Goldstein and Kintigh—the perceived SAA representatives—by making them seem very, very reasonable, and by implication, though perhaps not intentionally, made the SAA seem forward looking. In mid-1993, the commentary by Klesert and Powell (1993) finally appeared, but with its criticisms of Goldstein and Kintigh dramatically toned down.

Remythologizing among archaeologists was most apparent at the 1995 SAA annual meeting in Minneapolis. On the opening night, a past SAA president, identified by some Indians a few years ago as being obstructionist to reburial, gave a major address that sounded as if everything had not been as bad as it had seemed at the time. He had recently begun training programs at his university on how to work with Indian people and how to deal with NAGPRA's consultation clauses. During the sessions, with the SAA Executive Board's blessing, a group of First Nation archaeologists held an organizational meeting. At the closing plenary, an archaeologist from a major museum—who had quietly supported reburial all along—pointed out, to loud applause, the promise of working closely with Indian people.

In a related matter, SAA also began to work on revision of its ethics code. Its accountability principle proposes that archaeologists be more aware of and responsible toward the interests of nonarchaeologists with interests in archaeology. Supporting statements specifically dealt with Native Americans and reburial. Although they will not be in the actual principles, they were at least part of the formulation of the code and were published (Watkins et al. 1995). The final principles, as accepted by the SAA Executive Board at the 1996 annual meeting, only mention Indians in the public education section.

In 1995 I had the opportunity to address the annual meeting of Keepers of the Treasures, a national organization developed to protect and promote the living traditions of American Indians, Alaska Natives, and Native Hawaiians. I explained this remythologizing process to them. I suggested that on our part as archaeologists, we will sound like we have always been your strongest supporters and friends. We will say that we have always been willing to work closely with you. We will develop new and cooperative programs that will offer to train Indian people in archaeology. I was pleased when Northern Cheyenne elder Bill Tallbull, who had attended my archaeological field school in 1988 for two weeks, said to me afterward, "You know, I have seen this happening already." One can predict that this remythologizing will continue, probably to the point where it seems that archaeology was always in favor of reburial and really was just trying to seek clarification of certain points.

The remythologizing process among Indians with respect to their relationships with archaeologists is not as clear, but it is happening. In their recent dispute with the Nebraska State Historical Society, the Pawnee relied heavily on very traditional archaeological views of Pawnee origins to bolster their case for cultural affiliation of remains. A Pawnee tribal historian involved in that case, Roger Echo-Hawk, has recently had to defend his acceptance of this and other archaeology to a mixed-nation group of Native Americans in Colorado where he acted as a monitor for archaeology on construction of the new Denver airport (also see Echo-Hawk 1997). The fundamental problem for Indians is that many have gone to great lengths to distance themselves from archaeology. Many others, however, recognize the contribution that archaeologists have made on such issues as land claims and that when it comes to preservation of important cultural sites, Indians and archaeologists could be almost natural allies. Indians will probably not have to go as far in their remythologizing because their position is more understood by the public as being "right." Nonetheless, if they choose to deal with archaeology, they must go through the process. . . .

Covenantal Archaeology

Among the major Native American complaints about archaeology is that it has benefited only itself and its practitioners. Whatever the truth of this complaint, many archaeologists have worked closely with Indian people on land claims and in very successful heritage preservation programs. The exemplary, well-developed, and relatively long-term programs of the Navajo, Zuni, and Hopi in the Southwest have been extremely successful. Though no program is perfect, and some cannot incorporate even the entire range of Indian views or concerns, nonetheless the programs are at least administratively under Indian control, dealing with Indian concerns first and those of archaeology later.

As many archaeologists who have worked closely with Indian people have discovered, archaeology need not come to a screeching halt when it accedes to Indian demands. Many have discovered that if a relationship of trust can be built, archaeology may gain increased access to materials and sites. At the same time, control of the archaeology transfers to Indian hands, and they can see it as a benefit; their own questions about their own pasts receive primary attention. The kind of work done is essentially a covenant between archaeologists and Indians; this is fundamentally what indigenous peoples have asked for in the WAC ethics code. The approach *will* work, and I agree with Powell, Garza, and Hendricks (1993) that it will flourish as soon as its benefits are more widely realized.

The covenants will include not only research, but education. At first many archaeologists believed that if they could just educate Indians about what archaeology does, then Indians would come to appreciate it more. Many archaeologists still do not understand, however, that supposedly beneficial educational programs, such as the proposed scholarships offered by SAA and the Plains Anthropological Society, can be seen as an effort to co-opt Indian people and are viewed with suspicion by some. If the attitude, on the contrary, is to train Indian people in archaeology theory and method to apply these tools to their own research questions and *not* necessarily to get them to buy into archaeological interpretation, then these programs have a good chance of success. As an aside, I now chair the SAA's Native American Scholarship Committee, which has been slow to get off the ground due to lack of funds. Initially, I objected to the whole concept of an SAA Indian scholarship until I figured out that it was part of the remythologizing process.

If covenantal archaeology works, archaeological interpretation will change to better meet Indian interpretations of the past. This is a profoundly complex matter. As one editor of this volume pointed out, there may well be no pan-Indian interpretations of the past. There may even be conflicts, as in the case of the Hopi and Navajo differences of the settlement of the Southwest. Asked if archaeology could be made to meet both histories, which could grate on some Native sensibilities and draw archaeologists into the explosive political arena, I might counter by saying that archaeology as a profession is already there.

One might also point out that there is a substantive difference between archaeology as a profession and archaeology as a way of knowing. If one views archaeology as the former, then no, archaeology cannot meet both histories. If one sees archaeology as the latter, then the answer is absolutely yes. As a way of knowing, all archaeology provides is a basis of interpretation from material remains from a past. Archaeology does not seek or determine truth about the past; whether done by non-Indians or Indians, archaeology is a tool that helps people construct—not reconstruct—the past. In one sense this question betrays a fundamental epistemological issue in archaeology: that there is one correct view of the past and that it can only be known archaeologically. That view causes no end of problems in the archaeological profession's relationship with Indians.

On the other hand, if archaeology as a way of knowing is under the control of Indian people, then archaeology as a profession can change. What archaeologists teach the non-Indian public about Indians, for example, will perhaps downplay such solid archaeological dogma as the Bering land bridge migration route to the Americas and the like. Of course, this grates on archaeological sensibilities because archaeology *must* find grounding for interpretation in the material record from the past, not in peoples' belief systems about themselves and their origins. Some archaeologists suggest that this issue is akin to debates between scientists and creationists, but there is a major difference, because in archaeology and the associated issues of repatriation and reburial we are dealing with "archaeological colonialism." Pasts created by archaeologists have been imposed on Indian pasts without a chance for debate. There is, in other words, a major power relationship difference in the two issues. They are analogues, not homologues.

Ethnocritical Archaeology

So where does this leave us? Archaeology as a profession and Indian nations must both have their own stories from their own bases of knowledge. They need not be the same stories even if they are discussing the same past(s). To reiterate, however, power relationships are crucial. Archaeology has been a dominant society tool, viewed by Native Americans as part of the western tradition's repression of the "Other," the "Rest" of humanity. The reburial issue has been and remains a forum for Indian declarations of their victimization by the West, and they have a right to complain loudly about that treatment by the profession of archaeology. Although archaeology has a right to its own stories, if archaeology and Indian relations have a chance to improve, then archaeology must be the one to change the most. An approach like that suggested by Arnold Krupat (1992) might be beneficial.

Krupat writes from the perspective of literary criticism, especially of Native American literature. He is suspicious of any scientific theory or position that looks like a metaphor of social ideology or that can be construed as contributing to the alienation of any class or group, which is exactly what archaeology has done.

In essence, if Indians and archaeologists view all issues as oppositional sets, bipolar and black or white, we are bound to fail to change very much. Any compromise between archaeology and Indians still reflect the positions of the opposing sides. For archaeology, this has meant simply another way of telling "our" own story, of "turning 'their' [Indian] incoherent jabber into an eloquence of use only to ourselves" (Krupat 1992, 6). As an alternative, however, archaeology could apply what Krupat calls "ethnocriticism," which suggests that scholars work at the boundaries of their usual ways of knowing. In this intellectual frontier,

> oppositional sets like West/Rest, Us/Them, anthropological/biological, historical/mythical, and so on, often tend to break down. On the one hand, cultural contact can indeed produce mutual rejections, the reification of differences, and defensive retreats into celebrations of what each group regards as distinctly its own. . . . On the other hand, it may also frequently be the case that interaction leads to interchange . . . and transculturalization (Krupat 1992, 15).

Oppositional views are simply useless. As they once justified imperial domination, they now serve to justify postcolonial revisionist "victimist history." One can acknowledge that some people have been hurt by others in the colonial context and that they have every right to complain about their treatment, but to where does that lead except more rhetoric? Ethnocriticism is concerned with differences rather than oppositions; it seeks to replace oppositional with dialogical models where cultural differences are explored and where interpretations are negotiated rather than declared. Claims to accuracy, systematicity, and knowledge would reside in their capacity to take more into context, that is, to be more flexible and open to new ideas and approaches that deal with differences. Thus, if ethnocritical archaeology is a way of knowing, even two Indian nations such as the Hopi and Navajo might come to terms with their differences over origins and settlement of the Southwest.

The result is a relative truth, but one that does have rules. Archaeologists can still be scientific, but in ways meaningful to Indians, by negotiating the methods and procedures to be followed and by indicating the empirical and logical components of reasoning. How might this work? In truth, we hardly know yet because so little of it has been tried, but there are indications. One example from the Southwest is discussed in the thoughtful and provocative position paper by Anyon, Ferguson, Jackson, and Lane (1996) that looks at how oral tradition and archaeology can be coalesced (also see Anyon et al. 1997). What happens in ethnocritical archaeology is that the science is clearly articulated and is placed fully into an explicit social context. This is the essence of a covenantal archaeology, where research questions and methods are negotiated and support a mutually agreed upon agenda. As this approach becomes more commonplace, archaeological science will become more modest and very different from what it has been. It will be the end product of the syncretism begun with the reburial issue. . . .

8

Power to the (Indigenous) Past and Present! Or: The Theory and Method behind Archaeological Theory and Method

H. Martin Wobst

Why write about archaeological theory and method in a book on Indigenous archaeologies? Are these topics not at loggerheads in discussions of archaeological practice? Why do theory and method in archaeology and Indigenous archaeologies suggest an internal contradiction, if not an oxymoron, when used in the same sentence? In this paper I explore why theory and method in archaeology and Indigenous archaeologies continue be so far apart from each other that many archaeologists (see, for example, Friends of America's Past 2003) and a number of Indigenous representatives (for example, Deloria 1969, 1992, 1995) view them as inherently incompatible.

I am not an Indigenous archaeologist, by the definition used in this volume. I was educated in archaeology at a North American university, have done field work in the USA, France, and the former Yugoslavia, teach archaeology in the academy as part of an anthropology program, and train future archaeologists. My point of departure for this paper is not Indigenous archaeologies, or the goals and aspirations of Indigenous populations, but the archaeological mainstream. I am asking, what in its present theory and method separates archaeology from Indigenous interests, and what needs to change to overcome that separation.

We are witnessing the emergence of a new form of archaeology, an archaeology that is informed by Indigenous values and agendas. This

---

Excerpted from Wobst, H. Martin. 2005. Power to the (Indigenous) Past and Present! Or: The Theory and Method behind Archaeological Theory and Method. In *Indigenous Archaeologies: Decolonizing Theory and Practice,* ed. H. M. Wobst and C. Smith, 17–32. London: Routledge.

Indigenous archaeology moves beyond research "about" Indigenous peoples to focus on research that is conducted with, and for, Indigenous peoples. This interface between archaeology and Indigenous peoples is expanding and productive (Davidson, Lovell-Jones, and Bancroft 1995; Loring and Ashini 2000; McGuire 1994; Nicholas and Andrews 1997; Swidler et al. 1997; Watkins 2000; Zimmermann 1989). Much of its activity is useful for archaeology and Indigenous peoples. However, even if all such projects had been successfully completed, if all archaeologists had been sensitized to the agenda of Indigenous peoples, and all archaeology were carried out by Indigenous archaeologists, archaeology might still do violence to Indigenous peoples. That violence would have archaeological theory and practice as its source (Wobst and Smith 1999). A truly shared and constructive future for Indigenous people and archaeologists will come about only once archaeological theory and method is liberated from its First World bias. This paper is a stepping stone in that direction. . . .

The Emergence of Indigenous Archaeology

In the First World of the twenty-first century, the (Indigenous and other) pasts that archaeologists generate are of great interest to many people. People are more interested in these Indigenous pasts than in Indigenous presents. They constitute weapons for interfering in the present, and for generating alternative futures—futures that are not necessarily desirable. As the discussion has shown, archaeological practice is potentially quite deleterious to the future of Indigenous societies.

Archaeology came into the First World as a strategy in support of the state, an association that pervades its theory, method and data even today. In its present practice, archaeology makes it harder to envision logical alternatives to state societies, and it falsifies the archaeological records of non-state societies to look like incipient states or failures to reach statehood. Archaeological practice has done that, unthinkingly, at every decision point from applying for excavation funding to museum displays and curation following fieldwork and publication.

Archaeological practice with Indigenous pasts requires significant change in archaeological theory and method. Foremost is a broadening of archaeological vision. This broadening will make possible the theoretical integration of material culture studies with fields of study that have been concerned with "non-material" realms, such as historical linguistics, language, poetry, music, dance, place name studies, oral history, folklore, myth, and others. Another axis of theoretical integration will require de-emphasizing the difference between artefact and nonartefact and between "nature" and "culture," so that the entire visual (or even imaginable) scape is allowed to enter our vision of Indigenous and other pasts. This visual or imaginable scape may include stars and alignments, fauna and flora, geomorphology, and landscapes, colors, sounds and smells. We will have to allow for "natural" (that is "non-artefactual") and "cultural" (that is, "artefactual") variables to be enculturated, to be significant to human action, and to articulate, like artefacts, with social life. These kinds of broadening our theory will allow us to feel ourselves closer to pasts, such as the Indigenous ones at the center of this essay, that are significantly different from the materialities of the present. It will also allow us to decolonize the Indigenous past (and present).

Archaeological practice liberated from the context for which it was invented has significant roles to play in the present. It is a powerful tool for the Indigenous to liberate their pasts from the filter of colonizing ideologies, and thus to enable them to take control of their future as well as of their past. Such archaeological practice will also empower the people of the First World by presenting them with clear alternatives to the societies in which they are enculturated, thus broadening their room for action. In that way, archaeological theory and method can help us to feel ourselves to an understanding of social process that is shared and empowering, rather than partial and enslaving.

Indigenous societies of the twenty-first century have little patience with non-community members enriching themselves in their comfortable ivory-towers by establishing expertise over their past, while blinding themselves to the Indigenous present. Instead, they are reaching out for allies to help them build vibrant communities, in full control over their past, present, and future. To decolonize archaeology and Indigenous history requires non-Indigenous archaeologists to reinvent themselves so that they are thoroughly grounded in the problems of their Indigenous contemporaries, sensitive to Indigenous needs, and willing to further Indigenous projects and agendas. There can be little doubt that the point of departure for these projects must be contemporary Indigenous society, rather than the academies of the First World. Non-indigenous "archaeologists" are needed as allies, guest workers and mercenaries to help Indigenous populations with their plans, projects, and battles to the extent that they engage the Indigenous past. Ultimately, these battles will reshape archaeology in the First World as significantly as Indigenous communities.

9

Indigenous Archaeology as Decolonizing Practice

Sonya Atalay

Distance of Time, Distance of Worldview

One often hears archaeology described as being primarily concerned with a study of the unknown, of what has been lost or buried (e.g., Bourbon 2000; O'Connor 1995). The "lost" pasts that archaeologists seek to uncover are often distanced from them by time, culture, or both. In studying the past, archaeologists utilize the contemporary lens of their time to study "others." Thus, from its earliest beginnings, there has been a sense of "othering" involved in archaeological research that is based upon a quest for knowledge and understanding about those distanced from the present day by time (e.g., studying people and cultures from *pre*historic times, who are worthy of study because their lifeways are different and unknown).

Through the process of colonization, Westerners gained the power to study not only those distant from themselves by time but also the pasts of others who were distant from themselves culturally, and often geographically—those who had been subjected to colonial rule around the globe. In these colonial contexts, the othering by archaeologists not only entails the distance of time but also involves distance based on another, more cultural dimension, as it has created a power imbalance that allowed Western archaeologists to study the past lifeways of those who are not their own ancestors. Archaeologists have utilized Western epistemologies to view the practices and lifeways of others, many of whom held a very different worldview that operated on a different set

---

Excerpted from Atalay, Sonya. 2006. Indigenous Archaeology as Decolonizing Practice. *American Indian Quarterly* 30(3&4):280–310.

of ontological and epistemological principles, and this research was also carried out for the benefit of Western scholars, was (re)produced using Western methods of recording history (external from people, held in books, for purchase), and was taught in Western institutions of higher learning or sold to Western public audiences. . . .

Building an Indigenous Archaeology

The theoretical and methodological tenets and practices of Indigenous archaeology are currently being defined. The concepts and practices it professes have not been clearly defined, but rather are in the process of being articulated, with both Indigenous and non-Indigenous scholars contributing to its development. In my own view, Indigenous archaeology includes research that critiques and deconstructs Western archaeological practice as well as research that works toward recovering and investigating Indigenous experiences, practices, and traditional knowledge systems. George Nicholas has referred to Indigenous archaeology as, "archaeology with, for, and by" Indigenous people (Nicholas 1997, 85). I agree with Nicholas that an Indigenous archaeology should be engaged in conducting research that is beneficial and valuable for descendent communities, and I advocate such research to be carried out in full collaboration with community members, elders, and spiritual and cultural leaders. However, I argue that Indigenous archaeology is not only for and by Indigenous people but has wider implications and relevance outside of Indigenous communities. In my view Indigenous archaeology provides a model for archaeological practice that can be applied globally as it calls for and provides a methodology for collaboration of descendent communities and stakeholders around the world.

It is critical to make a distinction here between consultation, which is currently required as part of the NAGPRA legislation, and collaboration. Unlike collaboration, consultation does *not* necessarily allow for Indigenous people to play an active role in the *entire* research process, including research design, grant writing and funding processes, analysis and interpretation of results, production of reports, and sharing of research results in a culturally effective way with community members (Forsman 2004, 2–3). A growing number of scholars have been exploring collaborative methodologies and putting forth models for effective means of determining what is applicable and valuable in any particular community and their methods for carrying out such research (see, for example, Foster and Croes 2002; Lightfoot et al. 2001; Nicholas 1997; Nicholas and Andrews 1997; Robinson 1996). Such research is quite valuable, and I believe this is an area that requires a great deal of further exploration and investigation among Indigenous archaeologists in order to further develop effective methodologies. Whatever models are put forth, it seems clear that there will not be one definitive solution for effective collaborative practice but that each circumstance will require its own unique strategy. Some of the challenges to be faced in this area include how to determine the appropriate collaborative partners in each community, how to face the challenges of working with diverse groups within each community (who may each have different desires and aspirations in terms of research plans and agendas), how to fund collaborative projects, and issues of intellectual property rights—to name only a few. In my own research, I have found the participatory research and popular education model of Paolo Freire to be one worthy of further exploration, and I discuss this topic in greater detail later in this article. However, beyond a Freirian approach, there are a number of potential collaborative methodologies to be explored—each with challenges to be faced—but it is clear that any models of collaborative research must involve descendent communities and explore the methods and practices they see as culturally relevant and appropriate.

Beyond the issue of collaboration, identity and place are two of the issues related to Indigenous archaeology that I'd like to address here briefly—questions of who does, or can do, it and where is it carried out seem critical to address. While I agree that Indigenous archaeology is something that must involve Indigenous people, scholars as well as elders, tribal historians, community members, spiritual leaders, and other stakeholders, I argue that Indigenous archaeology is not simply archaeology done by or involving Indigenous people. One need not be an Indigenous person to engage in the practice of Indigenous archaeology—it does not include such essentialist qualities. Archaeology on Indigenous land, conducted by Native people without a critical gaze that includes collaboration, Indigenous epistemologies, and Native conceptions of the past, history, and time or that neglects to question the role of research in the community would simply replicate the dominant archaeological paradigm. Such a noncritical archaeology would be part of an imperialist practice, one that disperses the methods of the mainstream (American and British archaeology) to the "other" (for a description of imperialist archaeology see Trigger 1984).

It may be the case that Indigenous people who become archaeologists will choose a nation-centered research agenda, one in which they focus on questions of interest to their own community. Some might view such an approach negatively, taking it to be part of a nationalist or revitalist project; however, I would disagree with this assessment and argue that a desire among Indigenous archaeologists to study the "self" is not part of a state-sponsored nationalism but rather part of a larger decolonizing project to develop counter-discourse. As part of a decolonizing practice, Indigenous archaeologists aim to challenge the master narrative and attempt to de-center standard archaeological practice, to bring back to Indigenous people the power to set the agenda for their own heritage, to ask the questions, to determine what is excavated, and to remain involved in interpretations and dissemination of knowledge that reflect their own traditional methods of cultural resource management. As Linda Tuhiwai Smith notes in her book *Decolonizing Methodologies*, such a research agenda might also include pointing out the power relations involved in mainstream archaeological practice and bringing the imbalance of power to the foreground.

Indigenous archaeology exists and is growing today because Indigenous people, marginalized and victimized by the early development and ongoing daily practice of anthropology, archaeology, and other social sciences, are finding ways to create counter-discourse that speaks back to the power of colonialist and imperialist interpretations of the past. This research is situated to work from the place of the "local," among the elders and people in our communities—to acknowledge their critiques of exploitative research practices, to name them, and deconstruct them. Our research may then examine ways of regaining lost traditions and use those to move beyond critique of Western archaeological practices to offer a positive plan of forward movement toward a more ethical practice that takes seriously the concern of Indigenous people with regard to their own heritage. Indigenous archaeology is thus part of a decolonizing process that aims to improve upon problematic aspects of mainstream archaeological practices by incorporating Indigenous concepts and knowledge forms.

Audre Lorde (1984, 112) writes that "the master's tools will never dismantle the master's house," and truthfully, some Indigenous activists might agree with this stance, arguing that archaeology (and archaeologists) are part of the problem of an ongoing colonization in Indigenous communities—a problem that must be tackled and dismantled by halting all archaeological research. However, I disagree and would argue that although mainstream archaeology requires critical reflection and considerable change in order to become decolonized, this work is beneficial for Indigenous communities because it will bring about positive and effective change from within the discipline that will result in a powerful research tool from which Indigenous people, and others around the globe, can benefit. A decolonized archaeology can play a critical beneficial role in the recovery of many other precolonization Indigenous practices that, as Angela Cavender Wilson (2004, 83–84) points out, once adapted to our contemporary world, can be important for our health and well-being. Some of these include foodways and harvesting, spiritual practices and ceremonial knowledge, methods of education and reproduction of knowledge, and land use and conservation practices. However, I agree with Cavender Wilson (2004, 83) that not all topics and areas of research are appropriate for investigation by outsiders, and the topics of research and emphasis for developing projects that seek to recover Indigenous practices and concepts must be those thought worthy and appropriate for sharing by Indigenous communities.

Centering Indigenous Concepts

In my own work, I have found it helpful to investigate the postcolonial concept of "de-centering." De-centering involves moving concepts from the margin to the center. In terms of archaeological research, I've found it useful to de-center certain dominant Western concepts relating to the linear and departmentalized view of time, systems of production and reproduction of knowledge, and the role of research in society. In bringing to the center of archaeological theory some of the concepts held by Indigenous people about the past, traditional ways of teaching about history, heritage, and ancestral remains, and the role and responsibilities of research knowledge for communities, we would be in a position to begin envisioning a very different type of archaeological practice—one that emphasizes ethics and social justice for a wider, more diverse audience. However, we must ask the question, if in working to de-center some of the problematic aspects of Western archaeological practice, are we then advocating for destroying one power structure (a Western one) to simply replace it with another, Indigenous-centered one? I ask this question because of a recent dialogue I had on this topic in which by suggesting the de-centering of Western concepts in order to center Indigenous views, I was labeled a "colonist," someone who was doing nothing different than what Western scholars had done before me (i.e., forcing my Indigenous worldview onto others). In response to such an argument I feel it is critical that we think carefully about what it is that we are calling for in decolonizing archaeology, and other Western-dominated forms of discourse and practice (history, museums, sociology, etc.). In addressing this issue, I argue as both Abiola Irele (1991) and Peter R. Schmidt (1995) have that we must sometimes use the master's tools (in this case critique and academic scholarship) to create a counter-discourse to Western approaches that have consistently worked to destroy or silence our Indigenous ways of knowing (both discussed in Schmidt and Patterson 1995).

There are numerous concepts and areas of traditional Indigenous knowledge that deserve further attention and research as part of Indigenous archaeology and a wider decolonizing archaeological practice. I offer here one example of de-centering that seems critical in an Indigenous archaeology—the Anishinaabe concept of *gikinawaabi*. *Gikinawaabi* is an Anishinaabe concept that describes the passing or reproduction of knowledge, through experience, from elder to younger generations. It relies on the oral tradition and on practice, in daily life. After exploring the implications and practices of this concept in past and contemporary Anishinaabe life, I argue that *gikinawaabi* is a concept that should be centered in an Indigenous archaeology, particularly for what it implies about the communal access to knowledge.

In Ojibwe culture, while certain people have greater access to some forms of knowledge than others, there remains a sense that knowledge, particularly that related to our history, is shared by the community. It is not stored externally, in books on shelves, but is *internal*—held inside the people themselves. Knowledge of this sort might be put in the care of certain individuals whose responsibility it is to exercise knowledge stewardship in protecting and passing on that knowledge. Yet, it is of critical importance that tribal history be for the community, not something external from them. It is passed from elders to youth, via the oral tradition through face-to-face interactions and in daily life practice.

If archaeology is to take a lesson from *gikinawaabi* practices, then archaeological collaboration with Indigenous and local communities must become standard practice, as questions of ownership and stewardship of cultural property in the form of historical knowledge, access to it, and the processes by which it is reproduced in the community are brought to the center. Although this concept is from an Ojibwe tradition and holds particular relevance and importance in that cultural context, I argue that it is also an example of the way in which traditional Indigenous knowledge holds wisdom and relevance for the larger global community of which it is a part. In this way, *gikinawaabi* as a centered and central part of mainstream archaeological practice holds important implications for the theory, methods, and practice of archaeology globally, outside of Ojibwe, Native North American, or Indigenous settings. It has relevance for an ethical and decolonized practice globally, which brings history back into the hands, hearts, and minds of a wider audience of diverse stakeholders, descendant communities, and publics. Borrowing from Ojibwe literary scholar, Gerald Vizenor's (1984) poetical description, it allows for an archaeologist as a teller of stories to "relume the diverse memories of the visual past into the experiences and metaphors of the present" as "original eruptions of time." Thus, archaeologists become critically engaged storytellers of sorts, who might utilize a range of scientific methods for examination yet retain an understanding, appreciation, and respect for the importance of the past in the present and the ethical implications of practice that entails. In the approach I am advocating for, Indigenous forms of science, history, and heritage management would be researched and then blended with Western concepts to produce Indigenous archaeology methods, theories, and practices that are ethical and socially just and put forward as models of a decolonized archaeology. . . .

Wider Implications: Traditional Indigenous Knowledge to Transform Research

Part of the practice of decolonizing archaeology is to research Indigenous traditional knowledge and practices and to utilize them, as Cavender Wilson (2004, 75) describes, "for the benefit of all humanity." There is a great deal of knowledge and wisdom in these practices and teachings that has the power to benefit our own Indigenous communities as well as others globally. Traditional Indigenous knowledge holds in it a wisdom, some of which is appropriate to share and can help to build strength for other communities. Thus a decolonizing archaeology must take as one of its goals the work of bringing these concepts to the academy and working toward their legitimization in areas of research that have a dramatic impact on Indigenous people globally, such as archaeology. Beyond that, we must also engage in the struggle to put these concepts into practice in our own scholarship, producing models that those working with descendent groups around the globe can follow.

Integral to this work is the realization and acknowledgement that Western ways of knowing are not in any way superior or natural—they are produced and reproduced through daily practice. As such, these ways of knowing and understanding the world can be disrupted, changed, and improved upon. As all aspects of human life and culture, knowledge and practices associated with its production and reproduction are not static but are constantly changing. Through Indigenous archaeology research as part of a global decolonizing practice, it is possible to find effective ways to regain our traditional knowledge, epistemologies, and practices and bring that knowledge, when appropriate for sharing outside of Native contexts, to the fore. Currently, one value system and standard is used—one that views Western science, theories, and methods as the standard and goal with the aim of producing knowledge truths. Decolonizing archaeology entails researching alternative ways of viewing the past, history, and heritage and working to see that these are viewed as valuable and legitimate ways of seeing. Some might utilize the resulting methods and theories in Indigenous communities, while others see the value of incorporating certain aspects into archaeological practice more broadly, as part of a wider project of global decolonization.

Thus Indigenous archaeology is not marginal in its applicability but rather has implications for mainstream archaeological practice globally. It offers the potential of bringing to archaeology a more ethical and engaged practice, one that is more inclusive and rich without sacrificing the rigor and knowledge production capacity that make it such a powerful tool for understanding and creating knowledge of the past. . . .

10

Archaeology, Diaspora, and Decolonization

Ian Lilley

Archaeologists in settler societies live in interesting times. Thinking of those in Australia, most are politically supportive of colonized Aboriginal and Torres Strait Islander minorities despite broader community skepticism regarding assertions of Indigenous identity and claims

Excerpted from Lilley, Ian. 2006. Archaeology, Diaspora, and Decolonization. *Journal of Social Archaeology* 6(1):28–47.

to land, resources and cultural property. While most have close working relationships with particular Indigenous groups and individuals, as a group they continue to be confronted by skeptical if not hostile Indigenous reactions to their work on a more abstract, political level. This state of affairs has prompted sometimes radical efforts to decolonize archaeological theory and practice by encompassing Aboriginal and Torres Strait Islander interests and outlooks and their complex and often subtle interplay with those of the colonizers (Byrne 2003a, 2003b; Clark and Frederick 2005; David and McNiven 2004). Such initiatives have unquestionably made progress, but if the Australian situation is any guide, the circumstances in which settler archaeologists find themselves can still occasion a great deal of personal and professional angst. This state of affairs would be easier to cope with intellectually, ethically and emotionally if practitioners had a better theoretical grasp of the phenomena they are trying to accommodate. To that end I propose that with certain provisos they might usefully be approached as the products of a single social condition—diaspora—in a manifestation that is unique to settler societies because it positions both the colonizer and the colonized as diasporic.

The qualifications are as follows. First, I am not equating the historical or contemporary socioeconomic or political realities of settlers and colonized minorities. Unlike the case for Aboriginal people after European settlement, the dispersal of colonists to Australia was voluntary for all but those transported as convicts or ordered to accompany them as guards and administrators. Moreover, no amount of hardship subsequently endured by colonizers as a group—including grievous losses in overseas wars—would come close to the enormities visited upon native minorities. What is more, in Australia as in other settler nations the intersection of race and class continues to result in gaping sociopolitical differentials between these groups, as made abundantly clear by empirical indices such as the appalling health statistics that characterize many if not most Indigenous communities. The issue, though, is very much one of *perception*. As I will show, there is good reason to contend that settler Australians, particularly but not exclusively the large Anglo-Celtic majority, see themselves as victims of a capricious and unforgiving colonial fate. At the level of the social processes underlying it, this aspect of the settler mentality is not fundamentally dissimilar to the perception of victimhood quite justifiably present in the outlook of colonized Indigenous peoples owing to their history of dispossession. *Both* groups have been uprooted and relocated by the colonial process, undeniable differences in the nature of this experience notwithstanding, and *both* have thus been left with the very strong perception that they are victims of colonial circumstance. The decolonization of the discipline (and indeed the nation as a whole) demands that these shared perceptions are exposed and explained rather than ignored or denied, in recognition of the fact that they reflect a shared rather than a segregated colonial history.

While the quality of victimhood through dispossession suggests that colonized native minorities can be characterized as diasporic, it must be stressed as a second proviso that this identification is an exploratory one that remains controversial. For indigenous people and those who sympathize with them politically, the potential for controversy lies in two prospects. The first, elaborated later in the article, is that characterizing native communities as diasporic (i.e., dispersed) can imply that they have been cut off from the homelands with which they identify to ground their identity claims. The second is the opposite of the first—to the extent that the diasporic condition emphasizes links to a homeland, it can imply that contemporary indigenous identity *necessarily* entails ties to land, as, for example, Ingold (2000) contends in his discussion of "relational" indigeneity. This could decentre Aboriginal perspectives that emphasize dimensions of existence other than space (e.g., time) as more critical to social identity (as in the case in the US Southwest discussed by Bernardini 2005). For conservative political interests, on the other hand, the potential for controversy lies in the implication of diaspora theory that native peoples assumed to have been thoroughly deracinated and delegitimized can still claim an authenticity rooted in "traditional" lands and "traditional" ways of life. In contrast to the foregoing, the characterization of European colonialism as a diasporic process is commonplace, but the particular perspective on Australia that I take up may be somewhat contentious. . . .

Understanding how and why native people literally go to such extraordinary lengths to maintain attachments to distant family members and homelands despite "the relentless assault on indigenous sovereignty by colonial powers, transnational capital, and emerging nation-states" (Clifford 1994, 310) is critical to understanding the attachment of colonized indigenous people to their cultural heritage under the same conditions. Traveling to and through country along family beats is both a key symbol of Indigenous Australian identity and a means of creating or maintaining that identity in a world that has long been intent on seeing the end of it, either through frontier violence or later policies of segregation or assimilation (cf. Byrne 2004). In this, such travel is not unlike the "traditional" journeys through country along Dreaming tracks by senior men who embodied those Dreamings and who were reinforcing their connections to particular tracts of land (Sutton 1994 [1988]). It is also reminiscent of the travel over often-prodigious distances that was involved in "traditional" ceremonial exchange networks (McBryde 1987). As Clifford (1994, 310) puts it:

> If tribal groups survive [today], it is now frequently in artificially reduced and displaced conditions, with segments of their populations living in cities away from the land, temporarily or even permanently. In these conditions, the older forms of tribal cosmopolitanism (practices of travel, spiritual quest, trade, exploration, warfare, labor migrancy, visiting and political alliance) are supplemented by more properly diasporic forms (practices of long-term dwelling away from home).

It is only by grasping these sorts of articulations among different dimensions of modern and "traditional" life that the "need" accepted by J. Allen (1987) in relation to contemporary Indigenous links with archaeological material becomes truly "apparent" as something more than simple special-interest politics. Attempts to maintain ties with country and kin and attempts to control access to cultural heritage and knowledge about the past are closely related aspects of life in a diasporic condition. Ethnographic research makes it clear that many Indigenous Australians see their history as fundamentally—*physically*—constitutive of their distinctive identity, as are attachments to kin and country. People literally *are* their history, the latter being read as patterns of interaction among people and relationships between people and place over time. Sutton (1994 [1988], 254–55), for instance, found that "men not infrequently refer in ordinary conversation to [mythic] Dreamings [which govern proper behaviour and relate people to place] as 'me,' 'my father,' or 'my father's father' . . . [and in] the third person they may refer to particular Dreamings by the names of living people." It is on the basis of this embodiment of history that contemporary Indigenous Australians claim inalienable attachment to their tangible and intangible historical heritage despite the fact that they may have been geographically and even to varying degrees intellectually separated from that history for several generations. Because history is physically part of them, they see it as theirs to control in the way that knowledge was/is "traditionally" controlled through its embodiment in particular individuals rather than being an alienable public good in the Western Enlightenment sense. This leads Sutton (1994[1988], 261) to conclude that:

> In these terms, [contemporary Aboriginal] history construction is remarkably similar to the [mythic] Dreaming. The past is also the present, as one of its aspects. The past is not transcendent or remote, but underpins and echoes present and continuing reality. Just as the Dreaming is the person, in one facet of its complex nature, the

> Aboriginal person is likewise the historical Aborigine—not merely the survivor but the embodiment of the scarifying processes of conquest, dispossession, resettlement, missionisation, and welfareism.

I suggest this sort of visceral connection between history and identity, rather than just cynical politics, was behind the pointed question Aboriginal woman Ros Langford put to the Australia Archaeological Association over 20 years ago, to counter claims that "everyone and no-one" owns the past: "if we can't control our own heritage," she asked, "what the hell can we control?" (Langford 1983, 4).

It is interesting, in this context of embodiment, to consider an aside in which Sutton (1994 [1988], 261) describes how "the contemporary white Australian can sometimes also be defined and identified as the historic coloniser, not merely as their descendent or beneficiary." This means that, much to their bewilderment, settler-archaeologists can be publicly accused of personally doing unethical things they did not themselves do—or that archaeologists as a group, rather than, say, medicos or amateur antiquarians, did not do—only to be reassured privately by their accusers that they should not take it personally. This situation is perhaps best illustrated by the anecdote Sutton (1994 [1988], 261–62) himself uses. He was walking along the main street of his state capital when he saw a policeman arresting an Aboriginal man following a violent incident. Numbers of young Aborigines were looking on, and one shouted at the policeman "Captain Cook c[. . .]t!" Cook was last in Australia in AD 1770, and even then never came within 1000 kilometers of the locality in question. The youths would not have considered the policeman literally to be the individual Cook himself, but by the same token the reference was something more than metaphorical. The abstract notion of "the historic coloniser" is commonly grounded by Aboriginal people in the person of the most iconic of the continent's European explorers (Williamson and Harrison 2002).

To draw this part of the article to a close, I note that using diaspora theory to comprehend key features of the sociopolitical milieu in which archaeologists work in settler societies falls under the rubric of what Scham (2001) calls a "heritage recovery" approach to "the archaeology of the disenfranchised." Her language resonates very strongly with that of the diaspora literature, and indeed she specifically draws attention to parallels between the situation of colonized indigenous minorities and that of both the Jewish diaspora and the profoundly difficult situation engulfing Jews and Palestinians in the Middle East. She reminds us that "the clearest distinguishing factor in colonial disenfranchisement is the effective replacement of an indigenous past by a narrative that emphasizes the conquest culture," which "inevitably" prompts attempts to reassert an original culture usually not truly lost despite the efforts of the colonizer (Scham 2001, 188). "Permeating such tragic records of the past", she says, "is a sense of loss that must finally translate into material terms. The recovery of a heritage is futile unless accompanied by attempts to quantify that recovery" (2001, 196). Interestingly, in relation to the debate in Australia and elsewhere concerning the instrumentalist politics of indigenous heritage claims, Scham contends that "recourse for heritage recovery is always through established legal and political channels. . . . Heritage recovery is not just a heuristic exercise but also a compensatory one. This is why efforts to reclaim the past are so often misunderstood" (2001, 197). . . .

11

Dwelling at the Margins, Action at the Intersection? Feminist and Indigenous Archaeologies, 2005

Margaret W. Conkey

We archaeologists do not often consider how specific experiences have influenced or informed archaeological interpretation (cf. Bradley 2002; Kus 2002; Rubertone 2001, ix; Schrire 1995; Spector 1993; Tringham 1991).

Excerpted from Conkey, Margaret W. 2005. Dwelling at the Margins, Action at the Intersection? Feminist and Indigenous Archaeologies, 2005. *Archaeologies: Journal of the World Archaeological Congress* 1(1):9–59.

There is little doubt that for those archaeologists who adhere to objectivist ideals, it appears to be a slippery slope to bring in (or openly admit) "experience" as a source of evidence and potential meaning. And certainly there has been scepticism about how the contemporary world of experience—what a tribal elder, for example, may say about ancient rock art—can be brought to bear on activities and practises of the past (e.g., Woody 2000). Yet most of us do draw on not only our own experiences but also those of other cultures and settings, such as in much ethnoarchaeological work. In fact, some might claim that without ethnographic and historical experiences there could be little basis for much traditional archaeological interpretation, as the materials of archaeology do not, in fact, ever "speak for themselves."

But how often are the "experiences" of Indigenous peoples considered by archaeologists? What kinds of experiences "count," "matter," and are considered acceptable? Many who are willing to engage with this as a serious question know that it is more complicated (and interesting) than just adding the experiences of different researchers or of different (previously unrecognised) voices and social actors. We recognise that to appeal to some kind of incontestable evidence, such as "my experience," merely adds another foundational premise to a discipline already overburdened with undiscussed, unproblematised foundational notions—as Joan Scott (1992a) has suggested for the field of history. She points out that it is not individuals who *have* experience, but rather we are all subjects who are constituted *through* experience. We cannot, she suggests, just appeal to experience to explain something, no matter whose experience it is. Rather, we need to explain and, in fact, *historicise* experience (Scott 1992a, 25–26; see also Scott 1991; for an excellent example of the historicisation of experience, see Carby 1987).

When we engage, as we should, with "experiences" as a dimension of interpretation, as integral to our own epistemologies, and as having powerful potential, we begin an inquiry into the ways in which subjectivity is produced, and in which politics (broadly speaking) organise and interpret experience. The lesson, from feminist, Indigenous, and other critical archaeologies, is that we should be openly discussing what counts as experience and, furthermore, who gets to make that determination. We can then perhaps be better situated to historicise experience and to reflect critically on the history we write about rather than to merely premise our archaeological narratives upon it or dismiss it out of hand. When, as cited above, R. A. Williams (1989–1990) poses the question, "Consider for a moment the degree to which your own understanding of gender roles in Indian cultures might be distorted by the legacy of white patriarchy itself" (1029), he is asking us to historicise our experience in the service of our archaeology. What does "experience" mean in different settings, among different social actors, and at different times? Within "the West," what "experience" has meant and how it has been used and transformed is in itself highly variable and historical (Jay 2005; see also Butler 1990, 22–25 and R. Williams 1983, 126–29).

From the past two decades of "third-wave feminism," from the growth and expansion of Indigenous rights activism, and from some of the understandings of "the subjective nature of experience" (e.g., H. Moore 2001), it may be possible to *begin* our social analyses in archaeology with a reflexive and relational analysis that includes (or centres on) a theory of agency and representation that is based on experience, *but does not end there*. Rather, and this is what an intersectional approach may offer, we need an explicit understanding of experience and history within the broader sociocultural frames that have structured and do structure our lives (Russo 1991). Or, as Bannerji (1992, 94) puts it so succinctly, "we need to go beyond expressive self-referentiality and connect with others in time and space."

There may be some good lessons to be learned for both archaeologies from the evolution and critique (e.g., Mohanty 1987) of the use of "experience" in feminist history and analysis, even in a history intent on a history of difference. For example, this has led to a more explicit recognition of the historian/archaeologist as an active producer of knowledge, as having a subject position. This puts into motion the mandate to reflect critically on the archaeologies we write in regard to experience, rather than to premise our archaeologies upon "experience," even if the experiences invoked are only implicit but nonetheless foundational. A critical perspective on experience requires that we take concepts and identities as historical events in need of explanation; in fact, it requires that we denaturalise experience and take all categories of analysis as being contextual, contested, and contingent. In most archaeology, we all too often assume our categories (but see Meskell 2001a; Snead 2002; Spector 1993). In fact, it is not so much a matter of how "visible" women, gender, difference, or the Indigenous perspective might be, but first, what does it mean for archaeologists to study the past in terms of these categories, for some of us to think of ourselves/themselves now—or in the past—in these terms?

While experience is and can be a powerful and important concept, it perhaps warrants at least scrutiny (not unquestioned and foundational acceptance), if not redefinition. Since experience is always contested, as both feminists and Indigenous researchers have found, it is therefore always political. Thus, the role and place of experience in the production of archaeological knowledge is not what might appear to be the straightforward generation and communication of knowledge that is said to be arrived at though experience but, rather, the analysis of the production of that knowledge itself. This is why one of Linda Tuhiwai Smith's goals of Indigenous research is "to tell the history of Western research through the eyes of the colonized" (Smith 1999, 2). What we want to explain is the experience that we invoke, observe, and draw upon—"experience" cannot stand as the source of our explanations and accounts. . . .

Working with community partners in the research process has emerged as one of the most efficacious ways to get "in" to the local stories and the previously unanticipated connectivities, and to understand how, on the ground, we are increasingly accountable to the specific case at hand, including a deep consideration for how we present research, how we represent the past, and how we represent ourselves in the research process (e.g., Loring 2001, among many). As feminist archaeologists continually ask what we have to offer, not just to wider feminisms (e.g., Brumfiel 1998; Conkey 1993) but also to our own social and cultural worlds; the project-specific coalitions between previously unconnected but equally interested parties require identification of and collaboration on the common grounds. Perhaps the emergence and articulation of the intersections between Indigenous and feminist archaeologies will push the "working together" of the past decade towards an even more transformative coalitional consciousness.

Gender Roles

Since gender roles have been one key focal point of feminist and gender archaeologists (e.g., Crown 2000), this may be one research area that might particularly benefit from an intersectionality, or from coauthoring. The legacy of white patriarchy is likely to function quite differently in different cultural contexts. We should, for example, direct our attention to the possibility that gender roles in some Indigenous cultures "might be understood differently and in ways unfamiliar to white patriarchal values" (Williams 1989–1990, 1037; see also Jacobs 1999; see for a more specific example Chato and Conte 1988 concerning the destructive aspects of white patriarchy on Navajo conceptions of gender roles). These "white patriarchal values" are not easily or automatically overcome, even by feminist convictions and principles (e.g., Lâm 1994).

Many Indigenous women and men—for example, among Indians in North America—are caught in the legacy of a set of gender roles and gendered values that have been historically generated by the white patriarchal societies, often stereotyping males as lazy and women as hardworking (e.g., Williams 1989–1990; Young 1980), or overlooking and ignoring Indigenous systems of gendered power and influence, especially those of women. And yet it is interesting to note how, despite four or five "centuries of the legacy of white patriarchy, many gendered cultural patterns of apparent matriarchal power and influence in Indian tribes appear to enjoy some continuity" (Williams 1989–1990, 1034; see also Deloria in Denetdale 2004, 140–42). In an important comparative approach, Rothschild (2003) shows how gender roles in two different situations of colonial encounters with Native Americans were at work in what are very varied experiences of colonialism. Mihesuah (2003) remarks that most who write today about Native women are not aware of or do not understand the very powerful legacies that women have within tribal traditions, and yet Native women are very much concerned with looking to their past for motivation. This is something to which feminist archaeologies can contribute.

Indigenous views can offer to feminists some very differently articulated visions of the relations between gender and power in the lifeways of a people. In his compelling article on "outsider jurisprudence," R. A. Williams uses the Iroquois example to suggest that a better understanding of gender roles *in an Iroquois cultural context* has the real possibility of engendering valuable insights and strategies immediately relevant and useful to "the outsider jurisprudential project of dismantling white patriarchy in our own society" (Williams 1989–1990, 1043). This dismantling project is, of course, one that feminists would share.

The Archaeology of Space

At a somewhat different analytical level, an archaeology informed by both feminist and Indigenous perspectives could reconceptualise and reframe how we approach, understand, and interpret "space." On the one hand, there is an extremely rich literature from the feminist perspective in geography (e.g., Currie and Rothenberg 2001; Massey 1994; McDowell and Sharp 1997; Moore 1986). On the other hand, there has been innovative work in archaeology that has questioned the taken-for-granteds of imposing Western and colonisers' notions of space onto archaeological materials and settings (e.g., Byrne 2003a; Rose and Clarke 1997), while recognising, at the same time, the ways in which spatial practices—such as those of spatial containment in the colonising processes (e.g., Byrne 2003a; Casella 2000; Voss 2000)—impose foreign, disruptive, and alien spatiality on the subjects of study and in how we then represent them. To a certain extent, one must question the (usually undiscussed) application of "our" spatial concepts onto prehistoric sites and settings as well as in "activity area" research. Archaeology itself is a practise of spatial containment, where more or less bounded sites are the preferred object of inquiry, even for very mobile humans of the past, and where research practices—such as site excavation—are more highly valued than survey, with its presumed "messy" artefact "scatters" (e.g., Moser 1996).

Byrne (2003a) makes two powerful points to illustrate these issues. First, he shows how the heritage archaeology of the postcontact period in Australia, and the places it inventories, privileges loci of spatial containment: mission stations, massacre sites, institutional "homes" for Aboriginal children. These are places, he suggests, where Indigenous peoples rarely went unless they had to, and are places that certainly do not represent the spaces of everyday Aboriginal experience. In fact, an entire spectrum of Aboriginal postcontact experience within the larger colonial landscape is *not* visible, and these are the landscapes that are both the most interesting and the most crucial in the everyday practises and the "nervous" spaces of race relations (see also Gill, Paterson, and Japanangka Kennedy 2004).

Thus, the second relevant point finds us, once again, confronting the epistemological and interpretive challenges of "visibility." Just as feminist archaeologists and those engaging with gender continue to be challenged about the very "visibility" of sex and gender, so, too, are Indigenous archaeological inquiries into contact/postcontact times. These were times of racial segregation that appear to have rendered a specific "invisibility." In North America, many so-called contact archaeology studies have privileged the more obvious colonial imprint, and, as pointed out above, the very historiography has rendered much invisible, and intentionally so (e.g., Handsman and Richmond 1995; excerpted in Chapter 21 this volume).

In Wylie's introduction to the important volume *Working Together: Native Americans and Archaeologists* (Dongoske, Aldenderfer, and Doehner 2000), she identifies three "persistent themes" for those collaborative projects that seem to work. Certainly her first theme has been central to the feminist project as well—both in archaeology and more widely—namely, "a willingness to consider other ways of knowing" (Wylie 2000, viii). Many feminist and other postpositivist philosophies of science have discussed and debated this, and Wylie has pointed out that, in fact, this attitude is actually integral to the scientific process that archaeologists have themselves championed for many decades. Minimally, we gain a more critical appreciation of the strengths and limitations of our own systems of knowledge by engaging with the "empirical knowledge systems" of other cultures (Harding 2003, 63). We must engage with the reality that there are a variety of epistemic bases for researching and understanding the past, something that has come only slowly (if at all) to many archaeologists.

From the perspective of the Indigenous scholar and the Native woman, feminist scholars "must abandon being an expert on what counts as important knowledge about Native women. If feminist scholars can engage in reciprocal, practical dialogue with their informants, then Native voices, too, will become part of feminist discourse" (Mihesuah 2003, 8). The same general observation applies to archaeologists, and, in fact, Wylie's second persistent theme that she sees in the successful collaborative projects is a commitment to the "cultivation" not only of this reciprocity but also of "accountability in both an intellectual and political sense" (Wylie 2000, ix; see also Watkins et al. 1995).

What Are Some of the Problems and Tensions?

While both Indigenous and feminist archaeologists would share critiques of Western science, what to do about this will vary and even differ. Both will face different challenges and present different responses to negotiating some sort of connection (or not) between feminist and Indigenous commitments, on the one hand, and the broadly scientific ones that continue to prevail in contemporary archaeology. There will be some suspicions about how one perspective may be trying to (even unconsciously) co-opt the other; after all, what justifications do I have in making some of the statements that I have laid out here, especially in regard to Indigenous scholarship, research, and peoples?

It would be unusual if what feminists and what Indigenous scholars took as their "bottom lines" were the same, once we move beyond our mutual concerns for survival and human rights. For Indigenous peoples, self-determination and revised definitions and practises of "protection" and "ownership" of cultural resources, heritage, histories, and integrity are likely to be "bottom line." They are not likely to prioritise how knowledge of their specific pasts and cultural histories can contribute to an overarching understanding of humanity: of the "human career" or "what it means to be human." For feminists, an analysis of gender, but as a very different and constantly evolving concept, is perhaps a "bottom line" (Longino 1994)—at least until we better understand how social inequalities have emerged and societies today can be transformed. "Feminism is not simply a struggle to end male chauvinism or a movement to ensure that women will have equal rights with men; it is a commitment to eradicating the ideology of domination" (Collins 1990, 37–38).

Indigenous peoples are unlikely to respect the "territorial" notions that some scholars have about "their" subject area when it involves Indigenous knowledge, place, history, and people. In fact, intellectual property has emerged as one of the most critical fulcrums of debate (e.g., Brown 1998, 2003, especially pp. 299–301; Nicholas and Bannister 2004 [excerpted in Chapter 12 this volume]; Riley 2004; and references therein). The most sensitive issues of concern, for example, to American Indians have been cited as the use of oral histories as source material, remuneration to tribes for information received, and the question of who benefits from research on Indians (Mihesuah 1998, x). Nicholas and Bannister (2004, 330) point out that, despite the perception that most outcomes of archaeology have limited practical application, these outcomes increasingly have potential applications and they very much "matter" to those who are descendant groups—groups who may themselves be caught up in twenty-first-century political, legal, and cultural contestations. Thus, there will be, or should be, tensions and contestations over such things as "ownership of, copyright in, or trademarks related to the artefacts, designs, or marks uncovered during archaeological research," as well as "fiduciary duties related to the secrecy of sacred sites, which could also include copyright in maps" (Nicholas and Bannister 2004, 330).

The very nature of an "archaeology of difference" (but see Torrence and Clarke 2000) is likely to be contested, especially if the approaches are based on a somewhat neoliberal pluralistic stance and/or emphasise static identities at the cost of really probing the structural dynamics of the social relations of appropriation. All too often the impression is that there is or can be a positive coexistence among different subject positions, and that some approaches to "difference" and "diversity" tend to allow for multiple subjectivities, yet enclose them into static identities (Anzaldúa 1990, xxi–xxii). "Lacking an analysis of forms of consciousness and social relations, theories of 'difference' lack the potential for a revolutionary politics" (Bannerji 1992, 86). This is a potential trap that feminists perhaps once already fell into, as was much critiqued by third-wave feminists—a trap that should be anticipated by the intersectionalities of feminist and Indigenous archaeologies. . . .

12

Copyrighting the Past? Emerging Intellectual Property Rights Issues in Archaeology

George P. Nicholas and Kelly P. Bannister

Archaeological Research Products as Cultural and Intellectual Property

Every human society is the embodiment of a particular system of knowledge. The cultural knowledge possessed by contemporary Indigenous societies is part of a compendium of wisdom that extends back through time, a significant portion of which is represented in archaeological materials and information. This information not only reflects what happened and when it happened in the past but is symbolic of cultural identity and worldview still important to many of the descendants of the sites' creators. Archaeological sites thus constitute not only cultural property but intellectual creations, raising questions of how archaeologically derived knowledge contributes to cultural identity and what aspects of cultural identity qualify as intellectual property. Here we are referring not to archaeological approaches to cultural identity (i.e., using archaeology to define ethnicity [e.g., Shennan 1989]) but rather to the appreciation of archaeological material as a component of cultural identity (Jones 1997) that makes the products of archaeology potential forms of intellectual property. Archaeological sites and materials fit the abovementioned definitions of Indigenous cultural and intellectual property proposed by Janke (1998) and Hampton and Henderson (2000) in their contributions to cultural identity, worldview, cultural continuity, and traditional ecological knowledge.

Excerpted from Nicholas, George and Kelly P. Bannister. 2004. Copyrighting the Past? Emerging Intellectual Property Rights Issues in Archaeology. *Current Anthropology* 45(3):327–50.

Cultural Identity

Archaeological artifacts and sites have long served as symbols of national identity worldwide. Stonehenge is not only one of the best-known archaeological sites in the world but also strongly associated with British identity (see Golding 1989). When Rhodesia gained independence in 1980 and became Zimbabwe, it took its new name from an archaeological site and chose as its national symbol a carved soapstone bird from that site. In many parts of the world, Aboriginal communities relocated by government mandate, epidemics, or other factors have retained a strong association with their former homes, whether through occasional visits or through oral histories (e.g., Kritsch and Andre 1997; Myers 1986). Artifacts and heirlooms also play a vital role in the identity of Indigenous peoples, serving as a link both to past generations and to the systems of knowledge that sustained them. This may help to explain the widespread use of, for example, arrowheads—objects that have likely not been in use for a century or more—in the contemporary logos of many Aboriginal groups in North America.

Aboriginal peoples may choose to represent themselves or seek confirmation of their cultural identity by continuing to use (or, in some cases, adopting) precontact objects or traditions (e.g., Merrill, Ladd, and Ferguson 1992). These may include architecture, traditional foods and cooking practices, and rock art imagery. In the Interior Plateau of British Columbia, the image of the semisubterranean pit house is widely used by the Secwepemc (or Shuswap) people on letterhead, signage, sweatshirts, and promotional items. Full-scale reconstructions of pit houses are found in Aboriginal heritage parks and communities; some individuals have even built and seasonally use their own pit houses. Underground pit-cooking (a practice well-documented in the archaeological record) continues, although only infrequently, and pit-cooked food is prized (Peacock 1998). Pictographs are also widely viewed by Secwepemc and other Plateau peoples as an important part of their heritage (e.g., York, Daly, and Arnett 1993), although no new ones have been painted for many generations. Among other things, pictographs provide an expression of worldview and clear indications of a distinctive Aboriginal presence in the landscape.

Worldview

Certain types of archaeological sites and artifacts, such as pictographs, petroglyphs, medicine wheels, vision quest sites, and burial sites, have long been associated with the worldviews of Indigenous peoples. While few of these are still in use today, those that are reflect continued use since precontact times; offerings are left at sacred places today much as they have been for possibly millennia (e.g., Andrews and Zoe 1997). In Australia, the National Aboriginal Sites Authorities Committee distinguishes two types of Aboriginal sites: (1) archaeological sites, whose significance is defined "on the basis of scientific enquiry and general cultural and historical values," and (2) "sites which are the tangible embodiment of the sacred and secular traditions of the Aboriginal peoples of Australia." It is noted that the latter sites may include the former and that the "relative significance of these sites may only be determined by the Aboriginal custodians" (NASAC 1991, cited in Ritchie 1994, 233).

The role of these types of sites is not necessarily static but reinterpreted or even augmented to meet current needs. Dreamtime sites are places in the landscape where ancestral beings went about creating the land and all it contained, including themselves (see Stanner 1998). To Aboriginal Australians, the Dreaming is a timeless phenomenon relayed through oral traditions linked to specific places and objects. While most of these tell how things came into being, they also reflect contemporary issues. As noted by Chatwin (1987, 12) almost anything "can have a Dreaming. A virus can be a Dreaming. You can have a chickenpox Dreaming, a rain Dreaming, a desert-orange Dreaming, a lice Dreaming. In the Kimberleys they've now got a money Dreaming." Contemporary influences on traditions are also found in North America. Offerings left at sacred places often include tobacco, pebbles, and food, as well as coins and other "modern" items. Such versatility is also seen in rock art, which may include both an objective record of life in the past (e.g., animals seen) and a subjective one (e.g., personal visions, dreams, magic). These images may be interpreted differently today from when they were created. In some places, the tradition continues of repainting or even painting over old images (e.g., Chaloupka 1986).

Mortuary practices and the treatment of human remains are also expressions of worldview, and the reburial issue goes to the core of worldview and cultural identity in indigenous societies everywhere (e.g., Bray 2001; Carmichael et al. 1994; Davidson, Lovell-Jones, and Bancroft 1995; Zimmerman 1997). Cemeteries have long been important places in the cultural landscape and served as territorial markers. Some cemeteries have been in use for thousands of years (O'Neill 1994). Such locations are of importance to the associated contemporary Indigenous communities and may also play a significant role in land claims and political movements.

Cultural Continuity

Cultural continuity may be reflected in the occupation of the same lands for millennia, in the retention of the technologies used in the past to produce the same household goods (e.g., ceramics in the American Southwest) and in other ways (e.g., Jones 1997). Archaeological sites serve as important personal and societal touchstones (i.e., as links between past and present) that reaffirm basic values and provide a sense of place. This is indicated by Chase's (1989, 17) observations on the significance of precontact archaeological sites for North Queensland Aboriginal people in Australia. In cases where the colonial experience and a century or more of acculturation have dramatically changed the lives of Aboriginal peoples, there often remain core cultural values that indicate the persistence of traditional beliefs and worldview. These may take the form, for example, of a strong emphasis on family values and respect for community elders.

The strong connection between cultural continuity and Indigenous claims to land and cultural or archaeological materials has significant implications for the recognition of ownership in matters of repatriation and reburial. However, the continuity may sometimes be more apparent than real; as a result of population movements in the distant past or historic federal tribal relocation and the often capricious nature of tribal boundary recognition, one group may occupy a territory that contains the archaeological record of another. Even in central Australia, where until recently the effects of colonialism were limited, the degree of relatedness between the Aboriginal Australian groups mapped by Tindale (1974) and their late Pleistocene predecessors in the area merits examination.

Where cultural discontinuities are recognized in the archaeological record, residents of the area may deal with this information in different ways. For example, the group may lack any concrete knowledge of earlier residents and accept the entirety of the local archaeological record as its own; some Secwepemc people insist that their ancestors always lived in pit houses and harvested salmon when the archaeological record suggests that these are later Holocene developments (Nicholas 2003). Alternatively, the newcomers may recognize the legacy of an earlier occupation and integrate knowledge of ancient unrelated beings into their histories and worldviews as Hamann (2002) has documented for Mesoamerica. Finally, the group may consciously co-opt the archaeological record for cultural or political reasons, as is the case with current Navajo claims to Anasazi archaeological sites.

Traditional Ecological Knowledge

"Traditional ecological knowledge" has been described as an Indigenous system of knowledge that is based on observation, testing, and replicated results and therefore directly comparable with "science." Berkes (1993, 3) defines the term as "a cumulative body of knowledge and beliefs, handed down through generations by cultural transmission, about the relationship of living beings (including humans) with one another and with their environment. [It] is an attribute of societies with historical continuity in resource use practices; by and large, these are non-industrial or less technologically advanced societies, many of them Indigenous or tribal." Traditional systems of knowledge have become an important subject of intellectual property rights (e.g., Simpson 1999) and are increasingly recognized by both Indigenous and non-Indigenous people as a manifestation of the acquired knowledge of particular Indigenous societies. This body of knowledge includes not only the intellectual tradition itself (i.e., the information preserved and transmitted) but also the traditional use sites that are the geographic expression of that knowledge.

Archaeological sites by any definition are traditional use sites, and therefore the knowledge represented at these sites is worth considering in the context of cultural and intellectual property. Various types of sites (e.g., fish weirs) represent the operation or practice of past land-use and resource-harvesting practices that, in turn, are the embodiment of traditional ecological knowledge, while those of a particular region collectively reflect compositional and distributional changes that occurred over millennia as past occupants responded to shifts in the natural and social environment. Traditional ecological knowledge is also frequently used by archaeologists to locate archaeological sites (e.g., Greer 1997). Site information is typically obtained through interviews with elders and community members or from published ethnographies.

Should intellectual components of the archaeological record such as these be protected as proprietary? If so, by whom? No explicit protection exists under any provincial or state heritage protection mechanisms in Canada or the United States. Most archaeologists, in fact, may not recognize an intellectual component at all. However, the situation is likely very different for those with a vested interest in their own heritage sites. In Australia, for example, Aboriginal peoples have expressed concern that "the focus of cultural heritage laws is on tangible cultural heritage, such as specific areas, objects, and sites. The intangible aspects of a significant site, such as its associated stories, songs, and dreaming tracks, are not protected" (Janke 1998, xxiv; also Roberts 2003). Even if an intellectual component is recognized, an argument may be made that the great age of most archaeological sites puts this information in the realm of shared heritage, thus making its exploitation legally acceptable. In the following section we return to the two-sided issue of control of knowledge in archaeology and evaluate threats to Indigenous cultural and intellectual property rights through appropriation and commodification—taking and affixing a price to what many would consider inalienable and priceless. . . .

Who Owns the Future?

"Everyone now speaks of their culture," says Sahlins (1999, x) "precisely in the context of national or international threats to its existence. This does not mean a simple and nostalgic desire for teepees and tomahawks or some such fetishized repositories of a pristine identity. A 'naive attempt to hold peoples hostage to their own histories,' such a supposition, Terence Turner remarks, would thereby deprive them of history. What the self-consciousness of 'culture' does signify is the demand of the peoples for their own space within the world cultural order." A strong association between cultural knowledge and cultural identity is reflected not only in a society's material culture (e.g., the pit house in Interior British Columbia) but in the intellectual aspects of cultural traditions. Language, for example, is a very important contributor to Indigenous cultural identity (see Maffi 2000). Given the strength of this association, it is clear why control of knowledge is at the heart of the issue—not simply for economic reasons but because control is integral to the definition or restoration of cultural identity for present and future Indigenous societies.

It can be argued that whoever owns (or controls records of) the past also owns or otherwise shapes the future of that past. Archaeologists have, to date, controlled the dissemination of information derived from the archaeological record through publication practices, restriction of access to site locations, and other means. While this management of knowledge has done much to help preserve archaeological resources, it has had several drawbacks. For one, much information has been kept from Indigenous communities, often inadvertently. Since archaeologists are in the position to choose what they will or will not publish, information potentially useful to Indigenous peoples may simply not be available because it fell outside of the interests of the investigator and was not pursued. Access to knowledge is obviously the first of several key steps in establishing control of it. Yet publication itself is a double-edged sword in terms of sharing research findings versus protecting knowledge from third-party exploitation (see Bannister 2000; Bannister and Barrett 2001, n.d.; Laird et al. 2002). Beyond simply relying on heritage protection legislation, is it possible to increase Indigenous control of cultural knowledge and property through existing intellectual property laws and complementary non-legal tools? If so, what are the implications for future archaeological research? . . .

13

In the Spirit of the Code

Claire Smith and Heather Burke

An Ethical Dilemma: Indigenous versus Scientific Stewardship

The increased professionalization of archaeology has resulted in the relatively recent development of ethical codes. The American Anthropological Association (AAA) developed one of the first in the United States. Since then, the Society for American Archaeology (SAA) and a number of other national bodies in First World countries have also developed codes of conduct to assist their members in the recognition and resolution of ethical dilemmas. Each body has produced a formal document that distills the beliefs of its members, articulates the underlying assumptions and guiding principles of the association, and provides a fundamental framework for conducting research in an ethical and responsible way. While each of these codes in some way expresses the common core of group wisdom that originally created them, each was also created within its own social "bubble," resulting in widely differing core values. These vary enormously from code to code: from promoting the greater understanding of archaeology (Archaeological Institute of America) and the stewardship of heritage (SAA and New Zealand Archaeological Association) to recognizing a paramount professional responsibility to those who are being studied (AAA), or acknowledging the importance of indigenous cultural heritage to the survival indigenous cultures (Canadian Archaeological Association, World Archaeological Congress [WAC], and Australian Archaeological Association). While all of these aspects are undoubtedly a part of professional archaeological responsibility across the discipline, there is one very clear difference: As a first principle, stewardship of the archaeological

Excerpted from Smith, Claire, and Heather Burke. 2003. In the Spirit of the Code. In *Ethical Issues in Archaeology*, ed. L. J. Zimmerman, K. D. Vitelli, and J. Hollowell-Zimmer, 177–97. Walnut Creek: AltaMira Press.

resource privileges a completely different ethical standpoint than a principle that privileges the survival of indigenous cultures. This is not to say that one set of core values is more acceptable or "correct" than any another, simply that each code has been developed from the needs of a particular group at a particular time and place to deal with local situations in different parts of the world.

The existence of alternative ethical starting points, however, does mean that archaeological responses to ethical dilemmas in different parts of the world can have vastly different outcomes. Two relatively recent cases involving the custody of ancient human skeletal remains clearly demonstrate this divergence. The ongoing furor over the significance and ultimate future of the 9,800-year-old skeleton of the "Kennewick Man" excavated in 1996 near Kennewick, Washington, has become a symbol of a wider debate between scientific rights to knowledge and indigenous rights to control their cultural heritage. A similar controversy took place in Australia in the late 1980s and early 1990s in response to indigenous requests to rebury Pleistocene skeletal remains excavated at Kow Swamp, in Victoria, and in Lake Mungo, in New South Wales (see Bowdler 1992; Davidson 1991; McBryde 1986; Mulvaney 1991). While the final disposition of the Kennewick remains has yet to be determined, both the Kow Swamp and Lake Mungo remains were returned to the indigenous populations who have contemporary cultural affiliation to the places where the remains were found. In each case, there was a struggle between local indigenous groups, who wanted to have the remains returned to them, and a group of scientists, who argued for conserving the remains for future generations by keeping them in the custody of a museum. In each case, the local archaeological communities had to come to grips with alternative opinions on the ultimate meaning of these long-dead individuals and thus on the most appropriate solution for their future. Neither side was "wrong" in the position it adopted; rather, each was guided by its respective codes of ethics to argue from opposing first principles.

It can be argued that the most important attribute of ethical codes is that they provide a spirit within which to work through ethical dilemmas. But how do you work out the spirit of an ethical code? This is not straightforward, especially if, like most of us, you were not privy to the debates that were undertaken when that code was established. . . .

The Ethics of Archaeological Practice

The very existence of an ethical code can present certain dangers. Ironically, the very codification of behavioral standards can provide a means for escaping ethical requirements as well as enforcing them. Some people will act on the basis that it is legitimate to do anything that isn't specifically prohibited by a code. The counterargument is that simply because a behavior hasn't been proscribed doesn't make it ethical. The point here is that ethical codes are to be studied, not as strict of legal interpretation, but in terms of the spirit in which they were made and the principles that they were intended to further. Ethical behavior requires that individuals articulate their ethical values in practice. It means having a standard against which to assess the choices that archaeologists are continually required to make. It can be argued that the most important attribute of any ethical code is the provision of a spirit within which to work through ethical dilemmas. Such a spirit can only be defined in practice, however, as new situations develop and ethical challenges arise. Moreover, because each code of ethics only reflects the professional needs of archaeologists in that region at the time the code was developed, then codes of ethics must always be in flux. Professional debate is one of the most important aspects in this process of ongoing revision. Without it, the disjunctions between general codes and the specifics of daily archaeological practice have no forum for resolution.

Once entered into, any debate over the ethics of practice will raise significant, and potentially unanswerable, questions. What happens if you are a member of WAC, the SAA, and the AAA? Do you pick the most appropriate code of ethics to suit either yourself or the situation? How do you determine what is "most appropriate"? At a more general level: What use is archaeology? Who does archaeology serve and whom does it disempower? Do archaeologists have a right to create and control the past of others? As archaeologists, we assume the answers to these kinds of questions. We take it as self-evident that archaeology is useful, and that we have a responsibility, as well as a right, to create the pasts of others. It seems clear to us that this needs to be done and that it needs to be done in the scientific, rigorous manner that is archaeology. Rarely do we question the agendas that are furthered by our work and what groups are disempowered as a result. While archaeology is a powerful tool in the creation of cultural identities in the past, and we know that evidence is chosen selectively and interpreted according to our own biases and inclinations in the present, we still work on the assumption that our work should be considered as being beyond politics.

Looking to the future of ethics in archaeology, it is clear that we need a more systematic evaluation of the consequences of what we propose as "ethics" before we assume that our strategies are effective. One real problem is that few organizations have established procedures for evaluation of their ethical codes. Though WAC, for example, has had a profound impact on the development of other codes, it is difficult to assess what "real" impact these codes have had in terms of implementation. In fact, most codes are deficient when it comes to operationalizing them, enforcing them, or adjudicating purported violations. This raises the question of how much these codes actually inform the behavior of archaeologists. Do we have ethical codes only for moral authority? What do we do when there is a violation, either obvious or more ambiguous? The SAA Ethics Committee, for example, has no authority or mechanism to investigate complaints, even though there have been charges of ethics violations brought to its attention. Neither do other organizations, such as WAC, the Canadian Archaeological Association, or the New Zealand Archaeological Association. The RPA (2002) and the Archaeological Institute of America are better positioned here, as each has a tribunal system that confidentially deals with ethical violations, but these are exceptions rather than the rule (see Davis 2003).

The existence of so many potentially conflicting ethical codes also brings into question the possibility of ever having common international ethical standards. While we may hold certain moral tenets in common (e.g., respect for others and for archaeological material), if our ethical codes provide such widely divergent starting points, will it ever be possible to reconcile our different approaches to ethics in practice? This is an important issue not only in theory, but also in practice. American Indians may never have the control that is currently held by the Aboriginal and Torres Strait Islander peoples of Australia, but if American archaeologists wish to work in Australia, they had best be prepared to deal with local expectations of ethical behavior. This means they would have to be prepared for a level of indigenous control over their work, especially if the work receives support from Australian funding agencies. For Americans, who are accustomed to the notion of free speech, this can create a serious ethical dilemma. Should they submit to Aboriginal approval of their results, simply because they want to conduct research in Australia? From an American point of view, this could seem like "censorship" but Australians are more likely to consider it as being "edited for content." Moreover, many Australian archaeologists would consider the obtaining of indigenous approval of publications, especially photos, as exemplary ethical behavior on the part of the researcher. . . .

SECTION IV

Oceania

The Indigenous peoples of Oceania, identified by themselves and others as Aboriginal ("aborigines" in much of the anthropological literature), trace their history on the Pacific islands back thousands of years. For more than two centuries, they have contended with the legacies of European colonialism: dispossession from their territories by the colonial policy of "terra nullius" (the perception that their territory is an uninhabited "no-man's land"), endemic racism and violence, and little recognition of their human rights. Despite these challenges, Aboriginal peoples have maintained strong communities built on intimate and inalienable connections between land, culture, and history. Much of the decolonizing work in this region is driven by the sentiment summed up by Lois O'Donoghue (Yankuntjatjara), Chairperson of the Aboriginal and Torres Strait Islander Commission, before the United Nations in 1994: "The past cannot be changed: our future is in our hands. We will empower ourselves" (1994, 74).

The development of Indigenous archaeologies and decolonizing practice is deeply rooted in Australia and New Zealand. Many archaeologists in the region have been responsive to Indigenous criticism of the discipline's poor treatment of Aboriginal communities, and significant numbers of practitioners are now applying community-based approaches and decolonizing methods while working with and for Aboriginal communities. Decolonizing practices have been formalized in the ethics statements of the Australian Archaeological Association (2004), which requires the negotiation of equitable agreements between archaeologists and the Indigenous communities whose cultural heritage is being investigated.

Many of the issues faced by Aboriginal communities and archaeologists in Oceania are similar to those faced in North America. These include reburial, repatriation, Indigenous land title, heritage protection, and intellectual and cultural property rights (for example, see Smallcombe 2000). The four excerpts in this section have been selected not because they are comprehensive but because they touch on a range of issues and practices that link archaeologists and Aboriginal communities in the region. Indigenous archaeologies are laborious and complex, and we chose to reproduce significant portions of several pieces to give the reader a sense of this. Together, these excerpts provide theoretical and practical grounding for regional transformations and exemplify productive collaboration among Indigenous and non-Indigenous practitioners.

This section begins with an excerpt from Claire Smith and Gary Jackson's "Decolonizing Indigenous Archaeology: Developments from Down Under," which offers a practical account of Indigenous control over research. Drawing on their research with the Barunga-Wugularr communities of the Northern Territory and the Ngadjuri people of Burra, South Australia, they trace decolonizing trends while exploring how the languages of science, archaeology, and bureaucracy silence and disempower Indigenous Australians. To mediate this violence, they advocate decolonizing languages and other measures that implement Indigenous control over heritage. They recommend straightforward practices such as obtaining permission and requiring proof of community support for research and fieldwork, ensuring community control of access to Indigenous sites and knowledge, and establishing community involvement in disseminating scholarly results. Smith and Jackson note the importance of reciprocity—conceptualizing research as shared intellectual property and redistributing the long-term benefits of research.

A selection of excerpts from case studies highlights the experiences of Indigenous and non-Indigenous peoples engaged in archaeology and heritage work. The excerpt from "*Nukun and Kungun Ngarrindjeri Ruwe* (Look and Listen to Ngarrindjeri Country): An Investigation of Ngarrindjeri Perspectives of Archaeology in Relation to Native Title and Heritage Matters" explores the intersections of archaeology, social practice, and lived experiences. Co-authors Amy Roberts, Steve

Hemming, Tom Trevorrow, George Trevorrow, Matthew Rigney, Grant Rigney, Laurie Agius, and Rhonda Agius reflect on the core values of Indigenous archaeologies: collaboration on every aspect of projects. The paper is a collaboration of six Ngarrindjeri people and two non-Indigenous researchers. Together, they present the "lived experiences" of Ngarrindjeri peoples as a means to encourage ethical, sensitive research relationships in the future. They suggest reshaping archaeology as a tool in Aboriginal self-determination, while chronicling some of the failures such as the well-known Kumarangk/Hindmarsh Island conflict. They acknowledge the significant potential for symbolic violence when archaeology is used as a tool for continuing colonization, but they chart a more productive course where Indigenous connections are recognized and given a central role in the development of research, planning, and assessment. The authors introduce us to a powerful document (the "Kungun Ngarrindjeri Yunnan Agreement: Listening to Ngarrindjeri People Talking Agreement") that recognizes the Ngarrindjeri as the traditional owners of the area, expresses regret for injustices, and challenges the conventional history. This agreement stands as a model for how Indigenous values, knowledge, and epistemologies can shape heritage policy and on-the-ground practice.

Like Roberts and associates, "*Wāhi Ngaro* (the Lost Portion): Strengthening Relationships between People and Wetlands in North Taranaki, New Zealand" is a collaborative effort among non-Indigenous scholars and the Māori Ngāti Mutunga community. Co-authors Harry Allen, Dilys Johns, Caroline Phillips, Kelvin Day, Tipene O'Brien, and Ngāti Mutunga relate a project that integrates a landscape approach to conservation and heritage with Māori traditions and contemporary issues. Wetlands, as places to obtain food resources and store cultural materials, play a significant role in past and present Māori cultural life. Wetlands are also the focus of contemporary conservation efforts, though frequently overlooked in heritage management policy. Allen and associates discuss the dispossession of Māori peoples, the intersections of cultural and ecological landscapes, and the problems of conceiving of them as separate entities. They highlight efforts to strengthen relationships between the Ngāti Mutunga community and wetlands through a research program directed by Māori concerns and needs. Their consideration also touches on the role of museums in the care and conservation of Māori artifacts, and the broader social context that complicates collaborative efforts.

This section concludes with an excerpt from Christopher Wilson's "Indigenous Research and Archaeology: Transformative Practices In/With/For the Ngarrindjeri Community." As an Indigenous archaeologist, Wilson describes the tensions of working between two different knowledge systems during his "lived experiment" of conducting research with/by/for his community. His research focuses on a sensitive and political issue: the impact of the removal of human remains from Ngarrindjeri communities and the implications of their repatriation. Wilson's self-reflexive process is a model in that his hybrid practice applies academic conventions (for example, analysis, comparison, critique) and integrates them with Indigenous expressions (for instance, histories, art, photography), and the uniquely Ngarrindjeri process of speaking and listening.

14

Decolonizing Indigenous Archaeology: Developments from Down Under

Claire Smith and Gary Jackson

Indigenous Control over Indigenous Culture

One of the principal issues facing contemporary archaeologists working in Indigenous Australia is that of Indigenous control over research. If the outcomes of research are jointly owned, then it follows that they are also subject to joint control. This position is consistent with the United Nations' Draft Declaration for the Rights of Indigenous Peoples (part 6, article 29), which affirms:

> Indigenous peoples are entitled to the recognition of the full ownership, control and protection of their cultural and intellectual property. They have the right to special measures to control, develop and protect their sciences, technologies and cultural manifestations, including human and other genetic resources, seeds, medicines, knowledge of the properties of fauna and flora, oral traditions, literatures, designs and visual and performing arts. (United Nations, "Draft Declaration")

After several years of conference debate, this issue became powerfully imprinted on the consciousness of Australian archaeologists when Ros Langford, a member of the Tasmania Aboriginal Community published her views in the mainstream journal *Australian Archaeology*:

> You seek to say that as scientists you have a right to obtain and study information of our culture. You seek to say that because you are

---

Excerpted from Smith, Claire, and Gary Jackson. 2006. Decolonizing Indigenous Archaeology: Developments from Down Under. *American Indian Quarterly* 30(3&4):311–49.

> Australians you have a right to study and explore our heritage because it is a heritage to be shared by all Australians, white and black. From our point of view we say you have come as invaders, you have tried to destroy our culture, you have built your fortunes upon the lands and bodies of our people and now having said sorry, want a share in picking out the bones of what you regard as a dead past. We say that it is our past, our culture and heritage, and forms part of our present life. As such it is ours to control and it is ours to share on our terms. (Langford 1983, 2)

As with Vine Deloria, Jr., in the United States, Langford's views set one of the parameters of archaeological debate in Australia (see, e.g., Deloria 1992). This paper is widely quoted in discussions of Australian archaeology: by writing within the discourse of the discipline, Langford engaged directly with its practitioners, in the process shaping how Australian archaeology would develop (Hodder 1999). In some ways, her paper laid a foundation for the level of control that Indigenous Australians now have over their cultural heritage.

The question of Indigenous control over research has simple and complex dimensions, according to whether the form of control depends on action by an Indigenous person or the researcher: while it is a relatively simple matter for scholars to accept that Indigenous people control their research through withholding certain types of information, the issue becomes more contentious when it enters the realm of intellectual property rights, especially those relating to dissemination of the results of research. Australian archaeologists take their guidance from the Code of Ethics of the Australian Archaeological Association, revised in 2004, and the First Code of Ethics of the World Archaeological Congress, which formed the original basis of the AAA Code of Ethics (Australian Archaeological Association 1994; World Archaeological Congress 1991). The World Archaeological Congress's Vermillion Accord on Human Remains also comes into play here (World Archaeological Congress 1989). All of these ethical codes contain various provisions that recognize the rights of Indigenous people over their cultural heritage. These codes are reinforced by guiding statements within the discipline, such as that on the cover page of Rock Art Research, which affirms the promotion of Aboriginal custodianship of sites as one of its principal objectives. While the rights of Indigenous peoples to control their cultural heritage are not supported by all Australian archaeologists, there is no doubt that this is the consensus view, and these values are reinforced by archaeologists who highlight relationships with Indigenous communities in their conference presentations and publications and by occasional books (see, e.g., Beck et al. 2002; Davidson, Lovell-Jones, and

Bancroft 1995; May et al. 2005; Smith and Wobst 2005a). Recognition of Indigenous rights over Indigenous cultural heritage is an important factor in what is accepted as ethical archaeological research in contemporary Australia.

Obtaining Permission for Fieldwork

It is at the level of fieldwork that Indigenous people have the greatest control over archaeological and anthropological research. One of the biggest changes over the last thirty years involves the process of obtaining permission to work with Aboriginal communities. Prior to the return of lands to Aboriginal control with the Northern Territory Land Rights Act of 1976, researchers obtained permission to work in Aboriginal communities by applying to the Department of Aboriginal Affairs. Permission was negotiated between the non-Aboriginal researcher and the non-Aboriginal government employee, and Aboriginal power structures were unrecognized and circumvented. Today, permission for fieldwork in remote Aboriginal communities must be obtained directly from Aboriginal groups and organizations.

Obtaining permission to conduct research in Aboriginal communities is not a simple matter. Our own experience, undertaken initially in the early 1990s, involved a preliminary visit of ten days, followed by many months of waiting and written applications, which we still fill out every year. The preliminary visit was important because it gave people a chance to meet us and decide if they wanted to have us living in their community for a full year. During our initial visit, Phyllis Wiynjorroc, the senior traditional owner, gave us permission to return to conduct fieldwork the following year. Afterward, we submitted a formal application to the Barunga Council, requesting permission for extended fieldwork. After about six months without a response, we phoned Cyril McCartney, the council president, and he gave us verbal approval to conduct the research. After that, we also had to obtain a permit from the Northern Lands Council, which has to be signed by the community's permit officer, at the direction of elders, and after we had been in the community for some months, our stay was ratified at a community meeting. It is also wise to contact the Jawoyn Association, though it does not formally ratify research in this region. In recent years, at the request of the community we have written a formal letter outlining the particular project and how community members will benefit from it.

The point here is that the contemporary process of obtaining permission to work on Aboriginal land is one in which the researcher has to negotiate with many levels of authority, all of which are composed of

Aboriginal people. The intricacies of the process and the time it takes is one that empowers Aboriginal people since it demonstrates to the researcher the fact that he or she does not have an intrinsic or irrevocable right of residence. The process of renewing permits is an annual reminder of Indigenous rights over Indigenous lands.

Indigenous Control via Institutions

One of the most important changes that have occurred in Indigenous studies in Australia is that today Indigenous control over research is exerted via institutions. Many institutions seek written proof of community support for research on Indigenous subjects, including university ethics committees, museums, government departments, and funding bodies. Aboriginal permission is needed for a permit to excavate Indigenous sites or conduct research on human remains that are still held in museums (though there are active repatriation programs in all major museums) and secret-sacred material held in museums cannot be accessed, even by museum staff, without permission from Aboriginal elders. At the South Australian Museum, for example:

> For sensitive areas of the collection, i.e., parts involving burials, ceremonial material, access to human biology records etc., the researcher must provide evidence of their consultation efforts with relevant communities (i.e., Indigenous Australians, Māoris, Papua New Guineans, etc.). Without them demonstrating that they have gained at least some community support for their project, access will be declined.
>
> For access to less problematic parts of the collection, we consider that most researchers who are already established in their field (or are at least externally supervised by someone who is) do not pose a risk to the Museum's collections or to cultural sensitivities in general. . . . When the situation is unclear I have even insisted that researchers approach state Aboriginal heritage committees and university ethics committees to demonstrate beyond any doubt that the intended research with our collections is not going to cause alarm in any quarters. Of course, access by people involved in court matters can legally truncate some of our demands. (Philip Clarke, personal communication, January 24, 2005)

Another important way in which Indigenous control over research is exerted is through funding bodies. In Australia, the major bodies that fund research into Indigenous subjects are the Australian Research

Council, the National Health and Medical Research Council (NHMRC), and the Australian Institute of Aboriginal and Torres Strait Islander Studies (AIATSIS). The *Guidelines for Ethical Research in Indigenous Studies* published by AIATSIS state:

> 1.8 Informed consent, community support, and ethical clearance
>
> Refer to the AIATSIS Guidelines for Ethical Research in Indigenous Studies document, and the Ethical clearance checklist and Part 3 (Questions 9 to 11) of the AIATSIS Application Form. Applicants must provide evidence of community consent and support for their research project, and consider issues of private, personal, or cultural information. Failure to supply evidence of Aboriginal or Torres Strait Islander support may jeopardise the applicant's chances of being awarded a grant. (Australian Institute of Aboriginal and Torres Strait Islander Studies, "Research Grants Program")

Occurring across a wide range of institutions, measures such as these transmit a message that ethical research is that which is community supported and in which Indigenous people are fully cognizant of the implications, costs, and benefits of the research, the basis of "informed consent."

The "Selection" of Aboriginal Colleagues

The question of informed consent is not one that informs the anthropological literature on the "selection" and reliability of "informants" in field-based research (see, e.g., Becker and Geer 1986, 241–22; Bernard 1988, 179; Hammersley and Atkinson 1983, 116–17). Generally, this relates to the ideal qualities of such people—reflective, articulate, and possessing formal or informal power—especially in terms of "key informants" (see, e.g., Burgess 1986, 73–75; Whyte 1986). However, much of this literature does not appear to recognize the intrinsic power that individuals and social structures within the research community have over the choice of colleagues. Our own experience, for example, involved having the people with whom we might work selected for us by the senior traditional owner, Phyllis Wiynjorroc. Our first day of fieldwork was spent with Phyllis visiting each of the major population centers and being introduced to the appropriate people with whom we could work. Elsewhere, we have argued for a comparable process occurring when other researchers have conducted fieldwork with Aboriginal people and have thought about how this affects the kind of information that is collected (Jackson and Smith 2005). Our point here is that the objective "selection" of Indigenous colleagues by field researchers is a scientific myth.

Access to Sites and Knowledge

Aboriginal people have always controlled the research process through restricting access to sites and knowledge. In cases where Aboriginal people assist researchers in the location of sites, they have power to direct them toward some sites and to bypass others. In Australia, this is recognized by researchers as a legitimate and effective way of caring for country (see, e.g., Lewis and Rose 1985). Moreover, Aboriginal people have always had control over the knowledge they impart. In the Australian situation, the classic paper on this is Neville G. W. Macintosh's revelation that when he and A. Peter Elkin each visited the Beswick Creek cave rock art site, near Barunga (then known as Beswick Creek), in the late 1940s, they were given different information by the senior traditional owner, Charlie Lamjerroc. Macintosh concludes:

> Retrospectively I came to think of these two sets of explanations as being in the first instance a lay interpretation sufficiently satisfactory in his opinion for me. In the second instance an erudite interpretation for Professor Elkin, going much beyond the first, and appropriate to the depth of knowledge and length of association and understanding between Landerod [*sic*] and Elkin, on matters of Aboriginal inner lore. (Macintosh 1977, 191)

This incident shows that information was given out according to the specific relationship between the researchers and the individuals with whom they worked. Even though they were working with the same person in the same place at the same time, Elkin and Macintosh were given substantially different stories. It is likely that a third researcher would have been given a different explanation again. This does not mean that one story is necessarily correct and another incorrect. They may all be true, each one accessing or emphasizing different aspects of a multi-faceted central story, which itself is not a single overarching truth. The point here is that Aboriginal people clearly used their ability to control Elkin's and Macintosh's research through restricting their access to information. . . .

Control over Publications

One of the major developments that has occurred over the last thirty years is Aboriginal people obtaining control over the publication of material concerning their culture. Much discussion has focused on Indigenous control over the publication of secret or sacred information, and this informs views of general publications on Indigenous cultures (see Aboriginal and Torres Strait Islander Commission 1998). Up until the 1970s, Indigenous peoples had virtually no control over the material that was published on their societies. Early research was conducted during a time when Aboriginal people were expected to either die out or be integrated in the dominant society. Based upon the assumption that information not recorded in writing would be lost forever, many scholars appear to have assumed the position that by publishing important (i.e., secret) information, they were caring for future generations of both Aboriginal and non-Aboriginal people (see, e.g., Mountford 1976). There was no notion that Aboriginal systems of knowledge could flourish or recognition that such flourishing would depend on control of Aboriginal cultural and intellectual property. There was also an assumption that Indigenous people would not see the published product (as is evident in the earlier discussion by Evans-Pritchard).

In Australia, a turning point was reached when the Pitjantjatjara people used a breach of confidence action to successfully contest publication of Charles Mountford's *Nomads of the Australian Desert*, which contained secret-sacred information that could not be viewed by women, children, or uninitiated men. In *Foster v. Mountford*, members of the Pitjantjatjara Council obtained an injunction to prevent the book being distributed in the Northern Territory on the basis that the information it contained could only have been shown or exposed to the author in confidence. In addition, the plaintiffs successfully argued that the "revelation of the secrets contained in the book to their women, children and uninitiated men may undermine the social and religious stability of their hard-pressed community" (Australian Government, "Stopping the Rip Offs"). While this case was not argued on the basis of copyright, another major step occurred in 1988, Australia's bicentennial year, when the artist John Bulun Bulun and other Aboriginal artists from the Northern Territory brought an action concerning the unauthorized reproduction of their artworks on T-shirts. Throughout Australia, Indigenous designs and imagery are owned by Indigenous artists and are therefore subject to Indigenous intellectual copyright. A series of copyright cases was the subject of a groundbreaking exhibition curated by Vivien Johnson of Macquarie University, which brought enormous public attention to the matter, informing the views of both Indigenous and non-Indigenous Australians (see Johnson 1996).

There can be no doubt that these high profile cases influenced both Indigenous and non-Indigenous attitudes toward publication. In terms of our work with the Barunga-Wugularr community, elders exert control over our research in two ways: by encouraging us not to read early publications that contain secret information and by having direct control over the content of publications from our research (see Jackson and Smith 2005). When publishing a paper or book we seek formal permission for both text and images, firstly on the draft and secondly when we have proofs. Permission is sought on return visits to the community, and copies of all publications are returned to the community councils and associated organizations (such as the Jawoyn Association). Elders and community members are paid for any images used when the material is published, in recognition of their intellectual input into the publication and as a means of sharing the long-term benefits of research. We have found that the elders show particular concern about the use of information through photographs or other visual media such as videos. In a society that still has sectors that are nonliterate, photographs and other visual material are particularly subject to scrutiny.

The Dissemination of Results

A recurring criticism voiced by Indigenous peoples is that researchers do not involve them in the distribution of research results (e.g., Everett 1990; Willmot 1986). One problem for Indigenous peoples, as Price remarks, is that the researcher's necessarily selective written account of a system of knowledge, especially if it is supported by archival evidence to which people living in the society may not have access, has the potential to be established as a "canonical" or "authorized" version, even by individuals from within that society (Price 1983, 23). This issue articulates with concerns about the representation of Indigenous peoples, an issue under discussion globally (see, e.g., Mihesuah 1999). Lynnette Riley-Mundine argues that Aboriginal people should have control over or, at the very least, involvement in the formulation and dissemination of results: "Aboriginal people, *as people*, surely have the right to be involved in what is said about them, how it is said and what research is carried out" (Riley-Mundine 1998, 13, emphasis in original).

There are many benefits of having Indigenous people involved in the dissemination of research results, and since 1992 people from the Barunga-Wugularr community have traveled with us to conferences in Australia (Armidale, Darwin, and Cairns) as well as overseas (Cape Town, South Africa, and Washington DC, San Francisco, and Los Angeles, USA). In addition, we have toured rock art sites and visited collections from the community held at the Smithsonian Institution's National Museum of Natural History, in Washington DC. For the discipline, an obvious benefit is that [of] people having direct access to

Aboriginal views. Instead of asking the researcher, "What does Dolly think about . . .?" as one of us heard at an American Anthropological Association conference presentation, it is possible to ask Dolly herself, obtaining an answer that is not skewed by the selective memory and the interpretative and culturally shaped lens of the researcher. For Indigenous peoples the value is not only in having their voices heard and their views discussed but also in obtaining an understanding of the ways in which information is disseminated within a conference environment. Conference participation illustrates what researchers actually do when they leave communities. As Peter Manabaru said while attending a conference in Cairns, they "go away and talk about us." One outcome of this process of education can be the revocation of permission to use certain images or disseminate certain information, but this is due to consent becoming genuinely informed (Jackson and Smith 2005, 344). As with non-Indigenous scholars, the Indigenous people who attend conferences obtain a deeper understanding of the research process and have an opportunity to participate in the shaping of the discipline. This has to be an essential element of decolonizing archaeology.

Sharing the Benefits

Also fundamental to the decolonization of archaeology is recognition of Indigenous peoples' rights to protect their cultural and intellectual property, to share knowledge on their own terms, and to share fairly in the benefits that derive from research (see Blakeney 1999; Janke 1999, 2003). The system inherited from colonial structures, however, is one in which academics accrue the long-term benefits of research, while Indigenous people get no benefits, or only short-term benefits. Yet much archaeological research is informed by Indigenous knowledge, and a great deal of it could not be produced without the assistance of Indigenous people. While researchers bring skills to a project, often they do not provide the primary data. It follows that both Indigenous people and archaeologists have rights in the intellectual property that arises from such research, since both were essential to the outcome. One way to conceptualize this is to think of research as a kind of soup in which different people provide essential ingredients. Though there may be a "chef" (the researcher, either non-Indigenous or not), that particular soup could not exist without the full range of ingredients (both Western and Indigenous knowledges), and all the people who provide those ingredients have rights in that soup. It seems logical, then, to assume that all people involved in the research should benefit from its outcomes. . . .

The critical point here is that the benefits of research emerge some time after the fieldwork has been undertaken, sometimes many years afterward, and that the financial benefits of research are accrued indirectly. The time lapse between fieldwork and research outcomes contributes to researchers forgetting or minimizing Indigenous contributions to the research. This is facilitated by the fact that researchers normally live away from the communities they research. Regular visitation can be expensive, and as the ties of communication are loosened, so too is the researcher's sense of obligation to the community. This situation is exacerbated by the fact that the benefits of research are accrued indirectly. While academics rarely get paid to publish an article, their publication record contributes to promotion and higher salaries. Each article that an academic publishes is an increment toward financial reward in the form of higher salary. That the reward is delayed, not immediate, does not mean that the Indigenous people who were essential to the process should not participate in it. . . .

One consequence of recognizing Indigenous peoples' rights in research outcomes is that archaeologists will have to share the benefits that accrue from the Indigenous past. These benefits can be financial, such as salary and book royalties, or non-financial, such as travel and status. This need not be a difficult matter. For a start, it is a relatively simple matter to ensure that Indigenous communities get direct financial rewards from archaeological publications. For example, if society underwrites academic salaries for experts on Indigenous populations, it is reasonable for Indigenous populations to demand that part of that financial benefit is passed on to the primary sources of information, the Indigenous experts on those topics (Wobst and Smith 2003). One way this can be done is through inviting Aboriginal elders to give university classes and paying them at the same rate as other expert guest lecturers. Another way is for academics to contribute a tithe on their salary to the elders who have taught them or to a community fund. This would have the benefit of being tax deductible as well as being tied to the promotion structure of the academy.

Archaeologists also get funding from publications—directly, from book royalties, and indirectly, through their publications contributing to their obtaining employment, tenure, and promotion. While the Indigenous people who contributed to the archaeological research normally do not receive these indirect forms of payment, they do have a right to receive remuneration. It is a simple matter to share the financial rewards that come from publication, simply through directly royalty payments and paying a fee permission to publish images or articles. If the book derives from work with one particular community, it makes sense that the royalties be directed to that community, which we have done with a video documentary and book based on our work at Barunga. However, if the research is situated in more general discussions, the royalties can be directed to an Indigenous fund. David Hurst Thomas for example, directs the royalties from *Skull Wars* (2000) to the Society for American Archaeology's Native American fund. Along similar lines, royalties from the World Archaeological Congress's Indigenous Archaeologies Series with AltaMira (now "Archaeology and Indigenous Peoples" with Left Coast Press) are used to support Indigenous attendance at meetings of the World Archaeological Congress.

It is also reasonable for an Indigenous community to receive payment whenever an image or article is published. In our research with the Barunga-Wugularr communities of southern Arnhem Land, Northern Territory, and with the Ngadjuri people in South Australia, we pay for each image that is published of the people, or their land. The amounts range from $A100 (about $US75) to $A400 (about $US300), with the lower rate for each photo of an individual or site and the higher rate for cover images for books or images of several people. Payment is made to the senior traditional owner, the senior traditional custodian, or the individuals in the images, and permission has to be resought any time we wish to republish the image. For an entire book, this can be expensive, but it is possible to apply for publication subsidies to cover these costs—and as a last resort, to pay this from the salary that derives from doing research with these Indigenous people. . . .

Another measure that can be implemented to share the benefits of research is that of obtaining funding for community members to travel to participate in, or co-present, conference papers. The benefits of travel are in addition to those regarding control of Indigenous cultural and intellectual property, outlined in the preceding section of this article. Travel is a high status activity in both Indigenous and non-Indigenous cultures, as it broadens people's experiences and enriches their knowledge. When people travel to present their knowledge they accrue status in both Indigenous and non-Indigenous spheres. Apart from this, travel has long conferred status in many Indigenous cultures (see Henriksen 1993; Loring 1997; Shotridge 1920). Also, there is an argument to be made for a reciprocity in which scholars return the hospitality of Indigenous people on Indigenous lands through hosting these people in the scholar's community.

We have attended several conferences with the people with whom we conduct fieldwork, as discussed earlier. The presentations have taken a range of formats: joint presentations, sole presentations by the researcher, and sometimes presentations solely by Aboriginal people. While there are many benefits, there also are substantial challenges in such collaborations. For us, this has ranged from helping people get birth certificates and passports to making certain that there are sufficient funds to cover their travel costs and daily expenses. When we are at conferences together, it means looking after people, as they are operating in a different culture, rather than networking with our own archaeological colleagues. It involves going to the beach or a market rather than a conference session or meeting—and sometimes this does feel like a sacrifice. But the most challenging aspect of this is that of helping people to succeed in a presentation environment that is unfamiliar. Giving a conference presentation is daunting to anyone who is new to it, and this is exacerbated for people who are from a different cultural environment. For Aboriginal people, especially people from small communities, there can be considerable stress involved in leaving the security of their country and in being judged by others in a formal situation, especially one that is shaped by the rules and cultural assumptions of the academy.

For the researcher, the overriding challenge is that of making certain that the format is structured so that Aboriginal people are able to present their ideas successfully. In our presentations with Barunga-Wugularr people, who come from small communities of around four hundred people in a remote part of Australia, we have experimented with a range of formats. We have found the formats that work best are those closest to their normal configurations. Outdoor settings, culturally informal to the Western scholar, are formal to many Indigenous peoples. In the Barunga-Wugularr region, for instance, community meetings, including important meetings with government officials (when those officials are not structuring the meeting format) are held outdoors. Moreover, elders sit on the ground when they engage in discussions of an issue of importance or gravity and which may take an extended time. Normally, they sit down for positive discussions; if they want somebody to go, the discussion is undertaken whilst standing as an indication that the decision is made and the conversation will be brief. It is possible to transfer an Indigenous format to a conference setting, and this has been done in several conferences in northern Australia, including the Kultja Business conference, held in September 1996, and the 1997 Fulbright symposium "Indigenous Cultures in an Interconnected World," where most of the discussions were held outdoors and accompanied by cultural demonstrations and workshops that showcased Indigenous expertise and cultural knowledge (see Smith and Ward 2000). For conferences in less amenable climates, we have found that the format that works best for people from remote communities is one of small settings rather than large conference halls, which can be intimidating.

While implementation of the measures outlined in this section involves a commitment by the researcher in terms of time, funding, and organization, we do not feel that this is unreasonable. It seems only just to expect researchers to share the benefits of research fairly with the communities who provide the intellectual basis for their work. . . .

Given that differential access to power is at the core of colonial relations, it follows that the decolonization of Indigenous archaeology involves a rethinking of power relations between archaeologists and Indigenous peoples. It must involve a movement from the colonial assumption of a right to acquire knowledge to recognition of Indigenous peoples' rights to protect their cultural and intellectual property and to share knowledge on their own terms. It must move Indigenous concerns and values from the "outside" to the "center" and be committed to the survival and strengthening of Indigenous knowledge systems. The archaeological and anthropological practices outlined in this paper do not "empower" Indigenous peoples, they simply refrain from disempowering them.

15

Nukun and Kungun Ngarrindjeri Ruwe (Look and Listen to Ngarrindjeri Country): An Investigation of Ngarrindjeri Perspectives of Archaeology in Relation to Native Title and Heritage Matters

Amy Roberts, Steve Hemming, Tom Trevorrow, George Trevorrow, Matthew Rigney, Grant Rigney, Lawrie Agius, and Rhonda Agius

The "Discovery" at Goolwa and the *Kungun Ngarrindjeri Yunan Agreement*

In September 2002 the Alexandrina Council unearthed the remains of two "old people" in the area of the contested land near Hindmarsh Island (Kumarangk), in the Goolwa Wharf precinct. This "discovery," as Grant Rigney and Lawrie Agius point out, served to reinforce their belief that archaeologists and governments should cease to think in terms of "archaeological sites" and instead should recognise the interconnectedness of sites and therefore view "country" as an interconnected cultural landscape that cannot be segmented.

The "discovery" at Goolwa also reignited painful emotions about the Hindmarsh Island Bridge Royal Commission, as well as the Federal Court case, and posed some real problems for the Alexandrina Council

---

Excerpted from Roberts, Amy, Steve Hemming, Tom Trevorrow, George Trevorrow, Matthew Rigney, Grant Rigney, Lawrie Agius, and Rhonda Agius. 2005. Nukun and Kungun Ngarrindjeri Ruwe (Look and Listen to Ngarrindjeri Country): An Investigation of Ngarrindjeri Perspectives of Archaeology in Relation to Native Title and Heritage Matters. *Australian Aboriginal Studies* 1:45–53.

due to the unfortunate way in which the "old people" were unearthed. These problems revealed the need for formal agreed processes to deal with, and respect, Ngarrindjeri people, culture, knowledge, and heritage (Hemming and Trevorrow 2005; Liddle 2002).

The *Kungun Ngarrindjeri Yunnan Agreement* is an historic and powerfully symbolic document that recognises Ngarrindjeri people as the traditional owners of the Goolwa area, and acknowledges and respects their right to care and speak for their traditional country in accordance with laws, customs, beliefs and traditions (Liddle 2002). The agreement also expresses sorrow and regret for the injustices that Ngarrindjeri people have experienced since colonisation. The agreement states (in part):

> We accept your frustrations at our past ways of misunderstanding you. . . . We are shamed to acknowledge that there is still racism within our communities. We accept that our words must match our actions and we pledge to you that we will work to remove racism and ignorance. . . . We ask to walk beside you, and to stand with you to remedy the legacy of 166 years of European occupation of your land and waters and control of your lives. . . .

Importantly in relation to archaeological processes, the agreement commits the parties to consulting and working together to protect Ngarrindjeri sites, objects and the "old people." Equally importantly, it also inserts a new history into the public space: a history that recognises the traumas experienced by Ngarrindjeri people as a result of European invasion; the continuing problems of racism and ignorance; and the continuing Ngarrindjeri "traditional ownership" of the lands and waters of the Lower Murray region. This new history is very different from the more conventional history built around important archaeological "sites" and an implicit story of cultural extinction. A recent natural resource management plan for the Lower Murray region identifies "Blanchtown, Fromm's Landing, Devon Downs and Nildottie" as key "sites of Indigenous cultural and historical significance." In making this selection of "sites," the authors of the report justify themselves by arguing that "they [the sites] are known to have aboriginal artefacts more than 6,000 years old" (SA Murray-Darling Basin Integrated Natural Resource Management Group 2002, 24). This common act of privileging archaeological significance, and in particular what has been described in archaeological discourse as "prehistoric" significance, may have damaging consequences for contemporary Indigenous rights and interests to country.

As Rhonda Agius points out, the events surrounding the *Kungun Ngarrindjeri Yunnan Agreement* reveal that there is a way past the sensationalism that has dominated recent media reports and led to a negative perception of Ngarrindjeri people by many non-Indigenous people. Furthermore, Tom Trevorrow believes that through negotiation local-level agreements can be reached between Indigenous peoples and other parties. Indeed, as was shown in the *Kungun Ngarrindjeri Yunnan Agreement,* these documents can be powerful expressions of Indigenous peoples' rights to "country."

Discussion

While recognition of native title continues to be an important goal for many Indigenous communities, the recent *Ward, De Rose Hill* and *Yorta Yorta* decisions highlight the unpredictable nature of litigation as well as the importance of negotiations at the local level. Indeed, because of the success of the *Kungun Ngarrindjeri Yunnan Agreement* the Ngarrindjeri Nation has begun negotiations with other local councils.

The agreement has meant that Ngarrindjeri people can begin to be in charge of archaeological research. Tom Trevorrow believes now that they will be able to use archaeology as a tool towards their own self-determination, rather than it being used as a weapon in their continuing colonisation (Hemming and Trevorrow 2005).

In order for archaeology to be used as a tool by Indigenous communities, it is crucial that archaeological research, in this era of native title and heritage management regimes, attempt to ensure that Indigenous places be understood through their Indigenous epistemologies. Indeed, the discipline of archaeology has been guilty of imposing its own systems of categorisation around concepts such as time, space and culture (e.g., Attwood and Arnold 1992; Colley and Bickford 1997; Gosden 1994). This is particularly contentious in native title research and litigation. It is important to be aware of the ways in which archaeological knowledges can be useful to those opposing (vexatiously?—as opposed to "testing") Indigenous title claims.

Anthropologist Deborah Bird Rose has written about a process she describes as "deep colonizing." She refers (2001, 115) to:

> [a] cluster of practices which, under the guise of self-determination or self-management, probe ever more deeply into the conditions of Aboriginal people's lives and bodies, severing people from the sociality of connections within which they are embedded and reconstituting them as defenceless individuals. Current practice for land claims, including native title claims, and for the protection of Aboriginal heritage have the potential to further deep colonising; they are curtailing the social

> reproduction of Aboriginal culture by confining it in a prison of tradition, external documentation, consistency and consensus.

Archaeologist Denis Byrne (1996) has argued that, since the 1960s, archaeology has used the language of heritage to appropriate the Indigenous "past" in an attempt to provide a deep history for the young settler nation. This invented, pre-colonial, archaeological past combines with what many Indigenous leaders and scholars have long recognised as colonialism's dependence on the construction of an "Aboriginalist," colonial past to secure it legitimacy (e.g., Anderson 1995; Deloria 1995, 2000; Langford 1983; Langton 1981). Indeed, as English (2002a, 219) notes, the perception that cultural values were steadily erased after settlement has obscured Indigenous peoples' post-invasion experience and the complex processes of cultural change and adaptation.

Archaeology has also become a useful tool for governments attempting to limit Indigenous interests in land and waters. Archaeological "site clearances" have a finite character. They are limited to the physical and historical characteristics of a particular space. In considering heritage from an Indigenous perspective, social, economic, political and cultural interests are crucial. Use and enjoyment are other crucial factors and become even more important in native title cases. However, Indigenous peoples are often expected to relate to their country in what can be described as an archaeological way. This creates a restricted subject position for them in the Aboriginal heritage regimes of southern Australia (Hemming 2002). Such a form of symbolic violence has real effects on the Indigenous people engaged with the system (see Bourdieu 1984).

State and federal governments conceive of Indigenous rights to country in much of southern South Australia as fundamentally different from those in the north of the state—it is in these southern spaces that Indigenous traditions and political interests are translated into something called "Aboriginal heritage." This conception masks the ongoing political, economic, social, spiritual and cultural relationship that Indigenous people have with their land and waters. Ngarrindjeri people carry out a range of "conservation" practices, such as sharing resources, caring for land and revegetation. Burning-off is still also practised on occasions and has been a fundamental part of the "land management" regime. People hold social and cultural activities on their country and teach their children about their culture, history and the history of race relations in Australia. Camp Coorong, Race Relations and Cultural Education Centre, provides a focus for many of these activities (see Hemming 1993). Identities are formed through cultural practice and are often tied to particular places, experiences and knowledges. This opportunity has often been somewhat restricted on land alienated by farming or other purposes. Working on clearance teams, however, provides Ngarrindjeri people with the opportunity to engage with places, their stories, and the spirits of the ancestors. This activity is culturally productive and to some extent undermines the restrictive nature of the archaeological survey and its report outcomes. The culturally specific ways in which Ngarrindjeri people relate to their country are not generally considered important in the heritage clearance but are crucial for native title claims.

It is also important for archaeologists to be aware that governments and other parties may be using them as tools in the continuing colonisation of Indigenous Australians. In southern South Australia there appears to be a clear preference for archaeologists to work on heritage and native title clearances. This type of research often focuses on tangible objects, thereby avoiding the complex values associated with people's connections to place and their interaction with the landscape around them (English 2002a, 219). As a result, such research outcomes can be restricted and finite. The cultural, economic, social and political interests of Indigenous people, which are all part of their heritage and native title, will not emerge in this process. They have no space in the archaeological survey—the contemporary Indigenous person does not exist here. This is an invented space, framed by archaeological discourse and valuable to the interests of non-Indigenous peoples and their state apparatus. The experience of the "survey" or "site clearance" can be overtly disempowering for Indigenous people, and symbolically violent, and the powerful messages of extinction and assimilation can permeate the subject positions provided to Indigenous people engaged in these processes.

Paradoxically, the experience, as already mentioned, can also be culturally productive for Indigenous people, as they engage with country that may have previously been out of bounds to them. This process can be largely invisible to the archaeologists, or if visible may not be counted as important to the survey process and the understanding of Indigenous connections with country. Unfortunately, the survey or clearance process also imposes a short time frame for decision making about country. This can be very difficult for Indigenous native title/heritage committees as they often suffer from a lack of funding.

Thus, in order to avoid these pitfalls archaeological approaches must be designed with Indigenous peoples to recognise the links between heritage, identity and community wellbeing (English 2002b, xiii). Indigenous interpretations of places must be given a central role in "site clearances." There is a need to negotiate the introduction of Indigenous values that may be intangible (English 2002b, xi). It is imperative that there is development of research, planning and assessment processes that span the artificial divides between numerous disciplines that work in the cultural as well as natural heritage arenas. Indigenous scholars are bringing

Indigenous perspectives and theories to disciplines such as archaeology, sociology, anthropology and history and are often at the forefront of the engagement with new international theory (e.g., Moreton-Robinson 2000; Smith 1999; Te Hennepe 1993). Hard questions also need to be asked in archaeological research and political agendas, aimed at building self-governance and the recognition of sovereignty and state-sponsored heritage research that can be interpreted as continuing the "mapping" and colonisation of Indigenous space (see Hemming 2002; Hemming and Trevorrow 2005).

In conclusion, it must also be recognised that the new types of approaches that are needed to introduce Indigenous values into archaeological research require a deep commitment by all participants. It is acknowledged that these approaches are certainly more time-consuming and expensive. They also introduce new issues such as intellectual and cultural property rights (see Battiste and Henderson 2000; English 2002a, 226). Such approaches, however, will undoubtedly provide a richer record and will improve the ways in which archaeologists understand and value landscapes. They will also serve to ensure that Indigenous peoples' native title rights and interests are respected and protected.

16

Wāhi Ngaro (The Lost Portion): Strengthening Relationships between People and Wetlands in North Taranaki, New Zealand

Harry Allen, Dilys Johns, Caroline Phillips, Kelvin Day, Tipene O'Brien, and Ngāti Mutunga

North Taranaki: Land and History

Taranaki district is situated on the western side of the North Island of New Zealand, and is dominated by an active volcano, Taranaki. The mountain itself has a complex natural history and there is a similarly long history of interaction between the landscape and its human inhabitants. . . .

The *Māori* history of north Taranaki over the past 200 years, since the European colonization of New Zealand, has been one of war, confiscations, migrations, repatriations and loss of lands (Lambert and Henry 2000, 15–27; Prickett 1990, 9–12; Smith 1910; Waitangi Tribunal 1996). The efforts of Taranaki tribes to obtain justice are documented in their claim to the Waitangi Tribunal, the court set up to hear *Māori* treaty claims against the Crown (Sharp 1991; Temm 1990). The Tribunal found that Taranaki *Māori* had been "plundered of their resources. The little left to them cannot sustain the cultural basis of their society for the future" (Waitangi Tribunal 1996, 311). This history has had the effect of separating Ngāti Mutunga from their cultural wetlands. The sale of land and the modification of the wetlands by drainage have accentuated

Excerpted from Allen, Harry, Dilys Johns, Caroline Phillips, Kelvin Day, Tipene O'Brien, and Ngāti Mutunga. 2002. Wāhi Ngaro (The Lost Portion): Strengthening Relationships between People and Wetlands in North Taranaki, New Zealand. *World Archaeology* 34(2):315–29.

this separation, creating a disjunction between the *Māori* community, landowners, wetlands and associated artefacts. . . .

Wetlands incorporate at least three sets of values. First, there are *Māori* values, relating to the *mauri* (life essence) of the wetland, whether or not it remains as swamp or is still in *Māori* ownership. Second, there are archaeological values, where wetlands are a repository of environmental and historical information concerning the past. Finally, there are ecological values, where wetlands provide environments for important species of plants and animals, and act as water reservoirs. Currently 99.8 per cent of wetlands on privately owned lands in Taranaki have been drained (Taranaki Regional Council 1998, 73–74). Surface waters have been removed, and changes have occurred for aquatic plants and animals, resulting in the loss of ecological values. Fortunately many *Māori* and archaeological values remain, as Taranaki's drains are mainly shallow and the landscape remains patchily damp. The environmental indicators present in tephra and silt layers, charcoal and peat still survive, as do artefacts. However, if farmers install deeper and more efficient drainage systems, further damage to wetsites and the information they contain will occur.

Within a few decades of organized European settlement of the Taranaki region in 1841, waterlogged artefacts were being discovered in wetland areas. Initially these finds were infrequent, as the drains had to be dug by hand. After World War II, the use of mechanical excavators meant that swampy areas, previously deemed unproductive, could be drained for dairy farming. During the late 1950s and for the next two decades, a number of wetlands in the western and northern areas of Taranaki started to yield artefacts. Household or utilitarian items were commonly found. The more spectacular finds of carved or decorated pieces were less frequently discovered, though a recent survey (Day 2001) of *Māori* wooden carvings from the Taranaki region includes many such examples. . . .

Artefacts and Museums

The collection and removal of cultural materials from New Zealand commenced in 1769 with the first voyage of Captain Cook (McKinlay 1973, 13). Signed in 1840, the Treaty of Waitangi included a commitment by the Crown to safeguard *Māori* possessions (Kawharu 1989, 317, 321). Despite this guarantee, the Maori Antiquities Act (first passed in 1901, see McKinlay (1973, 13–43) was aimed at controlling the illegal export of cultural items. There were no provisions to control the fossicking of *Māori* places for artefacts neither did legislation assist *Māori* to retain control of cultural items.

It is significant that this legislation came up for review because of the chance finding of carvings near Motunui, north Taranaki, and the failure of the government to prevent their illegal export. This review led to the current Historic Places and Antiquities Acts (Day 2001, 39; McKinlay 1976, 38–40).

The Antiquities Act 1975 formalized procedures for museums by setting up a system of registering collectors, licensing exports and making all newly found *Māori* artefacts to be *prima facie* the property of the Crown (except those recovered from known graves). *Māori* artefacts found after 1975 must be registered and deposited in a regional museum, generally as part of the ethnological collections (R. Wilson 1984). There is little provision in the Act for *Māori* control of artefacts recovered from within their tribal areas.

Over the past twenty years, the incorporation of the Treaty of Waitangi into legislation and *Māori* claims before the Waitangi Tribunal has created a new view of the Treaty as a legal contract between *Milori* and the Crown (Sharp 1991, 86–103). Today, the idea that the Crown would assume ownership of *taonga* (valued possessions) on behalf of *Māori* is interpreted as a breach of Treaty obligations (Williams 1989, 75–76) (for a discussion of the meaning of *taonga,* see Kawharu [1989, 321], Mead [1984, 21], Tapsell [1997, 333]).

Mead comments:

> What is important for the owning group is that the taonga is "brought home" so that it can be slotted into an art style, the history, and oral traditions (korero) of the people. When the taonga is not brought home into the tribal territory but rests instead in some museum hundreds of miles away, the object and its associated korero remain lost to the owning group. Such objects are part of the wahi ngaro (the lost portion) of Maori culture. (Mead 1984, 29)

The relationship between Ngāti Mutunga and objects held in the Taranaki Museum reflects the general situation described above. The museum, originally formed in 1847 (Lambert and Henry 2000, 28), is now the responsibility of the New Plymouth District Council (NPDC). Its collection of around 5,000 Māori objects was built up through chance finds, gifts and purchases. Between 1960 and 1989 formal *Māori* involvement with the museum was limited to one or two representatives from the Taranaki Māori Trust Board. This changed in 1996, when the NPDC incorporated a Komiti Maori of representatives from each of the eight Taranaki *iwi* (tribes). This committee was to advise on a new institution known as Puke Ariki (the combined museum and library) on issues relating to biculturalism, *matauranga Māori (Māori* knowledge), intellectual and cultural property issues and the physical and spiritual care of *taonga*.

In 1997, a Tauhora Curator (Maori Curator), O'Brien, was appointed to the staff of the museum to ensure the appropriate care of *taonga* and to liaise between *iwi Māori* and the museum. In the same year, Ngāti Mutunga ratified a Memorandum of Understanding with the museum, which specified that Ngāti Mutunga held *rangatiratanga* (sovereignty) over *taonga* in the museum collection that had been found in their tribal territory or *rohe*. Ngāti Mutunga visit the museum regularly to view artefacts from their area on display or in storage.

Ngāti Mutunga and the Conservation Laboratory

One of the positive implications of state ownership under the Antiquities Act is that the Ministry of Culture and Heritage takes responsibility for the conservation of newly found *Māori* artefacts. Through this scheme, Johns at the Wet Organics Conservation Laboratory has conserved one hundred and fifty artefacts for the Taranaki Museum over the past fifteen years. Many of these were discovered in Ngāti Mutunga territory.

These at-risk artefacts, which require immediate attention if they are to survive, provide an ongoing link between Ngāti Mutunga and the laboratory. Protocols have been established with Ngāti Mutunga to guarantee that the artefacts are conserved in a respectful manner. Ngāti Mutunga elders accompany artefacts on their journey from the museum to the laboratory and conduct the appropriate ceremonies. At the same time, Ngāti Mutunga take the opportunity to inspect the Conservation Laboratory and to familiarize themselves with its operations.

Having re-established a relationship with artefacts from north Taranaki, Ngāti Mutunga became concerned about the number of *taonga* being recovered. During 1998 a collection of waterlogged artefacts, which were found in the Mimi area of Ngāti Mutunga, led to a meeting at Urenui Marae with Allen and Johns from the University of Auckland. Issues raised at this meeting included site protection and the conservation of wet organic artefacts, conservation science, the effects of waterlogging on organic materials, laboratory treatment for recovered artefacts and the need for further research on the wetlands.

North Taranaki Wetlands Project

Early in 1999, a group of researchers from the University of Auckland and elsewhere, consisting of three archaeologists, a conservator, an ethnologist, a palynologist, a radiocarbon dating specialist and a Māori researcher (i.e. the authors together with Nigel Prickett, Auckland Museum, Janet Wilmshurst, Landcare Research, and Tom Higham, University of Waikato), submitted a preliminary proposal to the Royal Society of New Zealand Marsden Fund to study the cultural significance of north Taranaki wetlands. The intended project area was between the Waiiti Stream and Onaero River, bounded on the west by the coast and by dissected hill country in the east. This is the majority of the coastal area within Ngāti Mutunga *rohe*. It was selected on the basis of the number of waterlogged artefacts recovered from the area and the strength of the relationships built up between the tribe, Taranaki Museum and the University Conservation Laboratory.

The general goals of the research project were to renew systematic research into wetland archaeological sites in New Zealand, to draw together information from wetland and dry-land sites within the context of a *Māori* settlement system and to use archaeological methods to study wetlands. The intention is to use a landscape approach to integrate this information with *Māori* traditions.

Ngāti Mutunga gave provisional support, and explained that they were principally interested in co-operative research where members of Ngāti Mutunga could work alongside the team and where permission for investigations could be obtained only on a case-by-case basis. The success of the application was announced in September 1999, and a Memorandum of Understanding (MOU) between the research team and Ngāti Mutunga was signed at Urenui Marae in May 2000.

The main points made in the MOU were, first, that Ngāti Mutunga retained the rights to intellectual property concerning *Māori* traditions, place names, locations and other information which they might make available to the researchers. Second, that proprietary rights to intellectual property created by the research were subject to negotiation between Ngāti Mutunga and the researchers. Third, the researchers could investigate wetlands subject to agreement about specific places. Fourth, if *koiwi* (human remains) were discovered, the researchers would cease operations in the vicinity and contact the *tangata whenua* (people of that place), who would respond with directives on how the situation would be managed. Fifth, the researchers acknowledged the rights of Ngāti Mutunga as owners of artefacts recovered from locations within their *rohe*. Finally, the researchers agreed to consult with *tangata whenua* prior to the publication of the results of the research and that the *tangata whenua* could include *Māori* perspectives in these reports. . . .

In February 2001, a meeting was held at Urenui Marae, attended by Allen, Johns, Phillips, Day and O'Brien, to report the findings of the project to date, discuss the archaeological survey programme and ask for members of Ngāti Mutunga, who might like to learn about archaeological techniques, to assist with the survey. It was at this stage that previously unknown difficulties came to the surface. Some sections of the tribe were convinced that the purpose of the fieldwork was to locate and remove *taonga* from the wetlands. This was to some extent motivated by an unfortunate newspaper report, which represented our project as a hunt for buried treasure. Following discussions, the issues and concerns of *iwi* present were addressed, a consensus was reached and it was agreed that we would proceed with the survey as planned.

In March 2001, a team of experienced archaeological surveyors led by Phillips arrived at Urenui Marae for an informal welcome, and they were met by a deputation who repeated some of the concerns that had been discussed the previous month. The main issues raised were, first, there was still the belief that the archaeologists were going to search and dig for *taonga.* Second, there were areas where they did not wish the team to go because they were *tapu* (sacred and dangerous). In this sense they were especially dangerous for *tangata whenua* if they allowed others to go there. The last concern was the control over the information recovered. They argued that, if knowledge of important places became widespread, then others might come in and dig for *taonga* and disturb *köiwi.* Many of these points were within the MOU, and as part of that agreement *rangatahi* (younger members of the *iwi)* had been asked to join the survey team. It was hoped that this would allay any continuing fears or misgivings.

Resource management decision making in *Māori* tribes is complex. While major issues might require consensus of all tribal members, the exercise of authority over local areas is at the kin group level (M. Kawharu 2000, 355). This means that some areas might be open to the archaeological survey while others might be closed. It was on this basis that the project could continue.

Agreement was reached, and the survey began the next day with four teams comprising five Auckland archaeologists, O'Brien and Day from the Taranaki Museum and the two *rangatahi,* who had been told the areas that the survey team were not to visit. Surveying started [on] either side of the Mimi River mouth, where contact had already been made with several farmers. Two full days of surveying went without incident. Unfortunately, on the third day a miscommunication arose between a farmer and one of the *rangatahi.* We decided to postpone the survey to give us more time to re-negotiate access. In the brief period of surveying undertaken, a block of land approximately 5.6 km^2 had been intensively covered. This provides a pilot survey of the project area, giving an indication of the true range of visible archaeological sites on the landscape.

A New Direction

A further meeting between the project team and Ngāti Mutunga took place in November 2001 to see if support for the project remained. A new agreement based on the original MOU was negotiated in which large-scale archaeological operations were suspended and the research focused on the conservation of specific wetlands where we had both landowner and *iwi* support. This involved a monitoring schedule to evaluate sites and to determine the conditions needed to maintain optimal environmental parameters for site preservation. Work at present has concentrated on understanding factors that control physico-chemical processes and seasonal variations. Allied to this was the need to build on the palynological and environmental data already obtained. Therefore, it was planned to take more pollen cores and bring in a geomorphologist to provide further evidence about the history of the wetlands. The *Māori* historical research was to continue as before, and in order to facilitate any permissions that might be necessary, a member of Ngāti Mutunga was chosen to liaise between the team, relevant *hapü* and the *iwi* as a whole.

Discussion

The colonization of New Zealand has resulted in the physical separation of *Māori* from their places, artefacts and the landscape. It has also resulted in a conceptual separation, where wetlands, archaeological sites and artefacts are dealt with through separate environmental and cultural legislation and organizations. This is unhelpful from a *Māori* perspective, where natural, cultural and economic realms are embedded within a unified spiritual framework (Harmsworth 1995, 27–29). It also creates difficulties for effective resource management. Maintenance of cultural relationships between the *Māori* community and the wetlands is necessary to allow the fulfillment of their *kaitiaki* role, the responsibility to safeguard their ancestral inheritance (M. Kawharu 2000). Acceptance of the Treaty of Waitangi as a legal treaty between the parties has been pivotal in starting a process of change in practices and attitudes concerning ancestral relationships throughout New Zealand.

The project attempted to join Ngāti Mutunga's growing awareness of the artefacts being uncovered with their concerns for wetland conservation. It also attempted to link their wish to reclaim lost *taonga* (both knowledge and artefacts) with the archaeologist's concerns over the destruction of archaeological evidence and the need to understand the context of the artefacts being recovered. In attempting this, the project created conditions for learning on both sides. The linking of the terms archaeology, wetlands and *taonga* in our proposals convinced a section of Ngāti Mutunga that we were intending to excavate and remove cultural treasures. While they would like accidental damage to wetlands through drainage to be kept to a minimum, Ngāti Mutunga accept such damage as a fact of farming life. They are more concerned about investigations that intentionally expose the past. The ICOMOS New Zealand *Charter for the Conservation of Places of Cultural Heritage Value* (1995) allows that non-intervention, which maintains undisturbed constancy of spiritual association, may be more important than intervening to protect the physical aspects of places of indigenous value. This is close to the conservation sentiments expressed by Ngāti Mutunga. Those who supported the project have had to risk the consequences of any culturally inappropriate actions by the researchers. Finally, the process of *iwi* decision making meant that, when a large-scale archaeological survey was planned, the area to be surveyed incorporated most of Ngāti Mutunga territory. This involved all members of the tribe, including those who supported the investigations and those who remained unconvinced about our aims.

Other factors have made the research harder than it might have been. North Taranaki is a distant research location for most of the researchers. *Māori* prefer face-to-face relationships *(kanohi ki kanohi)* and these are more difficult with a multi-disciplinary team that arrives and departs irregularly. Taranaki is also distant from most universities and hence has not received the research attention it deserves. As a consequence, both the local *Māori* and *Pākehā* community are largely unfamiliar with academic research. In addition, several local events have heightened tensions between *Māori* and their *Pākehā* neighbours. In September 2001 the owner of a newly purchased farm block bulldozed a track through a Ngāti Mutunga *pā* and this caused local disquiet. Matters were very tense in north Taranaki for other reasons. On 30 April 2001, a policeman shot and killed Steven Wallace, a young Ngāti Mutunga man. Since then, there has been a series of police inquiries and court cases, which have not allayed the Wallace family concerns.

The project is taking place during a period of change. These wider events have made a co-operative research programme timely, but more complex. In response to these issues, the researchers have developed new protocols to minimize the impact of their investigations on the wetlands and to work in a manner consistent with their *tapu* status, Ngāti Mutunga have maintained their support for the project. The research now has a conservation and environmental focus as this supports the *iwi's* role as custodians of their land and heritage by providing a better understanding of the wetlands.

17

Indigenous Research and Archaeology: Transformative Practices in/with/for the Ngarrindjeri Community

Christopher L. Wilson

As both a Ngarrindjeri person and an archaeologist, my position within any research project involves different dimensions to those experienced by non-Indigenous students, archaeologists and researchers. I have realised that as an Indigenous person I need to expose part of who I am in order to teach others, including researchers, about the complexities which surround Indigenous peoples in the broadest sense. Explicitly exploring the research process and the way I approach it is an important aspect of working with my community and follows the approach of many other Australian-based archaeologists (Colley 2002; Pardoe 1990; Ulm 2006; Wallis, Hemming, and Wilson 2006; Webb 1987).

My approach became increasingly multifaceted as the research progressed, offering one example of a culturally appropriate research methodology for anyone conducting research within the Ngarrindjeri community. This self-reflexive practice is useful for "all" as it considers the complex issues the researcher experiences as a part of working with Indigenous communities and thus exposes the politics of the research process. As a result, I argue based on my experience, that Indigenous research projects developed within archaeology should always be focused towards working in, with and for Indigenous communities and thus contributes to the broader socio-political context. . . .

As is a common academic convention, I analysed, compared and critiqued written records to provide an historical context for the research

Excerpted from Wilson, Christopher L. 2007. Indigenous Research and Archaeology: Transformative Practices in/with/for the Ngarrindjeri Community. *Archaeologies: Journal of the World Archaeological Congress* 3(3):320–34. Reprinted with kind permission of Springer Science and Business Media.

I was undertaking. In addition, I also integrated this with Indigenous histories, photography, poetry and art written by and for Indigenous peoples. This approach highlights the importance of recognising "non-traditional" approaches within archaeology as well as values Indigenous knowledges and creative responses as part of the process of de-colonising archaeology. Within my research, I articulated these experiences through story, art and poetry and analysed how my position relates to the research process as a method for incorporating both western and Indigenous epistemologies (Wilson 2005). This "de-colonisation" of archaeological practice builds upon the perspectives developed in post-processual archaeology (Johnson 1999; Smith and Wobst 2005a). Furthermore, anti-colonial theory is critical to the deconstruction and decolonisation of academic literature and my ability to effectively undertake archaeological research within my community that is beneficial. This is a common approach adopted by many Indigenous academics that need to deconstruct colonial discourse and ways of knowing in their disciplines (see Langton 1993; Million 2005; Smith 1999; Watkins 2000; Watson 2002).

Once I considered these crucial issues and developed a broad research framework I contacted Uncle Tom Trevorrow, Chair of the Ngarrindjeri Lands and Progress Association (NLPA) and the Ngarrindjeri Heritage Committee (NHC). This initial visit to Camp Coorong Race Relations Centre required strong input by my supervisor Steve Hemming who was able to guide me in developing an ethical research relationship with my community. Owing to previous experiences with researchers, many Ngarrindjeri people are often reluctant to accept archaeologists into the community unless introduced by other researchers who have existing long-term relationships. Prior to meeting Ngarrindjeri Elders I was not aware of the research history of the community or that was associated with my background as an archaeologist. This lack of understanding, in conjunction with the fact that I grew up in suburbia, made me feel like the "outsider" entering into my own community. The research process facilitated this initial introduction to my Elders; my acceptance into the community was instant because people knew my family and my connections to them.

At Camp Coorong I was able to meet several members from the NLPA and NHC, as well as other Ngarrindjeri Elders. This provided the opportunity for me to introduce myself and, more importantly, meet people "face-to-face". Through discussing my research proposal with members of the committees we established the beginning of a partnership which would seek the support, opinions, and contribution of Ngarrindjeri to produce collaborative outcomes. After this meeting Uncle Tom expressed the importance of having a Ngarrindjeri person working on Ngarrindjeri issues in the area of archaeology, and agreed this project would therefore be beneficial to the community. . . .

During the course of this research and the development of a sound relationship with my community, I was invited by Uncle Tom to travel to Museum Victoria to bring home 74 Old People in August 2004. As I later learned from my Elders, Old People's remains must be returned to the community for reburial in accordance with Ngarrindjeri cultural practices. My involvement in the trip to Victoria allowed time to *Kungun* and *Yunnan* (Listen and Talk) about several issues with Ngarrindjeri Elders and begin to understand these views and opinions, which are largely based upon the concept of "respect." I was also able to participate in the capacity of a younger Ngarrindjeri person learning about the responsibilities that Ngarrindjeri Elders deal with on a day-to-day basis. This opportunity ultimately grew from the realisation by Ngarrindjeri Elders that my research agenda was driven by its importance to the community. Furthermore, it framed the overall research process and became the major "case study" for discussing the implications of repatriation for my community within the final production of my thesis.

The Semi-Standardised "Interview" or Discussion?

Another important component of the research process for me was the shift in use of language as well as my approach to "data collection." The importance of seeking the views and opinions of Ngarrindjeri Elders and community leaders was to highlight to others the impact of removal and repatriation of Old People's remains for Ngarrindjeri people today.

The semi-standardised (also referred to as semi-structured or focused) "interview" involves questions, which are predetermined, asked in a systematic order for each "interviewee," and permits the "interviewer" to expand beyond the answers supplied (Berg 1998, 61–62). Many disciplines, including archaeology, call the process of recording an individual for research purposes by the term "interview" or "oral history." In the context of my research project, however, the relationship between the "interviewer" and the "interviewees" is somewhat different to non-Indigenous researchers as the researcher is a young Ngarrindjeri male who is discussing issues relating to repatriation and cultural identity with Ngarrindjeri Elders. This created a space for dissemination of cultural knowledge through research. Adopting part of this approach I developed a set of themes for discussion with Elders.

All people involved in the discussions were Ngarrindjeri who have specific Ngarrindjeri cultural knowledge and/or have been involved in the repatriation of Old People to the Ngarrindjeri community. Although numerous people were identified as potential contributors early in the research project, discussions were only conducted if Elders had the time. This approach meant I did not necessarily have all relevant Elders contributing to all components of the project, but it was nevertheless a reality of conducting research with senior leaders who have several political responsibilities to deal with, and various existing commitments including community, work and family. Those who agreed to be involved in this project were provided with a letter which introduced them to the researcher; an information sheet that outlined the project; and a list of themes/topics for discussion. As a part of the Flinders University ethics process, Elders were required to sign a consent form to record the discussion and to use the recording and/or transcription in preparation for this thesis. Although Elders signed the forms for the research, I was provided with feedback in relation to the language and terminology in the forms, which made me re-consider the language used throughout my thesis.

The first two Elders who I approached to contribute towards this research were my grandparents. I decided to incorporate my grandparents' views and opinions into the research process because I value highly their source of knowledge about "lived experience" of growing up as Ngarrindjeri people in South Australia during the implementation of various government policies (i.e., assimilation, protection, segregation) which impacted upon their lives (see Sabbioni, Schaffer, and Smith 1998 for a brief overview). They were also the best source of knowledge in relation to family genealogy. Furthermore, I made the decision to privilege my grandparents' stories to allow an opportunity for them to pass down their experiences and knowledge, which "grounded" me as a young Ngarrindjeri person prior to developing relationships with Ngarrindjeri Elders at Camp Coorong.

Following this discussion I approached Ngarrindjeri people who had been involved in repatriation and, if possible, those who were involved in the repatriation of Ngarrindjeri from the Museum Victoria. Most of these people however are continuously dealing with other issues and my research therefore needed to be incorporated into their already busy agenda. Building the trust of busy Elders meant I had to become more involved with the community so they had an opportunity to make decisions about my ability to work on specific projects. It was also a case of being involved with the community and giving people an opportunity to get to know me. After several trips to Camp Coorong, attending meetings and community events, I was fortunate to formally discuss my research topic with three senior Ngarrindjeri leaders who have been involved in the process of repatriation.

In order to consider the advice and information provided to me by Elders in a sensitive and culturally appropriate way, I had to firstly understand my role and position within the whole research process. Drawing upon post-modern theory and the approach to reviewing the archaeological literature enabled me to raise political and ethical issues relevant to my research (Howells 1999, 122). This included an examination and deconstruction of texts including the language used for my own ethics application, which revealed distinct differences in comparison to the language used for the final version of my thesis. This shift suggests that I have undergone a significant cultural, spiritual and personal transformation from a "student of archaeology" to "Ngarrindjeri person/archaeologist" which contributes to the common experiences between Indigenous peoples and archaeologists and the development of an Indigenous archaeology [as] has been described by a number of Indigenous academics (see for example Million 2005; Watkins 2000).

De-Constructing Language: Transforming Practice

In light of discussions above, a critique of the pro forma used for discussions with Elders highlights an internal shift in language for the Ngarrindjeri archaeologist. This in conjunction with the overall process of *Kungun* and *Yunnan* (listen and talk) with the Elders further demonstrates the importance for transforming practice in archaeology.

As a part of the original methodology for my project it was proposed to conduct a series of "interviews" with "participants". A total of five themes were developed to discuss with the Elders who would become contributors to this research project. Although the intention was to provide Elders with a guide for discussions, it became clear upon reviewing my ethics application that it added little value to the actual research process because Elders were sharing information that they deemed important. I ultimately framed my language to suit the ethics committee rather than for Elders contributing to the research project. For example *Topic 1* used terminology such as "participant" and "researcher" (Wilson 2005, 37). Smith (1999) has described the relationship between the practice of "research" and Indigenous peoples as problematic. As an example, the "researcher" has historically been a "white Anglo-Saxon male" with the sole purpose of recording and distributing Indigenous knowledges for their own benefit. Hence, the use of "participant" and "researcher" becomes highly inappropriate in the context of a Ngarrindjeri person/archaeologist carrying out a discussion with Elders.

Poor or inappropriate research practices and methodologies were further reinforced in the pro forma through the use of concepts including "gathering information" and "data collection" which I used in describing *Topic 2* (Wilson 2005, 38). Research with Indigenous peoples should not be a process of "gathering information" or "collecting data". These concepts lie within the domain of past archaeological practices of "collection" including collecting the remains of the Old People. A more culturally appropriate research practice such as *Kungun* and *Yunnan* with the Elders would have been a much better selection of phrasing. *Kungun* and *Yunnan* is an important Ngarrindjeri cultural message, which is transmitted to all Ngarrindjeri people and more recently the wider non-Indigenous community including researchers, as well as local councils and government bodies (see Hemming and Trevorrow 2005).

Furthermore, *Topic 4* asked "participants" to spend some time thinking about the implications that repatriation of "human remains" has had upon the community and/or the individual (Wilson 2005, 38). Two problems emerged from this. Firstly, Elders do not use the phrase "Ngarrindjeri human remains"; instead the term Old People was preferred. The use of the latter term is more culturally appropriate, as well as respectful to the Old People and to their living descendants. Secondly, Elders would have already thought through the positives and negatives as a result of repatriation and are instantly affected by such actions.

This critique also brings to light the context within which the discussion operates. For example, Elders would share information depending on a range of factors including those that cannot be controlled (age, gender, family background) and those that can (time of the day, the place the discussion occurs). Understanding the context in which a discussion may occur is as equally important as understanding the relations between the Elder and the young person. Furthermore, the process of recording the discussion becomes less important to the process of *Kungun* and *Yunnan* as the Elders contributing to research processes are also assessing Indigenous researchers working with their own communities.

Upon reflection, it was crucial that an appropriate research question was negotiated that would be valuable for the Ngarrindjeri community, the discipline and me. Further, my research process was more complex than for a non-Indigenous researcher. This is partly because I would be representing my family in addition to my supervisors, the university and myself as a researcher and Ngarrindjeri person. This situation creates additional layers of responsibility, which may have a range of impacts (both positive and negative), for various parties depending on the progression and outcomes of the research.

For example, my role as an archaeologist working with Indigenous peoples involves developing relationships, conducting research for the community, collaboration with various Elders and committees as well as upholding my ethical responsibilities to the community within whom I work. As a Ngarrindjeri person and community member I am also involved in the broader social and political issues that impact upon the community that are not "archaeological" or "heritage" related matters. These "factors" are exclusively a part of the community and have a cultural and historical context, which are not separate from the archaeological record or Ngarrindjeri people today. As both a Ngarrindjeri person and archaeologist, I take on a majority if not all the roles above and possibly many more at various levels. At an individual level I am accountable to my community and at risk of being excluded if I do not follow appropriate protocols. At the "community" level I am intertwined in a broader effort for self-determination and reclamation as the community continues to battle against changes in government policy. At a national and international level I become a representative for the community, thus placing enormous responsibilities upon me as the young Ngarrindjeri person and archaeologist who has recently embarked on an academic career.

The issues that arise from my experiences are only one example of how Indigenous peoples/archaeologists are working within their community. There are other Indigenous peoples/archaeologists in similar positions who continue to share their perspectives and others who work outside their own community and thus identify a whole set of separate experiences that must also be considered and strongly acknowledged (see Norder 2007 for an American/First Nation experience). Similarly, the reasons for undertaking research and the questions that direct it are diverse and distinct depending on the "researcher" and community context.

In my context, I choose to privilege a unique Ngarrindjeri process of *Kungun Ngarrindjeri Yunnan* (Listen to Ngarrindjeri people talking) in place of the standard "interview." As a result, information exchanged through conversations between me (the young Ngarrindjeri researcher) and community Elders produced valuable perspectives into the social, cultural, spiritual, political and economic implications of repatriating Old People. After realising this distinction, I have been able to place my position into perspective. I am not only being assessed as a "researcher" under the structure of the university, but I am also undergoing cultural training as a "learner" through the assessment and examination of my Elders. Elders in the community have ultimately taken on responsibility to ensure that I am aware that Ngarrindjeri protocols exist and that university processes are not the only ethical guidelines with which I must comply. . . .

Section V

North America

In North American contexts (particularly the United States and Canada), Indigenous peoples are referred to as American Indians, First Nations, Native Americans, Tribal Nations, and various tribal names derived from their multitudinous cultural, territorial, and linguistic groupings. Their long habitation on the continent (extending back at least 12,000 years) is evidenced in material remains and oral traditions that document complex networks of seasonal movements, resource-gathering activities, and political and social relations over time. As in Australia, New Zealand, South America, and elsewhere, the North American Indigenous peoples who survived to the present have maintained intimate and inalienable connections to their lands and cultures and have (with varying degrees of success) resisted European colonization, domination, dispossession, and other threats to their sovereignty and survival.

Indigenous involvement in professional archaeology in North America is not new. During the nineteenth century, Indigenous people were hired as guides, porters, research assistants, and informants; during the early twentieth century, some became practicing archaeologists, most notably Arthur Parker (Seneca), employed by the New York State Museum, and his daughter Bertha Parker Cody (Abenaki and Seneca), employed by the Southwest Museum (Colwell-Chanthaphonh 2009). However, non-Native archaeologists largely dominated the discipline, and the routine excavation of Indigenous sites—including sacred places and gravesites (regarded as public property and archaeological resources)—continued unabated until the mid-twentieth century.

Indigenous protests against archaeological disturbances were well underway when Maria Pearson/Running Moccasins took a stand against the Iowa State Archaeologist in 1970 (Pearson 2000). Since then, concerns over repatriation, reburial, Indigenous land title, heritage protection, and intellectual and cultural property rights have been prominent in American archaeology, resulting in multiple opportunities for both conflict and collaboration. New legislation emerged, notably the Archaeological Resources Protection Act (1979) and the Parks Canada Agency Act (1998), which, like the National Historic Preservation Act (NHPA 1966), identified Indigenous sites as historic and irreplaceable.

Most tribal, state, and provincial governments now maintain offices devoted to historic preservation, but regulations for protecting, reporting, identifying, and repatriating materials and human remains from Indigenous sites and disturbed burials are inconsistent if not contradictory. Even the United States' Native American Graves Protection and Repatriation Act (NAGPRA 1990) is only a partial success story. Under NAGPRA, the skeletal remains of more than 38,600 individuals have been repatriated, but the remains of more than 115,900 Indigenous individuals and unknown thousands of objects remain in the control of museums and federal institutions. The vast majority of repatriations have involved only American federally recognized tribes; non-federally recognized tribes and Canadian First Nations have benefitted to a much smaller degree from this legislation. In addition, many thousands of Indigenous remains and artifacts continue to circulate among looters, collectors, and art and antiquities dealers in national and international venues, out of reach of federal laws (Bruchac 2010).

The focus on repatriation has led to substantive change in the practice of archaeology in American contexts, in particular requiring that archaeologists consult with Indigenous communities. As a result, a spectrum of decolonizing collaborative and participatory practices and novel analytical approaches are becoming prevalent across the continent (see, for example, Colwell-Chanthaphonh and Ferguson 2008; Kerber 2006; Martinez 2006; Silliman 2008). However, the emphasis on repatriation has also drawn attention away from other injustices committed against Indigenous people in North America. Efforts at increasing heritage protection in North America have met with a surprising degree of resistance from mainstream archaeologists and the general public. Other countries, such as Australia and New Zealand, have greater protections against site destruction and stronger ethical protocols that insist on Indigenous consulting and collaboration. Native Americans and Canadian First Nation peoples are thus hard pressed to prevent further archaeological disturbances, having limited lands in reserve, limited control over ancient ancestral lands, and limited funding for site protection.

This section takes us to the far north, the northeast, the northwest, and the southwest to explore Indigenous relations, past and present, with landscapes, materiality, and archaeologists. These excerpts have been selected not because they are comprehensive in their coverage of the geographical region but because they touch on some of the key issues and practices that link archaeologists and Indigenous peoples.

The section begins with an excerpt from Joe Watkins (Choctaw), one of the first self-identified Indigenous archaeologists, and one of the earliest to publish the term "Indigenous archaeology" (Watkins 2000). Watkins explores the privileging of Western epistemologies in archaeological approaches to Indigenous histories, discusses the state of relations among Native American and First Nation peoples and archaeologists, and identifies threats to Indigenous sovereignty. He also introduces readers to some of the key events and legislation that forced shifts in archaeological practice, including the "Kennewick Man" or "Ancient One" case.

Collaborators from Mi'kmaw territory in Nova Scotia—Donald M. Julien (Mi'kmaq) Tim Bernard, and Leah M. Rosenmeier—offer a critique of archaeological language, for example, "paleo" and other homogenizing terms ("Maritime Archaic Indians," "Woodland Indians") that are commonly deployed to distance contemporary Indigenous peoples from their ancient ancestors. The authors dissect and refute the taken-for-granted notion that technological change is a marker of cultural separation. They ground traditional knowledge in metaphorical and analogical reasoning and experiential learning, traditionally expressed as *msit* ("all knowledges together"). Our understandings of the past will, they argue, increase exponentially, if Mi'kmaw ontologies are integrated with archaeological practices.

Also writing from the far north are Andrew Stewart, Darren Keith, and Joan Scottie. In "Caribou Crossings and Cultural Meanings: Placing Traditional Knowledge and Archaeology in Context in an Inuit Landscape," they discuss the enduring relations among humans and migratory animals in a landscape that has remained essentially unchanged since the middle Holocene. They describe the Inuit use of stone markers that record and communicate features of seemingly "uninhabited" taskscapes that have long been points of crossing. The organization and spatial adjustments of Indigenous hunting camps over time reflect a deep knowledge of and relationship with the caribou. The interplay between enduring and time-transgressive forms (like the stone markers) and the elusive movements of the caribou informs a "never-ending present of seasonal cycles of activity," recorded in oral traditions and honored in the deposition of animal bones that further contextualize the landscape.

In "Confronting Colonialism: The Mahican and Schaghticoke Peoples and Us," Russell Handsman and Trudie Lamb Richmond (Schaghticoke) introduce the concept of Indigenous "homelands" as the cultural mapping of familiar landscapes over time. They note the importance of this model for envisioning Native peoples in the past and documenting Indigenous continuity during the nineteenth century (a time when northeastern Native peoples are popularly imagined to have vanished). Historical erasures are often enabled by archaeological disturbances, and "the language of scientific analysis and interpretation is so dehumanized that it becomes easy to forget that the archaeological record represents the memories and heritage of living people." They challenge the multicultural approach to telling history as a collection of stories and insist on a critical analysis of the power dynamics that shape which stories are told.

In "Working on Pasts for Futures: Eastern Pequot Field School Archaeology in Connecticut," Stephen Silliman and Katherine H. Sebastian Dring attend to the detail and method of archaeological practice and pedagogy. They describe the process of negotiating and modifying standard procedures to address specific local cultural traditions without altering the essence of their archaeological work. Although challenges are posed by cross-cultural social relations in the field, they stress the importance of *relationships*, particularly when conducting archaeological surveys intended to address questions that are raised by and immediately relevant to the partnering native community.

George Nicholas, author of "Decolonizing the Archaeological Landscape: The Practice and Politics of Archaeology in British Columbia," provides training in archaeological practices and cultural resource management for First Nations archaeologists on the Kamloops reserve in Canada. Secwepemc students are trained to view archaeology not as the source of all past knowledge but as a tool that can be useful in preserving heritage and influencing policy. Research-based fieldwork focuses on local cultural history and chronology, archaeobotany, territorial boundaries, and long-term land use patterns. Nicholas notes the generational shifts in heritage management and public education, pointing to the success of Indigenous archaeologists who now promote "internalist archaeology that enriches and validates traditional history, as defined by narrative and folklore."

The section ends with the work of three archaeologists who, through their blended identities as "Indigenous" and "archaeologist," call our attention to issues of authority, relationship, and meaning. Tara Million

(Cree), from Alberta, Canada, applies traditional precepts of knowledge and kinship to archaeological field methods. Through deceptively simple shifts in practice (digging round instead of square holes in the earth), she highlights archaeological social relations and everyday practices that shape the construction and movement of knowledges, categories, boundaries, and meaning. Dorothy Lippert (Choctaw), questions both the authority of archaeologists and the transformation of Indigenous objects into commodities. She points to the necessity for bridging techniques in the discipline to reconcile gulfs among Indigenous and non-Indigenous. Davina Two Bears (Navajo), from the American Southwest, relates her experience as a tribal member and an archaeologist. As a tribal insider, she acknowledges the necessity of archaeology, and the potential knowledge to be gained, in the face of community suspicions. She also notes the difficulties of working within the federal cultural resources framework. These three represent just a few of the many Indigenous archaeologists laboring to insert Indigenous epistemologies, human rights concerns, and local kinship relations into the theories and practices of archaeology in North American contexts.

18

Beyond the Margin: American Indians, First Nations, and Archaeology in North America

Joe E. Watkins

The Land of Prehistory

David Hurst Thomas (2000, 4) wrote about the impact of naming geographic features as part of the "discovery" and conquest of the Western Hemisphere—"The names established an agenda under which the rest of the encounter would be played out. . . . The power to name reflected an underlying power to control the land, its indigenous people, and its history." This passage might just as well have been written about the discovery and conquest of the indigenous past by archaeologists, for bibliographies of archaeologists are filled with the discovery, conquest, and naming of archaeological sites that established an agenda that has acted to control what Kehoe has called *The Land of Prehistory* (Kehoe 1998).

Archaeologists, based on their credentials as scientists, have consistently considered themselves to be the authorities when it comes to decisions concerning the archaeological record. Their training in the scientific method, generally accepted as the basis for scientific research, requires that they consider information objectively. Additionally, because of society's emphasis on formal education and the role of scientists within the society of which they are a part, archaeologists are generally seen to possess knowledge that is somehow beyond the understanding of nonscientists; they are the keepers of that knowledge.

This, of course, is not a situation that is unique to archaeology but is a characteristic of the growth of Western thought in general. In *Conjuring Science*, Christopher Toumey examines the way that the American public

Excerpted from Watkins, Joe, 2003. Beyond the Margin: American Indians, First Nations, and Archaeology in North America. *American Antiquity* 68(2): 273–85. Reprinted by permission of the Society for American Archaeology and Joe E. Watkins.

perceives science and scientists: "American citizens respect science as a kind of religion in the sense that it supposedly has a plenary authority to answer all of our questions and to solve all of our problems" (Toumey 1996, 153).

As the "recognized" authority on the scientific record held within archaeological and heritage sites, then, archaeologists have substantial power over resources associated with the culture history of indigenous peoples, and members of descendant communities often feel powerless about what happens to their ancestors and the archaeological sites associated with them. Because of this power differential, archaeologists often are perceived to be arrogant and insensitive by native people, while at the same time native people often are perceived to be antagonistic toward archaeological research.

Archaeologists practicing heritage management in the United States have specific legal requirements. Numerous publications outline these laws and the responsibilities of the archaeologist under each (e.g., King 1998, 2000), and these laws will not be presented in detail here. However, a cursory review of selected laws illustrates the extent that archaeology has been able to assert its wishes and desires over cultural resources, including the excavation of pre-Contact American Indian sites.

Beginning with the passage of the Antiquities Act in 1906, archaeologists (perhaps unintentionally) began to co-opt the American Indian's unwritten history and material culture. The United States government deemed archaeological and historical sites of past cultures in the United States as worthy of protection for the benefit of the public, but it ultimately developed a permit system that centered protection of the past within the scientific community rather than in the hands of those whose ancestors were responsible for its creation. It wasn't until the passage of the Archaeological Resources Protection Act (ARPA) in 1979 that American Indians were given the explicit right to participate in regulating the excavation and removal of archaeological resources on land under the control or ownership of American Indian tribes, organizations, or American Indian individuals.

Even then scientists maintained control of the legislative process, as demonstrated by the inclusion of human skeletal material as "archaeological resources" within the definitions section of the act. While the uniform regulations developed to carry out ARPA required consultation with tribal groups who own the land upon which the archaeological resources were located, the intent of these regulations was as much to govern the issuance of permits as it was to involve American Indian groups more within the process.

Interactions between archaeologists and indigenous peoples in the United States are defined by formal consultation as mandated by heritage and historic preservation legislation such as the Native American Graves Protection and Repatriation Act (NAGPRA) of 1990, the National Museum of the American Indian Act (NMAIA) of 1989, and the National Historic Preservation Act (NHPA) of 1966, as amended. Consultation (defined in the federal regulations that govern the NHPA as "the process of seeking, discussing, and considering the views of other participants, and where feasible, seeking agreement with them regarding matters" arising in the compliance process [King 1998, 94]) is required at various stages in the historic-preservation compliance process. Different laws define consultation differently, and archaeologists engaged in cultural resources management and repatriation in the United States need to have a thorough understanding of the regulatory framework governing archaeological projects if they hope to fulfill their legal obligations to indigenous communities.

In the United States, the status of land ownership or federal involvement in a project determines which (or even whether) cultural resources protection laws apply. Federal laws apply to projects that occur on federal or tribal land, if there is federal funding involved in a project, or if a federal permit of any kind is required for the project to occur. Privately funded projects on private land are not required to follow federal laws regarding cultural resources *unless* a federal permit is required.

Indian tribes are recognized by the United States government as domestic dependent nations that retain sovereign powers, except as divested by the United States, and Indian sovereignty is a key issue defining the interaction between Native Americans and archaeologists on Indian-owned or controlled land. Indian sovereignty means that all archaeological research undertaken on Indian land requires the approval of the tribal government, and that a tribe retains the right of ownership of all cultural materials found on their land.

The 1992 amendments to the NHPA authorized Indian tribes to develop Tribal Historic Preservation Offices and assume the historic preservation functions that are otherwise the responsibility of a State Historic Preservation Office regarding projects on their land. For many tribes, the assumption of these responsibilities is an issue of tribal sovereignty because it removes a state official from the decision-making process managing heritage resources on tribal lands and reinforces the government-to-government relationship between the United States and Indian nations. Tribal groups have different reasons for accepting these responsibilities (Anyon, Ferguson, and Welch 2000; Ferguson 2000), and as of November 2002, 36 Indian tribes had appointed Tribal Historic Preservation Officers (www.achp.gov/thpo.html). Many of these tribes have hired archaeologists to provide administrative support services to their Tribal Historic Preservation Officers.

Assumption by tribal programs of these historic preservation functions, however, may prove both detrimental and beneficial. While the assumption of such duties does allow the tribe to fully participate within the established federal historic preservation system, it often places a burden on tribal administration and forces the tribe to adhere to federally defined concepts such as mitigation, qualifications of personnel, and significance. Consultation becomes more formalized and must follow federal guidelines rather than proceeding along more informal pathways. Finally, tribal programs for tribes without a large land base (such as tribes in Oklahoma where there are no reservations and only fractionated or minimal amounts of tribally owned land) are severely underfunded and must try to deal with floods of consultation requests.

On the federal level in Canada, cultural resources management programs operate primarily through two agencies: Parks Canada, a Federal Crown Corporation responsible for administering all aspects of Canada's 29 national parks and more than 100 monuments and forts; and the Archaeological Survey of Canada, a branch of the National Museum of Man, which operates an archaeological salvage program to minimize the loss of archaeological resources and information caused by construction projects.

There are no nationwide heritage laws that govern the practice of archaeology in Canada; rather, laws relating to heritage are implemented primarily on provincial, municipal, and corporate levels. Additionally, the absence of a Canadian national law means that "there is no leverage to hold the province accountable for bilaterally funded projects, no precedents for the provincial politicians to become used to funding large scale mitigation projects, and no heritage legislation for federal lands, including reserves" (Syms 1997, 54).

However, the relationships between First Nations and archaeologists are relatively strong. In British Columbia, for example, the relationship between Simon Fraser University and the Secwepemc (Shuswap) Nation has led to a strong collaborative program (Nicholas 2000); in the Yukon, the Yukon Heritage Branch has worked collaboratively with First Nations such as the Carcross/Tagish (Hare and Greer 1994), the Inuvialuit (Friesen 1998), and the Kwanlin Dan (Gotthardt and Hare 1994).

In spite of this lack of a national perspective on heritage issues, Canadian relationships with First Nations are seen to be stronger than in the past, primarily as a result of archaeologists directly taking into consideration the wishes of the indigenous populations in the research arena rather than performing through a regulatory or legal framework. George Nicholas, writing about the situation in British Columbia, notes that "consultation with the appropriate First Nation is now a prerequisite for obtaining an archaeological permit. This requirement occurred in response to demands for greater aboriginal representation, and overall, has had a positive impact on the discipline as it makes archaeologists more responsive to contemporary needs and their work more relevant" (2000, 163).

Archaeologists working in North America also need to recognize that native peoples and scholars often have different concepts of heritage resources and their relation to the past. Archaeologists generally conceptualize the archaeological record as inanimate deposits of artifacts and sediments that offer information about the "past." Many indigenous peoples, however, view archaeological sites as places where ancestors and spirits still live and continue to have a profound influence in contemporary life. In many indigenous cultures, the boundary between the past and present is not as clearly demarcated as it is in the scientific worldview (Naranjo 1995; Nicholas and Andrews 1997; Rappaport 1989).

For archaeologists, the principal values of the archaeological record are derived from its ability to yield scientific data about past human behavior. While some indigenous people might appreciate the scientific values of the archaeological record and the information it can offer, indigenous values for archaeological sites are primarily derived from their association with ancestors and tribal history—traditional values seen to transcend scientific data. The desire to preserve archaeological sites in situ as monuments that attest to tribal history is often more important to indigenous people than the information that can be gained through archaeological excavation. Given the cultural and spiritual importance of ancestors, some indigenous people want all ancestral graves threatened with destruction by development to be located and moved if avoidance is impossible, and many indigenous groups allow nondestructive analysis and documentation of osteological material as part of the process of excavation and reburial. Despite the fears of scientists, some scholars (Rose, Green, and Green 1996) believe that NAGPRA might lead to more, rather than less, osteological study, even if it means only minimal data are collected. In some ways this may be true, since such data must now be collected at the time of exhumation (if at all), rather than left to be collected from sets of remains stored in museum collections, as was the case in the past.

To their credit, however, more and more archaeologists are trying to accommodate indigenous values. This is being done in a variety of ways, including focusing on the identification and study of archaeological sites using nondestructive survey techniques; excavating only those sites that are threatened by land development, vandalism, or some other form of destruction; providing training to native students in an archaeological field school situation; and involving native communities in excavations of cultural sites. Cultural heritage laws in the United States provide archaeologists engaged in cultural resources management an avenue to become involved in recovery of information from threatened and endangered sites in creative research programs that can be complementary to the wishes of tribal groups, and cultural heritage programs within the Parks Canada Corporation (as well as in provincial, municipal and corporate programs) allow and encourage tribal groups to be active participants in salvage research relating to sites of their culture.

Balancing scientific and tribal values within archaeology is a difficult and challenging task but there are many examples of projects in the United States and Canada that have successfully managed to do this (Dongoske, Aldenderfer, and Doehner 2000; Nicholas and Andrews 1997; Swidler et al. 1997). For many years, the Society for American Archaeology has published a "Working Together" column in the *SAA Bulletin* (www.saa.orglpublications/saabulletinlindex.html) that explores these issues, and which now continues in the new publication that has replaced the *SAA Bulletin*, *The SAA Archaeological Record* (www.saa.org/Publications/thesaaarchrec/index.html). These projects provide models for how archaeologists and indigenous peoples can work together to attain goals that are mutually beneficial to all parties involved, as well as outlining some of the problems and pitfalls associated with trying to develop such programs.

More archaeologists are recognizing that professional responsibilities to scholarship and science need to be balanced with ethical responsibilities to indigenous peoples, and that this is not an easy or straightforward task. Because different values, sometimes hard to reconcile, are involved in this balancing act, the inclusion of indigenous groups from the onset of archaeological projects is necessary. For instance, archaeologists are taught that the dissemination of knowledge through scholarly publication of research is an ethical responsibility, yet this often conflicts with the desire of indigenous people to maintain the confidentiality of esoteric cultural information. Additionally, assertion of intellectual property rights by indigenous communities is often seen to be at odds with academic notions giving scholarly authors ownership over their written works. . . .

Tribal and First Nations Programs

The development of the Navajo cultural resources management program should be seen as a watershed event in the history of American Indian archaeology. The establishment of the Navajo Tribal Museum in 1956 was the beginning of tribal involvement in an archaeological and historical research program. With the formal establishment of the Navajo

Nation Cultural Resource Management Program in 1977, the Nation developed "professional anthropological expertise combined with regional archaeological experience and an understanding of Navajo customs" (Klesert 1990, 116) to conduct federally mandated archaeological surveys in the American Southwest. Even though the program was developed and has been managed primarily by non-American Indian archaeologists, it is not a tribally operated carbon copy of the dominant Euro-American scientific culture: the Navajo use traditional religious practitioners in the identification of project impacts on sacred sites, shrines, and other localities of importance to the Navajo quite apart from any other archaeological or ethnographic professionals (Begay 1997; Doyel 1982; Martin 1997).

The Zuni, another tribe in the American Southwest, have been involved in cultural preservation programs since the formal establishment of the Zuni Archaeology Program in 1978 (Anyon and Ferguson 1995; Mills and Ferguson 1998). Although the program through the years has been managed primarily by non-Indian archaeologists, the tribe is able to protect its cultural resources in the manner it wishes through a blending of culturally appropriate scientific procedures and the involvement of traditional leaders. Seven Tribal Council Resolutions affirm "the need for and benefits of cultural resources management, and outline the active role the Pueblo of Zuni wants to play in the federal cultural resources management compliance process" (Mills and Ferguson 1998, 32). Additionally, the 1991 formulation of the Cultural Resources Advisory Team of the Pueblo of Zuni added another process by which cultural resources are protected by the Pueblo. Mills and Ferguson note that the "Zuni Tribe is fortunate to have its own on-going archaeological program because it provides an interface between the historic preservation bureaucracy and the tribal structure" (1998, 40) in such a way as to help alleviate conflict between the tribe and outside interests.

In 1989, the Secwapemc Cultural Education Society (SCES) of the Secwapemc of south-central British Columbia collaborated with Simon Fraser University (SFU) to initiate an educational program to "establish a native-administered, native-run, postsecondary educational institute" to, among other things, "preserve, protect, interpret, and promote their history, language, and culture" (Nicholas 2000, 155). The program offers a bachelor of general studies and a bachelor of arts degrees with both a major and minor in archaeology and anthropology, and, with 15 archaeology courses offered, provides strong methodological and theoretical grounding in archaeology. Additionally, a field school offered jointly between the SCES and SFU provides field experience to interested First Nations individuals (Nicholas 1997, 2000).

Of course the above examples are not the only tribal or First Nations programs actively pursuing archaeological research. As noted, 36 tribal programs in the United States are actively attempting to influence archaeological research on their tribal lands through initiating cultural resource inventories, monitoring compliance proceedings, and reviewing the professional work of archaeologists, and the Kwanlin Dan First Nation of Yukon has taken an active role in the excavation and interpretation of their heritage.

In addition to the tribally operated programs, some governmental agencies such as the United States Department of Agriculture Forest Service offer programs that provide training to indigenous people in archaeological techniques and subsequently employ them as cultural resource technicians on Forest Service projects. Some programs combine academic and on-the-job training as a means of providing indigenous people with opportunities to participate more fully in the archaeological enterprise. Davina Two Bears (2000) discusses how the Navajo Nation Archaeology Department, in conjunction with the Department of Anthropology of Northern Arizona University in Flagstaff, operates a student training program to provide formal credentials to Navajo people. An agreement was set up in 1988 whereby Navajo and other Native American students are eligible to receive training from the Navajo Nation Archaeology Department in archaeological field methods and techniques.

However, the number of American Indians or First Nations members in the field of archaeology is small, with less than 15 individuals with a doctorate in archaeology and perhaps 50 with a master's degree. Because of this small number, archaeologists with American Indian or First Nations heritage often feel singular in large gatherings of professional archaeologists. Two Bears writes, "At anthropology conferences, I often feel like a walking specimen to be photographed, documented, measured, and dissected. . . . It makes one feel as though a Native American is not even a person or human, but just a very complex, interesting thing" (2000,16).

In spite of this feeling of "Native American archaeologist as a nonhuman object," and because of the variety of programs aimed at helping Native Americans develop archaeological skills, an increasing number of indigenous people are working as professional archaeologists. Some of these archaeologists earn graduate degrees, and are employed by universities, museums, and governmental agencies. Other indigenous archaeologists gain their knowledge through on-the-job training and spend their entire careers working for tribal heritage programs. Many more indigenous archaeologists have substantial knowledge and skills, direct fieldwork, and author reports that meet professional standards, yet lack the academic credentials to provide them academic standing equivalent to their non-indigenous counterparts. While there are many non-Aboriginal archaeologists who are in similar situations, the cultural background that many Aboriginal archaeologists bring to the study of the past would seem to warrant additional consideration from archaeologists and anthropologists. . . .

Future Possibilities

This paper has discussed some of the differences between American Indian/First Nation perspectives on archaeology and that of non-Indigenous practitioners of the discipline. American Indian and First Nation perspectives concerning archaeology have had some minimal impacts on its practice in the United States and Canada, but there are other concerns that archaeologists could address in order to strengthen their relationship with American Indians.

Archaeologists must recognize that stewardship, the first principle in the Society for American Archaeology's Principles of Archaeological Ethics, must be shared between themselves and Indigenous Nations throughout the world. It makes good economic and professional sense for archaeologists to "work for the long-term conservation and protection of the archaeological record by practicing and promoting stewardship," (Kintigh 1996, 5) because, without the archaeological record, archaeologists would soon run out of resources that they could study. However, this failure to include Indigenous Nations as equals in that stewardship role implies that it is only archaeologists who "'speak' for the people of the past and who are the only ones truly capable of doing so" (Zimmerman 2001, 169). This "scientific colonialism" effectively removes American Indians and First Nations from the cultural resource protection sphere, and forces them to compete with archaeologists for the right to protect their own heritage. While the SAA's second principle of archaeological ethics acknowledges that archaeologist have "accountability" to the various publics that have interests in the archaeological record (Watkins et al. 1995, 33), this is a different concept than accepting those publics as equals. Archaeologists must try to integrate North American Indigenous groups more effectively into their attempts to conserve and protect the cultural heritage that is the focus of archaeological study if they are to remove the competitive "us-vs.-them" atmosphere that has permeated the relationship between archaeologists and Indigenous groups.

Additionally, North American archaeologists must find a way to initiate legislation that would extend cultural resources protection laws over heritage sites nationwide over all land, including private land. If archaeologists want to develop stronger partnerships with American Indians and First Nations, extending legal protection over cultural sites on private property would be a major step forward. It is ludicrous to talk of a "national heritage" while at the same time allowing its destruction because of private-property issues. Private-property rights within the United States are closely held and protected by a myriad of laws, but the idea that individuals can "own" heritage sites is foreign to most people worldwide—and North American archaeologists need to find some way to bring their publics into the twenty-first century.

The disjunction between private-property rights and tribal heritage is important because of the removal of Indian tribes from the eastern states and later governmental land allotment policies. What used to be tribal land in the east is now privately owned property, and what used to be tribal heritage is now considered to be privately owned property. Tribes in the eastern United States were socially and physically removed from their homelands, their ties to the land forcibly severed. Indian tribes from the east gave up the ownership and control of their lands. One can argue that the archaeology programs of American Indian groups in the Southwest on the whole are advanced compared to other American Indian groups in the United States because they have been able to maintain physical connection with their land, more than the fact that southwestern cultures have a longer history of contact with Europeans, that they have an easier time demonstrating cultural affinity to the pre-Contact past, and that they have stronger oral histories that tie them to the area.

North American archaeologists also must find a way to better integrate oral tradition into heritage management programs, specifically, and into the scientific enterprise, more generally. As mentioned earlier, some tribes do not wish their oral traditions to become part of the written record (see Anyon et al. 1997), but others are actively using their oral traditions to demonstrate the time depth and variety of their cultures to a sometimes-skeptical scientific world (see Echo-Hawk 1993; Zimmerman and Echo-Hawk 1990). The use of oral traditions can demonstrate the geographical and cultural complexity of indigenous cultures over time. At the same time, scrupulous use of these traditions perhaps can allow archaeologists to extend the focus of their research from one depending on the interpretation of material culture to one that can better illuminate social structures of pre-Contact culture groups. Of concern to many Indigenous groups, however, is the wholesale appropriation of these oral histories into the anthropological record without consideration of the intellectual property rights of the group as cultural stewards of that information. . . .

19

Paleo Is Not Our Word: Protecting and Growing a Mi'kmaw Place

Donald M. Julien, Tim Bernard, and Leah Morine Rosenmeier, with review by the Mi'kmawey Debert Elders' Advisory Council

Paleo Is Not Our Word

The fact that no Mi'kmaw people were involved at the Debert site when it was excavated in the 1960s is a puzzle for many, reflecting the isolation of academic inquiry from Mi'kmaw values and cultural practice. While the parallel nature of academic research and life in Mi'kma'ki is not new, it remains true that Mi'kma'ki is the homeland of more than 30,000 Mi'kmaw people living in more than 33 communities. Presently, more than 50% of First Nation people in Nova Scotia are under the age of 25; Mi'kmaw people are the fastest growing population in the Atlantic Provinces (Patten and Associates 2006, 51). Recent community development work shows the highest priorities of Mi'kmaw communities are to understand Mi'kmaw culture and history and to bring healing to both the individual and community levels. Given these demographics and priorities, transferring cultural knowledge, language, and community histories to the next generation is critical to the health and well-being of individuals and communities. It is from these priorities that the Mi'kmawey Debert project has grown.

Excerpted from Julien, Donald M., Tim Bernard, and Leah Morine Rosenmeier, with review by the Mi'kmawey Debert Elders' Advisory Council. 2008. Paleo Is Not Our Word: Protecting and Growing a Mi'kmaw Place. In *Archaeologies of Placemaking: Monuments, Memories, and Engagement in Native North America*, ed. P. E. Rubertone, 35–57. Walnut Creek, CA: Left Coast Press.

The vision for Mi'kmawey Debert is a unique cultural center, guided by the Elders' principles, where the sites are protected, understood, and honored by the Nation, all levels of government, academia, and the general public. The plans for the Centre redefine conventional museum practices, integrating Mi'kmaw knowledge, practice, and educational approaches to meet the needs of both Mi'kmaw and non-Mi'kmaw audiences (Lundholm Associates Architects 2007; Patten and Associates 2006). We conceive of visitor experiences as journeys—whether they are journeys of knowledge, leisure, spirit, healing, or exploration. Mi'kmawey Debert is to be a place where learning, transformation, and healing are possible and fostered. Current planning studies project up to 80,000 visitors a year in a 3,300m² (36,000 sq. ft.) facility—individuals and groups who will come as casual visitors, educational groups, or cultural tourists attending specially designed and prebooked programs. Visitors are invited to a landscape, not just a building. The landscape encompasses multiple interpretive trails, a viewing platform from which to understand the millennia of environmental and climatic change, and a healing lodge. The archaeological sites will be carefully protected within this landscape with appropriate visitor programs as opportunities arise.

Early on in the development process of Mi'kmawey Debert, the Confederacy convened the Mi'kmawey Debert Elders' Advisory Council. The guiding principles for the project speak directly and indirectly to the Elders' sense of past and place in Mi'kma'ki and to the distinct values of the Nation in protecting and growing Debert as a Mi'kmaw place. We use these principles for the remainder of the chapter as a way of demonstrating the character and distinction of Mi'kmaw perspectives of the sites as ancestral places in the larger landscape of Mi'kma'ki.

As Mi'kmaq, We Are Descended from the People Who Have Come before Us in Mi'kma'ki

Of all the messages the Elders want conveyed, this one of descent is perhaps the most important. It is also perhaps the most likely to be misunderstood in current academic and legal contexts, as well as by the general public. If there is one shared sentiment across Mi'kma'ki, it is that people share a homeland—we come from this place. This statement does not mean that people have been exactly the same for 11,000 years. It does not mean that there has been no linguistic, cultural, or biological change amongst the people who have lived in Mi'kma'ki since the last glaciation. It means simply that relative to other groups of people who live in North America, Mi'kmaq and First Nations people descend from this place in a way no other groups of people do. Yet, the vocabulary of Paleo Indians, Paleo Americans, and now even "Early Americans," grows out of assumptions of populations bounded by time. The vocabulary ultimately contradicts what many Mi'kmaw people believe on a broad scale: that we come from this place in a way that other (non-First Nation or Inuit) groups of people do not. Again this is not to say that there is no change through time, but instead that the crux of being Indigenous is descending from human occupations in North America since the last glaciation, and potentially prior to the last glaciation.

In part this message is important because language, terminology, and categories that alienate people from their ancestry also alienate people from the landscape and places of those ancestors. From this perspective, it is easy to understand that the Elders' statement signals that breaking the relationships of people temporally means breaking them spatially as well: to disconnect the populations through time necessarily means disconnecting people from homelands and ancestral places. At a display about Debert and "Paleo Indians" mounted during annual celebratory events of Treaty Day in the provincial capital of Halifax several years ago, the most common question to the Mi'kmawey Debert staff was, who were these Paleo Indians? People thought of them as another tribe, like Cree or Mohawk, rather than as a very old, largely technological category of ancestors in North America. If you had asked these same people if they were related in some way to the ancestors who lived in Mi'kma'ki—shared their homeland at some point in the past—the likely answer would have been yes. However, in this case the language served to say not only that people weren't related, but that the place itself was not connected to the people.

In many ways, the Elders' statement inverts the commonly asked question of where did people come from to ask the question, where did they go? To which the archaeological answer at some level has always been that "Paleo Indians" descended in some way and at some geographical scale—the Western Hemisphere, North America, or even Mi'kma'ki—to present-day Indigenous peoples. And this descent from the Archaic onward, as the discipline reflects, has been dynamic and complicated, but always contained within the boundaries of the continent—that is until Leif Eriksson and his Norse brethren arrived somewhere around AD 1000 and then others more permanently after the fifteenth century. The Elders' statement asserts that the age-old disciplinary question of where people came from is much less significant than what has transpired since then within Mi'kma'ki. The more important question is, what has made us who we are? What are all the myriad ways that our culture, language, and knowledge have grown up in Mi'kma'ki? What is the dominant shared landscape and experience of people in the last 11,000 years? The question where do you come from? is one that dominates and originates in countries of immigrants. More often in Mi'kma'ki, the question is not where you come from, but to whom are you related? The issue of to whom you are related is critical because it determines the extent of shared experience and establishes the personal and cultural relations among people.

Certainly the Elders' statement rejects the new term "Paleo American" to indicate that people living in North America more than 8500 ^{14}C yrs BP (~10,000 cal yrs BP) are not Indian or Native American (although the term "Indian" is not a favorite either). The basis for the recent distinction in the literature is largely biological rather than historical. Life since the last glaciation—the 11,000 years of shared historical experiences—has been the basis for defining Native American or First Nation, not presumed biological groupness, whose boundaries and transitions are fuzzy at best. This debate has come out most clearly in the legal proceedings and academic discussion about the origins and identity of the Kennewick Man and the suggestion of European origins for Native American peoples (Bradley and Stanford 2004, 2006; Bruning 2006; Chatters 2000; Fiedel 2004; Owsley and Jantz 2001; Straus 2000; Straus, Meltzer, and Goebel 2005; Swedlund and Anderson 1999, 2003; Thomas 2000). Unfortunately, in popular media the academic debates were often either exaggerated or corrupted into one of Native Americans being racialized as "European" (Egan 1998; Kluger and Cray 2006; Lemonick and Cray 1996; Lemonick, Dorfman, and Cray. 2006; Murr 1999, 2005; Preston 1997, 1998; Sanders 2004; Wilford 1999).

The intense degree of attention the debate received from mainstream press and media, including hour-long television episodes on Nova and CBC, exposed deep cleavages between the attitudes and perspectives of Native and non-Native North Americans. Sadly, this attention speaks volumes to the differential treatment ancient histories receive from the general public when they are perceived by that public as their "own." The point to emphasize with regard to Debert is that at the temporal and spatial scales on which these terms have meaning, the Elders' message rejects the notion that a postulated biological group of people 11,000 years ago is more important than the 11,000 years of human experience that has transpired in North America—experience of which the Elders and the rest of the Mi'kmaw Nation are descendants. No one is arguing that biology isn't part of groupness or that it does not change through time, but people are asserting that the historical experience of descending from a place over 11 millennia trumps any particular point of origin.

The Elders are directly and indirectly asserting their own experience, which says we are still related even when we change biologically and technologically—something most Mi'kmaw people know and take for granted in their everyday modern lives where biological and technological change is a reality. Most importantly, by prioritizing, in particular, biology over history as "more" essential, the new vocabulary of "Paleo American" eschews the devastating losses that characterize the colonial experiences for Indigenous people throughout the Americas. It remains the case, however, that a historical basis for categorizing individuals defines most aspects of life for Indigenous peoples in the Western Hemisphere—today people's lives are much more historically contingent than they are biologically contingent. It would be difficult to overstate how much history has determined for people, and specifically the history of colonization. From land loss (and retention), to residential schools, policies of removal and relocation, cultural and linguistic repression, loss as well as recent renewals and applications of treaty rights, and the language and culture Mi'kmaw people share today, history has played a much greater role than biology.

While most archaeologists would agree that the largely technological bases for archaeological culture histories are *not* biological or even cultural groups, the reality is a pervasive confusion in academia, legal proceedings, and the general public about what really defines groupness within the archaeological record—and how archaeological culture histories inevitably shift into "people." Given that much of what archaeology tells us is about technology and materialism essentially, it is perfectly understandable that technology is what underlies categorizations through time. These categories serve the discipline well in many respects. The problem is that when archaeological culture histories transition into "people" and migrate into legal and popular contexts, First Nation people confront culture histories that disconnect present day people from the broader ideas of descent that lie at the heart of people's understanding of who they are and what it means to be Mi'kmaq or Indigenous to this place. Take for example this excerpt from a Parks Canada press release of April 2006 describing Kejimikujik National Park, located in southwestern Nova Scotia:

> The park is in the midst of traditional canoe routes that Parks Canada says were first used by Maritime Archaic Indians about 4,500 years ago. Woodland Indians then lived in the area, making seasonal campsites along the rivers and lakes before their descendants, the Mi'kmaq, made Keji their home for about 2,000 years.

This paragraph is a prime example of the way archaeological periods suddenly become "people," even though generally academics understand and agree that cultural history periods are not meant to describe a people per se. There were no "Maritime Archaic Indians" or

"Woodland Indians" (i.e., "Ceramic Indians"). There were people who lived during the Archaic and Woodland/Ceramic Periods as well as the other archaeological periods. A present-day analogy would lead us to a discussion of the "horse people" and then the "car people," or better yet, "wood people" and now "steel people"—soon to be the "fiber optic people." Technology doesn't tell us about descent or ethnicity at this scale in this way. Most great grandparents in North America used horses in their lives, and people drive cars today, but they are still related—biologically as well as culturally. Roger Lewis (2006), then archaeologist at Kwilmu'kw Maw-klusuaqn (the Mi'kmaw Rights Initiative), worked with Mi'kmaw Elders across Nova Scotia to suggest new names, reflecting this perspective of relatedness and descent, for the archaeological periods.

While the naming of the culture histories does not change the basic technological categories through which the history is understood, the language places the ancient people in relationship to those who have come afterward, emphasizing descent.

The archaeological language that blurs the distinction between technology and people has come to symbolize the breaking of the relationships of people through time. As the human relationships are broken, so are the relationships to the land where sites are located and where people assume all Mi'kmaq have lived. Many people understand that rupturing the relationship between people and the land, temporally or spatially, is what characterizes the most destructive historic events and processes, and therefore lies at the heart of community illness and historic trauma. If Mi'kmaw people are more related to—more descendant from—these sites than the waves of people who have arrived in the Americas in the last 500 or so years, then the experience of disconnection results in replicating traumatic historical processes and events that are much more well known and recent in community lives, even though most archaeologists do not intend to alienate present-day Indigenous people from their own understandings of the past in this manner. . . .

Throughout the summer of 2005, the project undertook a surficial geology map under the direction of geologist Ralph Stea, who has worked extensively in the area on late glacial geology (Stea 2006; Stea and Mott 1989, 1998). While paleo shorelines were not identified in the summer of 2005, the initial research tentatively identified that fluvial deposits near the sites were riverine, not lacustrine, and that further research would be required to determine a site model (Rosenmeier et al. 2006). The project has benefited greatly from the collegiality of Stea and Brewster, who continue to work on these outstanding research issues (Brewster 2006; Stea 2006). While this research does not overtly establish relationships between Mi'kmaw individuals and the sites, it has laid the basis for ongoing research at the sites, and, importantly, it derives from the Confederacy's mandate to both protect and to understand the sites. Pursuing research such as this within a Mi'kmaw context challenges us to develop an approach that integrates conventional archaeology and geology with Mi'kmaw practice, knowledge, and perspectives.

Such integration is not always quick and easy business. It is part encouraging and mentoring young Mi'kmaw people who are interested in archaeology, geology, and related sciences; part outreach to other Mi'kmaw scholars and researchers in related fields; and part allowing for the relationships to emerge over time. One of the most exciting areas of new research is the reevaluation and interpretation of meaning in the Mi'kmaw stories of Kluskap (the Mi'kmaw culture hero) (Rand 1971[1893]). The stories about Kluskap and the giant beaver, the fight with winter that Kluskap lost (when it was winter all year long, although Kluskap brings summer back at another time), and his transforming large mammals into small ones have garnered particular attention. Some researchers are following up on how the Kluskap stories mark lithic sources and define climatic events (either the periodic "little ice ages" or the end of the last glaciation) and changes in the landscape across Mi'kma'ki (Gloade 2007; Sable n.d.); for others they tell of the extinction of Pleistocene mammals (Paul 2007).

We also look to other models for integrating Indigenous and Western sciences. One of the most promising aspects of the project to date has been the growing partnership with the Toqwa'tu'kl Kjijitaqnn/Integrative Science Program at Cape Breton University. The program seeks to integrate Mi'kmaw world views and perspectives with Western science approaches. The Toqwa'tu'kl Kjijitaqnn/Integrative Science Program is based on the idea of *msit,* meaning "all knowledges together." The concepts relate themselves meaningfully and directly to the historical sciences of geology and archaeology. The central roles of pattern recognition, metaphorical and analogical reasoning, and inquiry-based learning stand out as primary examples of the compatibility between the Toqwa'tu'kl Kjijitaqnn/Integrative Science Program and archaeology and geology in particular. The approaches being nurtured at the Toqwa'tu'kl Kjijitaqnn/Integrative Science Program support very much the urging of Dena Dincauze, who in 1993 (cited in Curran 1999, 5) called for archaeologists to "overcome the constraints of thinking only in secular time or radiocarbon centuries; temporal units such as seasons (Curran and Grimes 1989; Spiess 1984) and generations should be employed in interpretation because they were the spans of time experienced by Palaeoindians themselves." Using experience as a source for research questions is exactly what the Toqwa'tu'kl Kjijitaqnn/Integrative Science Program does.

For many researchers, what distinguishes a Mi'kmaw archaeology, or even "Indigenous" archaeology, remains an intellectual question, if not a fabrication. In our experience, the integration of Mi'kmaw perspectives, language, and cultural knowledge with conventional archaeological and geological practice broadens the scope of what might be known, simply by changing the origin of the research questions people consider. Just as with allowing for healing relationships to the sites to be acknowledged and fostered, encouraging questions that are derived from traditional knowledge means new ways of thinking about the past. Finding new questions in new places will always raise the ontological questions about what is possible to know, but it does not (as is sometimes claimed) corrupt the practice of the sciences that may (or may not) shed light on these new questions. Most importantly, the project sees these new questions and new partnerships as critical to growing the Mi'kmaw context for understanding the past in Mi'kma'ki. . . .

20

Caribou Crossings and Cultural Meanings: Placing Traditional Knowledge and Archaeology in Context in an Inuit Landscape

Andrew M. Stewart, Darren Keith, and Joan Scottie

Features That Signal Enduring Relationships between People and Animals

The landscape is organized in ways that reveal relations among human beings, animals, and land. The south side of the river, for example, is extensively modified in ways that distinguish it from the north side. *Inuksuit* [upright stone markers in symbolic human form] account for half the number of features on the north side, whereas they account for only 15% of features on the south side (Stewart et al. 2000). Many of these *inuksuit* occur in lines that clearly were meant to influence the movements of caribou moving along the north side of the river. Not only is the north side the least culturally modified of the two sides of the river, its feature assemblage is dominated by stones that have a "natural" function—one of communicating directions to animals. The river divides the country into realms of greater and lesser human involvement in the landscape. A similar opposition between areas of greater and lesser activity is repeated in a number of other ways in the landscape.

Oral accounts of life on the land mostly describe warm season activities. Most evidence of cultural activity is contained within 1 km of

Excerpted from Stewart, Andrew M., Darren Keith, and Joan Scottie. 2004. Caribou Crossings and Cultural Meanings: Placing Traditional Knowledge and Archaeology in Context in an Inuit Landscape. *Journal of Archaeological Method and Theory* 11(2):183–211.

either side of the river (though archaeological survey beyond this zone in the Harvaqtuuq has not been systematic). The material evidence located within 1 km of the river includes the settlement record of both summer-fall crossing sites, which are located on the river itself, and spring season sites, which are located inland from, and high above the river (Stewart et al. 2000). Hence, activity during the warm season is represented in both traditional and archaeological accounts as occurring almost entirely along the river. The cold season, when people lived in snow houses, is, so far, missing from the record. Oral accounts place cold season houses all over the landscape, many of them on smaller lakes in the interior far from the river (e.g., Aasivaaryuk in Mannik 1993, 29).

A third distinction made explicit in oral accounts concerns places to avoid when caribou are crossing the river and, more generally, during the season of caribou migration. Dense concentrations of tent rings, caches, hearths, and other features and artifacts occurring within 1 or 2 km of the landing places of caribou attest to these areas being a strong focus of settlement. Oral accounts suggest, however, that crossing sites were viewed as special places requiring adherence to rules, comparable to Iñupiat views of ritualized places on North Slope Alaskan beaches where whale carcasses were worked on (Bodenhorn 1993). Along the Kazan River, places where caribou could be spooked, causing them to miss a crossing, were avoided:

> Inuit used to try and not catch or hunt caribou on the other side of the river crossing from their camp so that if they have been killing and skinning caribou, the caribou might smell odour or see the difference of land and turn back, or go through a different route. (Aasivaaryuk in Mannik 1993, 37)

This injunction applied to places along the north shore where caribou were likely to start crossing, but it was also considered important to restrict activity and to keep a low profile in camp on the south shore, where caribou were likely to land during their southward migration in July and August:

> When Inuit are camping at the crossing, they are very cautious of what they do. When they see caribou . . . appear from the distance, they try to be quiet and motionless, along with their dogs. They also keep the tent entrance closed . . . because the tents face towards the river, sometimes the entrance to the tents are wide open . . . so that the caribou won't suspect there's people on the other side. . . . So camping around the crossing is hard work and you have to be cautious about . . . [every] thing. (Aasivaaryuk in Mannik 1993, 25)

This restriction sometimes meant keeping tents and people out of sight behind boulder ridges that are pushed up at places along the shore by ice moving down-current during spring breakup. Area 6 at Piqqiq is an example of such a low-profile camp (Stewart 1994, 61). Places along the shore exposed to view from the north side were places to be avoided during the crossing season.

With open space around crossings, there appears, on first consideration, to be little restriction on where people can live or work. The distribution of features seems to confirm this impression. Yet proscriptions on local land use, and an examination of types of features, remind us that land use occurs in the context of an enduring relationship between people and animals that is honored in practices like bone disposal and in stories. Activities privileged in oral accounts—for example, the anticipation and pursuit of caribou at the crossings—are conceived to occur mainly on the south side, and in lower areas, protected from sight-lines across the river. Removed from these intensively—used areas are two kinds of higher locations. One is the spring-season site, referred to only obliquely in oral accounts and, thus, relatively invisible in the traditional record. Two of these camps, Akunni'tuaq and Qavvavaujarvik, are located on slopes above the crossings and contain hundreds of features (Stewart et al. 2000), but are not associated in oral accounts with any known occupations or families. Akunni'tuaq, the "big interval," alludes to its relatively weak or subsidiary location between two powerful crossing sites. Qavvavaujarvik, the "place of ghosts," also suggests a kind of transitional existence. The other kind of higher location are places with features such as graves, monumental *inuksuit,* and waiting places. These places are, conversely, highly visible in oral history, being associated with enduring stories. These kinds of prominent features transcend a never-ending present of seasonal cycles of activity.

Oral accounts simultaneously support the notion of permanence of crossings like Piqqiq and the unpredictable element—the awareness that caribou may pass over a certain crossing in a given year to use another one, or that they might not come at all (Aasivaaryuk in Mannik 1993, 31; Tiktaalaaq in Mannik 1993, 54). The enduring forms, like Ipjurjuaq's stone and Utaqqivvigjuaq, are time-transgressive. They seemingly defy change over the long period, whereas habitation areas in the camps are subject to change: Abandoned areas of habitation evince changes in patterns of annual reoccupation. Caribou are an enduring presence but their elusive quality, inherent in their migratory behavior, attests to the need for constant knowledge of their behavior and spatial adjustment of response. The history, placement, and internal organization of camps reflect this necessity and awareness. In the country surrounding the camps, on the other side of the river, and on hilltops and places in between the camps, the landscape is relatively unchanged, or lightly used, and human activity has been mitigated and naturalized through the presence of enduring forms.

Conclusion

Archaeologists working in regions like northern North America, where land use has not been severely disrupted from earlier hunter-gatherer patterns, are fortunate in being able to contextualize sites within oral traditions set within a landscape largely unaltered since the middle Holocene. Since the 1980s, indigenous people have increasingly participated in archaeological research. Efforts have been refocused on recording knowledge of the recent past, through oral histories, and the more distant past, through oral traditions (Andrews and Zoe 1997; Hanks 1997), recalling, in some ways, research that was conducted by anthropologists employing native assistants before the 1960s (Greer 1997, 147).

Inuit-driven research in Baker Lake has resulted in a new perspective on the archaeological record of the Kazan River, highlighting the lower part of the river, the Harvaqtuuq, closest to Baker Lake. The locations of major crossings have been identified, and the families that used them. These sites are foregrounded in a "traditional" landscape in which other camps, representing other seasons of the year, are backgrounded. Enduring principles of orientation are expressed in binary sets of names and in maps and also in land use, as reflected in areas of greater and lesser daily human involvement in the landscape. Places that project moments or events of the past contrast with places with evidence for cycles of seasonal activity. Chronological resolution is suggested where oral and archaeological accounts conflict, where occupation is remembered for some sites and site areas, and not for others.

Returning to the question of meaning, how can archaeologists contextualize their finds in the presence of oral traditions? By describing the types of material forms in a landscape, archaeologists may be able to identify cultural traditions or conventions that provide a context for features—structures, artifacts, and locations of camps. This context conveys meaning, if not specific meanings. Traditions of performance underwrite, or certify, the authenticity of narratives (Chamberlin 1999, 88). They become habitual and therefore recognizable (Layton and Ucko 1999, 12). Oral presentation of stories follows traditions of performance—the use of narrative frames, for example, or patterned repetition of content (Dauenhauer and Dauenhauer 1999), though these conventions may and do change over generations. Monuments like Ipjurjuaq's stone and the circular feature at Utaqqivvigjuaq, which stand apart from other *inuksuit* and waiting places, respectively, due to the large size and prominent positioning of these features, affirm the stories associated with them. They also affirm the existence of earlier generations of Harvaqtuurmiut, as they do the place of Inuit on the land. Elder George Tataniq, referring to standing stones in the Harvaqtuuq, says: "We were told never to move the position of those rock markers because they were fixed up by our ancestors . . ." (Tataniq in Mannik 1998, 231). Prominent landmarks in the Harvaqtuuq signal feats of strength, possibly also the assertion of authority and control among competing individuals and groups. Distributions of archaeological features on either side of the river, or between high and low places in the landscape, also follow conventions that are echoed in oral traditions.

Assessing particular meanings is problematic. Our understanding of them depends on how these stories were told and recorded. It is, therefore, continually evolving (cf. Fienup-Riordan et al. 2000). Particular meanings change over time and may be inaccessible in the absence of specialized cultural knowledge. But recognizing the form of the tradition, and its authenticity through generations, is at least as important. It is frequently the patterned form, rather than the meaning of the form, which is most striking, visible, enduring, recognizable, and culturally distinctive to the archaeologist and historian. Having said this, where specific meaning or historical knowledge is available, it should not be ignored. We might be tempted to overlook traditional knowledge when it seems to conflict with scientific knowledge. Both kinds are subject to critical evaluation and can be assimilated into explanations of the past (Whitley 2002).

21

Confronting Colonialism: The Mahican and Schaghticoke Peoples and Us

Russell G. Handsman and Trudie Lamb Richmond

By thus underrepresenting the number of native people, as well as denying their early and continuing presence, Berkshire County's historians argued that their colonial ancestors settled lands only sparsely occupied and scarcely used. And because there were so few Mahican Indians living there in the early eighteenth century, or so they argued, the effects of colonial settlement on native people were assumed to have been both negligible and short-lived.

This same, seemingly trustworthy argument had been used somewhat earlier by Charles Allen, attorney general of Massachusetts, in his 1870 *Report on the Stockbridge Indians*. Writing in response to a petition from Stockbridge Mahicans living in Wisconsin, Allen (1870, 3) dismissed their request for an allowance, declaring that the state had already, and for a long time, aided the Mahicans "by its watchful guardianship." The state must not make itself responsible for land deeds given earlier for which little or no consideration was paid. It did not really matter, Allen argued, that the country was never rightfully obtained. After all, long before the colonial settlement of the Berkshires, the Mahicans "had become reduced in number and scattered" (C. Allen 1870, 23).

Significantly, such nineteenth-century misrepresentations are now being corroborated and thus made to seem more scientifically valid

---

Excerpted from Handsman, Russell G., and Trudie Lamb Richmond. 1995. Confronting Colonialism: The Mahican and Schaghticoke Peoples and Us. In *Making Alternative Histories: The Practice of Archaeology and History in Non-Western Settings*, ed. Peter R. Schmidt and Thomas C. Patterson, 87–117. Santa Fe, NM: School for Advanced Research Press.

and objective through two archaeological models of late prehistoric and post-contact land use and settlement proposed for the Berkshires. In one study (Shaw et al. 1987), early Mahican peoples are redefined as Connecticut River Algonkians who occupied and used the lands of the Berkshires only on a seasonal basis for hunting and gathering. The second model tries to interpret the undeniable and highly visible historic Mahican settlement around Stockbridge as a recently arrived community of native people whose purpose was to procure beaver pelts for sale at trading posts along the Connecticut and Hudson rivers (see project summaries in Hasenstab 1989, 5–6).

Among Mahican peoples, counterhistories, both oral and written, have existed for a long time. In 1734, as John Sergeant traveled north to begin his work in Stockbridge, his Mahican Indian interpreter-guides stopped along the Housatonic River somewhat north of the Massachusetts border. There they walked into the woods until they reached a "large heap of stones," already, according to Sergeant, more than ten cart-loads in size. As was their custom, the Mahicans placed more stones on this memorial pile every time they passed (Butler 1946). When questioned by Sergeant, they explained that "their fathers used to do so, and they do it because it was the custom of their fathers" (Hopkins 1753, 11; Taylor 1882, 44–48).

Somewhat later, in the 1790s, another body of Mahican oral tradition was recounted to Hendrick Aupaumut, himself a Stockbridge Mahican, presumably by Elders then living among the Oneida Iroquois (Belknap and Morse 1796). These stories told of the ancient origins of the Mahicans and spoke of how their ancestors came to the traditional homelands in eastern New York and western Massachusetts a long time ago. There they found abundant game and fish and rich planting fields: "They seldom felt much want and were very well contented." After "the chuhko-thuk, or white people, settled amongst them," the story continues, "they were subject to many disorders and began to decay" (E. Jones 1854, 15–16). Unlike the town histories written so frequently after 1850, the Mahican traditions make obvious and confront the catastrophic effects of colonialist policies of expansion and occupation. The very fact that such oral histories and cultural memories continued to exist and to be passed on to succeeding generations also means that the Mahicans had not renounced or repudiated their traditions as desired by John Sergeant. . . .

Metichawon, located along the falls at the junction of the Housatonic and Still rivers in the Weantinock homeland, was used as a traditional fishing site and sacred place long before the coming of white people. Archaeological evidence suggests that this locality began to be visited, at first perhaps on a seasonal basis, more than 3,000 years ago. Over successive millennia, settlements became more permanent; by the seventeenth century Metichawon was the residence of one of the Weantinocks' important clan leaders. Today, this long-term pattern of settlement and sacredness is represented by an extensive archaeological record covering more than 50 acres (Handsman 1991).

The archaeological visibility of places such as Metichawon, like that of the memorial piles built across Indian New England, is evidence of how the cultural meanings of homelands have survived for thousands of years. Yet despite the enduring importance of homelands to Indian people, their cultural meanings and historical presence are often obscured or ignored by regional archaeologists. For example, when New England archaeologists study the late prehistoric period (between 1,000 and 1,500 years ago), they rarely write about ancestral homelands. Instead, one reads stories about decreased mobility, changes in the utilization of habitats, or the intensification of trade networks (Feder 1984; Lavin 1988; McBride and Bellantoni 1982). Indian people themselves are rarely mentioned. Indeed, the language of scientific analysis and interpretation is so dehumanized that it becomes easy to forget that the archaeological record represents the memories and heritage of living people.

> I wish I could think of a better term to provide for gathering. Because when people think of gathering, well, we're going to gather berries or we're going to gather nuts. . . . And it's not given the importance that it should be given, because in terms—I mean, the women were responsible for the gathering of plants; they had to know a great deal. . . . My grandmother had a lot of knowledge, for example, about plant life and how they were used in terms of medicines and foods and things. And I know some of these things. —Trudie Lamb Richmond (testimony from oral history interview, "Native American Gathering," collected and transcribed by Jeremy Brecher for Connecticut Public Radio, January, 1989)

That very same archaeological language can also prevent or inhibit the exploration of continuing traditions of settlement and land use in ancestral homelands. Archaeologists normally assume that Mahican peoples and their kin, including the Schaghticoke and Weantinock, lived in centrally located, nucleated villages of between three and sixteen bark-covered long houses and dome-shaped wigwams; population levels varied between 45 and 260 people (Brasser 1978; Snow 1980, 88–90, 319–35). Such settlements are understood to be well above the threshold of archaeological visibility. Yet New England archaeologists have only rarely discovered late prehistoric villages (Thorbahn 1988), and their maps of regional site densities strongly suggest that many interior regions in southern New England were either unoccupied or used solely on a seasonal basis between 1,000 and 300 years ago (see Thomas 1976 for an important exception). . . .

"According to our Law and Custom"

That Native Americans sometimes consciously decided to continue living in their ancestral homelands is a fact seldom mentioned in town histories or in the writings of colonial historians today (Merrell 1989). Yet even as parts of Mahican and Weantinock homelands were appropriated, surveyed, divided, and fenced, some native people resisted by making themselves less visible, resettling their families and communities beyond the fringes of colonial settlements (Handsman 1989). Less accessible settings such as the tops of ridge lines and small upland valleys became new home sites. Often such places were in disputed areas along the borders between the colonies of Massachusetts or Connecticut and New York, far removed from administrative centers. Because, at least initially, no one colony had systematic knowledge of or control over these lands, or access to the resources in them, those who lived there—Native Americans, African Americans, and others who were dispossessed—often survived as cohesive multicultural communities into the twentieth century (Feder 1994; Wetherbee and Taylor 1986).

Such localities had long been familiar to Indian people; their paths had traversed them for centuries, linking hamlets in the valleys to locations where raw materials (stone outcrops), food resources (groves of nut trees and sugar maples), or medicinal herbs had been gathered for generations. In these newly occupied places, Native Americans could continue to live within or close to ancestral homelands without making their presence known—unless they so desired. . . .

Conflicts like those between the Schaghticoke Indians and the state of Connecticut or between the Stockbridge-Munsee people and the Trustees of Reservations are often viewed as involving only indigenous people and "the law." But nowadays, struggles for equality and against systematized prejudice increasingly involve the domains of science, cultural politics, knowledge, and writing (Gordimer 1988; Said 1985). In these struggles, which will continue long after 1992 and the supposed "end of history," there is both space and need for scholars to take responsibility for their work and actions and for the consequences of them. Rather than continuing to declare our innocence, we need to see and confront the ways in which our words and actions contribute to the silencing and dispossessing of other people.

Working against colonialism in the future means that we have to interrogate, challenge, and break apart the emerging ideology of cultural difference. The ideology of difference obscures and deflects our critical gaze so that relations between different cultural traditions are not easily seen as matters involving hierarchy, alienation, domination, and control. Instead the ideology implies that the very real inequalities in power between peoples in the Americas are simply a matter of differing points of view, requiring that we need only learn to be more respectful and tolerant of the "stories" others wish to tell. . . .

22

Working on Pasts for Futures: Eastern Pequot Field School Archaeology in Connecticut

Stephen W. Silliman and Katherine H. Sebastian Dring

Collaborative Methodologies and Pedagogies

We can illustrate these various points about pedagogy and methodology with examples from the Eastern Pequot Archaeological Field

Excerpted from Silliman, Stephen W., and Katherine H. Sebastian Dring. 2008. Working on Pasts for Futures: Eastern Pequot Field School Archaeology in Connecticut. In *Collaborating at the Trowel's Edge: Teaching and Learning in Indigenous Archaeology*, ed. S. W. Silliman, 67–87. Tucson: University of Arizona Press.

School. The student-intensive archaeological research has hinged on efforts to emphasize the social, as well as the practical, aspects of field methodology. The methodology is designed to "do work" in the field, the community, the collaborative environment, and the educational setting. The features include modifications to standard archaeological practice that meet community needs without radically altering data collection and welcome interjections of Eastern Pequot cultural traditions into the archaeological work. The modifications have gone a long way toward forming a relationship of trust, mutual respect, and cooperative learning. The latter is critical because just as the Eastern Pequot community had little familiarity with the actual practice of archaeology at the outset of the project, the archaeological team also had minimal knowledge of Eastern Pequot preferences and perspectives. The realization of this learning process meant that we needed to maintain open dialogue about even the most mundane of archaeological tasks.

The standard procedure for a New England archaeological field project focused on preliminary reconnaissance is to excavate shovel test pits at regular intervals, fill them in with backdirt when done, and move on to the next one in the series. Although care must be exercised in choosing the sampling interval, depth of excavation, and screen mesh size for recovery, archaeologists take the practical side of dig-fill-and-move-on for granted, particularly when they complete a large number. However, the Eastern Pequot perceived the methods differently—they saw each instance as disturbance to their ancestral lands. They wanted to place an offering of loose tobacco at each location that we excavated, an act performed by the tribal historic preservation officer, to honor the disturbed earth. This compliance required a new sense of vigilance of otherwise mundane shovel test pits. The students played a key role in regularizing this process, for it had to become routine while retaining its cultural significance.

The collaborative field school may also be an introduction for archaeologists and students to unrecorded Native American history, cultural knowledge, and traditions concerning their Indigenous land. Very often, "at the trowel's edge," archaeologists focus their attention on what may lie beneath the earth and often disregard that which is a natural part of the earth. Eastern Pequots and many other Native Americans believe that Mother Earth consists of living things and natural objects, all of which are sacred. They hold that Mother Earth has sustained their people, history, and culture since the beginning of time. Mother Earth holds the spirit of ancestors and is available to nurture and inspire those who honor her. All people and Mother Earth are a part of the Circle of Life, where all contribute and all receive in the process.

People have the responsibility to be aware of this process. Therefore, archaeologists and students who work on the reservation land must respect and try to understand Eastern Pequot ancient history and cultural ways so as not to disturb this balance. In this manner they may truly develop a more responsive archaeology and gain a broader educational perspective. The collaborative field setting reveals the ways that past and present merge in the exploration of the land, of Earth itself. What lies in the Indigenous land besides dirt, stones, and artifacts? Some Eastern Pequots have noted that it is "peace" that they find when walking or working the land of their ancestors. As a result, Eastern Pequot tribal leaders were thankful when students made efforts not to unnecessarily harm animals and plants impacted by the excavations and when the archaeological team would cover excavation units overnight to keep animals from injuring themselves by falling into them.

To further orient the students to the social and cultural context of the field school, all participants go through an orientation with several tribal members on the first day before actual fieldwork begins. This orientation involves tribal members sharing thoughts on archaeology, history, and the reservation; personal introductions between all students, archaeological staff, tribal interns, and community members present; and, in recent years, a potluck meal. At the close of this orientation, an Eastern Pequot designee (Mark Sebastian in 2003; Royal "Two Hawks" Cook in 2004 and 2006; Bobby "Little Bear" Sebastian in 2005) conducted a smudging ritual, which involves lighting wrapped sage and other herbs and wafting the smoke over students and staff members for spiritual cleansing. To complement the initial orientation in 2005, we also arranged a meeting of the field school students with the Eastern Pequot Elders' Council to ensure that students understood how Elders felt about history, archaeology, and the land.

As we began to sort and clean the artifacts both during the field season and back at the University of Massachusetts, Boston, during the semester, the status quo of lab work shifted to accommodate a special request from the tribal council. Standard practice in archaeological laboratories involves going through bags of items collected in the field to sort, clean, and catalog artifacts and then to discard any objects—usually unmodified rocks!—collected in haste or uncertainty that proved, under more controlled observations, to be noncultural items. Again, archaeologists tend to consider this a process unworthy of reflection, but we encountered a new twist after discussing this with the tribal council: Any items that we would have normally discarded into the trash needed to be returned to the reservation. These natural objects constituted part of that historical and cultural landscape, and many tribal members held the perspective that they rightfully belonged there. Ultimately, all artifacts and other items collected will return to the tribe, but we now include these noncultural items for basic repatriation. We have also designed the flotation protocol on campus to capture as much sediment as possible from processed soil samples to then return it to the reservation. It is no exaggeration to say this poses significant logistical difficulties.

The tribal council also instituted an oversight procedure with respect to removal of artifacts from the reservation. North American archaeologists take for granted that what they remove from the ground goes to the laboratory for later cleaning, identification, and analysis, but a standard contract that Silliman was to sign with the Eastern Pequot had a clause about not removing any natural or cultural objects from the reservation. Silliman had anticipated that Sebastian Dring would say to just cross out that clause once the process was explained more clearly, but instead she reported back that the tribal council agreed to our temporary removal of cultural materials only if we provided a daily count of artifacts being removed. We reached a compromise that met the spirit of that request but was attuned to field logistics. Archaeologists collect many artifacts in the field, but often do so in bulk with little time to count and identify every piece collected. Once Silliman explained this protocol and noted that in-the-field tabulation would probably cut productivity in half, we agreed on a daily bag count instead. This daily accounting was regularly monitored by the tribal historic preservation officer and witnessed, if not also participated in, by field school students, allowing them to see the ways that archaeological research practices were also constituted as social and cultural practices. North American archaeologists may abide by codes of ethics, such as those published by the Society for American Archaeology, that would prohibit absconding with artifacts and never accounting for them, but real-world communities want their own assurances of ethical and respectful conduct.

Like most field schools, our project requires students to keep daily journals. The journals served one purpose of maintaining quality checks on data recovery (as a complement to field forms) and of encouraging students to keep detailed notes on their activities during the day (cf. Perry 2004, 241), but they began to serve another purpose in that students were encouraged to write down nor just findings and interpretation but also critical reflections on collaboration and tribal involvement. These latter reflections proved to be some of the most illuminating of all entries, as students recounted interactions with tribal members, wondered about politics, thought about cultural representation and identities, and reflected personally on how transformative the collaborative aspects of the field school had been for them. These journals are, therefore, like those used in classroom settings for pedagogical reasons. "Perhaps the most important contribution of the journals is that they encourage students to see education as a life-transforming experience, a journey of self discovery, rather than simply a race to acquire usable, saleable skills and competences" (Hamilakis 2004, 300).

Many of these elements tap directly into a central but often neglected feature of collaborative archaeological research: *relationships*. Everyone knows that archaeological fieldwork is an inherently social endeavor, but the collaborative and indigenous environment offers unique challenges and possibilities. Understanding relationships means recognizing that archaeology is a "cultural science"—or more pointedly for North America, is still a kind of anthropology—in the social and political present and that it takes place between people with varying interests in the process, content, and outcome. Consequently, the collaborative process must be monitored to ensure that all participants work toward a willingness to consider, respect, acknowledge, and include diverse perspectives, philosophies, and interpretations during the project. Each participant comes to "own the project" in his or her individual ways, which is a better metaphor than simply trying to "own the past." When the voices of archaeologists, students, Native leaders, and tribal participants are heard and valued by all involved, the educational, professional, and personal benefits expand in unique directions. We are reminded of a student who responded to a question from Eastern Pequot tribal members about what she gained from the project. She did not say historical knowledge or archaeological skills; she answered "self-development." If personal or community transformations occur during a collaborative archaeological project, then the project has an impact well beyond—or before—its final output of "interpretation." This is fundamentally important, since many participants in the archaeological process, whether students or tribal members, do not or cannot follow through to that end point (see also Berggren and Hodder 2003). They draw out their own experiences during the collaboration. We can understand these social, political, and even personal dimensions only by paying critical attention to the *process* of collaborating. . . .

23

Decolonizing the Archaeological Landscape: The Practice and Politics of Archaeology in British Columbia

George P. Nicholas

Training First Nations Archaeologists

An important avenue of decolonization is education. Today there are a host of opportunities for First Nations members to receive formal training in archaeology in Canada, the United States, and Australia. In British Columbia these include provincial training programs, such as the Ministry of Sustainable Resource's Archaeological and CMT Inventory Training for Crew Members certification, and degrees and certificate programs offered through universities, colleges, and outreach programs.

As one example, from 1991 through 2005, I have directed a university-based archaeology program on the Kamloops Indian Reserve that offers both classroom and field training (see Nicholas 1997, 2000). Each of our eleven archaeology field schools on the Kamloops reserve has provided training in the practical aspects of archaeology, including cultural resource management and public education. The fieldwork has been research-based, oriented to refining local cultural history and chronology, tracing the development of plant use through archaeology and archaeobotany, and investigating long-term land use patterns. The results will hopefully be utilized by the Secwepemc themselves when they chose to write their own histories. In fact, many of the students are learning to do archaeology on their own ancestral sites. My philosophy is to

---

Excerpted from Nicholas, George P. 2006. Decolonizing the Archaeological Landscape: The Practice and Politics of Archaeology in British Columbia. *American Indian Quarterly* 30(3–4):350–80.

provide Native students with the knowledge and means for them to use archaeology as a tool to use as they see fit; I don't expect them to do my kind of archaeology.

Only a percentage of our graduates are actively involved in doing archaeology on a regular basis. John Jules, for example, is cultural resource manager of the Kamloops Indian Band and regularly reviews AOAS and AIAS; Nola Markey (O-Chi-Chak-Ko-Sipi Nation) is in a doctoral program at Simon Fraser University but also teaches on the Kamloops campus and does consulting archaeology. Another graduate, Carrie Dan (Kamloops Band), is now an archaeologist for both her band and Golder Associates, a consulting firm recently working with the Neskonlith Band to excavate and study human remains from a site being mitigated before a railroad twin-tracking project (Nicholas, Jules, and Dan 2008). Recently, when a group of Native protesters demanded that excavations cease and the remains be immediately reburied, Carrie was uniquely situated to negotiate with the protesters on behalf of both the Neskonlith Band and Golder Associates.

Of equal or even greater importance to university education for Native people is learning their heritage directly from their family and community elders. First-hand knowledge of plant harvesting, moose hunting, and other traditional activities aids in locating and interpreting similar activities represented at archaeological sites. Such an education also conveys the non-materialist elements of the Aboriginal world that inform and stimulate. For example, in a recent field school trip to a sacred site—a spring that emerges from a hollow rock—student Randy Jim (Xaxlip [Fountain] Band) related both the medicinal uses of the water and the dangers associated with such places.

The emergence of Indigenous archaeologists such as Markey, Rudy Reimer (Squamish Nation), Eldon Yellowhorn (Peigan Nation), and others will have a significant influence on the discipline (Markey 2001; Reimer 2001; Yellowhorn 2002). These scholars challenge old ways of thinking and offer new perspectives. Reimer, for example, conducted a site survey in the alpine and sub-alpine environments of his traditional territory, and his results indicate that without including the traditional use patterns associated with high-elevation sites, land use models remain incomplete and nonrepresentative of the range of activities conducted in the past. Yellowhorn, now an assistant professor at Simon Fraser University, has promoted an internalist archaeology that enriches and validates traditional history, as defined by narrative and folklore. As he notes, "there is no point of going through the pretense of having a dialogue if Indians only echo mainstream archaeology" (Yellowhorn 2002, 349). This point is vitally important to promoting an archaeology that is attuned to non-Western perspectives.

Heritage Management and Traditional Use Studies

During the last two decades, many First Nations groups in British Columbia became involved in inventorying and managing their own cultural resources. Many established heritage policies, bylaws, and guidelines and developed protocols that established new arrangements or agreements for archaeological and heritage resources. The Heiltsuk, Kamloops, Musqueam, Squamish, Sto:lo, and other First Nations governments have established their own heritage permitting processes. These initiatives mark a significant development, establishing Aboriginal people as heritage managers, not just collaborators in provincial management schemes.

Related to the inventory and protection of archaeological sites was the development of the Traditional Use Studies (TUS) Program as a result of the 1995 *Delgamuukw* decision and later expanded through the Forest Practices Code of BC Act (1996). Under the provisions of the Forest Practices Code of BC, which required the government and the forest industry to consult with First Nations, baseline inventories would thus be developed for communities that would include locations associated with traditional beliefs about origins, culture history, and worldview, as well as location of trails, sacred sites, and resource-gathering areas, territorial boundaries, and other such information (Markey 2001). These were conducted in many First Nations communities, with First Nations staff, until the program ended in with the repeal of the Forest Renewal Act in 2002.

Data were collected through literature research, interviews, production of map biographies, and ground truthing. These projects compiled much previously unrecorded information about trails, traplines, place names, sacred places, animal migrations, family histories, and many other elements of land use that seldom appear in the archaeological record. For example, the TUS undertaken by the Kamloops Band in 1998–99 identified 120 traditional use sites,

> including 81 named places; 28 plant gathering sites; 29 hunting sites, 1 trapping site; 36 fish sites; 2 sacred sites; and 10 other sites, including a trail, several cabins, logging areas, and several historic sites . . . [along with] a comprehensive overview of botanical species with traditional Secwepemc cultural roles. (Gardiner et al. 1999, v–vi)

The information produced by these projects, and the skills acquired by community members, provided the means for bands to participate more effectively in consultations and negotiations with the government and industry. However, despite Aboriginal participation, the TUS program failed to achieve its promise, and the quality of the products was generally poor, certainly not defensible in court or at the negotiating table for land claims, or even for First Nations decision making. Although millions of dollars were spent, most went to building capacity, so little monies went into the actual studies. Projects were also constrained by flawed methodology, poorly trained workers, and other problems. More important, however, was the fact that the products were assumed to be complete and accurate by those who employed them for planning and management purposes—as has been the case with GIS modeling. In addition, these projects were restricted to recording site-specific information, with only very limited interpretation of the data. The approaches employed in TUS are not comparable to ethnographic methods, nor can ethnographic data be recorded on the type of database utilized in a TUS. Nonetheless, this initiative provided many First Nations with much value and could serve as a platform for future programs. . . .

24

Developing an Aboriginal Archaeology: Receiving Gifts from White Buffalo Calf Woman

Tara Million

I am an Aboriginal archaeologist. In this book I hold the hands of my sisters and brothers; young and old, Indigenous and non-Indigenous, academic and community based. Together we are creating a new, dynamic archaeology. In this chapter, I will discuss and summarize my archaeological theory and research.

In traditional Cree and Stoney cultures the spiritual figure of White Buffalo Calf Woman embodies guidance, learning, and teaching. She continues to provide a role model for Aboriginal women; women who both listen and speak. It has been my experience that, when Aboriginal women speak as Elders and leaders, they clarify what will happen. Their voices are respected and their guidance is followed. With these precedents established, Aboriginal women archaeologists are in a strong position to spearhead a paradigm shift within archaeology and, in fact, are obligated to actively do so. For these reasons, and because my practice of archaeology is based on an understanding of what is appropriate for Aboriginal womanhood, I use feminine pronouns throughout this chapter and White Buffalo Calf Woman as the overarching metaphor.

When I began to practice archaeology within the context of Aboriginal philosophy, I realized that to engage in archaeology is to create a powerful physical nexus point that replicates traditional Aboriginal architecture. Through the physicality of an archaeological site, the immanence of all

Excerpted from Million, Tara. 2005. Developing an Aboriginal Archaeology: Receiving Gifts from White Buffalo Calf Woman. In *Indigenous Archaeologies: Decolonizing Theory and Practice*, ed. H. M. Wobst and C. Smith, 43–55. London: Routledge.

times, and the relationship webs contained within those times, can be explicitly recognized and experienced. Therefore, when approached with an Aboriginal worldview, an archaeological site functions in the same manner as a North American sweat lodge and provides a similar arena for the ancestors to be present with both the living and the unborn.

Practicing archaeology within an Aboriginal philosophy transforms the person of the archaeologist. The archaeological site becomes a ceremonial area and the archaeologist a ceremonial practitioner. In addition to being the holder of a sacred site, the archaeologist is the holder of artefacts and ecofacts—all sacred objects, given by an aware archaeological record. White Buffalo Calf Woman gives these archaeological gifts in the same way as she gave our ancestors sacred objects and teachings and they carry the same spiritual and cultural meanings.

Within Aboriginal philosophy, the practice of archaeology is the creation of the world with the *axis mundi*, or the place of linkage between disparate elements, flowing through the archaeologist. An Aboriginal archaeologist is the locus for a relational web that incorporates past, present and future, living and non-living, academic and community, Aboriginal and non-Aboriginal. As an embodiment of the *axis mundi* she receives powerful gifts from the animate archaeological record that carry the obligation of redistribution and reciprocity throughout all of these relationship networks. In other words, as well as bridging contrasting worldviews, an Aboriginal archaeologist embodies the interrelationships between multiple worldviews and facilitates their unified functioning.

The principle of reciprocity that emerges from her relationship with the archaeological record extends into her relationships with human communities. In order to redistribute the gifts she has received, an Aboriginal archaeologist is obligated to speak within the Aboriginal and archaeological communities. From this point of view, I have concluded that the practice of Aboriginal archaeology gifts an archaeologist with the appropriate forms of authority and knowledge that are necessary in order to engage in egalitarian discussions within Aboriginal and academic cultures.

I have also concluded that archaeology is both a science and an art form. Aboriginal archaeology includes replicable methodologies and the systematic investigation of questions. Simultaneously, Aboriginal archaeology is an undertaking that incorporates creativity, truth, and beauty. An Aboriginal archaeologist strives towards precision, creation, and transcendence. In my opinion, the practice of Aboriginal archaeology is one avenue for creating the time prophesized when White Buffalo Calf Woman will restore what was lost and lead the way into a revitalized cultural era.

The Aboriginal philosophy I have discussed thus far grounds my archaeological research. I will now turn to summarizing this work. This is followed by my definition of Aboriginal archaeology. The chapter ends with three conclusions: archaeological, Aboriginal, and visual.

Developing the Archaeology

In order to develop an Aboriginal archaeology, I began by examining how traditional Western archaeology is perceived and practiced both by archaeologists and by outside observers. The basic concepts that underlie archaeological theory and method, as well as the dominant scientific paradigm of Western archaeology, were considered. I then explored my reactions of disengagement and dissatisfaction with Western archaeology and made the decision to re-frame my archaeological practices within an Aboriginal value system as a means of resolving these conflicts with the discipline.

This analysis resulted in a model for my research program and fieldwork that reflected the paradigm shift within my work from a Western linear worldview to an Aboriginal circular worldview. The traditional medicine wheel is the basis for my model. Its definition and use within Aboriginal culture, including the typical division into four quadrants, was explored. As further validation, I presented examples of Canadian Aboriginal scholars from other disciplines who have used variations of circular models and employed the significant concept of "four quadrants" in their research.

Following my research model, I sorted the various aspects of my fieldwork analysis and thesis discussion into four quadrants. The first quadrant was primarily academic. It included the academic basis for initiating my research; namely, the development of post-processualism within archaeology and its general movement towards fostering archaeologies that present alternatives to the dominant paradigm used in mainstream archaeology. In this quadrant I compared the underlying paradigms of power and time that emerge from a linear and a circular worldview. The archaeological ethics that result from linear and circular paradigms were also contrasted. In addition I continually re-engaged these issues throughout my project, as well as the broader implications of practicing archaeology and being an archaeologist in the context of a circular Aboriginal paradigm.

In the second quadrant, I explored my working relationships with Alexis First Nation, an Aboriginal community in Alberta, Canada. I focused on explaining how my interactions with Chief Francis Alexis and Council, community Elders, adults, and youth were both informed by and embodied Aboriginal circular paradigms. In addition, I provided specific examples within the context of each relationship that demonstrated circular conceptions of power and time, such as obtaining permission for archaeological excavation only from the Chief and Council, rather than from the provincial licensing body, Alberta Community Development.

The third quadrant of my thesis addressed the relationship that I initiated with the archaeological record. As I mentioned earlier, this relationship was based on an understanding of the archaeological record as an animate entity capable of negotiation and reciprocity. Traditional Aboriginal women's ceremonial protocol presented examples for culturally appropriate behavior with regard to the research and, more specifically, the archaeological site. For example, I closed excavations down during my menstrual periods and abstained from alcohol use throughout the research process. I described explicitly how my understandings of an animate archaeological record resulted in methodological changes for locating, laying out, and excavating an archaeological site. . . . Finally, data analysis, interpretations, and reporting methods were placed in the fourth quadrant. The modifications to artefact handling, cataloging, unit profiling, site dating, and the rationales for these procedures were all explored in this quadrant. . . . Also, my interpretations and recommendations for the Lac Ste Anne site (AFN-1) were described in detail and an analysis of calcium carbonate was identified for future research. . . .

Note: The archaeology that is summarized in this chapter is based on the author's Master's fieldwork and thesis. She refers those interested in a more developed discussion on the Aboriginal philosophy of circularity that grounds her work, the spiritual figure of White Buffalo Calf Woman, the traditional medicine wheel and its four quadrants, or archaeological methodology to this work (Million 2002).

25

Building a Bridge to Cross a Thousand Years

Dorothy Lippert

Attempted Transformations

In general, archaeological objects are grounded in a time other than our own. As Gosden and Marshall (1999) point out, they are also grounded in a separate context. An object may have a "cultural biography" that references its setting within a culture. Through the life of the object, meaning and relationships may evolve, "as people and objects gather time, movement and change, they are constantly transformed, and these transformations of persons and objects are tied up with each other" (Gosden and Marshall 1999, 169). By the time an object comes to be in a museum collection, it has gone through many different identities, from cultural object intended for use of one kind to a scholarly object intended for use of a very different kind.

Like medieval alchemists, archaeologists have taken base material, the everyday relics of individual lives, and transformed it into a scholarly commodity. The resulting product is, of course, valuable, but we cannot say that we have effected an absolute transformation. Unless subjected to destructive testing, the object generally maintains its physical characteristics, and unless we are willing to believe that scholarly thought amounts to destructive analysis, the object must maintain its cultural characteristics as well. Physically, the sherd that exists in a collections facility is part of the same clay object that was used by a Mississippian woman when feeding her family. Culturally, two different identities exist.

Excerpted from Lippert, Dorothy. 2006. Building a Bridge to Cross a Thousand Years. *American Indian Quarterly* 30(3&4):431–40.

Archaeological artifacts are defined primarily through the process of the relationship that an archaeologist enters into with them. By this, I mean to say that any object that was created by a human being may become an artifact, but it is the interaction between an archaeologist and that object that creates it as such. A bowl may be just a bowl, but when it is taken into an archaeologist's care and defined, it becomes a Barton incised bowl and becomes a marker for a certain time and place that are also defined by the archaeologist but that may never have been recognized by the creator or user of that object. That Mississippian woman likely never envisioned an interaction between her cooking pot and an archaeologist; however, it is not unreasonable to think that she may have thought that her children or children's children would keep, use, and appreciate her treasured possessions.

Many Indigenous archaeologists are unable to view objects from Indigenous cultures without recognizing that a multitude of contexts exist. An object may be at the same time a Catlinite disc pipe but also an object worthy of respect because of its placement within a Native culture. The awareness of the multiple contexts for the object can be understood through Michel Foucault's term "heterotopia." Miriam Kahn (1995, 324) defines this as "combinations of different places as though they were one." She focuses her analysis of heterotopias on museum exhibitions, which create meaning "through intentionally designed artificial contexts based on imposed logic" (Kahn 1995, 324). I would argue that besides exhibit space, the actual storage place of *artifacts* is another *artificial* context. A storage drawer may contain objects of many different categories, with different biographies and different contexts. Yet, they may all be viewed by an Indigenous person within a human context, that is, as objects made by people related either by blood or by cultural experience.

Heterotopias exist in many areas of archaeological work but go largely unrecognized because most archaeologists do not seek them out and have been trained to view situations through an obscuring, "scientific" lens. For Native Americans who choose to participate in this scientific practice there exists a certain degree of risk that by taking on the mantle of science we are agreeing to hide a part of ourselves that we know allows us to focus our gaze on the past more clearly. Indeed, Native archaeologists exist in a sort of heterotopia ourselves in that our work within archaeology is viewed by some Natives as an act of treason and by others as an act of revolution. As archaeologists we maintain and protect the scientific world, but as Native Americans we strive to change that world so that it will deal with our people in a fair and respectful manner.

The awareness of heterotopia exposes the potential for conflict. A specific location in the landscape may be at the same time an ideal place to practice rock climbing and a sacred location for many Indian tribes. At Devil's Tower National Monument, the National Park Service has had to mediate between groups who seek to impose differing identities on the same location. In the end, the Final Climbing Management Plan requests that climbers voluntarily refrain from climbing during the month of June, which is when many tribes hold cultural activities involving the site (U.S. Department of Interior 1995).

The repatriation issue is another example of heterotopic identification. Material that was legally defined as "objects of antiquity" was re-identified by Native Americans as loved ones and ancestors who deserved respect and proper burial. In both of these examples, the conflict had to be resolved through legal means. . . .

I examine . . . the nature of museum collections of objects that have been defined by archaeologists as artifacts but that to Indigenous people maintain their cultural context. In reestablishing the cultural context of the object, I believe that archaeologists return the full identity of the object to it. The process that an object goes through while being identified as an artifact adds another layer of identity to it. The recognition of multiple identities and contexts for objects in museum collections need not result in conflict as long as the parties involved do not try to deny the existence of the alternate identities. In fact, acknowledging the multiple identities should lead to a richer appreciation for the objects. I would argue that we must work to reestablish connections between Indigenous people and Indigenous objects from their past, in part because if we don't, we ignore the full cultural biography of the object and see only a small part of that object's life. . . .

26

Navajo Archaeologist Is Not an Oxymoron: A Tribal Archaeologist's Experience

Davina Two Bears

It is ironic that many tribes, like my tribe, the Navajos, find ourselves having to demonstrate our connection to our own ancestors and cultural items and that we must become "legitimate"—that is, credentialed in the eyes of the federal government—in order to protect our ancestors and sacred places on tribal homelands, but such is the outcome of a history of colonialism in this country. Begay (2003, 43–46) points out that Navajos practiced cultural resource management for centuries, as is true for many Native Nations of this continent. For Navajos many "archaeological sites" are recognized in Navajo oral history as places of clan origins and history, the homes of Navajo deities, and also feature prominently in Navajo religion and ceremonies (Begay 2003; Frisbie and McAllister 1978; Goddard 1933; Haile 1938a, b; Kelley and Francis 1994; Luckert 1977, 1981; Matthews 1994 [1897]; O'Bryan 1956; Preston 1954; Wyman 1970). These special places were, and still are, taken care of by Navajo people, who harbor great respect for Nahasdzaan (Mother Earth), Diyin Dine (Navajo holy people), and Anaasazi (all ancient peoples of Dine customary lands) (Begay 2001). Because Navajo people must find ways to continue to show respect to their traditions and culture, which includes the care of "archaeological sites," within the confines of modern Western society that is, America as well as the bureaucracy of the United States, clashes in cultural values occur.

For instance, when most Navajos hear the word "archaeology," they understandingly assume the worst thing one can do in Navajo culture, which is to "dig" where our ancient and recent ancestors have lived and

---

Excerpted from Two Bears, Davina. 2006. Navajo Archaeologist is Not an Oxymoron: A Tribal Archaeologist's Experience. *American Indian Quarterly* 30(3&4):381–87.

died. Regarding the student training program, it is important for Navajo students to share the requirements of their job with their families to receive support of their career choice as an archaeologist. For the most part, Navajo extended families do show support, but it is also true that families of Navajo archaeologists take special precautions. Often NNAD (Navajo Nation Archaeology Department) Navajo archaeologists have traditional Navajo protection prayers or ceremonies done in order to avoid any ill effects to oneself and one's extended family, which might occur as a result of being an archaeologist and handling objects that belong to someone now deceased or walking over a deceased person's house, whether one hundred or thousands of years old.

Although most of the work that NNAD does consists of archaeological survey work, which records and avoids "sites," rather than excavation or digging, the Navajo public usually does not know this until we tell them. The general Navajo public for the most part does not understand that as Navajo tribal archaeologists our job is to identify "archaeological sites" on the landscape, record them, and avoid them during construction. More important, the Navajo public usually does not know that Navajo tribal archaeologists also identify Navajo traditional cultural places, which are the Navajo sacred places, plant and herb gathering areas, or places of Navajo cultural, religious, and ceremonial significance. Given the bleak history of American archaeology in the eyes of most Native people and the fact that in Navajo culture areas where people once lived should be respected, protected, and left alone, the customary negative reaction to archaeology is not surprising. Once it is explained, however, to Navajo people, *most importantly in the Navajo language*, exactly what it is we do, the Navajo community and Navajo Nation Council members come to understand and appreciate the job of a Navajo archaeologist. One must consider that if a Navajo archaeologist is not fluent in the Navajo language, which I am not, then we are at a distinct disadvantage; however, Navajo archaeologists are encouraged to learn and speak, or to become better speakers of, the Navajo language.

Another equally damaging stereotype of archaeology on the Navajo reservation is that archaeology holds up the development process. The Navajo Nation Council passed tribal laws and policies that require protection of cultural resources, such as the Navajo Nation Cultural Resources Protection Act. Additionally, any federal undertaking on the Navajo reservation requires compliance with federal laws. Therefore, as part of development process, since the mid-1980s, a cultural resources inventory, or "archaeological clearance," must be conducted prior to any construction on the Navajo reservation. It is difficult for people to accept more red tape in the already lengthy preconstruction process that exists on Navajo lands. It must be understood that more than half of the Navajo households on the reservation don't have running water or electricity, a luxury that is taken for granted by most Americans. Many of the roads on the Navajo reservation are not paved. When it rains and snows, travel on the Navajo reservation becomes problematic or nonexistent because of the hazardous conditions like flash floods that obliterate existing dirt roads. Quite regularly, Navajo archaeologists are falsely accused for the delay in receiving services such as water, electricity, and paved roads. Archaeology has become the scapegoat in many instances for a road not being paved, when in actuality, the Bureau of Indian Affairs, one of the major builders of roads on the Navajo reservation, may not have the funding to pay for the construction costs for years. It is often difficult to be at the receiving end of misconceptions about archaeology, and it requires of Navajo and non-Navajo archeologists never-ending patience and good public relations. Also, since Navajo Nation Council members are elected every four years, re-education of the newly elected Navajo leaders, including the Navajo Nation president, must be done on a continual basis if NNAD desires continued community and tribal governmental support. . . .

Section VI

Mesoamerica and South America

This region is characterized by large populations of Indigenous peoples, particularly in Brazil, Bolivia, Ecuador, Mexico, and Peru. Arbitrary national boundaries, some of which hark back to the Spanish colonial era, have divided Indigenous communities and restricted their access to significant places. For generations, Western archaeologists have routinely conducted excavations in this part of the world, promoting colonial conceptions of pre-Columbian state formation and removing artifacts and knowledge without the permission of Indigenous peoples. Mesoamerican and South American nation-states have made efforts to preserve and promote some aspects of the Indigenous past, particularly the monumental architecture and high-value objects of gold and jade created by societies that are often framed as antecedents to modern nations (for example, Classic Maya, Aztec, Inca). Here, as elsewhere, archaeology has been used as a tool to promote national identity and state interests, often at the expense of Indigenous populations.

Heritage tourism provides a significant amount of revenue to the region, and state-sponsored tourism initiatives often appropriate Indigenous knowledge and symbols to provide "authenticity" for commercial purposes (see, for example, discussion in Ardren 2004). The approach to heritage tourism is largely "top-down," with state and private corporations making decisions about what is considered significant, how heritage sites are treated, and how Indigenous peoples—past and present—are represented. The financial and tangible benefits are reaped by states and private corporations, and they rarely benefit Indigenous and local communities (Clancy 1999; Pi-Sunyer, Thomas, and Daltabuit 1999). As Traci Ardren argues for a Mexican context, representations of the archaeological past (at heritage sites and as design motifs) perpetuate the inequalities of the tourism industry (Ardren 2004, 106).

Archaeologies of liberation are emerging in the region, and laws and protocols that require non-local archaeologists to partner with local scholars and institutions and insist that excavated materials remain in country have been enacted. This section provides examples of work in this direction. Indigenous and non-Indigenous authors consider ways of integrating Indigenous knowledge and archaeological science, discuss the potentials and pitfalls of multinational and multicultural cooperation, and call for reconsideration of the notion of social complexity and equality as applied to Indigenous pasts. They question the imperialist legacy of archaeology and its impact on contemporary human rights.

The section opens with an excerpt from Avexnim Cojti Ren (Maya) of Guatemala. In "Maya Archaeology and the Political and Cultural Identity of Contemporary Maya in Guatemala," she addresses the unequal position of Maya people with respect to economic, social, and political arenas, especially around cultural property and identity. The Maya are the subject of worldwide fascination, but many juxtapose praise for Maya achievements in astronomy and architecture with criticism of supposed societal excess and collapse. Cojti Ren critiques epigraphers who create and disseminate stereotypical and discriminatory pictures of the Maya past, thereby damaging Maya relations with tourists, governments, and educational institutions. She criticizes habitual models of "collaboration" as merely providing employment for locals as laborers and touristic performers, not as knowledge-producers. Summarizing the scientific principles in statements by UNESCO (United Nations Educational, Scientific, and Cultural Organization) and WAC (World Archaeological Congress), Cojti Ren's writing is a call to action. Archaeologists are urged to help decolonize Maya history by recognizing the persistence of ritual and social practices, incorporating Indigenous protocols, and training Indigenous archaeologists as equal partners.

Randall McGuire's case study from México is excerpted from his recent book *Archaeology as Political Action*. The Trincheras Tradition Project highlights collaboration among four communities from both sides of the international border (American, Mexican, Norteños, and

Tohono O'odham). McGuire describes the complexities of working with multiple communities and the process of re-evaluating the records produced by imperialist archaeologies. Archaeologists have been complicit in constructing national ideologies that have, in turn, limited Indigenous rights and realities. The participants in this case study struggled with the politics of "double colonialism" on the American/Mexican frontier, where the negotiations concerning practices and protocols for excavation, display, and analysis ranged from "bitter conflict to cordial cooperation." McGuire emphasizes the building of emancipatory praxis that can transform archaeology by forcing archaeologists to "confront the political, cultural, and economic difficulties of living communities."

Kevin Lane and Alexander Herrera, in Peru, propose incorporating traditional kin relations and rituals into archaeological practice. In "Archaeology, Landscapes, and Dreams: Science, Sacred Offerings, and the Practice of Archaeology," they explain the concept of landscape as animate in Indigenous farming practices. Narratives of the so-called superstitions of local communities are juxtaposed with the cynical assessments of archaeologists. The authors reflect on their personal positions as excavators of ancestral remains and their mistaken identities as dangerous shape-shifters. While acknowledging their own position as "Others," they have learned that belonging, in an Indigenous sense, requires shared "understanding of place . . . as embodied in a living and active landscape." Their efforts to participate in offering rituals to mountains and rivers facilitate deeper understanding and enable more productive relationships with local communities.

Archaeological dismantling of the Indigenous can also be addressed by re-appropriating Indigenous materials and values. A case study in Columbia, by Cristóbal Gnecco and Carolina Hernández, titled "History and Its Discontents: Stone Statues, Native Histories, and Archaeologists," examines the symbolic reclamation of significant sites and histories buried under layers of colonial meanings by Indigenous Nasa and Guambiano people. The Guambiano complain that the archaeological interpretation of ancestral peoples as "alien enemies was a colonial imposition and that their symbolic and physical recovery as ancestors is a political move of the greatest importance." Similarly aiming to subvert colonialist discourse about the past, the Nasa eagerly reclaim stone statues from the university museum. For these Indigenous people, history is inherently cyclical, and disasters are necessary for maintaining order and clearing the way for periodic renewal. Archaeological interventions can, at times, be conceived of as useful "disasters." Public outreach is necessary for conceptualizing and communicating these kinds of Indigenous "history in the making."

In Argentina, Alejandro Haber writes of "Reframing Social Equality within an Intercultural Archaeology." His paper problematizes the Western tropes of complexity and categorical reasoning. Western theory generally conceives individuals and groups as being autonomous. Haber introduces, *uyaña*, a theory of related-ness based in Indigenous ways of knowing and shaped by reciprocal, nested relations. He then applies this theory to interpreting the archaeological record of the precolonial Inca town of Ingaguassi and two neighboring towns, to articulate and illustrate the physical structures and social relations of reciprocity.

The final chapter in this section is "Indigenous Knowledge and Archaeological Science: The Challenges of Public Archaeology in the Reserva Uaçá," by Lesley Fordred Green, David R. Green, and Eduardo Góes Neves. The authors engaged the local community in archaeology by overtly seeking informed consent and appropriate permission and openly discussing negotiations of power on the reserve. Seeking to integrate archaeological research with Indigenous ways of doing history, they interviewed storytellers and transcribed oral traditions, aiming at preservation as much as discovery. While rethinking and reworking questions and practice, they conceived of new ways to communicate archaeological research as *ikiska anavi wayk,* studying "things left behind in the ground," with the goal of *ivegboha amekenegben gidukwankis,* "reading the tracks of the ancestors." In sum, the experience of involving local people in research provides a means to reflect on unequal levels of empowerment in collaborative processes.

27

Maya Archaeology and the Political and Cultural Identity of Contemporary Maya in Guatemala

Avexnim Cojti Ren

Colonisation left Maya people in an unequal position compared to Ladino people in the economic, social, political, and cultural arenas in Guatemala. This experience is not different from the experience of other Indigenous nations in Latin America. Like these other Indigenous nations, Maya people have a history of resistance that has continued to develop, as every generation creates new strategies to overcome its disadvantaged position.

Archaeology can be used to write history, providing essential benefits or detrimental stereotypes of Maya communities. Archaeologists who practise in Guatemala have a call to be more ethical toward the descendant communities that they work in, especially in the field of interpretation and creation of theories about Maya history. Maya people are affected by the knowledge produced in archaeology, and they have an inherent right to forge their own identity through history. . . .

In Guatemala we have responded to the situation of internal colonisation and assimilation with a movement of resistance that seeks to affirm our cultural and political identity and the right to maintain it. We are looking for commonalities that can unify us in a national culture. It has been a difficult task, since our culture is varied and undergoes constant change, as does any other society. Yet we are unified as a people, as a community in the Guatemalan state and other states in which we live, and even with other Indigenous nations around the world through our

---

Excerpted from Cojti Ren, Avexnim. 2006. Maya Archaeology and the Political and Cultural Identity of Contemporary Maya in Guatemala. *Archaeologies: Journal of the World Archaeological Congress* 2(1):8–19.

common history: millennia of independence and sovereignty followed by 500 years of resistance to colonisation. History shapes our present cultural and political identity individually and collectively. The history behind our individual experiences is, in the end, our collective history. Our historical identity is then the common identity we need.

Sadly and unfortunately, the history of our people has also been colonised. That is, the history of the Maya has been distorted and is told by others. The colonial system guaranteed the continuation of its legitimacy by erasing the records (written, material, cultural, and oral) that could be used to support the historical legitimacy and the cultural distinctiveness of Indigenous people (Wylie 1995). As a result, our unequal position of power in Guatemalan society and other states is explained variously as a result of colonial and capitalist systems. As Victor Montejo (1999) writes, the last five centuries of Maya history is a history of racist discrimination and degrading colonial representations of our people. Such racist and colonial history was used and continues to be used to justify land expropriation and relocation and assimilation of Indigenous people today.

As Indigenous people generally, we are blamed and even blame ourselves for the lack of progress, poverty, and violence in our countries, communities, families, and our own lives. This continuous colonialist blaming of the oppressed results in low self-esteem, self-alienation (regarded as our natural passiveness), and the practise of discrimination against our fellow Indigenous people and their cultures. Non-Indigenous Ladino and Western cultures are seen as naturally superior, and their model of modern life is supposed to be the one to embrace if Indigenous people want to progress socially and economically and be acknowledged as human beings and authentic citizens.

In order to unite as people who share a common identity, we must celebrate our common history, but in our respective countries our history and heritage are appropriated and exploited as "national patrimony." Maya sites, artefacts, documents, and so on have been constructed as characteristic of Guatemalan identity rather than the identity of the Maya. For instance, while the repatriation of archaeological remains and artefacts in North America means returning them to the Indigenous community, in Guatemala repatriated archaeological materials go to the Ladino state rather than to the Mayan communities (Cojti Cuxil 1995). We do not have control of our material culture or the history that is embedded in it. State governments deny us the right to our cultural heritage and the history that our material heritage represents. As a people, we need to recognise and understand both the historical basis and the continuing practises of colonisation that attempt to rob us of heritage, identity, self-esteem, and agency. But even more important is our reconnection to

Maya history prior to European invasion and colonisation; this is the history of sovereign nations with their own systems of government, literature and writing, languages practised at all levels of society, spirituality, leisure practises, family life, art, music, food, and so forth, just the same as exist in any Western developed society.

In the last century, practitioners of archaeology and more recently epigraphy have been participating in the writing of Maya history. We acknowledge that, in the interpretation of Maya calendrics, mathematics, and astronomical science and in making these interpretations available to the public, archaeology and epigraphy have contributed to a positive image of our people. Furthermore, these elements have been adapted to present Maya publications, *guipil* designs, individual names, art, jewelry, and so on, which also has positive connotations for our people's identity. However, there are serious drawbacks to the ways that Maya history is being written and presented to an increasingly large public.

Today the Classic Maya are being portrayed as a great ancient society with achievements in astronomy, mathematics, architecture, and other sciences, which existed for a certain period of time until, for unknown reasons, their civilisation collapsed and the people disappeared. One recent example is the book by Jared Diamond titled *Collapse: How Societies Choose to Fail or Succeed,* where ancient Maya society once again was said to have "collapsed" due to the greed of a ruling elite for a life of luxury and extravagance, which was the cause of its downfall.

Such an image of our people contains characteristics pertinent to a European and Euro-American idea of social complexity, technology, science, and cultural sophistication. In the example mentioned above, the Western values of individualism and capital accumulation, which are much emphasised in the United States, are portrayed in a Mayan context.

Precontact Maya history has also been divided into levels of civilisation: Preclassic, Classic, and Postclassic. The Classic period is considered the most important because during this time more writing, art, and architecture were produced. The other two periods are not considered as important, and therefore the people that lived during those periods are not thought to be as sophisticated as the Classic Maya. This "civilisational inferiority" is also applicable to contemporary Maya. That is, we might also believe that if current Maya do not produce the magnitude of art and architecture that Maya did in the Classic period, they cannot achieve the same greatness: "With awe-inspiring cities like Tikal and Chichén Itzá, the Classic Maya period, from A.D. 250 to 900, rivalled Egypt and Rome in its splendour and intellectual achievement" (Lovgren 2004).

In addition, to be considered "authentic Maya," we must conserve the cultural practises and traits of our great past, such as the rituals, the cosmovision, the art, and the agriculture. Even dress and physical traits must be maintained as the traits of "the real Mayas of the past." Otherwise our identity is questioned.

Theories of the Maya collapse have varied. Warfare and invasion, guilty elites, superstition, and environmental destruction together with population growth are some of the more popular ones (Montejo 1999; Wilk 1985). But in the end, the logical conclusion to which these theories lead is the same: the notion of a collapse is the notion of a failed civilisation, and it separates present Maya people from their past. Collapse denies our continuity as the original people of the countries in which we reside and undermines our claims to that historical continuity. The result of this discontinuation of our history is that Maya are denied a true identity; we are regarded still by the general public and even ourselves as just *Indios,* with no history or culture, no land title, but only customs and traditions, with dialects. In this view, past Maya civilisation deserves to be honoured but not the present *Indios;* our people are dehumanised and devalued, and any discriminatory or even ethnocidal policy against Indigenous people is thereby justified.

At the same time that we are separated from the accomplishments of our ancestors, we are subject to repercussions of another type of description of Classic Maya society. This characterisation, which focuses on the twin themes of rulership and violence, is exemplified in academic literature and popular media, including television documentaries like the recent *Nova* episode called "Copan, Lost Kingdom of the Maya." In these presentations, Maya kings are represented as historical agents ruling society and making war, yet they appear as two-dimensional autocrats rather than genuine leaders of a nation. We learn about rulers and their relations with other rulers, their conquests and the sacrifices made to them, but we do not learn about their family relations or festivities or how they governed our people. Their lives are constructed as based on violence and power and sacrifice.

As Victor Montejo (1999) has noted, the image of violence and sacrifice used to characterise our people in the past reinforces the justification for violence and oppression in the present. These interpretations lead us to believe that in preconquest times our people were already in a state of oppression from our own governors. This leads to the notion that our present situation as targets of violence and oppressive national policies is just a continuation of the past; we have just changed oppressors. Another possible implication from such a violent past is that we have been saved by the church, and now we enjoy, if not a perfect one, at least a better governmental system that came with the Spanish invasion.

As a people, we do not deny that warfare, violence, and human sacrifice were practised; this information is well documented by archaeology and epigraphy. But the emphasis made on this part of our past is so exaggerated, it seems as if no other society was or is as violent as the Maya. Archaeologists seem to forget that all past and present societies have warfare, torture, and violence. As is well documented in daily newspapers, violence is being practised to a degree never practised by our ancestors.

Our past society was composed of a variety of social, political, economic, and cultural processes, just as societies are today. The lives of the kings and spiritual leaders, warfare, sacrifice, and rituals cannot encapsulate the whole of past Maya society; no society can be narrowed to the separate aspects of life or individual agents.

Although disconnected from our ancestors' achievements, the image of a ritualistic Maya culture positions current Maya ideology as a continuation of the past with minimal changes. This portrayal of ritualistic contemporary Maya is what defines the identity of present Maya as Maya to archaeologists. In this sense, contemporary Maya are used to bring the dead past to the present, and the changes in our culture are ignored (Hervik 1998). People from my own community of Chichicastenango are represented as the true descendants of the great Mayas because of their rituals and sacrifices, but expressions of spirituality evolve while people still consider themselves Maya.

Past practises, events, and objects had certain meaning for our people at a certain point in time. The past spiritual and social practises and means of government have been known and shared among our people in the present, although with obvious changes over the past 2,000 years. Archaeologists know this fact and have used current Maya knowledge to describe the past. We have become good informants for reconstructing the language, spirituality, and cultural practises, but our views are not treated as equal to those of archaeologists when it comes to reconstructing our history. The information given by current Maya sources is selected and appropriated to fit the image and interpretation that archaeologists want to create, rather than considering Maya interpretation of past history as truthful and a suitable basis for further study.

Speaking about the past of other societies becomes an issue of who has the right to speak for whom, and who has the right to write whose history (Hanna 1997). Archaeological research reports are taken seriously as scientific investigation and receive positive media coverage and public acceptance with no questioning. Because archaeologists have legitimate authority from academia and governments to interpret the facts of the past, they are considered the scientific experts whose job is to share such historical knowledge with all humankind. The Maya past is considered a common good to be shared with the international community, rather than a cultural right for Maya to decide how our past will be shared with other people.

The distribution of historical information is usually aimed at a white, middle-class public, ignoring the fact that Maya people are getting more access to sources such as computerized media, literature, museum displays, and television documentaries in their home countries as well as in other countries around the world. Thus our representation becomes the description of "the other" to Western society through our mysterious, exotic, ritualistic, and violent life, while Westerners affirm their own identity as a society with modernity, a culture with logic, real history, good moral values, and so on. In short, our past and present life is sensationalised and sold to Western consumers as a newly discovered property (Echo-Hawk 1997). The archaeological image of Maya constructed as the culture of the other affects how non-Indigenous populations, corporations, and government institutions perceive us and treat us, as well as how we perceive ourselves.

Controlling the Maya past is tantamount to controlling our power in the present, for history is the basis for demanding respect for our political and cultural rights as a people. The reconstruction of our history by archaeology must benefit the interests and needs of living Maya, yet we are still excluded from archaeological research management and from the interpretation of our own past. Access to the Maya past through various media is becoming more available to Maya, and we want to relate to our history rather than being treated as objects, historical resources for the public and for the market. We want to speak on our own behalf; we want to tell our own history.

In this sense, it needs to be recognised that archaeology and epigraphy have been and will be political, for they have repercussions for the cultural and political identity of the people whose history is being studied. As Maya we want and need to reconnect with our past, a living father than a dead past which empowers our present struggles for decolonisation and allows us to have more agency in making our future. History is power for our people; history is the basis for Maya land rights, historical patrimony, education, language recognition, leadership, and so on.

Archaeologists can help to decolonise Maya history by being more ethically responsible to contemporary Maya peoples' needs and interests when reconstructing our past lives and the images of our lives. Anne Pyburn (1999) has stated that there is already a body of theory and guidelines in applied anthropology that could be adapted for a responsible archaeology. Similarly, Larry Zimmerman (1997, 66) proposes that archaeologists must be anthropologists first, meaning that archaeologists must consult with Maya people and get us involved in every level of research, acknowledging Maya alternative knowledge in the interpretation of the Maya past (66). . . .

Following is a summary of Ethical Principles of Archaeology towards Indigenous Peoples covered in the Canadian Archaeological Association and World Archaeological Conference (summarised in collaboration with Marvin Cohodas):

I. Respecting Aboriginal Interests in Their Heritage

A. Property Ownership versus Human Rights

WAC notes that while Indigenous peoples often have had the lands taken away that support heritage sites, and thus cannot claim legal property ownership, they have a moral or human rights title to control of their own heritage, especially since that heritage is still alive for them and important in their spiritual, political, and emotional lives.

B. Politics of Identity

Both statements of principle recognise that control over the excavation and interpretation of the archaeological heritage of today's Indigenous peoples remains essential for their well-being and cultural survival. These issues involve identity as it is constructed in several different spheres such as:

i. How they feel about themselves in relation to each other, the individual belonging to a nation.
ii. How others view Maya people as a group, which affects how they deal with Maya people. This includes not only touristic travellers and consumers but also state governments, intergovernmental organizations, multinational corporations, and so forth. This is a crucial political issue involving Indigenous rights to tell their own stories, versus the stereotyped characterisations produced by those who have colonised and exploited them.

II. Collaborative Excavation Procedures

A. Informed Negotiation and Consent

Collaboration with Maya people has been addressed primarily by negotiation with nearby communities over the labour of excavation, and over potential subsequent development of touristic infrastructure, which are positive for local economic benefits but do not reconnect present communities with their historical past. However, the WAC goes farther in requesting collaboration with Indigenous peoples, communities, or their representatives before excavation begins, in order to agree on questions, goals, and procedures, and they require that the community (or representatives) be kept informed at every stage of investigation.

B. Training Indigenous Archaeologists as Equal Partners

The training of Indigenous archaeologists as partners is a vital prerequisite so that both sides can engage in well-informed negotiations concerning excavation questions, goals, and procedures. We would like to have Maya archaeologists of the Maya past, but we do not want foreign institutions to produce archaeologists to be just physically representative. Rather, we want conscious archaeologists that can help Maya to reconnect to their past and their present needs.

III. Respectful and Deferential (Better Yet Collaborative) Interpretation

The WAC insists that interpretations be made with deference and respect to Indigenous descendants. Their main point is respecting Indigenous oral traditions. Respectful interpretations can only be accomplished if it is understood that Maya are part of the audience reading the interpretations and have the political power to reject degrading stereotypes (Pyburn 1999).

IV. Fair Trade

The WAC begins by noting that archaeologists have obligations to Indigenous peoples, and these moral obligations determine the principles and rules of their ethical behaviour. Speaking and writing ethically about the past of Indigenous nations in general, and especially the Maya past, is a political act that can repair the historical injustices toward Indigenous people and can benefit the needs and interest of Maya in their current struggle against colonialism.

In conclusion, history plays a key role in our peoples' resistance to colonisation and discrimination. We have an interest in reconnecting to our past because history can empower our present and our future. Archaeologists and epigraphers as scientists reconstructing the past of Maya people need to be aware of the implication of their excavation and interpretation work, since Maya are the subject of their study and part of their audience (Cojti Cuxil 1997). In this sense, archaeology and epigraphy are accountable to the Indigenous Maya in the countries where they reside, including the countries were they have immigrated. The implementation of already existing archaeological ethics codes is a starting point to decolonise Maya history, not only in the field of excavation but also in the field of interpretation.

28

México

Randall H. McGuire

In the mid-1980s I initiated archaeological research in northern Sonora, México, and threaded my way into the tangled skein of double colonialism along the border. I did so with a keen awareness of the imperialist archaeology that U.S. scholars traditionally practiced in México. I also had a developing sense of the colonialist nature of prehistoric archaeology in the United States. Since beginning this project, my Mexican collaborator Elisa Villalpando and I have tried to create a praxis of

Excerpted from McGuire, Randall H. 2008. Chapter 4: México. In *Archaeology as Political Action*, 140–87. Berkeley and Los Angeles: University of California Press.

archaeology that challenges both the imperialism and the colonialism that we encountered on the border. Creating emancipatory praxis will never be an easy thing to do. The realities of social relations and ethics are never so dear and distinctly defined as they are in abstract discussions. Splendid formulas for life simplify the real politics, conflicting interests, ambiguities, and contradictions of working with multiple communities. . . .

The archaeology of the Trincheras Tradition Project shows how praxis has worked out, albeit imperfectly, in one case. The project has involved four communities from both sides of the international border: U.S. archaeologists, Mexican archaeologists, Norteños, and the Tohono O'odham (the Papago). The relationship between U.S. archaeology and both Mexican archaeology and the descendants of Spanish settlers in Sonora, the Norteños, has traditionally been an imperialist one. Archaeology has played a role in the United States' economic, political, and cultural domination of México. The relationship of all three of these communities to the Tohono O'odham has been colonialist. The traditional lands of the Tohono O'odham straddle the international frontier, and O'odham live on both sides. México and the United States have subjugated the Tohono O'odham, and in both Sonora and Arizona the descendants of the conquerors study the ancestors of the conquered.

Double colonialism exists in two senses here. In the simplest sense it lies in the colonial relationship of both the United States and México with the Tohono O'odham. U.S. archaeologists crossing the border into Sonora also enter into an additional colonial relationship. Here they encounter a tradition of U.S. imperialist archaeology in México and they study the ancestors of a people their ancestors subjugated. An emancipatory praxis should seek to confront and transform these unequal relationships in both of these colonial relationships. Our efforts to do this in the Trincheras Tradition Project have met with uneven success. We have built a collaborative approach between the two communities of Mexican and U.S. archaeologists that mitigates the traditional imperialist U.S. archaeology in México. We have also entered into an educational dialogue with the Norteños of Sonora. But our consultations with the Tohono O'odham remain problematic.

The border creates a distinctive context for our research. The frontier between the United States and México west of the Río Grande is an unnatural line defined only by the artificial grid of longitude and latitude. For the people who live and work along this line, including archaeologists, the international frontier is in one sense very artificial but at the same time a very compelling reality (Alonso 1995). A mix of Español and English, tortillas and white bread, Norteño and country-western tunes, and El Pollo Feliz and Kentucky Fried Chicken defines a zone that is culturally neither U.S. nor Mexican but simultaneously both. Yet, there is nothing fuzzy about the line slashed through aboriginal territories, dividing native nations and leaving the archaeological record of ancient pasts unnaturally sundered. This line is a rigid social institution made up of walls, fences, and checkpoints and patrolled by agents of the state with guns, dogs, jeeps, and planes.

This line both impacts and structures the social relationships that generate the four communities of the Trincheras Tradition Project. Europeans created the United States and México by conquering and subjugating aboriginal peoples. The elite of each nation developed a national ideology that legitimated this conquest and defined the place of Indian peoples in the heritage of the state. Archaeologists participated in the development of the national ideology in both countries, and archaeology was also defined by these ideologies. The respective ideologies delineate very different relationships among archaeology, Indian peoples, and the state. Furthermore, the two nations are not equal. The Treaty of Guadalupe del Hidalgo ended the U.S. war of conquest that took approximately half of the territory of México (Griswold del Castillo 1990). Within México a distinctive subculture known as Norteño arose along the frontier. The unnatural line defined the limits of two nations but split a third, that of the Tohono O'odham, in two. Even though both the Norteño and the Tohono O'odham communities share the common history and reality of the border, they experience that heritage and reality in different ways. From those experiences spring different relationships to and interests in the past of the region. . . .

The Trincheras Tradition Project—Building Praxis

The international border arbitrarily cuts the Southwestern-Northwestern culture area in half. It had no meaning for the aboriginal history of the culture area, but it has had a profound effect on the archaeology of the region (McGuire 2002). The amount of archaeological research done north of the border greatly exceeds that undertaken in northwest México. Today the southwestern United States could be the most intensively researched archaeological region in the world. To the south of the culture area, Mesoamerica is also an intensively researched archaeological region. Sandwiched between these two areas, northern México may be, archaeologically, the least well-known region in North and Central America.

The paucity of archaeological research in Sonora provided an opportunity for our goals of creating a praxis of archaeology that challenged the traditionally imperialistic practice of archaeology by North

Americans in Mesoamerica. When we began the Trincheras Tradition Project, there was no established imperialist tradition of North American archaeologists working in northwest México. Previous U.S. projects had been expeditions that entered and then left the region. The same was true of most Mexican projects before the founding of the INAH center in Hermosillo in 1973 (Braniff and Felger 1976). We had an opportunity to build a new praxis of archaeology without having to confront an existing local practice and well established prejudice on either side. . . .

Indians and Archaeology on the Border

The Indians who lived along the Río Magdalena have not vanished. A handful of the Tohono O'odham still live in Sonora, and many thousands live in Arizona. They form the other half of the double colonialism that confronts the archaeologist on this frontier. We tried to confront colonialism through consultation with Tohono O'odham people. These efforts occurred in a context of shifting political interests.

When we started our work in Sonora, a French archaeological project was already ensnarled in a double colonialism. From 1984 till 1987, the French Center for Studies of México and Central America conducted an ethno-archaeological project at Quitovac, Sonora (Villalobos 2004, 77–109). The French researchers obtained permits from INAH's Consejo de Arqueología in México City, but they did not contact the traditional authorities of the local native communities in Sonora or Arizona. The project ultimately ended in bitter conflict with the Tohono O'odham.

Tohono O'odham from Sonora and Arizona gather at Quitovac each year to celebrate the Wi:gita ceremony, but in the late 1980s, the only O'odham actually living there were one elderly couple. With no Indians nearby who could witness their work and object to it, the French researchers excavated graves from the cemetery, and they collected materials from the blessed cave where the Tohono O'odham keep the sacred eagle feathers for the Wi:gita ceremony (Villalobos 2004, 80–85). In 1987, the French also found a skeleton of a mammoth which they uncovered and removed to Hermosillo for stabilization (Villalobos 2004, 85–87). The skeleton was eventually returned to the community, but then the local Norteños took charge of it, constructing a case to display it. Also in 1987, after the Wi:gita ceremony, the French systematically mapped and collected the ceremonial ground without permission of the Tohono O'odham.

In 1988, we began our first project in Sonora. The institutional and bureaucratic mechanisms that NAGPRA would inspire to facilitate cooperation between Native Americans and archaeologists did not yet exist. Confrontation was still the norm for such relationships. Nevertheless, Elisa and I felt that a radical praxis of archaeology in the region required that we involve Indian communities, so we sent copies of our grant proposals to the O'odham communities of southern Arizona (the Tohono O'odham Nation, the Gila River Indian Community, the Salt River Indian Community, and the Ak Chin Indian Community). We asked for comments and offered to host representatives of these communities if they wished to visit our project in the field. Only one community replied. I visited and talked to the leadership of the San Xavier District, of the Tohono O'odham Nation, before we went to the field. These individuals were sensitive to the archaeological issues because of their involvement with the Arizona State Museum during the San Xavier Bridge Project (Ravesloot 1990). Later, a delegation from San Xavier visited our survey project in the Altar Valley of Sonora. After all was done, we sent each of the communities copies of our reports.

In 1991, when we began our mapping and surface collection of Cerro de Trincheras, we followed the same procedure. This time, none of the communities responded. During the field season, all our research involved survey and surface collection. We had little chance of encountering human remains or sacred objects, and we did not. Following the 1991 field season, as we planned our excavations at Cerro de Trincheras, we realized that the situation had changed, both in the United States and in México. We did not plan to excavate in the cremation cemetery we had found at the site. We knew, however, that we might nevertheless encounter human remains.

After the passing of NAGPRA, archaeologists and Native Americans in southern Arizona developed institutionalized means and procedures for consultation on archaeological research. All of the Native American nations and communities of southern Arizona established either a committee or a designated individual within their governmental structure to handle this consultation. At this time, relations between archaeologists and Tohono O'odham people in southern Arizona ranged from bitter conflict to cordial cooperation. The Tohono O'odham had generally allowed the nondestructive analysis of skeletons and mortuary goods before their return and reburial (Ravesloot 1990).

In México, all archaeological materials are legally the heritage of the Mexican people. The national government owns all archaeological sites and artifacts, regardless of the ownership of the land they are found on. Any negotiations concerning the disposition of burials and sacred goods must be made with INAH, and only INAH has the authority to repatriate these things to Native American nations or communities. INAH had never done such a thing before the French project at Quitovac.

In designing the excavation project for the spring of 1995, we felt that we had to make a greater effort at consultation with the O'odham than we had in the past. We came to this position both because we would be excavating and because of the changing relations between archaeologists and Native Americans in the region. We thought that the repatriation and reburial at Quitovac gave us precedent for future repatriation and reburial in Sonora.

We were optimistic. The experience of the French was foremost in our minds, because we wanted to avoid the misunderstandings and abuses that had happened at Quitovac (Villalobos 2004). The Centro INAH de Sonora had played a leading role in returning the burials and sacred objects to the Tohono O'odham. The center was also involved in negotiations with the Tohono O'odham Cultural Affairs Committee about plans to develop the Sierra Pinacate as a Mexican national park. Because of the changes wrought by NAGPRA, we felt that it might be easier than in the past to initiate and maintain a process of consultation. The cultural affairs committees and offices of the Native American nations and communities of southern Arizona made it more convenient for us to contact key individuals in those communities. Once initiated, we also thought less effort would be required to maintain the process with standing committees or offices that would survive changes in tribal governments.

We made initial contact with the Tohono O'odham Cultural Affairs Committee by sending them a copy of our grant proposal for the project. We then arranged to meet with representative of the committee in Trincheras during September 1994. One member of the committee and an Anglo lawyer who represented the committee came to this meeting, along with representatives of the Comunidad de Trincheras and INAH. The meeting was very cordial, and the Tohono O'odham were quite appreciative that we had sought to consult them about a project in México. We agreed at the meeting that if we encountered any burials in our excavations, we would excavate them so they would not be looted and then contact the Cultural Affairs Committee.

The Tohono O'odham recommended that we should contact other indigenous nations and communities in Arizona in addition to the O'odham governments we had contacted in the past. They suggested we also inform the Pasqua Yaqui Indian Community and the Hopi Nation of our project. We subsequently sent all of the O'odham groups, the Yaqui, and the Hopi copies of our proposal. Only the Ak Chin community and the Hopi Nation responded to our query. Both indicated that we should deal directly with the Tohono O'odham Nation.

We started fieldwork at the beginning of February 1995. Within the first few weeks we had located several possible cremations, one definite cremation, and two inhumations. We left the cremations in place. They did not contain ceramic vessels, and we thought they were not obvious enough to attract looters. Our workers, however, immediately recognized the bones in the inhumations as human. Even though none of the inhumations contained extensive grave offerings, we excavated them on discovery to prevent them from being looted.

We notified the Tohono O'odham about our finds, then met with two members of the Cultural Affairs Committee and their attorney in Caborca, Sonora, on March 4. There, they agreed that we would be allowed to do nondestructive analysis of the inhumations and that afterward they would be reburied. The only point of contention was how long we would keep the bones before reburial. Since we had not yet talked to a physical anthropologist about doing the analysis, we wanted a year to get the work done. The Tohono O'odham wanted the work done more quickly.

On March 13, 1995, a delegation of four from the Cultural Affairs Committee and their attorney visited us in the field. The visit was quite cordial, except for one of the Tohono O'odham, who adopted a confrontational attitude. The Mexican archaeologists on the project had no experience with Indian criticism of archaeology, and the confrontational Tohono O'odham offended them greatly. They were, however, pleased with the cordiality and obvious sincerity of the other Tohono O'odham people who visited the site. Conversations at this meeting led to the decision to backfill the known cremations without excavating them.

After our 1996 field season, we had excavated a total of ten burials containing twelve inhumations from scattered locations in the site. We had made arrangements with biological anthropologists to analyze the remains. We anticipated that with the completion of this analysis, the remains and the few artifacts we had found with them would be repatriated to the Tohono O'odham and reburied at Quitovac.

In 1997, the Centro INAH de Sonora sought permission from the governing council of INAH, the Consejo de Arqueología, to repatriate and rebury the inhumations from Cerro de Trincheras (Villalobos 2004, 112–21). To our surprise, the *consejo* refused this permission. Despite a formal request from the Tohono O'odham Nation and further pleadings on the part of the center, the *consejo* would not change its position, expressing two basic reservations about the repatriation. Officials there felt that the requests represented an attempt to import U.S. problems into México, and they feared losing control over Mexican heritage. The *coordinador nacional de Arqueología* also raised legal issues. Under national law the skeletons and artifacts from Trincheras were part of the national heritage of México. The law vested responsibility for the analysis, interpretation, display, and curation of this heritage in INAH, and a local community could not co-opt this responsibility.

The regulations of INAH also required that such materials be kept in a recognized museum.

The *consejo* did not want a U.S. dilemma in México, and it took an anti-imperialist stance, withholding recognition of the Tohono O'odham Nation as having the legal or moral standing to request repatriation. INAH regarded the nation as U.S. Indians and U.S. citizens. Needless to say, this infuriated the O'odham, who see both México and the United States as invaders. The *consejo* accused the archaeologists at the Centro INAH de Sonora of being unduly influenced by North American archaeologists and of not representing the interests of the Mexican people and nation. They expressed concern that the North American archaeologists on the projects wanted to dictate policy to the INAH. Archaeologists from the Sonora center tried to explain that things were different on the border. Issues of heritage and legitimacy were much more complicated than they seemed in México City. But, for the *consejo*, issues of heritage and legitimacy were much broader than a few inhumations from the far end of the nation.

The national politics of heritage and legitimacy had shifted in México. Much had changed since the reburials at Quitovac in 1993. On the right, the Partido Acción Nacional agitated for the decentralization and privatization of heritage. This included the INAH, the ENAH, the museums, and the national monuments of the country. The right wanted a profit-making heritage industry, not nationalist lessons and scientific study. On the left stood the Zapatista revolution in Chiapas. The Zapatista program included an *indigenista* plank that refuted a pan-Mexican identity of La Raza. Zapatistas called for greater autonomy for indigenous groups. INAH feared that this call could come to include control of national monuments, such as Palenque, Bonampak, and Yaxchilán, in Chiapas. These fears raised the specter of other indigenous groups in the country demanding return of their heritage, the most important archaeological sites in the nation. Too much was at stake to risk any of it for a few inhumations in far-off Sonora. The situation remains much the same today.

In the end, our attempts to repatriate the inhumations from Cerro de Trincheras failed. Not surprisingly, the Tohono O'odham felt betrayed by the turn of events. In retrospect, we should have included the Consejo de Arqueología in our consultations with the Tohono O'odham from the beginning. The incident strained relations between archaeologists in northern Sonora (both Mexican and North American) and the O'odham, although dialogue continues. In addition to creating a situation in which we could not repatriate inhumations, the history, paradoxes, and ambiguities of three nations on the border also created a loss of trust.

Three causes lie at the heart of this lack of success. The first was our failure to establish a long-term and involved collaborative relationship with the Tohono O'odham as a community. Consultation was just not enough. The consultation model that we followed is typical of contemporary relations between archaeologists and native communities. Such a model may permit compliance with NAGPRA, but it does not build the trust and dialogue with native peoples that lead to true collaboration. The second was our failure to understand the shifting context of Mexican nationalism and the place of archaeology in it. Finally, the compelling realities of the border worked against us. In the absence of true collaboration and trust, there was no way to escape the snare of double colonialism.

Building an emancipatory praxis of archaeology requires more than splendid formulas for life; it requires that archaeologists confront the political, cultural, and economic difficulties of living communities. We have struggled to do this on the border with the Trincheras Tradition Project. We continue to build on the foundation of a collaborative binational praxis of archaeology involving U.S. and Mexican archaeologists. We persist in our dialogue with the Norteño people of northern Sonora and our programs of education. And we struggle to move beyond consultation to a true collaboration with the Tohono O'odham. . . .

29

Archaeology, Landscapes, and Dreams: Science, Sacred Offerings, and the Practice of Archaeology

Kevin Lane and Alexander Herrera

Case Study 2: The *Pishtaku* in Conchucos

After six years of fieldwork in central Conchucos (1996–2002), several months of which were spent working and living in the hamlet of Huagllapuquio, I (Alexander Herrera) find it intriguing that a Peruvian archaeologist such as myself should still be suspected of being a *pishtaku*. In this section I chart five years of changing attitudes and relations between archaeologists and the rural population. I focus on how the rituals we engaged in impinged upon this process and conclude that rituals at archaeological sites provide a crucial context for exploring and negotiating social bonds with the "other." Underlying tensions surrounding perceived economic dependence and "unfair" principles of labour organization can fuel demands for the reiteration of rituals and fuller engagement in ritual cycles.

In 1996, weeks after hearing the dream of my teenage guide, I made my first journey from the small hamlet of Huagllapuquio, six hours on foot from the end of the last dirt road, to the area around the saline spring of Yangón. Preliminary reconnaissance indicated investigations at Yangón and Gotushjirka would be archaeologically fruitful, albeit logistically and socially challenging. The site of Yangón lies at the bottom of the gorge-like lower Yanamayo valley (2000 m), two hours down and three hours up a steep path from the one score of houses that comprises Huagllapuquio. All tents, tools, equipment and supplies would have to

Excerpted from Lane, Kevin and Alexander Herrera. 2005. Archaeology, Landscapes, and Dreams: Science, Sacred Offerings, and the Practice of Archaeology. *Archaeological Review from Cambridge* 20(1):111–29.

be carried first down then up, either on the backs of mules or people. Excavations at the hilltop site of Gotushjirka, only thirty minutes from Huagllapuquio, would be far less challenging in comparison.

In the village, I had met and stayed with Francisco Samaritano and his family. Despite their welcoming friendship I was aware of being a foreigner in my own country, and that some people in Huagllapuquio thought me to be a *pishtaku*. I initially put this down to my European physique, urban style of dress and the distrust towards outsiders that is often found in small, close-knit communities.

A year later I returned to begin work, accompanied by a colleague of a more thoroughly "Andean" appearance. We were pleasantly surprised that we quickly managed to hire a mule to transport equipment to Huagllapuquio, although no muleteer could be found. However, we soon found that hiring help was to remain a complex task. In Huagllapuquio we were now suspected of being a team: the *pishtaku* and his adjutant. No one would accompany us at dusk, on their own, past Torregaga, the massive vertical rock outcrop which is the landmark of the lower Yanamayo valley. It took weeks before a handful of people took up the offer of paid work (16 per cent above the average daily rate) at Yangón. During this first season no one spent a single night at our camp, preferring a long daily return journey on foot, despite the offer of free food.

It seems that *pishtaku* can act in teams; they can change their physical appearance and speak Quechua. Yet they are considered less dangerous during the day. Clearly, some action was required if excavations were to go ahead in the following dry season. In the nearby town of Yauya, I had learned how a teacher had recently been beaten close to death on the suspicion of being a *pishtaku*.

Months before the intended start of excavations I returned to the region and formally requested the permission of the district council. At the suggestion of the mayor I addressed open meetings in the district capital and a community meeting in Huagllapuquio. The legally binding official permit, issued in Lima by the National Institute of Culture, was of no interest to anyone. After I gained approval in both instances preparations for the excavation began.

However, when I arrived at Huagllapuquio on the agreed day with four Peruvian colleagues no one would accompany us to the valley bottom site. It would have been impossible for anyone to return after dusk. A young man volunteered to come the next day, so we pressed ahead alone. Of course, he never did. I suspect he feared going alone, and no one, it seems, was about to allay his fears.

Through the municipality we contracted a field assistant from the district capital. On the 11th of July 2000, a first *pago* offering ritual was made at Yangón. Under the guidance of a colleague from Cusco we ritually addressed the main surrounding mountains, the neighbouring Yanamayo river and Yangón itself. We requested permission to dig and asked for good data. Around a small hole in the ground we chewed coca leaves, smoked tobacco and took turns libating and sipping alcohol. Each of the participants had his excavation fortune read from coca leaves and chose leaves for two *k'intu* bundles, one of which was buried along with sweets as an offering, as a ritual feeding of the site. Alcohol libations were copious and the burning cigarettes stuck into the ground did not go out; seemingly our offering had been accepted.

A few weeks later a slightly larger ceremony was conducted on the prominent summit platform at Gotushjirka, this time in the presence of several people from Huagllapuquio, including potential field assistants, onlookers and a few children. Our colleague clearly enjoyed his role of *misayuq*, as shamen are referred to in the southern highlands. Our hosts, on the other hand, seemed impressed by the elaboration of the ritual, even though no one in Huagllapuquio can understand the Cusco Quechua dialect. This time every single named mountain around was addressed.

Relations with the community improved as excavations at Gotushjirka began. The local *curioso* paid one visit yet he became ostensibly nervous near our excavation pits. As soon as human remains were uncovered children were forbidden to come to the site, I presume by their parents, but some still they sneaked in when they could. On the basis of dreams, local field assistants have asked me to hold additional offering rituals. Because of the pressure of completing the season's excavations I have refused. Perhaps my refusal is related to the suspicion of being a *pishtaku*, a suspicion that some people in Huagllapuquio still hold.

The day metal finds were first and unexpectedly made a condor was spotted sitting on the summit rock where our libations and offerings had been made. Dark cloud cover gave way to slight rain, a rare occurrence in the dry season. Then a pair of condors long circled above the site. This singular and evocative series of events underscored, to me, the power of place as a setting for ritual.

Gotushjirka is a powerful place by virtue of its setting. It is prominently located above a narrowing of the Yanamayo valley and it has a 270° viewshed reaching from the glaciers of the Cordillera Blanca to the West, to the peaks of the Cordillera Oriental. Additionally the surface and environs of the archaeological site are littered with marine fossils, including some on the summit rock, where the condor sits. Gotushjirka evokes a symbolic link between the sea and the air crucially mediated by the summit rock. This link is probably as old as the earliest ceremonial platform erected on the summit, which may date back four millennia. In a way, our ritual, just like the condor's flight, reanimated this ancient landscape.

Conclusion

These first steps towards an anthropology of archaeology are the result of preoccupations concerning our role as social scientists and our "otherness" when engaged in fieldwork. Consciously or not, the incorporation of ritual into archaeological practice provides a platform for the negotiation and affirmation of such "otherness." Within an indigenous metaphysical framework rituals at archaeological sites can be about the reaffirmation of identity (Mamani Condori 1996) or about the temporary integration, no matter how fragile, of our "otherness" within the local ideological network. From a socio-economic standpoint, offering rituals executed before the start of archaeological fieldwork ease access to labour. In the case of Huagllapuquio a successful allegiance was established with a section of village kin. At Yurakpecho difference prevailed and the community asserted its collective authority, demanding briefings and regular reports.

The idiom of "otherness" extends to anyone outside the immediate community. In Peru, a large majority of current anthropology and archaeology students at national universities are themselves second or third generation immigrants from the highlands. They, in turn, consider themselves more "in-tune" with highland sentiments and beliefs. They see themselves as the professional spokespeople for these ill-represented and "mute" communities. The rural people we met, however, begged to differ; to them we are outsiders all. Any apparent reflexivity or empathy on our part is mere self-delusion. Full understanding of local culture, as archaeologists, is probably impossible considering our urban background, our distinct "otherness" apart from *campesinos*. More often than not proximity is proscribed by how much Quechua one knows.

Yet, as a counterpoint, we propose that a sense of belonging or "inclusiveness" is mediated by acute knowledge of the environs. This extends beyond a mere knowing or naming of the various physical landmarks, something considered worthy of respect in its own right. Belonging, however, is based on sharing an ideal understanding of place within a spectrum that encompasses the past and the present as embodied in a living and active landscape. Interactions within such landscapes—what might be termed "landscapes of identity"—are guided by multi-faceted cultural values and rules. We argue, that these rules are not reflections of an altruistic view of the world, but are anchored in practical tenets, which negotiate a series of social relations mediating the natural and human worlds, including property rights, risk-minimisation strategies, and rural economics.

If, as Starn (1994) states, anthropologists have moved away from an examination of people towards a more inclusive and multi-vocal perspective relishing in diversity and innovation, it is likewise true that there is a tendency to glorify cultures battered by centuries of marginalisation, isolation and despair. Nonetheless the question of preferential access to the past expressed by Mamani Condori (1996) looms large. Traditional knowledge about the past and professional archaeology differ radically in their social context, means and purpose. Their juxtaposition can provide a baseline for reflection about both, yet this baseline must be founded on mutual respect. Within a pluralist framework their hybridisation is not inconceivable.

30

History and Its Discontents: Stone Statues, Native Histories, and Archaeologists

Cristóbal Gnecco and Carolina Hernández

Native Histories: History in the Making

Colonialist archaeological discourse about native histories imposed the idea that indigenous peoples and cultures were part of the past. The basis

---

Excerpted from Gnecco, Cristóbal, and Carolina Hernández. 2008. History and Its Discontents: Stone Statues, Native Histories, and Archaeologists. *Current Anthropology* 49(3):439–66.

of this discourse, upon which the exclusion and subordination of ethnic alterity was largely predicated, was the idea that the subject matter of history is the past, not the present and the future. Native resistance to this discourse confronted a meaning-producing regime, that of national history, with local histories largely mobilized in the framework of ethnic struggle. The establishment of temporal continuity using material (archaeological) referents and the revitalization of social memories long silenced now become central elements of new social projects.

In the past two decades there has been a drift toward a restoration of the links with ancestral times that includes their material referents. In Colombia this still-developing process was started by the Guambianos, neighbors of the Nasa, who feared the *pishaus*, reputedly former inhabitants of their territory, as much as the Nasa fear the *pijaos*. The *pishaus* were a colonial-produced incarnation of a feared alterity. Yet the Guambianos have recently turned the *pishaus* into their own revered ancestors (Dagua, Aranda, and Vasco 1998), and in this task they have been decisively assisted by anthropologists and archaeologists (Vasco 1992). Material remains uncovered by collaborative archaeological research have been endowed with new meanings in the context of ethnic struggle for self-determination and cultural revival. From considering that "bones and burial goods are dangerous and can cause disease and even death upon entering in contact with them" and that "those remains do not belong to Guambianos but to *pishaus*" (Vasco 1992, 181), the Guambianos came to say that "all the pottery and all the traces found in our territory are our own and not of other people. . . . The *pishau* are our ancestors and not strange people" (Vasco 1992, 188). In a manifesto coauthored by an anthropologist and two respected Guambiano elders a year after these remarks were made, any doubts about the cultural affiliation of *pishau* were dispelled (Vasco, Dagua, and Aranda 1993, 14–15):

> The *pishau* were not other people; they were the very same Guambiano. . . . White historians come now to tell us that the traces of the ancients that remain in our territory do not belong to the *pishau* but to the *pijao*, which were our enemies. With that story they want to snatch away our forebears, they want to cut off our roots from our trunk in order to assert their lie that we are not from here.

The manifesto thus makes it clear that the consideration of the *pishaus* as alien enemies was a colonial imposition and that their symbolic and physical recovery as ancestors is a political move of the greatest importance. This reassessment, an obviously conscious choice on the part of the Guambianos, sums up a moral story: the bad other disappears when the good other decides to confront domination, when subjugated alterity decides to become a respected and empowered self. Cultural meanings are historical and strategic.

There is yet another reason that this inverted semantics can occur: the bad other is certainly feared but also admired and made central to the symbolism of resistance (Taussig 1987). It embodies the power to confront the colonial order. Otherness is the locus of potential resistance, something the state has always known and that caused it to enlist the Catholic Church to curtail deviations from the norm of civilization. The bad other exemplifies everything feared and punished by the self, a moral void into which the good other is always at risk of falling, but the good other, no matter how afraid, finds in it a model, a positive morality, an icon of struggle. The ancestors fooled the Spanish by burying themselves in the underworld—a sign not of cowardice but of ingenuity—and thus avoided colonial subjugation. Burying oneself in the land or in the water (as Nasa myths say Juan Tama and other creation heroes did)—that is, patiently resting or hiding until the time arrives to return—is a pan-Andean trademark of the native messiahs eagerly awaited in the symbolism of these societies. Thus, the negative categorization of the bad other is, simultaneously, its sign of purity, the signature of the "true" native.

The indigenous organization in Cauca has recently set out on the path of the Guambianos. The celebration of the thirty-fourth anniversary of the CRIC two years ago began with a trip to San Andrés de Pisimbalá, site of the Tierradentro Archaeological Park—a significant move signaling the commitment of the organization to previously neglected archaeological referents. The current events taking place in the Juan Tama *resguardo* contributed to and deepen this move. Although the three stone statues uprooted from La Candelaria six decades ago are still housed in the museum in Popayán, in the past year several respected elders of the Juan Tama community have come to the museum to see them. Learning that they were taken from La Candelaria and that the university is willing to give them back has been a thrill for them. The university and the Juan Tama community have agreed that the statues will return to their original location. Their trip back to the Aguacatal River will highlight a planned collaborative research project involving archaeologists and native peoples in the production of local history, deepening a brief joint project carried out in 2003. The earlier project produced audiovisual materials showing the importance of getting to know the archaeology of La Candelaria and adjacent areas. Schoolteachers and students were especially active in this effort to strengthen and redefine ethnic identity.

Archaeology can find places where historical production is truly meaningful for local populations, politically and otherwise, beyond the grandeur (and, quite often, the local uselessness) of universal narratives.

Public outreach is becoming ethically mandatory and strategically necessary. Yet, for many archaeologists public outreach is still just a way of sharing results—that is, not a collective and collaborative enterprise but a one-way process by which expert knowledge is communicated to the public. Native peoples are included in this process with the idea that they may eventually find archaeological information useful for their own histories. In contrast, public archaeology (that is, archaeology for and by the public) is conceived not as a normally unidirectional process wherein wise archaeologists advise ignorant people about their own history but as a coproduction in which interested parties collaborate, learn from each other, and jointly (but not without productive conflict) produce history (Gnecco 2006).

From an academic perspective there is no doubt that history is crucial for the constitution and maintenance of the social fabric, but the situation may be different when one is dealing with communities experiencing living conditions on the margins of the well-being that the industrialized world takes for granted. In such cases mere survival and the fulfillment of basic needs (such as education and health) are more important or at least much more urgent than memory and its activation by history. It is one thing to talk about the importance of memory and history from the comfortable desk of a university office and quite another when the struggle for territory, economic self-sufficiency, and political recognition are at stake. Yet, when urgent agendas have already been fulfilled or when historical narratives can accompany them, there is room for hope that desire will eventually meet memory. Although this is currently happening in the Juan Tama *resguardo*, the meaningful appropriation of archaeological remains by indigenous communities in old and newly settled territories is a process that has to be promoted and in which archaeology is a prominent actor.

The Juan Tama community displays history in the making. Nasa history is cyclical, and one of its prominent features is times of renewal. It is also millenarist, and disasters are propitious for the restoration of order (Rappaport 1981). This idea seems to be widespread in Amerindian philosophy; the name it receives in the Andes is *pachacuti*, a cyclical, cataclysmic destruction of the world followed by the return of the right order. The millenarist movements of the eighteenth and nineteenth centuries in Tierradentro documented by Rappaport (1981), similar to others in the Andean realm, highlight the role of earthquakes in the reorganization of the world. The 1994 earthquake caused widespread destruction, but it was also a creative historical event: it has been thought of as a time of renewal and restoration, one capable of awakening history. This mythical renewal, moral in its postulation of the world as it has to be, combines with political struggle to produce a propitious time for the Nasa, a restoration of a lost order, a time in which historical meaning, through the symbolic appropriation of otherwise ignored and feared objects, can be paramount. As Rappaport (1981, 384) has noted, messianic thought is always present in Nasa culture, ready to become action when "available social conditions and cultural symbols coincide." In the case of the Juan Tama *resguardo*, the requisite social conditions exist in the strong involvement of the people in political consciousness-raising, bilingual education, historical revitalization, and the promotion of communal practices. Symbols are at hand, too, in the form (among other things) of archaeological remains that can be culturally appropriated and in the adoption of Juan Tama as the community's name: Tama was a messiah who defeated the *pijaos* and ended years of colonial terror, symbolically and proactively; he made the Nasa proud of themselves. This coincidence of symbols and conditions deepens an apocalyptic, millennarist native hope of a new opportunity to subvert the colonial order for the construction of autonomous, self-determining societies.

The native symbolic appropriation of archaeological remains, however, is marked by an approach that departs from that of most archaeologists. While for the latter the archaeological record is evidence of the past and therefore of vanished cultures worthy of being subjected to scholarly inquiry, for indigenous peoples an archaeological site is a living place (Mamani Condori 1989, 49–50):

> The archaeological ruins left by ancient cultures are not inert or dead objects: they have a reality which actively influences our lives both individually and collectively...The relationship we have with material evidence of our past goes beyond a simple "positivist" attitude which would treat them as mere objects of knowledge. Rather, they are for us sources of moral strength and a reaffirmation of our cultural autonomy.

It has been held that Nasa memory rests on material referents such as mountains, lakes, boulders, and waterfalls (Findji 1993; Gómez and Ruíz 1997; Rappaport 1990). In contrast to those of Western societies, these referents are almost exclusively geographical. Yet, indigenous communities can appropriate other material referents, even what we call archaeological materials, into their symbolic realm. They are even willing to explore the symbolic possibilities of alternative (even Western) mnemonic devices such as museums (see Vasco 1992). In this regard, the statues from La Candelaria can act as historical activators not only for the Juan Tama Nasa but also for many indigenous and local communities elsewhere. Material objects and features turned archaeological by academic or community-appropriated discourses can serve to strengthen the historical reflection that is needed to stimulate social participation. . . .

31

Reframing Social Equality within an Intercultural Archaeology

Alejandro F. Haber

Reciprocity and Relatedness

Western social theory tends to consider reality by dividing it into different realms of analysis. Relationships between human individuals and groups are explained by social theory, relationships with production are seen as economic, with practical devices as technology, and relationships with spiritual beings as religion. Each of these realms is analysed separately. As each realm has its own discourse, reality ends up being understood and managed in separated terms.

Social equality and inequality are analysed as if the relations between individuals themselves, or between individuals and groups, were autonomous from the broader network of relationships, or, in other words, as if the agents involved in social relationships were there before the relationships in which they came into being. Canonical within Western sociology, the assumption that social relations between social agents constitute an ontologically separate realm of reality (so justifying sociology as an epistemologically separated realm of knowledge) is part of a broader colonialist discursive formation. Once we view sociality and otherness as matters of discourse, the role of this discourse as a mechanism of colonialism becomes manifest.

Archaeological narratives about social difference among indigenous past societies cannot, therefore, be considered mere descriptions of something there to be known. Because colonialist actors produce social inequality (through the appropriation of land, resources and labour from

---

Excerpted from Haber, Alejandro F. 2007. Reframing Social Equality within an Intercultural Archaeology. *World Archaeology* 39(2):281–97.

indigenous peoples), any discourse that analyses indigenous societies on their own, that is, detached from their vital relationships to land and resources, is genealogically dependent on (and concurrent with) colonialism. While emphasis on social equality may counteract the strong insistence of archaeological narrative that indigenous peoples were basically unequal, it remains within the limits of the same intellectual framework supportive of colonialism unless it goes beyond the Western view of social relations as self-contained. . . .

Before going into the archaeological cases, I find it necessary to introduce some elements of the local—Southern Andean, Kolla—theory of relatedness, as a contribution towards a post-Western and de-colonizing archaeology. Several years ago Gabriel Martínez (1989) drew attention to the Aymara linguistic constellation around the root uyw-. The terms within that constellation in Bertonio's Vocabulary of 1612—*crías, los hijos y cualesquiera animales* ("o spring, the children and whatever animals")—are related to his present ethnography of Isluga (Martínez 1989). These terms make reference to upbringing, caring, loving, between parents and children, herders and llamas, living people and ancestors. "Uywaña has, in any case, a sense of bringing up that is a 'protecting,' with an implication of love, of loved thing and a very intimate and internal relationship, on which the good outcome of upbringing depends" (Martínez 1989, 26).

> Uywiri, active participle of uywaña is, thus, "the breeder," "the one who brings up," but conceived as an abstract entity, at a sacred level, with the underlined connotations. It is seldom applied, at this level, to the protector mountain or mountains of the house, which appear thereupon as the "breeders" of it; and the house, as a social group, as brought up by its uywiris. (Martínez 1989, 28) . . .

In the 1990s, departing from the essentialism implied in the theory of domestication, I worked on the idea of domesticity following the Aymara meanings displayed by the ethnography of uyaña (Haber 1999). Uyaña, which in other terms can be translated as "ownership," is not a relation but a relation between relations or, in Herzfeld's phrase, a meta-pattern (Herzfeld 1992). "[Cultural] rules . . . are . . . relations between relations, or what we might call metapatterns. These are what, for example, Fernandez . . . calls 'structural replications at various levels and various arenas in Fang life.' Such patterns allow individual agents to organize the otherwise chaotic indeterminacies of social existence" (Herzfeld 1992, 69). The fact that uyaña appears as technology or domestication, that is, as mediation between society and nature, tells us about the persuasiveness and naturalized character of such a relation of relations. If the Enlightenment assumption of nature as a pre-social arena has been criticized (Ingold 2000), the network within which beings come-to-being remains unchallenged. Putting aside the modern assumption of an asymmetry between man and the world, uyaña provides a framework of reciprocal conversations and nested relationships. But it also aids in the understanding of the deep cultural unity of the phenomena that from the outside are seen fragmented into economy, social relations, technology and religion. Uyaña is a theory of relatedness that emphasizes practice much more than discourse. Even if the term uyaña is derived from aymara aruni (Aymara language), uyaña is a practical and conceptual seed that grows among the Collau (Southern Andes) Quechua-speaking and Castilian-speaking peasants. This emphasis on the practice of uyaña and its reproductive potency independent of language is, at the same time, an indicator of its potential within an archaeological approach.

Uyaña is not an atemporal category, existing today and in the past in the same way; it is contingent on a particular area of the world and a temporality. The place and the time of such a theory of relatedness are not to be known in measurable and objective terms, but in relation to the place and the time of discourse about it. This means that the place and time of this text are structurally positioned in relations of power regarding its content, and not simply engaged in a relation of knowledge. The structural positions can be understood in relation to colonialism, which is, at the same time, constituted by knowledge. Discourses about the Other are textual mechanisms of coloniality. The description of social inequality is one feature of the construction of Otherness. The textual elaboration of the Indians as a social category at early colonial times was done through the narrative of "Inca tyranny," and Indians were understood as beings lacking the true religion to be reformed through religious conversion and state intervention. The assumption behind the colonial understanding of Indians was that they could be assimilated within a single category based on distance from Christianity, and detached from their particular and contingent, but vital and constitutive, relationships to land, souls, animals, plants and place. Academic discourses about the social inequality of colonial Others are rooted in such a colonialist genealogy. By contrast, local Kolla knowledge can be the basis from which to develop competing knowledge about Kolla history and culture. This knowledge is built in time (again implying that colonialism is constitutive) and implies long-term cultural resistance. Whether or not it originated in pre-colonial times cannot be objectively ascertained. It is not that this category authentically represents an objective past; its eventual appropriateness with regard to the past should be a consequence of its authenticity towards the present. . . .

Ingaguassi and the Architecture of History

A comparatively large amount of research has been done on Ingaguassi within both documentary history and archaeology, though independently of each other. Historians point to the fact that in the mid-eighteenth century Loreto de Ingaguassi was important enough to be considered an administrative section of the Spanish colonial state. The rich gold veins of Ingaguassi attracted several hundred people from different parts of the Peruvian viceroyalty. Ingaguassi had a considerable indigenous population as well as Spanish authorities, merchants and priests (Hidalgo 1978). From the amount of gold that the Cacique (indigenous chief) transported from Ingaguassi to the administrative town of San Pedro (Hidalgo 1987), relatively autonomous access by the Indians to mining resources can be deduced.

The main object of historians' preoccupation is the indigenous rebellion of the Carnival of 1775 (Hidalgo 1982; Hidalgo and Castro 1999). This has been considered variously as active resistance to the increasing tribute pressure by the colonial authorities, a dispute between colonial agents, the Corregidor (colonial political authority) and the priest, or a rebellion against the normal order in the upside-down, alcohol-abusive context of Carnival. Documentary history on Ingaguassi follows the descriptions included in written documents, where the colonial status quo is emphasized and the indigenous agency is presented as altering normality. For instance, Ingaguassi is considered in the texts as a town founded by the Spanish state for Indians to live in (a "pueblo de indios," or "Indian town"), with a checkerboard plan, a church and a plaza (Hidalgo and Castro 1999). In these versions planned architecture implies an already established colonial order, and the political action of the indigenous population is seen as altering normality; the very fact that texts were written by Spanish agents with particular colonial projects was not taken into account by historical reconstructions, which reproduce in their narrative the colonial textualization of indigenous people and resources. By not only ignoring the performativity of colonial texts but also adopting them as documentary evidence, objectivism reproduces the same colonial performativity (Haber and Lema 2006).

Archaeologists, on their side, have ignored not only documentary history but also each other, considering Ingaguassi to be a pre-colonial Inca town resettled by Spanish colonizers. Again architecture seems to be the clue for interpretation. Interpreting the plan of Ingaguassi as an Inca kancha (a rectangular enclosed compound), with several other supposedly typical Inca features such as two-way roofs, trapezoidal-shaped doorways, wall niches, interconnected roads and Inca state-produced pottery, the town was again considered to be the outcome of a state decision.

As my first steps in research into Ingaguassi, a complete plan survey of Ingaguassi and two neighbouring and contemporary towns (Agua Salada and San Antonito) was conducted, the sequential relations between each building event in each of the architectural structures of the three sites were described, and the complete area involved was surface collected. While not a single Inca potsherd was found in Ingaguassi, the road was found to connect the sites themselves and not a broader state network, and several architectural features were found to be non-existent or non-diagnostic. But the most interesting piece of research is related to the architectural stratigraphy. The church and the town enclosure were found to be built at late stages of the architectural sequence. Each of the compounds began as a single rectangular house with its long side aligned north-south and one eastward doorway. When the church was built, the houses immediately to the north and south of the church were changed by the addition of other rooms, the closing of the original eastward doorways and the opening of doorways to the church. Several similar changes occurred in other houses, but not all of them. An enclosing wall was then built around the church and the (now) main neighbouring houses.

By considering building events as social practice, architectural stratigraphy allows a completely different understanding of Ingaguassi, as settled by indigenous families in the first place. These families would have settled at the site attracted by its gold, with which they could pay the heavy tribute obligations. Afterwards, Spanish authorities, merchants and priests came in, as they knew of the wealth of gold, and struggled to appropriate it. Because the original indigenous houses are basically similar to one another, a general impression of social equality, afterwards altered by the colonial agents, arises. As with the case of Tebenquiche Chico, this kind of external view of social equality, although critical of former interpretations, is not enough to achieve an understanding history in culturally relevant terms.

The early indigenous houses in Ingaguassi, and the following architectural phases, are aligned in several north-south lines. This alignment aided the architectural and textual representation of the town as state planned, whether the state in question is precolonial Inca or colonial Spanish. But the alignment had nothing to do with town planning. The houses were placed directly on top of the surface quartz veins containing gold. More specifically, each house was built beside the pit dug in the quartz vein. While the mine pit went wherever the vein led the search of gold, its mouth remained by the house, where a maray (indigenous style) stone mill and a domed kiln were also placed. The family was closely associated with the means of mining production, and (as in Tebenquiche Chico with the canal) the house was built in the very place where the appropriation of the golden vein happened, that is, the mouth of the mine pit. Because each family had a mill and a kiln, the complete process of gold production was domestically controlled. Gold was a particularly important good in colonial times, and having or not having gold with which to meet tribute obligations could mean the continuity or not of indigenous families and/or communities. In a way illustrative of the colonial condition of existence, gold could mean the bringing up of the family as much as food staples did. To bring up gold through the proper acts of caring and feeding the vein could be actions as relevant for the family in the mining place as the other technical steps of gold production.

By understanding indigenous gold mining in uyaña terms, we are able to understanding the political actions of 1775 and their onset during the ritually significant time of Carnival, when the demonic being of the owner of the mine is the focus of the feast. The indigenous population at Ingaguassi may have been experiencing a progressive loss of their capacity to engage themselves in the proper relations of nested reciprocity with the gold vein. Their political action, implying the Corregidor flying away overnight with his family under the threat of death, the imprisonment of other Spanish inhabitants, and their voicing claims to their rights to the land and mine together with expressions such as "Spaniards should go to Spain" had the sense of an anti-colonial revolution, not because they wanted to restore a pre-colonial past, but because they wanted to free themselves from colonial oppression in their own present sense of proper relatedness of beings. When a couple of years after the rebellion a colonial army came to Ingaguassi to complete the military repression, the indigenous population departed. The Indians preferred to return to their communities of origin rather than remain in the mine under Spanish control.

Uyaña theory of relatedness aids an understanding of Ingaguassi, a site that differs from Tebenquiche Chico in political, technological, economic and even religious context (the church was presumably the place of worship of the image of Our Lady of Loreto by the Kolla miners also). Beyond those contextual differences, both cases belong to the same cultural and theoretical Kolla tradition. A powerful sense of such a tradition emerged when, a couple of years ago, while I was conducting research in Ingaguassi, a man from the local community asked me: "What do you think? Is it true or not that the vein grows at night?" . . .

32

Indigenous Knowledge and Archaeological Science: The Challenges of Public Archaeology in the Reserva Uaçá

Lesley Fordred Green, David R. Green, and Eduardo Góes Neves

Research Activities

Ethnographic enquiry—the responsibility of Green and Green—had the goal of collecting a comprehensive set of oral-historical texts and information about possible sites, as well as seeking to understand local power and practices that would need to be accounted for in any archaeological work. An ethnographic understanding of local lifeways proved vital, particularly with regard to the articulation of landscape, historiography and myth, sociality and approaches to power and the production and appropriation of local identities.

Over a dozen storytellers were interviewed in seven Palikur villages along the Urucauá River, with multiple versions of particular stories sought for comparative purposes. These were transcribed and translated into Portuguese by first-language Palikur speakers. Currently, some 230 performances of stories on digital video are in our database. Stories were grouped into "chapters of a canon" in a meeting with a number of Palikur elders and a poster display in Palikur formed the basis of a wider public communication about the nature of this analysis. Since the majority of stories refers to particular places in the landscape—of particular interest in an archaeological enquiry—a number of people were

Excerpted from Green, Lesley Fordred, David R. Green, and Eduardo Góes Neves. 2003. Indigenous Knowledge and Archaeological Science: The Challenges of Public Archaeology in the Reserva Uaçá. *Journal of Social Archaeology* 3(3):366–98.

invited to participate in the production of a large-format memory map of contemporary Palikur lands.

For several months in 2001, a programme of public education included setting up the poster display and a small library; as well as a television and video player powered by a solar panel to show videos on related subjects as well as footage from the sites.

After several months it was field-making season and people began to visit carrying fragments of pots, whole pots and stone axes that they had found in the ground where new fields were being planted; this was material that usually would have been thrown away. Among the most interesting finds was an ancient wooden paddle, the size, shape and decoration of which no-one remembered but which was remarkably similar to a seafaring paddle drawn in 1743, by P. Barrère (illustrated in Rostain 1994, Vol. II, Fig. 209). Photographs of ceramic figurines also elicited much interest, with indications from some that they had found similar items before but simply thrown them away. The number of visitors and the range of artefacts they offered was in marked contrast to sentiments in the early days of the work where secrecy and suspicion had been prevalent.

Archaeological investigations were directed by Eduardo Neves. The major goal in 2000 was to investigate sites that were identified in popular memory as those at which key events in ethnohistory took place. We sought to visit these and assess the conditions for further, systematic, research in the area. Recognising that the only way to ensure the preservation of remote sites would be if local people attributed value to doing so, we sought a process that would integrate archaeological research with indigenous ways of doing history, including local people in decisions and research activities. A key issue was that informed consent was almost impossible to assure in the absence of any prior exposure to archaeology. For that reason, three Palikur—Avelino Labonté, Tabenkwe Manoel Labonté and Ivanildo Gômes—were invited to attend three weeks of an archaeological field school near Manaus in July 2001 and on the basis of their report-back to local leadership, permission was granted to proceed with the first formal excavation work in November 2001. Accompanying Neves for the excavation work was a team of three Brazilian archaeologists who worked both as excavators and trainers. The location of the work was decided in conjunction with leaders and in consultation with residents at a public meeting.

At that meeting interested people were invited to sign up to work on an excavation of a large site at a place called Kwap. We sought to train as many people as possible and brought in a fresh crew of four every three days, with three working the entire period in order to provide some continuity. It was hoped that they could be trained well enough to join contract archaeological projects elsewhere, in the future. When the excavation was completed we held an Open Day. Four boat loads of people—about 100 in all, or one in 10 of the Palikur population on the river—made their way upriver to visit Kwap and were guided by Neves from test pit to test pit as he explained the soil profiles and described artefacts found and suggested links with oral history. The degree of interest and enthusiasm far outweighed our expectations. . . .

Rethinking Research Questions

The research questions with which we began fieldwork asked whether the Aristé-style artefacts found on two of the sites were more widespread, whether additional styles could be located at deeper levels on particular sites and whether archaeological research, supported by oral-historical research, could illuminate questions of the complexity of occupation in this part of the coastal Amazon region. In particular, we were interested in the possibility of anthropogenic landscapes that might indicate that complex societies had existed some 500 km north of the moundbuilding investigated by Roosevelt (1991) at the mouth of the Amazon. An additional interest was whether rumours of a shell-mound (known in Brazil by the Tupi word *sambaqui*) were true. Of all of these sites, we were interested in whether and how they are present in memories, their particular histories and whether they could be said to constitute heritage to local people.

Within days of arrival, in May 2000, we had learned the awkward truth that however important and relevant our research questions had seemed, the scholarly debates from which they emerge are worlds apart from everyday life in the Reserva. There, dominant concerns are the daily struggle to produce enough food; protect access to Indian lands; ensure health and, at least in 2000 in the biggest Palikur village, keep right with God in preparation for a Pentecostal rendering of Y2K and its possible apocalyptic outcomes (Capiberibe 2001; Passes 1998). In that context, our interest in the past and in ceramic shards that we claimed were worthless in monetary terms proved difficult to explain—especially given that we had money for wages, solar panels and an outboard motor. The constant fear of many Palikur that Brazilians were going to come and take their lands made some doubly suspicious. Thus, one of our biggest challenges was to develop research questions that have resonance and interest to local people, while trying to explain archaeological work.

One of the ways we chose to do the latter was by bringing with us a large format full-colour book on Brazilian archaeology, which we acquired at the exhibition known as the Brasil +500 Mostra de Redescobrimento, which had opened in São Paulo in 2000 as part of Brazilian celebrations of the 500th anniversary of its "discovery" (despite protestation from some of the more vocal indigenous groups that they had been there all along). Part of a celebratory discourse of the state's capacity to collect, the archaeological exhibition focused on the most prized ceramics in Brazil, most of which were labelled by place of origin, the contemporary collection from which they were sourced and, for the most part, the culture which they were purported to represent. Unfortunately, in this context the collection of photographs of urns and ceramics in the book (Scatamacchia and Barreto 2000) was interpreted as proof that archaeology was a seeking after treasures: implicitly promoting the idea of artefacts as commodities and undermining our claims that we were not there to collect pots or make a profit. Reflecting on our idea of archaeology, the phrase we came up with to describe archaeology, in conjunction with local leadership, was *ikiska anavi wayk* or the study of "things left behind in the ground." Eighteen months later when 22 people had been trained in excavation techniques and were learning to read soil profiles at the test pits, the dialogics of reciprocal-learning had produced a very different phrase: *ivegboha amekenegben gidukwankis*—"reading the tracks of the ancestors."

The switch of explanatory terms for archaeology reflects the extent to which participatory and ethnographic research had shifted our focus from material culture and ceramic types to questions of what it means, historically and contemporarily, to dwell in this landscape. This was far more than a learning of a new phrase. It marked a different understanding of a local way of doing history in which past and present are part of a continuous sequence of actions and in which history is a form of mapping and geography is stored in narratives. . . .

Reworking Research Practices

Mutuality, rather than control, is a delicate matter not easily achieved. This is particularly so when the goals of scholarship require methodologies that produce valid results. A number of issues became particular challenges that needed careful resolution: questions of power and empowerment; notions of consultation, debate and mutuality; the difficulty of essentialist histories and the encounter of archaeology with mythological historiography.

Power, Empowerment, and "Community"

The notion of "community" has been deconstructed by many scholars as well as several Urucauá residents who are all too familiar with the use of the word in development discourse. Some were quick to challenge our occasional use of the term, asking who within the community would benefit the most from the work we proposed. The questions pointed to an awareness that the power that comes with empowerment cannot be considered neutral or without a context. An entire community cannot be empowered simultaneously; certain individuals will be more empowered than others, with the implication that empowerment activities alter the social landscape as they proceed.

Over time, a series of difficult interactions with one particular individual who had initially become central to our work taught us that empowerment activities all too readily benefit individuals. This dynamic is exacerbated in a context where participating in paid archaeological or oral historical work is inevitably constructed as a route to the prized goal of sharing in the benefits and skills of what is spoken of as "outside": that is, modernity. A modernist version of individuality—of the individual as "an homogeneous, bounded, unitary entity" in Brubaker and Cooper's words (2000, 17)—is a highly desirable way of being for some who prefer to replace relations of reciprocity between household and/or kin groups with waged and hierarchical relationships that affirm individuality. In this context waged labour such as that practised in archaeological work tends to atomise people. Status accrues with wealth and, as a corollary, status accrues with the ability to become appointed to community development projects run by outsiders. If a person has an agenda of becoming a power-player in local society, participation in a project such as ours becomes a means to an end that can be disruptive to local social relations.

Notions of empowerment that are implicit in many models of participatory research rest on an assumption of the zero-sum model, where power is transferred from powerful to powerless. Stated thus, the naïveté is all too obvious. Yet only in-depth, long-term fieldwork can acquaint practitioners with the complexities of local power dynamics in a village setting, for very little of this is available to outsiders as discursive knowledge; it can only be discovered through observation and experience. Thus, without long-term fieldwork, one's inability to navigate networks of power makes hazardous activities such as public archaeology. It can take months for outsiders to understand local politics well enough to see how one's interests are being manoeuvred to serve particular agendas. To paraphrase the biblical injunction, public archaeologists should be as harmless as doves and as spry as snakes. . . .

Conclusions

While many archaeologists remain dismissive of public archaeology, in contexts like the jungles on an indigenous people's reservation in northern Brazil the only practical means by which archaeology might be pursued is via a process of public participation. Participatory research shifted our understanding of heritage from one that focuses on material culture to one that focuses on the heritage of skills that are required, historically and contemporarily, to dwell in this landscape. In our experience, this shift enabled an engagement with different ways of understanding time and land and compelled the rethinking of the production of archaeological knowledge. The work challenged notions of heritage, ethics, historiography, practices of research and assumptions about community participation. Such an approach to field research is challenging, but in the process both ethnography and archaeology can begin to engage in the production of knowledge that is grounded in principles of archaeological science as well as in indigenous knowledge.

Section VII

Africa

On the vast and diverse continent of Africa, the past has been mobilized to legitimize colonialism, serve nationalism, and provide a means for liberation. The histories and humanity of Indigenous peoples have been erased through colonialism and apartheid, and frozen in the "ethnographic present" by Western anthropologists and scientists who have treated the continent as a cultural and biological laboratory. (For a comprehensive review of the intersections of archaeology and politics in multiple contexts, see Shepherd 2002.) Moringe L. Parkipuny, Masai leader and human rights activist, articulated this concern to the United Nations: "We are looked down at as evolutionary relics of past primitive ages and considered an outright disgrace to the national image" (1994, 78).

Although the African past is relevant to people worldwide and humanity's heritage, archaeology and anthropology have largely been divorced from the interests of the majority of Africa's Indigenous peoples. While significant funding and media attention are given to efforts searching for human origins (due in large part to the work of the Leakey family) and the histories of domestication on the continent, little has been given to investigations of the more recent past. Beyond the realm of human origins searches, African scholarship has been widely marginalized on the worldwide stage. This was noted over a decade ago by archaeologist Peter Schmidt who stated: "The important and highly visible Leakey investigations assured the dominance of colonial archaeology in postcolonial eastern African and served as a powerful model of how archaeology should be funded for much of the continent, a model that influenced how African governments treated and viewed archaeology in subsequent decades" (1995, 123).

Colonial rule on the continent ended in the twentieth century, but its legacies persist in archaeology and anthropology. Since independence, African states have espoused policies of assimilation and expropriation of land, threatening Indigenous survival. Archaeology and anthropology have been employed to bolster nationalist endeavors, creating tensions between anticolonialist and nationalist agendas. Joe Watkins characterizes Africa as "relatively quiet concerning Indigenous perspectives on archaeology" (2005, 439). Indeed, in comparison to such regions as North America and Oceania, there is a notable lack of Indigenous writers and scholarship on Indigenous archaeological perspectives. However, as Watkins predicted, these perspectives are becoming visible as researchers increase their engagement with local communities (2005, 439).

This section begins with a consideration of ethics and practice on the African continent, providing a theoretical basis for collaboration, engagement, and sensitivity to context and politics. In the excerpt from "Situational Ethics and Engaged Practice: The Case of Archaeology in Africa," Martin Hall lays bare the complexities and interrelatedness of power, resistance, and rejection in the "new network society." Hall problematizes representations of Africa as a place of origins frozen in time, and traces archaeological approaches over the last two centuries. His specific focus is South Africa, where mid-twentieth century apartheid "took precedents of colonial control, underpinned them with a pervasive religious morality, and established a society organized by race and privilege that persisted long after similar systems of ethics had been discredited in other parts of the world and after all other African colonial regimes had been replaced by forms of majority rule" (Hall 2005, 181). He asks: "What ethics are appropriate for this contemporary network society, with all its crosscutting complexity?" Hall urges us beyond the ethics of the civilizing mission, of liberation and nationalism, and of scientific inquiry, arguing instead for situational ethics that account for context and power among researchers and communities positioned in social contexts. The relationality and situatedness that Hall highlights are central to decolonizing archaeological practice.

Peter Schmidt's "Using Archaeology to Remake History in Africa," published in the 1995 volume *Making Alternative Histories: The*

Practice of Archaeology and History in Non-Western Settings (Schmidt and Patterson 1995), directly addresses power relationships and the control of research. This formative piece challenged the historical erasures of African peoples and Western domination of African scholarship. Schmidt attempts to extract us from European epistemologies and colonial histories, while arguing that archaeology can be a tool to build a distinctly alternative and African history. State-supported museums and white prehistorians have long dominated the production of knowledge about the African past. To combat this inequality, Schmidt encourages us to revalue African contributions to science and technological innovations and to allow Africans to produce their own historical knowledge under the leadership of African scholars. Students must be trained to devise research problems that address important historical issues, to challenge interpretations of the African past, and to incorporate African epistemologies of time and space.

Sven Ouzman's succinct "Another World: Archaeology and Intellectual Property" highlights the important links between archaeology and intellectual property, globally and in an African context. He offers examples of commercial and intellectual appropriations, noting the tensions between protecting and sharing knowledge.

In "The Roles of Applied and Development Anthropology and Archaeology among the San of Botswana," Robert Hitchcock offers a reflective perspective on his surveys among the San people during the 1970s. He relates the dismay of San community members when they learned that the research team from the University of New Mexico Kalahari Project was not there to help with what they needed most. Questioning the value of archaeology in this context, he reshaped project objectives to respond to San needs, particularly land rights issues. Though Hitchcock acknowledges that the project yielded mixed results, it was successful in compiling archaeological, ethnohistorical, and ethnographic data that demonstrated the long-term San occupation of areas being turned into ranchland. In hindsight, it marked a pivotal shift in collaborative research practice as San communities began to set agenda and participate in the work.

A series of case studies (Berte; Moser et al.; Parker Pearson and Ramilisonina) illustrate engagement with Indigenous communities, innovative methods, and attentiveness to contexts, ethics, and relations. Sekou Berte relates efforts to mesh Indigenous knowledge with archaeological evidence in "Indigenous Perception of Cultural Heritage and its Management: A Cursory Blueprint among the Senufo in the Sikasso Region of Mali." As an Indigenous community member, Berte is in a unique position to understand and incorporate Indigenous concepts of landscape and memory, alongside mainstream archaeological techniques (for example, field walking) and ethnographic methods (for instance, interviews).

The Egyptian past has been appropriated by Western scholars since the nineteenth century (and by other colonizers, such as the Romans before that). Stephanie Moser, Darren Glazier, James E. Phillips, Lamya Nasser el Nemr, Mohammed Saleh Mousa, Rascha Nasr Aiesh, Susan Richardson, Andrew Conner, and Michael Seymour collaborated on "Transforming Archaeology through Practice" to report on a community-based archaeology project in the city of Quseir, along Egypt's Red Sea coast. This project was the first of its kind in Egypt, a place where local people have been systematically left out of processes of researching and stewarding the past. Moser and associates acknowledge the importance of heritage to people's perceptions of themselves, the places they live, and their place in the world. They recognize that local communities can make significant intellectual contributions to understanding archaeological sites, and they seek to engage this transformative potential. They present a practical discussion of their strategies—communication and collaboration, employment and training, public presentation, interview and oral history, educational resources, a photographic and video archive, and community-controlled merchandising—stressing not only the *why* of collaboration but also the *how*.

This section concludes with the first of two excerpts from "Public Archaeology and Indigenous Communities," in which Mike Parker Pearson and Ramilisonina explore distinctions and overlaps of "local" and "indigenous" concepts while discussing strategies of public involvement in the central highlands of Madagascar. They describe archaeology as complementary to Tandroy ways of knowing the past. Though Ramilisonina is Malagasy, they note the importance of collaborating with a Tandroy colleague who helps break through local suspicions of outsiders. They advocate for attentiveness to local contexts, recognizing that the "local" is inextricable from the "global" and acknowledging that decolonizing efforts require responsibilities to multiple communities at multiple scales.

33

Situational Ethics and Engaged Practice: The Case of Archaeology in Africa

Martin Hall

Ethics at the Margins

My approach to issues of ethics at the margins of the network society will be through the lens of archaeological practice in parts of Africa. Anthropology in Africa takes ethical issues to their limits: the moral claims of colonization and enlightenment and the subsequent castigation of such positions as the epitome of unethical practice, the extremes of apartheid and the case for a "militant anthropology" (Scheper-Hughes 1995), the rise of new nation-states built around historical identities and subsequent collapses into economic disaster, dictatorship, war, or genocide, the diaspora of African intellectuals to European and North American universities, the infinite needs of education, health care, and other social services, against which claims for resources for anthropological research appear obscene. Against this, Africa has a historical identity of unrivaled depth that includes the origins of both humanity and anatomically modern humans, the longest known tradition of art, which poses complexities of interpretation beyond the conceptual capabilities of Europe's languages, the independent domestication of plants and animals in several centers, and the development of complex societies along the Nile that connected equatorial Africa to the Mediterranean, early urban civilizations in West and southern Africa, and syncretic African/Arab cultures along the length of the east coast (Hall 1996). . . .

Excerpted from Hall, Martin. 2005. Situational Ethics and Engaged Practice: The Case of Archaeology in Africa. In *Embedding Ethics*, ed. L. Meskell and P. Pels, 169–94. Oxford: Berg.

What ethics are appropriate for this contemporary network society, with all its crosscutting complexity? What principles are appropriate for the practice of archaeology in Africa (and particularly—because it is the context from which I write—in South Africa), now and in the future?

Although Hardt and Negri's point that "clinging to the primacy of the concept of truth can be a powerful and necessary form of resistance" (2000, 155) still stands, it is also clear that simple dichotomies between relative and absolute knowledge are misrepresentations that serve as distractions. As Donna Haraway showed some time ago, claims that all knowledge is socially constructed lead to "a kind of epistemological electro-shock therapy which, far from ushering us into the high stakes tables of the game of contesting public truths, lays us out on the table with self-induced multiple personality disorder" (1991, 186). The issue was—and is—how to get the benefits of new knowledge, critique, and ethics in the same frame: "how to have simultaneously an account of radical historical contingency for all knowledge claims and knowing subjects, a critical practice for recognizing our own 'semiotic technologies' for making meanings, and a no-nonsense commitment to faithful accounts of a 'real' world, one that can be partially shared and friendly to earth-wide projects of finite freedom, adequate material abundance, modest meaning in suffering, and limited happiness" (Haraway 1991, 187). Bruno Latour develops Haraway's position further through a close anthropological reading of science-in-action. For Latour, questions of whether "reality exists" or whether scientific knowledge is "absolute" are irrelevant. The purpose of "science studies" is to assist science in "sorting out the 'cosmos' from an 'unruly shambles'" by developing a "politics of things" (Latour 1999, 22).

In considering the knowledge claims of the social sciences, Bent Flyvbjerg has argued that all effective inquiry will be contextualized and, consequently, that appropriate ethics will be situational. Flyvbjerg argues that social behavior is context-specific: "the problem in the study of human activity is that every attempt at a context-free definition of an action, that is, a definition based on abstract rules or laws, will not necessarily accord with the pragmatic way an action is defined by the actors in a concrete social situation" (2001, 42). His response is to develop Aristotle's concept of phronesis—practical wisdom—to include power. Building on the tradition of Nietzsche and following Foucault and Bourdieu, Flyvbjerg argues that social behavior is always penetrated by power.

What are the implications of this position for the ethics of practice? Because such research is always shaped by context, researchers necessarily position themselves, in one way or another, in relation to one or more reference groups within the social context they are studying.

This is evident in the overview of archaeological practice in Africa. With the wisdom of hindsight, we can see clearly how early archaeology was aligned with the reference group of explorers and colonial administrators, whether Napoleon's generals who directed the exploration of Egypt, social evolutionists who believed in Europe's civilizing mission in Africa, or district commissioners who believed that orderly categorization and scientific reports underpinned effective rule. We can also see how the nationalist archaeologies of the mid-twentieth century were aligned with the objectives of independence movements and newly independent governments—how interpretations such as Cheikh Anta Diop's argument for the southern diffusion of Egyptian civilization met the needs of postcolonial administrators attempting to build the instruments of civil society. More controversially, because it is a past that is still upon us, it can be argued that South Africa's dominant paradigm of archaeology-as-science appealed to a reference group of white academics caught between the opposing forces of a racist state, which they rejected, and black nationalism, to which they could not easily affiliate.

If one accepts the case for situational ethics and the inevitable alignment between the researcher and one or more reference groups within the society that is being studied, then it follows that ethical research will recognize the nexus of knowledge, power, and polities and declare its alignments explicitly. Again, this can be related specifically to the history of archaeology in Africa.

In rejecting a motion condemning apartheid at its Botswana meeting in 1984, the Southern African Association of Archaeologists was not saying that it supported the apartheid state. Rather, its South African and U.S. members were arguing that politics has no place in the pursuit of knowledge and therefore the resolution was unethical. Situational ethics turns this argument on its head. In failing to acknowledge that the creation of new knowledge in South African archaeology was the result of a play of interests and resources with political consequence, those opposing the motion were obfuscating the issue through an indefensible claim for context-free, absolute ways of knowing about the past; it was their position that was unethical. Ethical research requires an explicit consciousness of the role of power: "Who gains, and who loses? Through what kinds of power relations? And is it desirable to do so? Of what kind of power relations are those asking these questions themselves a part?" (Flyvbjerg 2001, 131).

Recognizing the role of power and politics in research is, then, central to an appropriate ethics. Such recognition also allows an appropriate position with regard to empirical evidence. Archaeology is a practical discipline in which fieldwork and the demonstrated ability to work with "hard evidence" are particularly valorized, a tradition that is further complicated by gender. A concern for politics and social context has often been caricatured as "soft" and "feminine," the recourse of those who do not have the endurance for excavations and prolonged data analysis.

But once we see (as Haraway, Latour, and others have shown) that the dichotomy between "reality" and "relativity" is an artificial construct, the requirement for situational ethics leads naturally into a requirement for ethics in assembling and managing evidence. This is because, as Flyvbjerg has shown, every interpretation in contextualized research must be based on claims of validity that are built up from the rationality of the detailed empirical data. Such validity claims are arguments that stand until better, empirically based arguments are developed. The objective of such work (and therefore its "morality," although Flyvbjerg does not use the term) is to increase "the capacity of individuals, organizations, and society to think and act in value-rational terms" (Flyvbjerg 2001, 130). In other words, because situational ethics requires that research be explicitly located in a social context, it is not enough to satisfy oneself (the "sovereign mind" or "brain-in-a-vat" of the Cartesian and Kantian traditions of absolute knowledge [Latour 1999]) or one's professional colleagues. Reference groups must also be satisfied and persuaded through interpretation and argument that is based on the rationality of evidence.

In making the connection with reference groups, "situational archaeologists" need to be particularly conscious of the insidious qualities of time. In the Cartesian tradition of archaeology-as-science, time is seen as an external dimension along with space, time is an axis of a graph on which archaeological observations are plotted. But time is a more complicated concept than this allows. As Fabian (1983) has shown, the denial of coevalness was one of anthropology's founding strategies, and, as this overview of archaeological practice has shown, this same denial has persisted to the present day. An ethical practice for the network society needs to recognize the importance of "intersubjective time" (Fabian 1983), allowing histories to interrelate rather than freezing "cultures" into "ages" or ethnically labeled boxes in the style of *Africa: The Art of a Continent*.

Understanding the role of empirical evidence sheds light on one of the stranger aspects of archaeological practice in southern Africa. Since 1994, when South Africa gained a postapartheid constitution and a representative government, the general interest in archaeology has declined. Student demand has fallen off, and university departments have closed. Museum budgets have been cut, and resources available for new fieldwork are at an all-time low. Many archaeologists have been surprised and shocked by this reversal, having expected the opposite, given that archaeology is the only route into precolonial black history. There is a stark contrast with earlier times that seems, at first glance, bizarre. Thus, when Gertrude Caton-Thompson presented the results of her fieldwork at Great Zimbabwe at a conference in Johannesburg in 1931, her report was headline news not only in the Transvaal but also a thousand miles to the south in Cape Town. Ian Smith's successionist Rhodesia of the 1960s and 1970s was sufficiently concerned to preserve the "white civilization" line of interpretation that Rhodes had initiated that the security forces took action against archaeologists who disagreed. But when this history of the role of evidence is set within its context, the paradox is solved. Caton-Thompson's reference group was politically and economically dominant and demanded to see and debate the evidence. Today South African archaeology, which eschewed the politics of context and is an overwhelmingly white discipline, has a reference group made up largely of its own practitioners.

But how should an appropriate reference group be identified? Flyvbjerg leaves this question open. For him the primary ethical imperatives are recognizing that research is contextual in the first place and then seeking to increase a society's internal capacity for "value-ethics" over contingent "instrumental-ethics." But in social contexts such as Africa's, where social and economic differentiation is far more acute than in the West and the North and where choices of research priority may be literally a matter of life and death, such an approach is incomplete.

Here it is helpful to combine Haraway's earlier formulation with Nancy Fraser's work on the "postsocialist position." In considering an appropriate agenda for feminist inquiry, Haraway proposes "a doctrine of embodied objectivity." This involves "seeing" from the perspective of the "subjugated" not because people who are oppressed are "innocent" but because "in principle they are least likely to allow denial of the critical and interpretative core of all knowledge . . . 'subjugated' standpoints are preferred because they seem to promise more adequate, sustained, objective, transforming accounts of the world" (1991, 191). For her part, Fraser is concerned with social justice and the reconnection of political economy and the "symbolic order." This project necessarily requires an ethical position from which forms of injustice are identified—a position that Fraser opens up by developing Habermas's concept of a public sphere, understood as "a theater in modern societies in which political participation is enacted through the medium of talk": "something like Habermas's idea of the public sphere is indispensable to critical social theory and to democratic political practice . . . no attempt to understand the limits of actually existing late-capitalist democracy can succeed without in some way or another making use of it" (1997, 70–71). Fraser argues that Habermas's founding concept needs elaboration and modification, allowing for a "plurality of competing publics" and, in particular, "subaltern counterpublics" where subordinate groups develop counterdiscourses that formulate "oppositional interpretations" of "identities, interests and needs" (1997, 81).

Taken together, Haraway's and Fraser's conceptualizations identify both the criteria for an appropriate positioning for an ethical, contextualized research and the channels in which this engagement can take place in the network society. In this view, anthropologists—and archaeologists—are not all-knowing experts who defend their rights as a privileged professional caste. Nor can they be divorced from the context in which they work; their contextualization is inevitable, if often unrecognized. Consequently, the issue is not whether the concept of ethics is still relevant—whether the practice of archaeology in Africa can be "beyond ethics." The issue is rather to make the ethics of practice explicit, empowering, in David Harvey's (2000) phrase, "insurgent architects" who can contribute to the competing publics and "counterpublics" that serve to challenge and limit the hegemony of dominant interests in our network society.

34

Using Archaeology to Remake History in Africa

Peter R. Schmidt

A major intellectual concern of African as well as some Africanist scholars since about 1965 has been how to liberate historical knowledge in Africa from the paradigmatic constraints of European historiography and the colonial library (Mudimbe 1988). Attempts have been made to develop new avenues of inquiry, new sources of historical evidence, and new theoretical perspectives. Each of these developments, beginning with an emphasis on African oral traditions and oral history and more recently finding expression in Marxist critiques of African history, has led to important new ways of constructing the African past. Each in its own way, nonetheless, is constrained by theoretical or analytical frameworks that arise out of European epistemologies or that remain bounded by evidence contained within the colonial library.

A prominent paradox in African historical studies is that archaeology's potential for developing alternative histories has not been fully realized. Because most of ancient African history is accessible only through archaeological approaches, there is compelling reason to refocus attention on archaeological constructions of the past as a means to build an independent, authentic, and distinctly African history. At the same time, archaeology is a distinctly Western activity. Its governing paradigms and epistemologies often conflict with African historical needs, views of the past, and ways of structuring time and space. Thus the paradox unfolds:

Excerpted from Schmidt, Peter R. 1995. Using Archaeology to Remake History in Africa. In *Making Alternative Histories: The Practice of Archaeology and History in Non-Western Settings*, ed. P. R. Schmidt and T. C. Patterson, 119–47. Santa Fe: School of American Research Press.

a repertoire of techniques and approaches that promise significant ways of recuperating African pasts heretofore obscured is accompanied by theoretical assumptions that are often out of tune with African sensibilities needs, and structures. . . .

Alternatives for Making History in Africa

One idea that holds hope for the future is archaeological inquiry into scientific and technological accomplishments in African settings, with the goal of understanding how and why distinctive technological innovations and variations arose out of the African environment. Innovation need not be measured relative to events and developments in other world areas; it must first be comprehended within its own cultural and historical contexts. Only archaeology has the techniques required to document ancient processes of innovation and scientific experimentation. The importance of this project lies not in potential revelations that might impact modern science. Rather, it lies in the recognition that it is possible to unearth original African contributions to science and, as Irele (1991, 68) put it, that "the fund of positive knowledge available to our traditional societies has yet to be seriously investigated and made available to the world." Irele sees this project as an African contribution to human knowledge about the past in which Africa takes neither a dominant nor a subordinate place but contributes in a way that revalues and recuperates that knowledge.

The revaluation of African scientific experience is one way to remove the science/intuition dichotomy and its science/ritual variant that perpetually diminish the African experience. Revaluation focuses on the pragmatic lessons that can be learned from the ways in which stress and difficulties were overcome in the past and from understanding what "inherent scientific values" underlie and unify successful experimentation with the natural world. It discovers a confident socio-scientific posture in the past that offers a model of success which in turn can help people confront the contradictions of the present (e.g., development failures attributed to insufficient technological know-how) and meet the challenges of the future.

This perspective was one of the guiding principles behind the development of archaeology in Tanzania. Another important principle was that an African archaeology should produce its own historical knowledge under the leadership of African scholars who value the search for an archaeology appropriate to Africa. This requires the training of undergraduate students working on African problems at the B.A. level within an African setting, a goal also pertinent to higher-degree training that is currently met at only a few African institutions. It also requires a focus on research problems that have the potential to address important historical issues, issues that challenge interpretations about the past of African science, trade, technology, urbanization, environmental relationships, symbolic life, and so forth. The curriculum at the University of Dar es Salaam incorporates a strong program of archaeological research design and implementation from the first year on, so students start early in their training to "think theory" and experience its relationship to field methods, laboratory analysis, and interpretation.

One proven way to proceed with student training was to continue making inquiries into the development of technologies that followed innovative tracks in Africa. The development of the preheating technique in iron smelting, for example, is a remarkable African contribution to technological innovation that demands to be understood more completely (Schmidt and Avery 1978). Techniques that overcame the presence of phosphorus in iron are another of the many aspects of ancient iron technology that invite further inquiry elsewhere in Africa (Childs 1995; Schmidt and Childs 1995). Archaeological evidence for the development of economic systems that degraded forested environments 1,000 to 2,500 years ago provides views reshaping previous ideas that African civilizations changed because of movements of ethnic and language groups. Such new views of the past encompass practical lessons to be learned from the early successes and failures of human societies to manage different environments and offer antidotes to nationalist tendencies to glorify complex societies in the past.

University-related research that first addressed these concerns in Tanzania took place in 1986 in the western Usambara Mountains, a locale suggested by students who observed similarities between the environment required for an early Iron Age technology as documented in western Tanzania and the well-watered Usambara Mountains of eastern Tanzania. Field research was structured so that students found most of the sites, among which was an early Iron Age iron-smelting site on the western and highly degraded slopes of the mountains. These finds were important in demonstrating that an early technology using preheating principles was also practiced on the opposite side of the country, in the area of an ethnic group (the Shambaa) that is close to and has some affinities with two of the most prominent ethnic groups (the Chagga and Pare) of eastern Tanzania (Schmidt 1988; Schmidt and Karoma 1987).

These initial research results, obtained under University of Dar es Salaam sponsorship, led to a perceptible softening of earlier subtle ethnic opposition to archaeology, with scholars from northeastern Tanzania taking particular interest in this trans-territorial phenomenon that linked widely separated parts of the country. The "national" characteristics of these discoveries, also represented in the ethnic diversity of the students pictured in a newspaper photo of the excavations, created for the first time an image of archaeology as a national enterprise with the power to make history that was African.

The success of the first research season was followed in the second year by research in an archaeologically unknown part of Tanzania's coastal zone, an area spurned by colonial archaeologists who were interested in the monumental sites of the littoral. The monumental sites, long known for their remarkable tombs, mosques, and coral houses, had come to be identified with the advent of urbanization and civilization along the East African coast. The growth of these complex communities was attributed to the arrival of Shirazi and Omani immigrants from the Persian Gulf during the first half of the second millennium A.D. This diffusionist explanation holds that Islam and trade were among the most important cultural forces leading to economic as well as community organization and coherence.

The history of archaeological research that incorporated this diffusionist package shows a steadfast fixation on the exotic, the imported, and the Islamic. Extensive archaeological investigations along the coast by Kirkman (1963) and Chittick (1974, 1984) at important urban "medieval" sites such as Kilwa, Manda, Mombasa, and Gedi had revealed evidence for earlier, first-millennium populations who also lived on these sites. But evidence of the earlier settlement was reported in very summary form, the ceramics were assigned pejorative labels such as "kitchen ware," and interpretation of the ancient remains was omitted (Chittick 1974, 1984)—an archaeological approach that effectively erased such communities from the landscape (see Handsman and Lamb Richmond 1995, excerpted in Chapter 21 this volume). Whatever interpretation did occur denigrated these early communities through negative naming of artifact categories. No questions about socioeconomic organization, population size, political organization, affinities with other settlements, industry, or diet—all conventional questions of the era—were asked about these indigenous communities. The only germane research goals were those of explaining the influences of foreign populations on trade conducted by these communities and of elaborating histories by explicating the few written historical accounts that touched upon them.

The "foreign civilizing" paradigm, while offensive to the sensibilities of African populations (Trigger 1990), nevertheless was still very much in vogue for the East African monumental sites and in no danger of collapsing when the second year's research under the university's new archaeology program began in 1987. Student researchers and instructors selected a "dead" zone that they thought would not soon capture the attention of investigators: low-lying hills with several small lakes approximately 10 to 20 kilometers from the Indian Ocean and located about 100 kilometers south of Dar es Salaam. The results from that season are significant from several perspectives. They revealed for the first time that during the late first millennium A.D., large communities with trade goods and practicing a local industry such as iron fabrication and possible fabrication of copper goods were located in the immediate hinterland adjacent to the littoral. These communities bore close affinities to the long-ignored communities buried under the coastal monumental sites and also found elsewhere along the coast (e.g., Chittick 1974, 1984; Kirkman 1963).

This research was also significant because it took place in an area in which there has been tremendous ethnic fluidity over the last century, with many ethnic entities located on the same landscape. The ethnic pluralism of the region and its significant change in ethnic makeup over the last century, when combined with the transformation of the landscape wrought by cashew farming, contributed to an erasure of history from that landscape. These characteristics meant that the archaeology could not be identified with a particular ethnic group and therefore could not easily be co-opted by any group. This in turn meant lessened political tensions over the development of ancient history for an area in which history had been mostly silenced. . . .

The Search for an Indigenous Archaeology

I want to return to the question of making histories that provide hope for a better future and that open African capacities for development. Much of the research just discussed touches on these issues, and they are also addressed by Bassey Andah, whose agenda clearly includes questions about control, identity, liberation, and the future (Andah 1990, 2):

> Authentic excavators of African cultural history need to descend into the burrow of Africa's invisible silent times . . . and strive for control of the text of our experience. Such excavation is thus motivated by the need to have the power to force others to recognize our African presence and rights to be Africans and to own what God has given us: namely, our African continent and identity as Africans.

The language Andah uses in this text (1990) emphasizes power and control over identity while also stressing that identification with "significant ancestors" is liberating, that it reveals how and why the past exists in the present and the value this has for a "future meaningful existence." Andah sees the key to constructing an Africa with "an enlarged future" as lying in the process of regeneration, wherein Africans "return or journey back to our African homes, natural, social and spiritual, of our yesterdays [so] that our present will accede to merge with our past, and to emerge from the past in an enlarged future" (Andah 1990, 3).

We have seen in the language of both Andah and Irele an emphasis on revaluation, regeneration, and return. Irele, though not an archaeologist, echoes his fellow Nigerian's concerns with the past and with a fundamental renegotiation of ideological relationships and languages of power to reclaim and recuperate the past for Africa. For Andah, this journey back depends on the strength of "spiritual" bridge building, an assertion apparently contradictory to his hope that a revolutionized historiography will result from a history transformed from storytelling into a vigorous scientific search for the truth through anthropology (Andah 1990, 4).

The contradiction between spiritual bridges and scientific searches is momentarily disorienting, yet if I understand Andah properly, his message lies in the language he uses—metaphors of ritual grounds in the past, spiritual journeys, identity with ancestors—all drawn from the deep wellspring of African life, sensibility, and history. Andah is recasting the archaeological discourse so that it is reconfigured to fit African mental constructs, a bold departure that promises to threaten those who control the production of knowledge about the past in Africa. Andah's program gives notice that there are now groups prepared to challenge those who control the production of knowledge, inevitably leading to negotiation for a new language of hegemony. As he observes, power depends on language.

Elsewhere Andah argues that there is a history of Africa that is distinctly African and that those who study it need to be uniquely equipped to unravel it. Andah explicitly argues that for any African history or archaeology to be relevant to an African audience, it must resonate effectively with an African cultural ethos. This view is more than the perspective that archaeology practiced in Africa must be aware of the historical sensibilities of the people among whom it is practiced (Schmidt 1983). Andah wants to push beyond this perspective to suggest that African archaeology needs to incorporate other "rich sources" with the goal of "re-enacting African cultural history" in such a way that it departs from "an archaeological discipline that often tries to create what may not have existed, rather than discovering and describing people, what they did and what happened to them" (Andah 1987, vii). We see here a view that resembles a "folkways" approach intended to construct a more animated narrative of everyday African life.

Andah's exploration of alternative methodologies assumes a commonality in the African experience, or an "African ethos." Although some will argue that making this assumption risks reducing rich variability in cosmology, belief systems, and historical experience among African peoples to a simple commonality, such a reaction would miss the importance of Andah's position. Though he fails to take his argument about what constitutes an African ethos farther, he makes clear that he thinks the cultural frames of reference in (most) reports and books written by Westerners about Africa assume that the "European cultural experience constitutes the image of universal man. As a result the framework is largely irrelevant for communicating the normative aspect of African cultural experience" (Andah 1987, viii).

Thus Andah's concern—as an African archaeologist—is the search for a normative African epistemology of time and space to which African practitioners of the discipline can subscribe. What room is there in which an Africanist archaeologist can operate successfully under these conditions? It is abundantly apparent that Andah is not arguing for a relativist view that assigns distinctive meanings to each archaeological region. The most important understanding arising from his discourse is that inferential interpretations in Africa, if they are to be assessed as pertinent and meeting criteria of reasonable fit, must be based on deep cultural understandings.

Foreign investigators are on difficult ground here, for they lack socialization in African languages and cultures. I believe, however, that there are domains of inquiry that may reveal important new paths allowing the merging of Western methods with African experience. Here I take inspiration from Irele as well as from a challenge Mudimbe (1988, 198) sets out when he suggests that there be a "reconceptualization of scientific method and the relationships that 'scientific knowledge' might have with other forms or types of knowledge." How then might we proceed to develop a science of archaeology that incorporates African ways of living and seeing?

Consulting with the ancestors and revisiting sacred ritual grounds, as Andah puts it, are essential components of African cycles of change and continuity that must be integrated into an African archaeology. For example, ritual events ordered by rhythmed time often leave behind clear and powerful physical signposts that are clearly remembered in the oral histories of African peoples. Such events are often remembered longer than events that may once have had a linear order, say, in clan genealogies, because such important ritual moments are marked by mnemonic devices such as sacred groves or trees that are preserved in the landscape today. Thus a royal shrine tree where a king was buried in a beer boat, or where a king was ritually buried during his installation rites, preserves the memory of the transformational event long after the waning of other oral records. Mnemonic systems present an enormously important extant record of rhythmed time in African cultures (Schmidt 1978). In many cases these indigenous African archaeologies are accessible to Western techniques of investigation. We must understand, however, the dynamics of social life that create the nonlinear characteristics of African ritual time, and our archaeology must be sufficient to account for a flow of events as rhythmic pulses that mark significant social and political transformations.

These ideas complement Andah's position and pose a challenge to both his fellow African archaeologists trained in the principles of Western archaeology and to those of us Westerners who have been exploring our own comprehensions of and reactions to African systems of thought and knowledge, insofar as they transform and inform our practice of archaeology on the continent. How do we respond to Andah's call for a new language within the African past? How can we carry out his more pragmatic suggestion that the past can inform African people about lessons the past holds for environmental management and appropriate ideologies of governance? The second question is more easily addressed than the first. Some archaeologists, including Africanists, are doing so by redirecting their study of past environments toward affecting management policy in the present and future (Marquardt 1994; Schmidt 1994).

But the question of a new language of archaeology, like that of a memory that returns to the African past, is an issue few archaeologists are prepared to face. Our distance from such issues is significant, even within the Africanist community. One measure of that distance is seen in the separation between Africans and Westerners that continues in the production of knowledge. While Andah and his colleagues struggle to produce the only continuous indigenous journal of archaeology in black Africa, white archaeologists have recently joined together (Robertshaw 1990) to write a history of African archaeology that includes a contribution by only one black African archaeologist (see Okpoko 1991). This is symptomatic of widely differing access to global information systems, but more disquieting, it also signifies the de facto peripheralization of Africans in the writing and dissemination of their own histories. Until we overcome such fundamental problems, the possibility for Western archaeologists to be able to read, understand, and accept African archaeologies remains distant.

35

Another World: Archaeology and Intellectual Property

Sven Ouzman

As archaeology matures, it becomes necessarily encumbered with more rules, protocols and codes of conduct. Our concerns and their codification are necessary because many of our techniques, methods, hypotheses and paradigms derive from other disciplines like anthropology, the biological and physical sciences and geology, and were never intended for uniquely archaeological uses and consequences. Such disciplinary self-examination forces practitioners to consider the wider ethical, legal and sociopolitical aspects of their work. Accordingly, the last decade has seen increasing interest in intellectual property (IP) issues in archaeology and related fields (e.g., Nicholas and Bannister 2004, excerpted in Chapter 12 this volume).

IP has always been present, both positively in researchers acknowledging others' work and negatively, with people jealously guarding sites and committing plagiarism. But the increased participation of indigenous people in archaeological fieldwork, revisionism and theory generation, together with the exponential growth of legal and institutional "audit cultures," has made IP a primary concern. Southern Africa's archaeological fringes have been at the forefront of this trend with, for example, the successful biopiracy suit against Pfizer Pharmaceuticals by the Khomani over IP attached to the *Hoodia gordonia* cactus (Geingos and Ngakaeaja 2002). Similarly, the National Research Foundation has an "Indigenous Knowledge Systems" focus area that is wrestling with the multiple definitions and intertwinings of indigeneity present in South Africa.

Excerpted from Ouzman, Sven. 2005. Another World: Archaeology and Intellectual Property. *The Digging Stick* 22(2):16–17.

Recently the Working Group of Indigenous Minorities in Southern Africa (WIMSA), stung by real and perceived abuses by the media and a minority of anthropologists and archaeologists, formulated a San Media and Research Contract to "ensure that all San intellectual property (including images, traditional knowledge, music and other heritage components as recorded in any medium) is controlled and protected" (WIMSA 2001, 3). Many of us might baulk at, for example, paying a research fee or agreeing "not to publish any facts or portrayals that might be harmful or detrimental to the San," which impinges on academic freedom. Yet the contract corresponds to many institutional contracts governing the use of archaeological materials and knowledge.

To place these local developments in broader perspective we could turn to similar post-colonial contexts in India, South America and Australia where the archaeological community has and is going through teething pains in trying to balance academic, indigenous and commercial concerns. In this spirit I spent the last six months attending a law course called "Archaeology, relics and the law" (Cunningham 2005) and remain amazed at the schizophrenia of US attitudes to heritage and IP. On the one hand, private property is sacrosanct. Landowners legally own all artefacts on their property to do with as they please—keep, conserve, donate, destroy, even sell. Go, for example, to www.ebay.com, type in "artifact" and see arrowheads, potsherds, Civil War memorabilia and rock art sell for between 99 cents and $750,000. On the other hand, a sixth of the USA's 9,166,600 km^2 is federally owned (in 2000 South Africa had a fifth of its 1,219,090 km^2 owned by the state) and stealing, trading or transporting artefacts from these lands carry substantive fines of up to $250,000 and possible incarceration—more if human remains are involved. But even here complications arise. The Kennewick skull—found on federal land and initially repatriated to a Native American coalition for reburial—was, on appeal, handed over to eight non-Native anthropologists for study, thereby harming generally good Native American-archaeologist relations.

This tension between physical objects and knowledge surfaced locally in a recent *Mail & Guardian* article that reported influential heritage personalities championing the repatriation of the Taung skull and the Mapungubwe rhino to their places of origin. Quoting the article: "What is the benefit to the African continent of these objects being colonised in Western institutions? They should not be the preserve of intellectual research and scholarship; they are our source of pride and identity" (Macleod 2005). Counter-arguments pointed to Taung and Mapungubwe's remoteness, inadequate curatorial care and loss of research potential. Furthermore, Taung and Mapungubwe have become icons for a much wider constituency than descendant communities—all of us in Taung's case—or specific findspots. While repatriation is an issue we have yet to face fully, knowledge and objects can lead separate lives, requiring a certain generosity of spirit to avoid unhealthily exclusive claims on "heritage."

The South African coat of arms is a case in point. Though many San, as genetic and moral inheritors of much of our rock art heritage, would like to have been consulted on the use of the Linton fragment's rock-painted human figure, most are satisfied that their specific heritage is part of an inclusive state symbol. They are less pleased with commercial and intellectual appropriations of rock art by way of T-shirts, themed shopping centres and the like that misrepresents IP, forcing the production of a *Handbook on Heritage and Intellectual Property Rights*. Similarly, some heritages are specific, private or what Gabi Dolf-Bonekämper calls "hurtful memories" (2002), and not everyone has rights of access to these. Southern African archaeology has similar concerns—what are we going to repatriate and under what conditions? This could range from ever-contentious human remains to following a "catch-and-release" policy for excavated and collected artefacts that have been studied, alleviating storage and curatorial pressures. Moving away from objects, the use of Creative Commons licensing (www.creative commons.org) for access to and use of images and databases is ideally suited for educational and academic use, ensuring dissemination of knowledge and due acknowledgement of work.

That skill in knowing when to shield knowledge and objects, and when to share icons and insights is what will distinguish a successful 21st-century citizen from one unable or unwilling to consider their position in the history of the human family.

36

The Roles of Applied and Development Anthropology and Archaeology among the San of Botswana

Robert K. Hitchcock

Over half a century has passed since the Marshall family began their ground-breaking research with Ju/'hoansi (!Kung) San populations in the northern Kalahari Desert region of southern Africa (see Marshall 1976). Their important field studies reflected significant shifts in anthropology toward detailed and long-term investigations of indigenous peoples who traditionally hunted and gathered for their livelihoods and who now are involved in diversified systems of production and income generation (see Hitchcock 2004b; Marshall 1999; Marshall and Ritchie 1984; Shostak 1981, 2000).

More recently, anthropologists, including a group of people who formed the Kalahari Peoples Fund (KPF), have been applying the results of their investigations to solving problems faced by the people with whom they work. This is especially important in the case of indigenous populations who are considered to be some of the most disadvantaged groups in the world today (Maybury Lewis 1997; Saugestad 2001).

Anthropologists have helped San and other indigenous groups in Africa gain title to their lands. They have designed, implemented, monitored, and evaluated economic development projects aimed at helping San. Social scientists, including linguistic anthropologists, have helped record indigenous languages, and have developed curricular materials for the education of people in those languages. In addition, anthropologists have assisted organizations and communities in disaster relief

---

Excerpted from Hitchcock, Robert K. 2004. The Roles of Applied and Development Anthropology and Archaeology among the San of Botswana. *Botswana Notes and Records* 36:125–35.

programmes, and have helped improve health and nutritional conditions at the local level (Lee and Biesele 2002; Lee, Biesele, and Hitchcock 1996; Van Willigen 2002).

In general, archaeologists have played less of a role in the lives of indigenous peoples. When they did participate in the activities of contemporary populations, it was usually through doing interviews to ascertain the purpose of a particular object or site. Relatively few archaeologists attempted to apply anthropological theory and method to improving the quality of lives of their informants.

This situation is changing. Archaeologists are increasingly called upon by indigenous groups to help document their histories and preserve their cultural heritage. School curricula are being designed by archaeologists so children can learn about their own societies' pasts. Ethnohistoric, oral history, and archaeological information are now used more and more in land claims and water rights cases. Biological anthropology and bioarchaeology offer clues about the diet, health, and physical status of people. The study of garbage dumps is providing insights into waste management. Forensic studies shed light on the fate of victims of genocide and other human rights violations. . . .

Anthropology among the San: A Personal Perspective

I first went to the Kalahari Desert of southern Africa in August 1975, as an archaeologist to undertake work with a team of anthropologists from the University of New Mexico. We were interested in looking at the impacts of social, economic, and demographic change among the San. We undertook various kinds of anthropological and archaeological surveys and compiled a wide variety of data over the period of a year in the field.

One afternoon in 1976, I was confronted with a group of angry Tyua San from the village of Manxotae on the Nata River in northeastern Botswana. They demanded to know why I was "wasting my time," as they put it, mapping camps and interviewing people about "the old days." They told me that there was a chance that the Botswana government might take away their land, and they demanded to know why I was not trying to help them keep from being removed from their homes. They also asked that I help them get a bridge built across the Nata River so that their children would not have difficulties attempting to cross the river when it was in flood. I found out that one of the daughters of a woman who was a member of the local Parents Teachers Association had almost drowned attempting to cross the river to my camp earlier that day.

When I went to the Government Land Board to ask for a bridge over the Nata, I was told that the people there could not get a bridge. When I asked why, I was told that they were hunter-gatherers and therefore did not have a need for land or a bridge since they were "nomadic."

It was at this point that I began to question the utility of archaeology. I asked myself over and over again, what is the purpose of archaeology? What good does it do for people? Does it provide them with the means to raise their standards of living and enhance the quality of their lives?

The archaeologist with whom I studied as a graduate student at the University of New Mexico, Professor Lewis Binford, stressed repeatedly that the purpose of anthropology was to gain an understanding of why human beings do what they do. As he pointed out, an expansion in ethnographic knowledge in itself cannot enable us to increase our understanding of the past. What we need to do, he said, is to investigate the processes that shape human behaviour. Knowing those processes, he argued, will enhance our abilities to confront some of humanity's central problems such as poverty, racism, and gender and class inequality.

For the rest of the time I was in Botswana during that field session (until November, 1976), I concentrated on gathering data relevant to specific problems facing San populations. In so doing, I collaborated with my colleagues on the University of New Mexico Kalahari Project, Jim Ebert and Melinda Kelly. I also worked closely with the Technical Advisor to the Ngwnto Land Board in Central District, Axel Thoma, and the Secretary of the Land Board, Malebogo Oabile (see Ebert et al. 1976). We shared our data among ourselves and provided reports to the people with whom we were working at the field level, including the sub-land board Land and Board in Central District and the Bushmen Development Programme (later, the Remote Area Development Programme) in the Ministry of Local Government and Lands. Throughout the course of our research, the University of New Mexico Kalahari Project took great care to ensure informed consent and to keep sensitive information confidential along the lines recommended by the ethics statements of the American Anthropological Association. We also worked closely with the Bushmen Development Officer (BDO) (later, the Remote Area Development Officer) in designing criteria for use in evaluating proposals for research among San in Botswana.

San Land Rights Issues

The first topic with which we grappled was that relating to land rights. It turned out that the San's land rights were not respected by the dominant populations in the region where they lived or in Botswana generally. We were told repeatedly that since the San were "mobile hunter-gatherers," they had no need for land. We pointed out that, in fact, foraging peoples needed large areas of land where they could obtain wild plants and animals and other important resources. Based on data we collected in the eastern and northeastern Kalahari, we learned that the blocks of land needed by groups ranged from 400 square kilometers to 4,000 square kilometers in size.

The Botswana Government eventually provided some land to the San in the form of what they called "communal service centres" or "communal cells"—generally located in the midst of blocks of ranches, as was the case, for example in the western sandveld region of Central District at Malatswae, or in the midst of the 72 Hainaveld ranches in the southeastern part of Ngamiland (North West District). The problem was that these areas were much smaller areas than people needed in order to survive, averaging between 25 sq miles (64 square kilometers, 6,400 hectares), and 20,000 hectares, where local people were expected to make a living as farmers, herders, and ranch and farm labourers. The positive thing was that the San got land at all.

The University of New Mexico Kalahari Project, in conjunction with personnel at the Central District Council, compiled archaeological, ethnohistorical, and ethnographic data that demonstrated the long-term occupational history of those areas being considered as potential cattle ranches. Using Tswana Customary law, we were able to argue that San had long-term interests in specific areas and that their rights should be recognized. There were problems, admittedly. The Attorney General's Chambers' Litigation Consultant issued a statement to the Land Development Committee in 1978 that ruled that the "Masarwu" had no rights except right to hunting (Will 1978).

What we found during the course of our work was that virtually everyone in the area of the western sandveld felt that they had rights to land in the area, and, by definition, the vast majority of them had customary rights to land, having lived there for over a generation. At the same time, we found that there were literally thousands of people residing in and utilizing natural resources in the east-central Kalahari Desert. Few of these people had water rights in the area, and as a consequence, it was likely that they would be required to leave the area once it was turned into commercial ranches. In order to counteract the argument that San lacked a concept of territoriality and that they moved randomly over the Kalahari, we began a series of investigations on mobility patterns and regional space use.

We obtained ethnographic and oral history information on land-use patterns and territorial claims by various groups. We questioned informants on the areas that they covered for various purposes. We also asked about the boundaries of their areas, and this information was cross-checked with that from other people in the region. The data we obtained were plotted on aerial photographs and maps. Once the map-making was completed, we took the results back to the local communities and asked them to check the findings. Only after revisions were made did we begin to assess the ranges and territories of the San. This information was provided to the District Councils and the Botswana Government for land-use planning purposes.

Some of the recommendations for areas to be made communal land instead of commercial (private leasehold) land were followed by the Government of Botswana, as was the case, for example, in parts of western Central District and in the Nata River region, and in areas surrounding pans in the Kgalagadi District (see Lawry and Thoma 1978). Had these recommendations not been made, it is likely that much larger portions of Botswana would have become commercial livestock ranches under Botswana's Tribal Grazing Land Policy and the various donor-supported livestock projects that Botswana implemented in the 1970s and early-mid 1980s.

At the same time, there were sizable numbers of people, certainly several thousand, who were required to relocate to places outside of commercial ranches. It should be noted that the compensation paid to those people who lost their land was minimal, usually they were paid only for the assets that they had to leave behind (houses, fences, and trees). The University of New Mexico Kalahari Project and government land use planners argued repeatedly that the compensation paid to people for their losses should be expanded and diversified, and that losses of hunting and gathering resource access rights should be considered worthy of compensation. These arguments had some effect, resulting in revisions in the Tribal Grazing Land Policy lease, the establishment of communal service centres, and the degazetting of some areas that originally were planned as commercial ranches. . . .

Conclusions

Anthropologists have had the opportunity to play a role in carrying out research and engaging in development activities which have gone at least some way toward assisting San to have their social, economic, and political rights recognized. Today, San are doing much of this work themselves, which is as it should be. Anthropologists now play more of a backstopping role, assisting San in their data collection, development planning and project implementation efforts. The agenda is now being set by the San themselves, and anthropologists are called upon by San and those supporting San interests to contribute in technical areas or as facilitators (Hitchcock 2003). . . .

37

Indigenous Perception of Cultural Heritage and Its Management: A Cursory Blueprint among the Senufo in the Sikasso Region of Mali

Sekou Berte

Data collection during April and June 2001 in the Sikasso region of southern Mali, West Africa, proved to be a journey of self-discovery, both from an individual and communal perspective. My fieldwork was primarily aimed at understanding how the indigenous Senufo perceive and manage their cultural heritage. Despite a long history of cultural contact, these people are found to be culturally heterogeneous, adhering to strong traditions and claiming common cultural identity. Given these continuing cultural traditions, my position as a community member

---

Excerpted from Berte, Sekou. 2001. Indigenous Perception of Cultural Heritage and Its Management: A Cursory Blueprint among the Senufo in the Sikasso Region of Mali. *Papers from the Institute of Archaeology* 12:105–09.

placed me in a unique position to provide useful insights regarding both the processes of establishing and/or assessing cultural identities over time and the understanding of local material culture from an indigenous perspective. The methodological approach therefore, consisted of *meshing* indigenous Senufo knowledge with archaeological evidence to attempt a cursory blueprint of the archaeological landscape of the Senufo inhabited area. The following report will aim to introduce the reader to some of the social dynamics underpinning this study and some preliminary results.

It has been argued by a number of scholars that the conceptualisation of the past continually anchors peoples to variable debates, irrespective of status and cultural backgrounds (Lowenthal 1985; McBride 1995; Schmidt and McIntosh 1996; Ucko 2000). Yet, although this does appear as a constant dynamic cross-culturally, the control of the globally widespread modes of access to the past such as history and prehistory remain a *chasse gardée* (vanguard) of a westernised mainstream of "experts," i.e., scholars and cultural resource brokers (Cleere 1989; Hartley 1997; Layton 1994; Lertrit 1997; Pwiti 1996; Shackley 1997). Historical and prehistoric accounts of the past draw upon scholarly contributions and remain by and large moulded by representations, which are in turn, partly impacted on by antiquarianism. Overall, the process seems to have made little or no attempt to consider alternative options, namely local viewpoints, which can potentially open up a wider understanding for discourses on the past (Ki-Zerbo 1981; Vansina 1985).

In Mali, as elsewhere, the widespread trends of debates have long ignored indigenous perspectives on the past and heritage studies. Archaeological involvement shows a long established legacy in northern parts of the country (Raimbault and Sanogo 1991; Sanogo 2000). By comparison, other regions, such as western and north-western parts, have received only episodic attention, whilst only the northern areas of the southern region have ever undergone any archaeological research. Cultural Missions, conceived to ensure the safeguarding of heritage places and resources have been enhancing local involvement in the Inland Niger Delta and parts of the northern regions in Mali since the early 1990s. In addition, a three-year project aimed at instrumental experimentation of integrated and sustainable protection has been initiated in the realm of heritage studies and management. Yet until now, an impact study, which can provide insights into this ambitious experimentation, has never been attempted (Diaby and Sanogo 2000; Sanogo 2001 pers. comm.). In contrast to previous scholarly works in the region, my fieldwork consists of the novel approach of combining archaeological research and ideological constructs of the past from indigenous perspectives.

Objectives of the Fieldwork

Broadly, the aims of the fieldwork fall into two levels: understanding and analysing the indigenous perception of cultural heritage among the Senufo people of the Sikasso region, and attempting an integration of conceptual approaches (both Senufo and academic) for the evaluation of archaeological and/or cultural resources among the Senufo. More specifically, the study aims at the following:

- Understanding how Senufo people define cultural resources.
- Identifying, locating and documenting archaeological sites.
- Documenting how the knowledge of the past is used in solving conflicts.
- Documenting access to and control of cultural heritage.
- Assessing the present state of preservation of cultural heritage in the Senufo region and the impact of merely passive care for cultural relics.
- Exploring how to suggest managerial strategies to stop destruction of cultural heritage or to alter passive care.

Methodology

The field survey took place in three study zones: the Kadiolo area (including southern Senufo territories, bordering Cote d'Ivoire); Sikasso and its environs (central Senufo lands); and the Dogoni area (comprising the extreme northern Senufo territories). The choice of these study zones aimed to most effectively integrate (from an indigenous perspective) a picture of the Senufo archaeological and cultural landscapes, focusing on the human-geographical concentration zone of Senufo people in Mali. The villages of Watialy, Mpela, Sokurani and Misirikoro were selected from the three study zones. The latter two villages claimed ownership rights over one important surveyed rock-shelter site, Misirikoro. During my survey, I followed parts of the trade routes dating from the early 15th century across the study region (Beleco-Sikasso and Sikasso-Tengrela-Khong) to gain a picture of the landscape of contact sites. I made frequent stops at different types of sites, such as tells and looted tumuli, to further explore the archaeological landscape.

As pointed out earlier, the methodological approach consisted of meshing Senufo definition of sites and archaeological evidence. Field walking was instrumental in identifying, locating and documenting the archaeological landscape. Basic archaeological techniques were used to document both sites and artefacts. In Watialy for example (study zone one), four sites of iron ore extraction, three sites of iron furnaces, hypogea sites, three rock art sites, and the south-western part of a city wall predating the 18th century, were recorded. The documentation process also included opportunistic surveys and guided exploration of both cultural and archaeological landscapes, to better match oral information with mapping and photography. Additionally, archaeological sites that seem to be significant for the Senufo were documented.

Interviews were conducted with "tradition bearers" (village elders and other representatives) from variable socio-cultural backgrounds about the social significance of "archaeological sites and the management of cultural" resources. Village assemblies were organized and the villagers themselves chose the informants from a wide range of age groups of several generations. This allowed the gathering of different viewpoints on cultural heritage issues. Archival information on the human-geographical distribution of Senufo communities and their material culture was collated from institutions in London, Bamako and Sikasso.

Results

Overall, the fieldwork activities led to what might be best described as a reconstruction of a votive archaeological landscape, which is viewed as sacred in its entirety by the Seoufo. The land is namely seen as a holy landscape, under temporal and spatial control of both ancestors and spirits. By contrast, the archaeological landscape is defined by the Senufo as that of a cultural locus of ancient events, things, and places. Indeed, the Senufo classify archaeological sites according to generic terminology. Among the Senufo, heritage sites and/or archaeological sites are termed as *KataaliEyi* or *kalaaliEyE*. Both these generic terms can be used interchangeably to stand for ancient settlement tells and other human activity areas making use of the natural landscape. Literally, these terms designate places of earlier events, things, and man-made and/or integrated natural features. Individual sites are defined according to their inherent past and present functional roles. For example *faasiike* and *tuwolwieegbe* stand, respectively, for agriculture lands and iron ore extraction holes/open but disused mines. In a broader sense, sites are those areas known for both natural and man-made heritage. . . .

Discussion

In each of the study areas, archaeological (and culturally important natural) sites are embedded within common folk memory. Across the study region, the perceived archaeological sites operate as cultural loci, associated not only with the occupational and ancestral identity but also with supernatural agency and present socio-cultural activities and meanings. These archaeological landscapes are characterised by artefacts, which are used by indigenous Senufo to ground corporate and individual claims over "patrimony." Two components can retain specific attention, one spiritual and the other political. For instance, settlement tells are constructs of cultural loci, within which people interact socio-culturally, as they are profoundly connected to the concept of common ownership, either for individual families and/or for communities at village and regional levels. These constructs are associated with ancestral figures and/or heroes and their belief systems.

The field survey contributed to the discovery of several new sites. These bring additional insights to archaeology, both at a regional and national level. Here it is noteworthy that these new sites are void of any modern management standard, as sites are actively used and subject to both natural and human pressure, such as erosion and agro-pastoral activities. The enthusiastic handling of the fieldwork activities also illustrates that, although it was the first time that locals ever had a chance to contribute to any archaeological involvement, indigenous Senufo would have been supportive of any activity that enhances our understanding of the prehistory in the area, and would have been more concerned about caring actively for their cultural heritage.

Future archaeological work and heritage management would benefit from sustainable and integrated conceptual approaches, with academia and indigenous Senufo, thereby providing a new page of prehistory that draws upon the contribution of both worldviews. Future research must also aim at a deeper integration of the indigenous conceptualisation of archaeological landscapes, as well as issues relating to the management of both archaeological and cultural resources, not only among the Senufo (and their neighbours) in Mali, but also in neighbouring West African countries, such as Burkina Faso, Cote d'Ivoire and Ghana.

38

Transforming Archaeology through Practice: Strategies for Collaborative Archaeology and the Community Archaeology Project at Quseir, Egypt

Stephanie Moser, Darren Glazier, James E. Phillips, Lamya Nasser el Nemr, Mohammed Saleh Mousa, Rascha Nasr Aiesh, Susan Richardson, Andrew Conner, and Michael Seymour

The Community Archaeology Project at Quseir began in 1999 as part of the large-scale excavation of the ancient harbour site known in Roman times as *Myos Hormos* and in the present as Quseir al-Qadim ("Old Quseir"). The aim of the project is to involve the local community in all aspects of the archaeological enterprise, culminating in the creation of a heritage centre that presents the findings from the excavations to the people of Quseir and tourists visiting the area. The project is the first of its kind in Egypt, seeking to bring about a change in the way archaeology is conducted in a country where local communities have been systematically excluded both from the process of discovering their past and in the construction of knowledge concerning their heritage. . . . The underlying premise of the project is that it

Excerpted from Moser, Stephanie, Darren Glazier, James E. Phillips, Lamya Nasser el Nemr, Mohammed Saleh Mousa, Rascha Nasr Aiesh, Susan Richardson, Andrew Conner, and Michael Seymour. 2002. Transforming Archaeology through Practice: Strategies for Collaborative Archaeology and the Community Archaeology Project at Quseir, Egypt. *World Archaeology* 34(2):220–48.

is no longer acceptable for archaeologists to reap the material and intellectual benefits of another society's heritage without that society being involved and able to benefit equally from the endeavour. We endorse the general goal of "community archaeology" to replace the traditional colonial model of archaeological practice with a socially and politically self-conscious mode of research, aiming ultimately to incorporate different cultural perspectives in the interpretation of the past.

There are several reasons why the community of Quseir should be involved in the archaeological investigations that are being conducted just outside the modern city. First, it has been suggested by many in Quseir that the findings from Quseir al-Qadim will play an important role in the formation of a sense of community heritage. Prior to the recent excavation of Quseir al-Qadim, it was not widely known that this was the location of the port of *Myos Hormos*. It is thus only recently that many local people have discovered that they are living in an area of international archaeological significance, and this has already started to affect the way they perceive their city, their past and themselves. It has also become apparent that the archaeological investigations will have an impact on the future economic status of the city, particularly as it seeks to reconstruct itself as the historical centre of the Red Sea. Following the demise of the local phosphate industry, Quseir has begun to occupy a unique niche in the Red Sea tourist trade as an upmarket resort combining marine and heritage tourism. The United States Agency for International Development (USAID), working in conjunction with the Egyptian government as part of their Environmentally Sustainable Tourism project, highlighted Quseir for special attention "because its cultural and natural resources offer a potential for the development of tourism" (Salama 1997, 3), while the Swedish philanthropist Peder Wallenberg has already invested substantial efforts into the regeneration of heritage locations in the city. Finally, and on a more general level, the residents of Quseir should be involved in the study of their own heritage simply because they, like most other Egyptians, have been excluded from Western scholarship in Egypt for so long. The historian Donald Reid (1985, 1997, 2001) has conducted detailed research into the hitherto neglected history of the efforts of Egyptian archaeologists to reclaim the past from Westerners, who appropriated it in the nineteenth century. While Egyptians have successfully taken control of Egyptian museums, the Antiquities Service and the export of antiquities from foreign powers, the majority of excavations are still conducted by Western archaeologists who do not involve local communities in their interpretations. This is also true of the heritage industry in Egypt, where, as Mitchell highlights (2000), the interests of multinational corporations, tourists and archaeologists are considered paramount, to the detriment of local communities (see also Meskell 2001b).

Furthermore, we believe that community involvement in the investigations at Quseir will transform our approach to, and interpretation of, the archaeological evidence. Indeed, one of the primary aims of the Community Archaeology Project is to establish the extent to which community involvement in the archaeological investigations affects the research process itself. Over the past four years we have learned that collaboration constitutes far more than simply showing respect for the values of another culture; the involvement of local communities in archaeological investigations from the outset results in better archaeology. Not only have we gained specific information about the site and the types of remains recovered, we have also been given access to different perspectives and interpretations of Quseir al-Qadim. These more diverse and culturally sensitive interpretations of the archaeological data provide a more comprehensive understanding of the site than would have been possible through traditional archaeological analysis alone.

It is nevertheless important to stress that Quseir is not an homogeneous community. An influx of economic migrants in the nineteenth and early twentieth centuries is reflected in the diverse make-up of the modern city, where a number of different groups, including Nubians, migrants from the Hajjaz, the Nile Valley and Suez, and the Ababda Bedouin, comprise a significant proportion of the population of some 45,000 people. This does not, however, negate the possibility of undertaking a community archaeology project in Quseir, as many members of the community have stressed their interest in both the project and the history of Quseir itself. . . .

A Strategy for Collaborative Practice

One of the key research objectives of the Community Archaeology Project at Quseir is to develop a methodology for conducting community archaeology. To this end we have identified seven components, which we suggest form the basis of this kind of work:

1. communication and collaboration
2. employment and training
3. public presentation
4. interviews and oral history

5. educational resources
6. photographic and video archive
7. community-controlled merchandising

While not intended as a "recipe" for doing community archaeology, this methodology may offer some useful ideas for others seeking to undertake work of this nature. It is, however, important to stress that this project is ongoing and that the details presented here, as with any project of this kind, are subject to revision. The latest updates on the progress of the project can be found on the website www.arch.soton.ac.uk/Research/Quseir. . . .

Partnerships with Local Organizations

Collaboration with local councils and heritage organizations is essential because it provides a framework for integrating the results of the archaeological investigations into community plans for the future. In this, we were fortunate to have the recently formed Quseir Heritage Preservation Society to establish a partnership with. Recognizing the potential of the excavation to have significant implications for future heritage-related developments in the city, Quseir Heritage has been extremely supportive of the project. The manager Adel Aiesh has taken a very active role in introducing us to various interest groups within the community and in keeping the Mayor informed of our progress. Our close relationship with Quseir Heritage not only provides a valuable source of feedback on all aspects of the project, but is also the vehicle through which future developments based on the excavations will be carried out.

Work Updates and Strategies

The production of regular reports on the project and proposals outlining each year's strategy for fieldwork is a fundamental part of the collaboration objective. Each year the team has produced a report summarizing the results of the project, with images of activities undertaken during the course of fieldwork. This is separate from the main excavation report submitted annually to the Supreme Council of Antiquities in Cairo, and is distributed to local organizations and individuals and published on the Internet. These materials give people a sense of how the project is evolving and serve to encourage feedback. We also produce annual outlines of our fieldwork objectives, which are submitted to Quseir Heritage for comment and revision.

Plain Language Reports

It is fundamental that the results of the archaeological investigations are communicated to the local community in a comprehensible format. The production of "plain language reports" in archaeology has been adopted over the last decade, particularly in Australia and North America. In his suggested method for this kind of public writing, Gibb (1997, 56) rejects the passive voice and contrived style of the third person, advocating the use of a narrative, rather than an analytical format, and the peopling of the "story" with site occupants, professional archaeologists and site visitors. To communicate the findings from Quseir al-Qadim in this manner, we produce an annual bilingual (Arabic-English) report that covers all aspects of the project, including both the excavations and the community archaeology work (Glazier 1999; Phillips 2000, 2001a, forthcoming). Prior to its distribution to schools, local authorities, hotels, coffee shops and other interested members of the community, a draft version of the report is presented to various members of the community to ensure that we get feedback on how it might be improved. The Mayor, for example, provided suggestions regarding the types of information he felt should be included, while Lamya Nasser el Nemr selected the images she deemed would be of most interest to the community. The distribution of the report to members of the local community employed as excavators on the site has also proved extremely positive. Not only has it provided them with an insight into the significance of the work taking place, it has also served to foster a sense of pride in their city. After consultation with members of the local community it was felt that the initial versions of the report were still too detailed and did not adequately explain archaeological research. To remedy this, the latest version includes a more general introduction to the project and a description of archaeological methodology.

Openness

Informing local residents about all the aspects of community archaeology work is imperative as local people should not feel that the members of the team are being selective in the information they divulge. In Quseir, we have sought to achieve this by employing local people to work as part of the Community Archaeology team (see below) and involving them in all the day-to-day activities of our work, in both Egypt and the UK. We have also adopted a policy of open communication, where we hide nothing about the work we are doing from the people we work with. On one level this includes conversations about the stresses of trying to negotiate the many levels of local politics that have implications for our work, while on another it includes frank discussions about aspects of our behaviour that may be considered inappropriate to particular groups in the community. In addition to talking openly, we have also placed great emphasis on doing jobs together, ensuring that the Egyptian members of the team are involved in every task, no matter how big or small. When the UK-based members of the team are not in Egypt, regular contact is kept via telephone calls, letters and an e-mail list through which each development relating to the project is communicated. This has resulted in far less suspicion about the presence of our team in the city, of particular importance at a time when increasing numbers of tourists in the region are offending sections of the local community with inappropriate dress and disrespectful behaviour. Furthermore, many individuals now feel comfortable about expressing their opinions of the project as we pass them in the street or stand next to them in a queue at the bank. Spontaneous feedback of this kind is essential to the success of the project, as people have begun to recognize that we are interested in the views of *all* sections of the community, not just those in authority or with a direct connection to the project.

Authorship and Ownership

A major concern in collaborative projects that culminate in some kind of public presentation is that the local community works closely with the curators or archaeologists to determine what is exhibited. If local people are not involved in the presentation of their heritage, their sense of ownership and concern for maintaining a site or museum will not be as great. We thus envisage our role as facilitators, presenting as much of the "raw data" from the excavations as possible to the local community and enabling them to decide what should be displayed and what stories should be told. One of the key problems in achieving this aim is that access to artefacts recovered from sites in Egypt is restricted. For instance, once unearthed, artefacts are recorded by archaeologists, registered with the Antiquities Service and sent to storehouses where they cannot be viewed by the public (in the case of Quseir, some 200 km away in Quft). Understandably, the Egyptian government cannot provide funding to establish local museums to display the vast amount of antiquities recovered by excavations throughout the country. Furthermore, physical access to the finds for those who cannot visit the dig and see artefacts *in situ* is extremely difficult as we are not permitted to take finds off site or out of our desert camp into the city to show people. Despite this, and prior to the application for permission to recover artefacts for display in a future museum, we have attempted to develop methods that ensure that people are aware of the types of material recovered. While viewing images of the finds does not constitute an ideal solution, we have created a digital artefact database that is accessible to the community before the final analyses are published. It is hoped that this will assist the community in making decisions about what kinds of artefacts they would like to learn more about and to see displayed.

Social Interaction

Successful collaboration demands that contact between the team and the people of Quseir is not simply perceived as a business relationship. During our visits, it has become increasingly clear that for many in the community it is desirable for us to make a personal investment in our work, developing friendships that involve regular and long-lasting contact. In other words, they want to know that we are coming back because we care about the place and the people, not just our research. This is also noted by the Australian team working at Brewarrina, who suggest that the "establishment and continual renewal of social communication provides the foundation of successful collaboration" (Field et al. 2000, 35), as well as by Native American archaeologists who have argued that the creation of partnerships beyond archaeology is essential in facilitating effective work within local communities (Watkins, Pyburn, and Cressey 2000, 73). Furthermore, researchers working in the archaeology of slavery in the United States have emphasized how successful collaboration depends upon long-term commitment and a "willingness to work through difficult issues *with* the community" (Derry 1997, 24). Related to this is the importance of making regular visits to the community, not just when excavations are taking place but in the intervening period. Although it is very expensive to get the team to Quseir outside the excavation season (because hotel accommodation, rather than camping, becomes necessary) it has been a priority to visit our Quseir colleagues at least twice every year.

Acknowledging Difficulties

It is important to recognize that difficulties will arise as a result of working so closely with community groups; to suggest that things progress smoothly with little disagreement would be misleading. As we highlighted earlier, there is no such thing as a homogenous "local community", and it is naturally difficult to engage every different interest group with the aspirations of the project 100 per cent of the time. However, by accepting from the beginning that tensions would be inevitable, the team is more prepared for conflicts when they do arise.

Employment and Training

A major priority in conducting a community archaeology project should be the employment and training of local people to work on all aspects of the project. This ensures that they will play a central role in the creation of a form of public presentation based upon the findings from the archaeological investigations. The passing on of skills related to archaeological study, heritage management and museum display is fundamental as it enables local people to co-ordinate the presentation of the site or the running of a visitors' centre or museum once established. The benefits of employing local people on the Quseir Community Archaeology team are many; not only does it ensure that there is continuity in project work when the European members of the team are absent, it also enables members of the community to play a critical role in making decisions about what will be displayed. Unfortunately, as Field and associates (2000, 43) have observed, securing funding for the employment of local people is one of the major problems that archaeologists face when engaging in community projects of this kind. Indeed, it is only because salaries are comparatively low in Egypt that our grants have enabled us to "indulge" in the luxury of employing individuals in this manner. By demonstrating the benefits of providing full-time employment to members of the local community we hope to convince funding organizations that such expenditure is necessary. Field and associates (2000, 43) have also emphasized the positive aspects of employing local people on the site itself during the excavations, where individuals are able to acquire skills that will enhance future employment prospects, learn something about archaeology, have input into the process of investigating their own history and become active in relaying information from the project to the wider community. This is already evident at Quseir, where many of the local people employed as excavators have expressed a genuine interest in the process and results of the investigation. However, while the employment of local people as excavators at Quseir al-Qadim has been crucial in involving the community and disseminating information, the employment of individuals to work with the Community Archaeology team has proved even more successful. . . .

Public Presentation

One of the fundamental objectives of community archaeology is the public presentation of archaeological findings, thus ensuring that the wider community is informed of the results and significance of work undertaken in their region. It is therefore imperative that research on representing information to people from different cultural backgrounds is taken into account, as the stories and modes of presentation we find important and interesting may have little relevance to people in different communities. This issue has been the subject of much discussion in literature concerned with non-Western collections; both Fienup-Riordan's (1999) account of an exhibition of Alaskan masks in North America and Specht and MacLulich's (2000) discussion of an exhibition on indigenous Australians in the Australian Museum provide valuable insights into the processes required to establish and maintain community involvement at all levels of exhibition creation. However, there is also a need to understand the nature of knowledge production in post-colonial contexts, and to appreciate how countries with a colonial legacy have responded to Western scholarship. As Hallam and Street (2000, 4–5) argue, understanding this kind of cross-cultural representation entails not only a self-reflexive and historical awareness of academic modes of production, but also an analysis of the ways in which "others" have themselves translated and subverted Western discourses.

The primary objective of the Community Archaeology Project at Quseir is to create a heritage centre in the city that will serve to bring the results of the excavation to the community (Moser 2001). Equally important, however, is that the heritage centre will function as a place where historical and cultural information about the community itself will be presented. The centre is therefore founded upon community involvement from the outset, with extensive "front-end" evaluation that will result in local people playing a key role in decisions regarding the themes and forms of presentation in the centre. The exhibition strategy for the heritage centre draws on the latest research in museology, where concepts such as multiple narratives, constructive learning, artefact life histories, audience knowledge and the exposition of the interpretative nature of exhibits have been promoted (e.g., Falk and Dierking 2000; Hein 1998; Hooper-Greenhill 2000; McLoughlin 1999; Moore 1997; Roberts 1997). To this end, a research project examining how to display the "life histories" of objects from Quseir has already been undertaken (Phillips 2001b). When the excavations at Quseir al-Qadim have been completed the team will also begin to prepare the site for presentation, incorporating it into the overall display strategy and thus ensuring a more holistic museum visitor experience. In undertaking this part of the project we shall seek guidance from successful "archaeological parks" such as Empúries in Spain (e.g., Pardo 2000, 16–17). . . .

Interviews and Oral History

Interviews with local people about their heritage should be a central component of any "community archaeology" project. Not only do they provide us with insights into how people respond to archaeological discoveries and how they experience and negotiate archaeology in the present, they also provide valuable opportunities to analyse how this information relates to established ideas about the heritage of the site being investigated. By focusing upon oral history and local perceptions of the past, interviews conducted in Quseir by Darren Glazier and Mohammed Saleh Mousa have enhanced our knowledge of Quseir al-Qadim, providing us with more diverse cultural interpretations of the evidence and facilitating the construction of a total life history of the site. Interviews with the community are also a vital means of communicating the aims of the project and thus engendering further community involvement. The oral history component of our project is founded upon research undertaken in fields such as the socio-politics of archaeology, anthropology and the construction of identities (e.g., Ahmed and Shore 1995; Anderson 1991; Gazin-Schwartz and Holtorf 1999; Gero 1989; Glazier 2001; Meehan 1995; Said 1989; Shankland 1996,1999). In addition to Darren Glazier's interviews about heritage, Lamya Nasser el Nemr has been recording the views of workers employed on the site, which will form a vital part of James Phillips' future displays on object life histories. . . .

Educational Resources

An important component of the Community Archaeology Project is the creation of educational materials that introduce younger members of the community to findings about ancient Quseir. Initially, this involved a series of school visits to the site, organized and carried out by Quseir Heritage and a postgraduate from Southampton, Susan Ballard. Currently, we are collaborating with teachers at the recently established Learning Development Centre of Quseir, which offers courses in English, computing and special needs, and which is funded by the Carpe Vitam Trust. An office in this centre has been generously made available for the Community Archaeology Project, and Lamya Nasser el Nemr is now working closely with the twenty local teachers employed within. In addition to tailoring our reports for the students at the centre, one of Lamya's main responsibilities is to consult the teachers about what kinds of archaeology-related teaching materials she can produce for use in their classes. . . .

Photographic and Video Archive

As part of the Community Archaeology Project at Quseir we have begun to create a photographic and video archive for exhibition in the heritage centre. The creation of a visual archive of the excavation ensures that the community has a record of both the event and the experience of the archaeological project. Furthermore, for those in Quseir who have not been able to visit the excavations—both in the present and in the future—there will be a permanent historical record of this key event in the history of the city. . . .

39

Public Archaeology and Indigenous Communities

Mike Parker Pearson and Ramilisonina

The Indigenous Community in Southern Madagascar

From an English perspective, the region of Androy is a dry, hot and desolate desert lacking in all the creature comforts that make life bearable. In the words of a Tandroy saying, it is "drier than a dog's crotch in the dry season." There is no electricity or running water and the tiny wooden

Excerpted from Parker Pearson, Mike, and Ramilisonina. 2004. Public Archaeology and Indigenous Communities. In *Public Archaeology*, ed. N. Merriman, 224–39. London: Routledge.

houses possess no furniture other than straw mats. There is scarcely any standing water in the nine-month-long dry season and the dry riverbeds are pockmarked by holes dug into the sand to seek out the hidden water below. There are fleas, lice, cockroaches, poisonous spiders, scorpions and (non-poisonous) snakes.

Most Tandroy are still pastoralists. People here in the arid south sometimes struggle to ensure that their families stay alive, as they watch their cattle herds dwindle and their crops wither. Drought and famine are ever-present dangers in this fragile and hostile environment.

Medical and hospital provision is exceedingly limited and there has been barely any provision for education since the government lost its ability to pay village teachers' salaries some ten years ago. There are Tandroy politicians in central government but promises of government aid and subsidies have largely come to nothing. Many have emigrated to find work in the plantations and cities in other parts of Madagascar, working as wage labourers, nightwatchmen and mechanics.

Tandroy attitudes to outsiders are largely antagonistic. The politically and economically dominant people of Madagascar's central highlands, more Indonesian in appearance than most southerners, have been referred to for centuries as "dog-pigs." The delicacy and politeness of the highlanders is alien to the Tandroy who pride themselves on speaking their mind, and being blunt and forthright in their dealings. Anyone who is not Tandroy is a *vazaha,* a stranger or foreigner, regardless of whether they are Malagasy or not. Like the relationship of Scottish to English culture, Tandroy culture is a distinct regional variant with its difficult dialect, its own economic practices (cattle pastoralism and manioc cultivation as opposed to the prevalent rice cultivation of the rest of the island) and its disdain for the soft life lived by other Malagasy, in opposition to which the distinctive lifestyle of the Tandroy has been forged.

The Tandroy know and talk about their fairly recent arrival in Androy. Genealogies list clan ancestors and oral histories tell how these ancestors came from the east and migrated across the south; archaeological survey places these migrations in the sixteenth to nineteenth centuries. It could be claimed that existing Tandroy notions about the past, manifested in genealogies, oral traditions and the presence of the ancestors, make archaeology an intrusive and unnecessary form of knowing the past. Much the same was once conveyed to the archaeologists working on South Uist Hebrideans (see Chapter 46 this volume) until people realized that there was an unknown and fascinating history being retrieved and reconstructed.

Our own approach is not that archaeology should serve to undermine traditional authoritative discourses but that it is a complementary and integral aspect of knowing the past. The past is important to people and archaeology is a way of broadening horizons and stimulating curiosity. There are certainly conflicts and contradictions between orally transmitted and archaeologically derived interpretations of particular archaeological sites but these are not to be shied away from. The Tandroy know that they have not always lived on the land they now occupy and seem to have no philosophical problem with accepting archaeological evidence of their own migrations or with the knowledge that there were other people living in the region before they arrived.

Public Archaeology in Southern Madagascar

Madagascar is the sixth poorest nation in the world. In this economic climate archaeology will seem to some to be an unnecessary luxury and yet the state supports a Musée d'Art et d'Archéologie, a Centre d'Art et d'Archéologie at the Université d'Antananarivo and a few archaeology and history posts in the provincial universities. Even during the years of Malagasy cultural reconstruction, when foreign influences and products were largely discouraged or unavailable, the Musée built up its international links and welcomed foreign archaeologists, ensuring that its research efforts went that much further through contact with French, American, and British academic institutions. Museum staff have worked intermittently in the south, and specifically in Androy, since 1961, carrying out field surveys of settlement sites and tombs, and excavations of major type sites dating from 1,000–500 years ago.

After 1984 there was a hiatus in Musée research in Androy until our own project commenced in 1991. However, Georges Heurtebize (a French resident of Androy, a geologist by training and an ethnographer by vocation) has carried out a certain amount of field survey and, together with the anthropologist Sarah Fee, has constructed an impressive museum of Tandroy life in the nature reserve and tourist attraction of Berenty in eastern Androy. He also encouraged and trained our Tandroy colleague Retsihisatse as an archaeologist and anthropologist.

Our work in Androy is not possible without Retsihisatse. There is a powerful social norm of hospitality throughout the south but people are very suspicious of outsiders. Retsihisatse's participation in the project enables us to break through this barrier. We have come across many stories of misunderstandings and confrontations between Tandroy and outsiders, both Malagasy and European, which have occasionally resulted in murder. There have long been tales of how "foreigners", especially white ones, will steal hearts, livers and tongues. In 1993 a new rumour began that white people were head-hunting to extract brains in the search for an AIDS cure. The rumour started in association with two Frenchmen in a red car ostensibly on a fact-finding mission into primary education—of which there is none. Within this climate of suspicion it was only a matter of weeks before the description of the suspects matched our team and Landrover—the head-hunters were now pretending that they were looking for old pottery . . .

The head-hunting rumour is still circulating today and has made fieldwork extremely slow and difficult. Few people know anything at all about archaeology, let alone what our research team is doing. In one sense this is a good thing because it means that we must spend even more time than we would ordinarily in talking to everybody about what we are looking for, and why. As one little girl asked when out fieldwalking with the team, "Are these the good foreigners or the head-hunting foreigners?" In Androy we are considerably restricted in terms of the media available for communication and dissemination of our fieldwork intentions or results. In a society which has a low rate of literacy and where paper is valued primarily for rolling cigarettes, the printed word is of little use in public presentation. Our only means of communication is face-to-face. There are no "village halls" so meetings take place in the open air within the framework of *kabary*, the Malagasy style of public speaking and debate.

Yet practice rather than talk is the best way of involvement and in the last eight years many more Tandroy than Hebrideans (see Chapter 46 this volume) have done some archaeology. Many people, especially the children, come fieldwalking. The novelty and interest tend to fade after the first day or so and yet there are some individuals who have a strong interest and a good knowledge of the archaeological remains in their locality. Several people, young and old, have shown the level of interest out of which may develop a life-long enthusiasm but there is no infrastructure of community funding or support which could ensure that Retsihisatse has protégés and a local "amateur" network for the future.

Tandroy manners are such that people are not slow in coming forward and the archaeologists are a known and reliable source of presents, medicines and free rides to market. Our bizarre behaviour is also a source of sometimes hilarious entertainment for both children and adults. Our financial input to the local economy is substantial through gift-giving, food purchasing, market shopping, accommodation payments, fees to guides and provision of animal sacrifices. Yet there are aspects of people's lives which we cannot begin to improve. Access to drinking water, professional medical and hospital facilities, a better transport infrastructure, bigger cattle herds, and even more enormous stone tombs are the things that people most want.

Our mission is primarily archaeological and can only provide a very intangible benefit. We think that our work is appreciated for two reasons. People enjoy telling us what they know about their history in terms of the places, traditions, genealogies and stories about the past. Perhaps our most significant role is in validation of Tandroy heritage. It is not only just as important as anyone else's but specialists have come from the national museum and from far away overseas to find out about it. Secondly, people are often interested in our discoveries but to a lesser extent and often only if they themselves have a pre-existing interest and aptitude. This is particularly the case with some of the men who have worked as paid guides and local helpers.

But, just as in South Uist, it is difficult to distinguish whether the communities with whom we have had contact are best described as "indigenous" or as "local." Working with Retsihisatse, an indigenous archaeologist by most definitions, we are able to explain our motives and the importance of the ancient settlements on Tandroy territory as well as calm any suspicions about what we are up to. Archaeologists working with "indigenous" communities are there at the behest of their hosts or by their agreement. This means participating on the community's terms, respecting their beliefs and traditions. Even though both of us were raised as Christians we are happy to participate in non-Christian rituals, such as sacrificing to the ancestors to gain their blessing before embarking on an excavation.

Despite a climate of fear in which our appearance has occasionally caused children to run away screaming, we have nevertheless managed to build good relations with many of the local presidencies and villages in Androy. But Androy is a big region of 5,000 square kilometres with a population of about a quarter of a million. Our worst problems, such as being held hostage, have happened when we were furthest from Retsihisatse's home village, in areas where no-one had ever heard of him or his family. Retsihisatse may be indigenous but, crucially, he isn't always *local*.

In both Androy and South Uist, people are intrigued by archaeological finds on their own land but expanding that local interest to encompass their entire region and ethnic group needs methods beyond personal contact, and becomes a goal which is difficult to attain in South Uist and currently still distant in Androy. In addition, much as we have obligations to the local communities with whom we work, we also owe duties to a myriad of different public audiences that archaeology serves. In national terms, for example, we have a responsibility to disseminate knowledge to the people of Madagascar. Although in 1989 there was an exhibition on Androy in the capital Antananarivo, prejudices against the people of the south, seen as fearsome, uncivilized and dangerous, are still strong throughout the rest of the country. In international terms we have an audience to reach amongst both scholars and the wider public. This is not simply because the long-term archaeology and history of Androy is fascinating for its contributions to understanding issues like megafaunal extinction and monumental tomb-building but because it is also a location where European and Malagasy history became inextricably entwined during the pre-colonial period of the sixteenth to nineteenth centuries.

How can this be expressed at a local level in Androy? Primarily through Georges Heurtebize's efforts, there is a growing sense of a history to be objectified and preserved. Oral traditions are being recorded, new archaeological sites are being discovered and there are the beginnings of a museum collection for the benefit of the local community in one of the oldest houses in Androy at Benonoke. Although the museum at Berenty is for the benefit of tourists, its very existence is a first crucial step which indicates to the Tandroy and the wider world that Tandroy culture and history are valued by people outside the indigenous community.

Just as tourism to the Western Isles has increased over the last ten years, so the numbers of American and European tourists to Madagascar have grown in tandem with newspaper articles describing it as a stylish adventure playground inhabited solely by cuddly lemurs. As our project's results are published to a wider European and American public so more people will want to visit Androy. Currently Androy is well off the beaten track of tourism. Public buses and tour buses pass through without stopping. Some non-Tandroy and Europeans live in the few small towns but otherwise the only white people to be seen, other than some of the archaeologists, are occasional aid workers and UNICEF water engineers, the Catholic priests and Protestant missionaries, some conservation personnel and the rare tourist who manages to explore beyond the roadside towns. The lemur reserve at Berenty is, however, specifically directed at overseas tourists. Many come to this insulated shady paradise unaware that they have the only running water, electricity, French food and cold beer for miles around. In Georges Heurtebize's museum there they can learn about Tandroy life without the discomforts of having to live it or, conversely, without inflicting themselves on the Tandroy.

In spite of their wariness of strangers, some Tandroy are keen that more visitors should pass through. There may not be a tourist infrastructure as such but there are marketing opportunities for women to sell the beautiful woven mats and locally made textiles that are distinctive to the region. This is a contradictory state of affairs in which tourists will be feared and welcomed at the same time. Many in the tourism industry consider that Tandroy culture would suffer from the exposure and that overseas tourism in Madagascar should be restricted as far as possible to the "honey pots" at places like Berenty. For better or for worse, our work will—to an admittedly minute degree—increase the influx of travellers who wish to encounter Tandroy life and culture for themselves at first hand. . . .

In neither South Uist (see Chapter 46 this volume) nor Androy do we claim to be working there for the indigenous community's exclusive and sole benefit: archaeology is driven by research which has to be multi-layered just as its audiences are multiple and globally dispersed. The world is too small to allow retreat into self-referential and closely circumscribed "parish pump" archaeologies which feed local chauvinisms about indigenous purity and exclusion of the wider world, erecting instead barriers of intolerance and misunderstanding. Yet in the practice of field archaeology, that parish pump may be all important. Local communities call many of the shots, and rightly so, but archaeologists must be conscious of the inherent dangers in any "indigenous" archaeology. Archaeology may sometimes lend itself to the redressing of great injustices but it will not always support beliefs held very dear by a dominated or disenfranchised community. In neither South Uist nor Androy, for example, can our research ever be used to confirm the present population as autochthonous. These indigenous communities live today on land once inhabited by others, people who were not their ancestors. These traces of past societies are nevertheless "their" history which they can learn about with pride and interest, recognizing that there are others in this world who also have the tight to know, either because they are the descendants of the thousands of enslaved Malagasy or impoverished Hebridean peasants shipped to North America, or because the projects were financed with public money, or just because archaeology fascinates them.

SECTION VIII

Asia

Indigenous peoples in Asia continue to experience the pains and disenfranchisement of colonialism, nationalism, and imperialism, including forced relocation and assimilation, exploitation, discrimination, and the denial of the right to self-determination. In many parts of Asia, Indigenous peoples struggle for even the most basic recognition by dominant governments. For example, Ainu peoples of the island of Hokkaido (Japan), and the Kuril Islands and Sakhalin (Russia), have only recently been acknowledged as distinct peoples by the Japanese government. At the same time, archaeologists in many parts of Asia, especially Russia, ignore the wishes, beliefs, and rights of local populations with regard to their cultural heritage (see discussion in Wobst 2004).

Throughout Asia, Indigenous peoples' land continues to be appropriated as resources (for example, timber, natural gas, oil, minerals) are extracted to fuel the global economy. The impact has been devastating on Indigenous communities economically and socially, especially in terms of heritage, community values, and ideology. Anderson Muutang Urud (Kelabit Tribe Sarawak) speaks of the devastation wrought by the timber industry in Sarawak, Malaysia: "Even when we mark our burial grounds, the logging companies bulldoze through them with no regard for our feelings. Hundreds of graveyards have been destroyed in this way. When we complain about the destruction, they sometimes offer us a small sum of money as compensation, but this is an insult to us. How can we accept money that is traded for the bodies of our ancestors?" (1994, 104).

Asia does not appear as a prominent node of Indigenous archaeologies in existing reviews (for instance, Nicholas 2008; Watkins 2005), though the currents of collaborative and engaged archaeological practice are growing stronger. Nicholas (2008, 1661) notes that although archaeology in such places as China has always been "indigenous," in that it has been practiced by Chinese scholars, it falls short of "Indigenous archaeology," because "it has been practiced by and for the powerful and has continued to colonize the disenfranchised." Grappling with the issue of power is central to decolonizing archaeological practice in Asian contexts, and there is increasing concern regarding people in positions of privilege and power dominating the practice of archaeology. Important steps have been taken to balance power and resource inequities (for example, funding, infrastructure, training) on a global scale, especially through international collaborations. Additionally, some scholars have begun to employ the theoretical and methodological principles of Indigenous archaeologies and decolonization, such as reflexivity, multivocality, and the recognition of the situatedness of knowledge. But more work needs to be done to achieve the kinds of partnerships called for by Ainu leader Giichi Nomura: "In Ainu language, we have a word, *Ureshipamoshiri*, which signifies our concept of the world as an interrelated community of all living things. In this new era in which the world is groping towards a redefinition of the international order following the end of the Cold War, we believe 'a new partnership' of indigenous and nonindigenous peoples which includes this worldview can make a lasting and valuable contribution to the global community" (1994, 71).

The four excerpts included in this section represent the contemporary currents in decolonizing archaeology in Asia. Each presents a critique of archaeological practice in a different part of Asia—from Israel and Palestine, to Korea, India, and Japan—highlighting the need for critical praxis in the region. Each offers a case study that illustrates the importance of archaeology as a tool for empowering marginalized peoples and pasts.

This section begins with an excerpt from Sandra Scham's "The Archaeology of the Disenfranchised." Here, Scham outlines different experiences of disenfranchisement in colonial contexts, which provides a useful framework for considering how peoples and histories have been marginalized throughout Asia. Her argument centers on a critical assessment of the postprocessual concept of "multivocality" as it applies to disenfranchised groups. Scham characterizes and evaluates various models within the paradigm she calls "the archaeology of the disenfranchised" and offers a case study of archaeology in this mode in Israel and Palestine. This case study situates archaeology in an occupied two-state political landscape, illustrates the significance of archaeological investigations to state construction and nationhood, and problematizes exclusionary efforts.

Like Scham, Minkoo Kim deals directly with the issue of power in decolonizing archaeological practice. In "Multivocality, Multifaceted Voices, and Korean Archaeology," Kim argues that the process of multivocality is not universally decolonizing but rather that it can continue to disempower marginalized voices. Korean archaeology has been a nationalist endeavor heavily influenced by Japanese colonizers and other foreigners. Kim illustrates how the voices of Korean peoples silenced during colonial period have become dominant, but also how these new dominant voices have legitimized nation-building efforts and promoted a particular view of the past that is itself marginalizing. She grounds her effort to understand the relationship between dominant and marginalized narratives in a discussion of the debate surrounding the Sorori site, an Upper Paleolithic site which may have the earliest evidence of rice cultivation known to date. Through this example, Kim demonstrates the symbolic power of "origins" research to national identity and makes the point that empowering marginalized voices does not necessarily mean disempowering dominant ones.

In "Decolonizing Methodologies as Strategies of Practice: Operationalizing the Postcolonial Critique in the Archaeology of Rajasthan," Uzma Rizvi presents strategies for decolonizing practice through a case study exploring the complexities of conducting a regional survey in the Rajasthan region of India. Rizvi's focus is methodological, but her discussion tacks back and forth between on-the-ground method and a theoretical grounding in the postcolonial critique. Rizvi describes the discussions and interactions among the international research team and collaborating communities and innovative ways that project participants redistributed power that traditionally resided with archaeologists. She also reflects on how her own social position and identity shaped some aspects of collaboration, and how the process transformed her perspective on knowledge production.

This section concludes with an excerpt from Hirofumi Kato's "Whose Archaeology? Decolonizing Archaeological Perspective in Hokkaido Island." Kato explores the potential for promoting Indigenous archaeology on Hokkaido Island, part of the homeland of Ainu peoples. He questions whether archaeologists in Japan have adequately recognized the rights of Ainu peoples to interpret and steward their heritage.

Highlighting a new initiative at a Japanese University—Hokkaido University's interdisciplinary Center for Ainu and Indigenous Studies—Kato describes a research project that mobilizes the principles of Indigenous archaeologies focused on the Shiretoko National Park, a UNESCO World Natural Heritage Site. Kato's discussion illustrates the crucial importance of Indigenous research centers and institutions as venues for cultural and historical recovery.

40

The Archaeology of the Disenfranchised

Sandra A. Scham

Colonial subjugation is perhaps the most devastating disenfranchising status because it affects almost every part of society and culture. Colonialism has a far-reaching impact on visions of the past—an impact that may continue in force long after colonial rule has been overthrown (Meskell 1998a). The clearest distinguishing factor in colonial disenfranchisement is the effective replacement of an indigenous past by a narrative that emphasizes the conquest culture. Inevitably this results in a movement to reestablish the hegemony of the older culture—within a newly formed, globally conscious paradigm (Bond and Gilliam 1994). Either because of demographic factors (where the colonized are as numerous or more numerous than the colonizers) or because there has been no geographic displacement, the indigenous predecessor culture and its history are usually not truly lost despite attempts by colonial powers to eradicate them (Said 1994, 210). There is an essential transmogrification of these cultures, however, stemming partly from modernism and partly from an unexpressed desire to learn something from the humiliating experience of conquest.

The disenfranchisement of minorities, the second most common type, results in a vision of the past that is primarily formed to counter the persistent messages from the majority culture that the minority culture is irrelevant (Gero 1995, 177). There are a number of conditions—immigrant, ethnic, and religious status, among others—that affect the rights of certain individuals to attain economic and social justice. It is important that this type of discrimination, which is subtler than that resulting from outright political subordination, be viewed as disenfranchising regardless of

---

Excerpted from Scham, Sandra A. 2001.The Archaeology of the Disenfranchised. *Journal of Archaeological Method and Theory* 8(2):183–213.

whether it is due to the overt actions of government or simply ignorance and neglect by the dominant populace.

The third disenfranchised group is less easily defined. It consists of the indigenous inhabitants of countries where foreign control over the past has been so extensive, all-encompassing, and damaging to local historical consciousness that a strong reaction has resulted (Bahrani 1998; Hamilakis 1999; Hassan 1998; Ozdogan 1998). Although some of these countries fit into the colonized group of disenfranchised peoples, there are others, Greece, Turkey, Lebanon, Egypt, and Palestine/Israel among them, where the inhabitants' experience of gaining control over their past has less to do with overthrowing political subjugation and more to do with abrogating alien cultural hegemony. "Cultural imperialism," a catchphrase of resistance literature (Said 1994), most clearly applies to the experiences of these countries whose national treasures have been consistently looted over time, whose ancient terrain has been marred with amateurish and destructive excavations and whose history has been defined largely by foreigners. . . .

Case Study: The Archaeology of the Disenfranchised in Israel and the Palestinian National Authority

> Perhaps the greatest battle Palestinians have waged as a people has been over the right to a remembered presence, and with that presence, the right to possess and reclaim a collective historical reality, a least since the Zionist movement began its encroachments on the land. (Said 1999)

Said's statement rather succinctly summarizes many of the bases upon which the archaeology of the disenfranchised in Israel and the Palestinian National Authority has been established. Calling up collective memory, historical reality, reclamation, and repossession, it touches on all of the premises in the complex relationship between Palestinians and their past. What Said does not state, however, is that Israel/Palestine comprises a rich variety of views of the past. Depending upon their political status, for example, Arabs here may see their past in highly different ways. For many Arab citizens of Israel, who, for economic reasons, generally believe that their fortunes are tied to that State, the past is bittersweet and irremediably lost. For Palestinians in the West Bank and Gaza, ready to throw off the yoke of occupation, the past can be revived, restored, and displayed in a whole new light. For the Palestinians of East Jerusalem, it is most important to challenge the prevailing myths of the dominant culture (Glock 1999).

In addition to these views, the ways in which Bedouin and Druze citizens of Israel look at their history must be considered (and they seldom are). Distanced from Palestinian Arabs in the first case by an age-old mistrust of *fellahin* Arabs (Hassan 1998) and in the second case by status as a (sometimes persecuted) religious minority, Bedouin and Druze have accepted Israeli sovereignty over their lives with seemingly little struggle. The prevailing view of these peoples among Jews in Israel is that they are loyal to the State, they serve in the Israeli Defense Forces, and they make very little trouble. The less prevalent view is that the Bedouin and the Druze have suffered tremendously in Israel from their status as second class citizens and that the State should not take them so entirely for granted.

It is the Jewish view of the past to which all of these views ostensibly provide alternatives (Abu El-Haj 1998). Jewish archaeology in Israel, however, is a rare case of a nationalist archaeology developing from what was fundamentally a heritage recovery model. Because of this and because the recognition of Jewish Diaspora history has heavily influenced archaeological interpretations, Israeli Jewish archaeology has retained some of these responses to the disenfranchising conditions of the past. Some of the peculiarities of site preservation in Israel can be explained on this basis. Recently, in a popular magazine, a long-time resident of Israel described how he once enjoyed taking groups of young people from the United States to the biblical site of Gibeon *(al-Jib)* in the West Bank, home of Ancient Israel's first king and site of a great biblical Israelite victory, but now he takes them to *Masada* instead (Roman 2000). Ostensibly he proposes that this was a reaction to political unrest in the area of the former site but there is also the factor of *Masada's* immense popularity with Jewish tourists in the intervening years.

Masada is a virtual shibboleth in archaeology here and represents very clearly a transitional phase from the Heritage Recovery model toward a vision of the embattled nation-state that Israelis have found so inspiring. Millions have been spent on the conservation and presentation of a site that essentially marks a disastrous, if legendary, defeat of the Jewish people by the Romans (Ben-Haim and Margalit 2000). Meanwhile, many famous biblical sites like Lachish, Gezer, Bethel, Mizpeh, and others have eroded and suffered damage beyond any hope of repair. Change from the *Masada* mentality, however, is already well underway. Modern Israeli Jewish archaeology has entered, with a vengeance, a very positivist and scientific phase that many archaeologists here will admit is itself a reaction to the ideological excesses of both Christian-inspired "Biblical" archaeology and nationalist archaeology (Dever 1999; Silberman 1998).

All of these different currents demonstrate the overlap of the heritage recovery archaeology, the archaeology of the colonized and reaction/

resistance archaeology in Arab and Jewish discourse about the past here. I recently attended an archaeological conference with Palestinian, Bedouin, and Israeli participants where this diversity of views was well represented. A paper by a Palestinian archaeologist from the West Bank discussed how he was able to interpret several interesting sites through ethnographic studies (archaeology of the colonized) of Palestinian village industries of today (Salem 2000). An archaeologist from East Jerusalem presented a paper that took issue with the suggestion that the so-called four-room house was in fact Israelite (reaction/resistance archaeology) since it seemed to be a widespread phenomenon throughout the Levant (Nur el-Din 2000). A Bedouin anthropologist who entitled his paper "Bury My Heart at Wounded Tree" (Abu-Rabia 2000) discussed traditional Bedouin burial practices, how modern encroachments upon traditional territories have irrevocably altered them, and the need for funds to protect Bedouin graves (heritage recovery archaeology). An Arab citizen of Israel, exploring in private conversation the popular notion discussed in the introduction to this paper that current Palestinian inhabitants of the land are descendants of Canaanites, Philistines, or Jebusites, discredited what he saw as an attempt by Palestinians to merely commandeer the prevailing Israeli mythos and stated the need for Arabs in Israel and Palestine to recapture their cultural identity and create concrete manifestations of their presence in the land (archaeology of the colonized *and* heritage recovery). Finally, an Israeli archaeologist, self-identified as a religious Jew, presented a paper based on the premise that the Iron Age "Israelite" settlers of the central hill country of Palestine had rejected imported dishes because they believed that foreign tableware was impure under the laws of *kashrut* (kosher; also, heritage recovery) (Faust 2000). Interestingly, the response to this last paper was noticeably more negative than the response to any other paper presented at that conference and came, not from Arabs, but from other Israeli Jewish archaeologists.

On one level, any archaeologist working in the so-called "historical" periods in Israel or Palestine is subject to criticism from many different sources and may, depending on the period on which he or she chooses to concentrate, be accused of blatant bias without ever having made a single interpretation. On another level, characterizations of the past are so fluid here that it is difficult to determine how anyone's ethnicity, political status, or religious affiliation can be considered as indicative of their ideology. The charge that Palestinians have made against Israeli archaeologists, that Arab and Islamic remains are routinely bulldozed in order to uncover earlier deposits is, as Kohl has noted, true "only in a few exceptional cases" (Kohl 1995, 241). Nonetheless, this remains a powerful and widespread notion primarily because, in terms of methodology and interpretation, Arab, Islamic, and additionally Byzantine and

Crusader, remains have in the past been disregarded if not destroyed. Israeli archaeologists will proudly declaim that they have never discarded a single Arab or Islamic artifact but will be hesitant to state how many such artifacts from their sites have actually been studied. On the other hand, the number of Israeli scholars interested in these nonbiblical historical periods appears to be increasing exponentially even as the individuals who had previously studied the remains from these periods, Palestinian scholars, have left Israeli institutions.

What is the future of Archaeology in Israel and Palestine? One scenario is that Palestinians and Israeli Jews will develop their own separate archaeological paradigms much as Jordanian archaeology has developed apart from Israeli archaeology even though sites in the two countries are quite similar. One can also envision a kind of economically driven combination of approaches. Certainly, the newly emergent Palestinian Authority will need tourist revenues from biblical sites within their jurisdiction and, just as Israel has to a great extent allowed considerations of tourism to color its own policy of site preservation, those sites may be given preferential treatment.

There is also the not negligible factor of past working relationships to consider. Many Palestinian archaeologists who have done fieldwork in the Levant have done so under the control of the Israel Antiquities Authority. Israeli Arabs in particular, familiar with the language of the dominant culture and well acquainted with its bureaucracy and social structure, have been involved in such projects. There is a notable camaraderie among some Arab and Jewish archaeologists, even while most other Jews and Arabs in the region remain apart. That many people are unaware of the degree of contact was brought home to me by a conversation with a Jordanian colleague at a conference. In the midst of voicing her opinion that there seemed to be little contact between the Arabs and Jews present, she turned around and recognized, in the row behind her, a Palestinian archaeologist sitting among a group of Israeli Jewish archaeologists and conversing in Hebrew. A scene that to anybody knowledgeable about Israel was quite common was to her utterly astonishing.

Inexorably, these relationships will come to depend more and more on the political factors in the region. Archaeology will come to serve the State in Palestine as it did and continues to do in Israel. Religion and nationalism both need the past to survive and to develop. As movements become nation-states, the mature passion that fuelled their success becomes the puerile sentiments of patriotism—conjured at will and concretized in "traditions"—that never saw the light of day before the creation of the state. Archaeology is a vital component in this process. Bruce Trigger's pronouncement that "most archaeological traditions are probably nationalistic in orientation" (Trigger 1984, 357), is a sobering thought for those of us who are archaeological practitioners in embattled lands and who often prefer to see ourselves as either politically neutral or struggling to "save" an endangered cultural identity (Glock 1999).

Discussion

The archaeology of the disenfranchised may well represent to some scholars the kind of ideological bias that they have long held to be inappropriate in the field. With the exception of postprocessual theorists, western archaeologists have not been welcoming of the various models described earlier for precisely this reason. In the Middle East alone, one can imagine any number of projects that could strike fear in the heart of the scientific investigator of the past: African American scholars investigating sites relating to Cleopatra to determine her racial identity; Palestinian archaeologists looking for cultural connections with Philistine sites; West Bank settlers being given complete autonomy over a neighboring site mentioned prominently in the bible; a *yeshiva* given control over important excavations in Jerusalem.

If the last two sound somewhat more familiar than the others, it is because they are real situations that have taken place, largely with the use of public funds, in Israel and the territories. The reason for placing them on this list is to make the obvious point that it should not be ideology itself that is the most alarming factor here but ideology that is supported by the State to the exclusion of other ideologies (Arnold 1990; Scham 1998). We have long proposed that the antidote to ideological biases in archaeology is to cease the funding of ideologically based projects. This is clearly not happening and perhaps never will as long as national self-interest dictates archaeological policies. . . .

41

Multivocality, Multifaceted Voices, and Korean Archaeology

Minkoo Kim

Korean Archaeology and Nation Building

Discourses about the past on the Korean peninsula have rarely been free of foreign influences. Yi (2001), for instance, shows that people during the Chosun (or Joseon) period (1392–1910) made sense of prehistoric remains by relating them directly to ideologies adopted from mainland China that were widely followed by the ruling class of the Chosun dynasty. For example, stone tools were called "thunder axes," and this term was directly adopted from China (Yi 2001, 60). Furthermore, the existence of stone tools was explained with reference to the Principle of Yin/Yang and the Five Primary Substances (metal, wood, water, fire, and earth) (Yi 2001, 185). The origin of thunder axes was explained according to the circulation of *gi,* a form of energy that is present in the five primary substances. According to the Principle of Yin/Yang and the Five Primary Substances, the *gi* of fire, at its extremity, becomes the *gi* of earth. A stone is simply a solidified form of earth. This framework explained why it might be "natural" to find strange stones where lightning, an extreme and peculiar form of fire, was present. This kind of explanation was considered rational and logical throughout the Chosun period and overshadowed other folk narratives by criticizing them as irrational, mystical, or subjective.

Over the course of the twentieth century, Korea has undergone a series of dramatic political upheavals. These political changes began with

---

Excerpted from Kim, Minkoo. 2008. Multivocality, Multifaceted Voices, and Korean Archaeology. In *Evaluating Multiple Narratives: Beyond Nationalist, Colonialist, and Imperialist Archaeologies*, ed. J. Habu, C. Fawett, and J. M. Matsunaga, 118–37. New York: Springer.

the Japanese annexation of the country in 1910. The liberation of the Korean peninsula in 1945 after the end of World War II was followed by the Korean War (1950–1953) and the subsequent establishment of two competing nations, the Republic of Korea and the Democratic People's Republic of Korea (commonly referred to as South Korea and North Korea, respectively). A series of upheavals in the political framework of Korea shaped a particular and unique social milieu, within which current archaeological narratives are situated.

The modem practice of archaeology in Korea started with Japan's growing political influence over the Korean peninsula and northeastern regions of China at the end of the nineteenth and beginning of the twentieth centuries. The first Japanese archaeologist to conduct archaeological site surveys on the peninsula was Shozaburo Yagi who entered Korea in 1893. He was followed by Japanese scholars such as Tadashi Sekino, Ryuzo Torii, and Ryu Imanishi. The Japanese colonial era (1910–1945) witnessed systematic archaeological surveys and excavations, the promulgation of a body of legislation regulating the protection and registration of cultural properties, and the display of archaeological collections in museums (Pai 1998). This was also the time when a rudimentary chronological framework was established for Korea and various prehistoric "cultures" on the Korean peninsula were identified. Throughout the colonial period, however, archaeological excavations and site surveys were exclusively carried out by Japanese scholars. No Koreans were adequately trained in excavation and analytic skills to conduct this work, and consequently, Korean voices that might have interpreted their own past were silenced. Until the liberation of the peninsula in 1945, Koreans only held nonacademic positions in national museums (Arimitsu 1996).

The colonial era is remembered by Koreans as the time when their past was "fabricated" and "distorted" by the Japanese colonizers. Scholars who have examined the history of Korean archaeological and historical work during this period of time argue that archaeological interpretations were predetermined by the agenda set by the Government General of Korea, which was the principal organ of governance during the Japanese colonial rule from 1910 to 1945. Pai (1994, 39), for instance, points out that four research themes were emphasized during the colonial period: (1) the common ancestral origins of the Korean and Japanese peoples; (2) the existence of Japanese colonies on the Korean peninsula in the past; (3) the overwhelming impact of Chinese cultures on the Korean peninsula; and (4) the backwardness and stagnation of Korean cultures (see also Pai 2000). Archaeological remains, which are intrinsically subject to a variety of interpretations, were easily exploited to justify the Japanese colonization of Korea. This use of the past to justify Japanese colonization was systematic and beyond the control of individual researchers.

Finally, the colonial period witnessed racist assertions partly justified by interpretations of archaeological evidence, which claimed that the Korean people were characterized by "a lack of independence" and "a servile attitude towards bigger nations." The argument was made, furthermore, that Koreans could become subjects of the Japanese emperor by overcoming their bad characteristics (Pai 1994, 40).

The Korean War (1950–1953), which swept the country 5 years after the 1945 liberation of Korea from Japan, killed approximately 2.5 million military personnel and civilians, devastated the economy, and completely destroyed the country's infrastructure. In the two nations that were established as a result of the war (North Korea and South Korea), archaeology was considered a legitimate scientific discipline, and archaeology has served similar purposes during nation building. Its main role has been to denounce colonial interpretations that emphasized the racial and cultural inferiority of the Korean people. As in many postcolonial states, Korean archaeology after liberation has taken a central role in refashioning national identity and restoring national pride. Given the scarcity of early historical documents and the opinion of scholars and officials that archaeological materials could provide "objective material evidence" for the effective deconstruction of colonialist claims, the role of archaeology in nation building was emphasized over that of other disciplines. Archaeology, however, was also expected to produce interpretations of the past that were compatible with the political ideology of each nation and, implicitly or explicitly, to serve each regime. Consequently, the theoretical perspectives and methodological practices that archaeologists employed were not politically neutral. This ultimately contributed to significantly different versions of the same history.

In both North Korea and South Korea, as in many other countries where nationalist archaeology dominates, a nation is conceived of as the natural unit of a people. Each unit has the right to constitute a natural political entity. This political entity is considered to have a past that can be studied and objectively described. In North Korea, a Marxist-oriented framework was used to understand the past of the Korean people. A Marxist framework was readily accepted because Marxism blended well with the communist ideology of North Korea, and because many Korean students, educated during the Japanese colonial period, considered the Marxist movement a powerful tool in the battle against imperialism. North Korean scholars described Korea's past as a history of continuous struggles between different classes of people, particularly the struggles of the common people against members of the bourgeois class, imperialists, and other oppressors. The perspective adopted in North Korea has generally presented the unilineal development of Korean culture as passing through various historical stages beginning with the Paleolithic and culminating with the current North Korean regime (Academy of Social Science 1977, 1991). In this model, present-day Korean people are considered a homogeneous population untainted by foreign lineages since the Paleolithic period. Interestingly, such claims about the "unilinearity" of Korean culture and the "homogeneity" of the Korean people were not overt in the writings of Yuho Do, a prominent archaeologist working in North Korea between 1946 and 1966. Rather, Do focused on describing artifacts discovered on the Korean peninsula and comparing them with similar artifacts found in neighboring countries (Do 1994 [1960]). Books and articles published after the early 1970s, however, have strongly and openly advocated unilinearity and homogeneity in Korean history (Yi 1992). Discussions of foreign artifacts, furthermore, have emphasized their differences from those of Korea.

The capitalist ideology of South Korea and the international politics of the Cold War period made most South Korean scholars deliberately avoid Marxist-oriented interpretive frameworks. On one level, archaeology in South Korea has been carried out in an ideological vacuum because it is heavily biased towards empirical studies of the temporal and spatial variations of archaeological remains. Inductive research and descriptive studies of archaeological materials are emphasized and are seen as important steps toward understanding the unique historical trajectory of the Korean people and their culture. In this sense, South Korean archaeologists have effectively dissociated themselves from any particular political ideology. On another level, however, selected artifacts and cultural traits are interpreted as evidence of migration and cultural diffusion throughout the Eurasian continent. Modern Korean culture is often described as the final product of a series of cultural interactions that occurred across this vast geographical region from the Paleolithic period onward. Such interpretations are common in South Korean archaeology. For example, the Chulmun period (ca. 8,000 [Im 1996] to 1,300 BC) is characterized by extensive migration and cultural contacts that encompassed the current regions of northeast China, Siberia, and Japan (see Han 1996 and Pai 2000, 77–81 for a critical review). The drastic cultural changes in the subsequent Mumun period (ca. 1,300 to 300 BC) are thought to be the result of immigration from the north (Kim 1986, 65; see Pai 2000, 82–87 and Roh 1996 for a critical review). Highlighting harmonious blending of different cultural traits and emphasizing cultural interactions over a vast region may appear to contradict claims in nationalist narratives that assume ethnic superiority. However, it should be noted that such interpretations implicitly describe ancient Koreans as people with a grandiose geographical scope whose lives were not confined to the small peninsula. Furthermore, describing cultural achievements that occurred in the Korean peninsula and their transmission to other regions often intentionally aims at suggesting creativity and superiority of the Korean people over others.

In both North Korea and South Korea, archaeology is considered a legitimate academic discipline that has become an integral part of nation building. In contrast with European countries where such developments occurred over centuries, the relationship between archaeology and nationalism in Korea has developed over only a few decades. The history of Korean archaeology during the twentieth century shows that the Korean people played an increasingly dominant role in archaeological research and interpretation. Korean archaeology is no longer organized around the colonialist/imperialist agendas of other powers, and the dominant narratives of previous periods have become less powerful. This demonstrates, using Hodder's phrase, that the "subaltern can speak back" (Hodder 2004, 4). This allows for "alternative agendas to be set and alternative perspectives to be explored" (Hodder 2004, 4). In a country where people have constructed nations in the face of a strong colonialist legacy, however, the place of archaeology is paradoxical. As Nelson (1995, 223) notes, "Koreans have not been interested in world prehistory, nor in the comparative history of humankind, but in unearthing and validating their own past." While local heritage and archaeological remains continue to be the sources of people's pride and identity, nationalist archaeology inevitably intervenes and manipulates or reshapes archaeological interpretations around the nationalist agenda. In both North and South Korea, these two processes seem to have happened over a relatively short period of time or even simultaneously. They are intrinsically intermixed and will be extremely difficult to disentangle. . . .

To understand the relationship between small groups and dominant nationalist narratives, I turn to the Sorori site, an Upper Paleolithic site in Korea that has evoked enormous controversy. The current debate about this site is an interesting case of how small interest groups may be empowered by creating their local heritage while simultaneously dominant voices presenting nationalist agendas remain powerful. The Sorori site derives its name from a nearby town, Soro-ri in Cheongwon County, South Korea. The site was discovered in 1994 by a site survey team of the Chungbuk National University Museum (Lee and Woo 2000). This archaeological site survey was conducted before the construction of an industrial complex planned by the local government of North Chungcheong Province. The site survey revealed that the entire region is rich in Paleolithic remains. In adjacent regions, Paleolithic stone tools were discovered from at least three other localities. The Sorori site is divided into three areas (Areas A, B, and C) and three research organizations participated in the site excavation: Chungbuk National University Museum (Area A), Dankook University Museum (Area B), and the University of Seoul (Area C). The total excavation area measured up to approximately 3.4 ha (Lee and Woo 2000). In 1997, the excavation that followed the site survey and small-scale test excavations led to the discovery of Paleolithic stone tools such as choppers, scrapers, flakes, and cores. Until the completion of the first excavation in early 1998, the Sorori site was nothing more than an ordinary archaeological site dated to the Upper Paleolithic period with an estimated date of approximately 30,000–20,000 years ago (Han and Son 2000).

In 2000, Yung-jo Lee, director of the Chungbuk National University Museum and Sorori site (Area A) excavation supervisor, claimed that his excavation team had recovered the husks of rice grains. He further claimed that the layer from which these remains had been found dated back to 13,000 years ago, and that the rice remains should logically be as old as the layer (Lee and Woo 2000, 608). He provided "scientific" data that supported this claim. According to an unofficial site excavation report of 2002, the radiocarbon (AMS) dates of charcoal fragments associated with the rice remains ranged from 14,820 to 12,500 uncalibrated bp (Lee and Woo 2002). A total of 13 charcoal samples were within this range. The dates were obtained by two independent research organizations: Geochron Lab in the U.S. and AMS Lab of Seoul National University. Allegedly, a sample of rice remain(s) was/were AMS-dated and found to be 12,500 ± 200 (SNU 01-293) uncalibrated bp (Lee and Woo 2002, 22). Lee compared the Sorori rice samples with rice remains from the Xianrendong site and the Yuchanyan cave site in China. These two Chinese sites had purportedly yielded the oldest evidence of rice yet discovered (cf. Higham and Lu 1998). He argued that because the Sorori rice pre-dated these remains by 3,000 years, it should now be considered the oldest rice in the world (Lee and Woo 2002, 18). He further argued that the recovered rice remains were in the early stage of domestication (Lee and Woo 2002, 18). . . .

Despite strong skepticism in academia, the story of the oldest rice in the world spread widely and rapidly. The Sorori site excavation team's findings were published in several major South Korean newspapers, although the story was not featured as a headline (Lee 2000; Shin 1998). By the end of 2003, most major South Korean newspapers had covered this story, generally as a short article in the culture or society section of the papers. The story was eventually covered by the BBC's Internet news site in an article entitled "World's 'oldest' rice found" (Whitehouse 2003). The coverage of the story by a foreign media outlet gave weight to the authenticity of the finding among some Koreans (see also Discovery Channel 2003).

The Sorori site successfully attracted the interests of people living in the region and became a source of local identity. In January 2004, the government of Cheongwon County, where the site is located, launched a virtual museum to introduce the findings of the Sorori site to the public. The Web site is officially entitled "Cyber Museum of Sorori Rice" (www.sorori.com). It presents the location of the site; a brief history of the excavation; pictures of excavated stone tools; the results of pollen analysis; photographs and description of organic remains such as wood and insect fragments; as well as dating results and photographs of the rice remains that were recovered from the site. The Web site also has special sections that introduce the Paleolithic period of the Korean peninsula and explain the social and ecological implications of agriculture in general. This Web site is intended to be interactive: it is linked to video clips, and visitors to the site can post questions and make comments about the findings. To attract a wider range of Internet surfers, the Web site is presented in English, Japanese, and Chinese in addition to Korean. In June 2004, the "Cyber Museum of Sorori Rice" Web site was selected by the Ministry of Information and Communication of the South Korean government as a recommended Web site for teenagers and, soon after, it was ranked among the top 6 of the 120 recommended sites (Kim 2004).

Around the same time in early 2004, the Sorori site moved to the center of debates that involved archaeologists, local people, and the general public. The Korea Land Corporation (KLC), the owner of the land where the Sorori site is located, decided to sell the property to a private company. This company planned to construct the industrial complex that had originally prompted the site survey and subsequent excavations of the Sorori site. The company's construction plans were opposed by many local people and organizations that thought the site should be preserved. They sent letters to government officials, contributed articles to newspapers and magazines, and made public statements. The various organizations and activist groups that publicly opposed the decision included the National Trust (NT) of Korea, a nongovernmental organization that protects historical relics and the natural environment (www.nationaltrust.or.kr); Citizen's Solidarity for Participation and Self-Government of Chungbuk (www.citizen.or.kr); the Hoseo Archaeological Society; the Korean Paleolithic Society (www. kolithic.or.kr); professors of the Chungbuk National University affiliated with the Collaborative Agricultural Research Group; and the local government of Cheongwon county (www.puru.net), to name just a few. Eventually, the local government of Cheongwon County filed a petition for the preservation of the site.

In November 2004, the Cultural Heritage Administration (CHA), a branch of the Ministry of Culture and Tourism (MCT) of the South

Korean government, convened their Cultural Properties Committee to discuss the preservation of the site. The committee rejected the petition from Cheongwon County to register the Sorori site as a national cultural property and to preserve it permanently. The reason for this decision was not made public. The evaluation simply stated that "the preservation of the layers associated with rice remains is not supportable, and additional preservation of the site seems unnecessary" (Yoo 2004). The members of the Cultural Properties Committee were likely unconvinced of the validity of the early date or the authenticity of the rice remains. In a domino effect, the Cultural Properties Committee of Chungcheong Province, where Cheongwon County is located, also rejected a petition from the county to register the site as a provincial cultural property (Chungcheong Province 2004). These decisions frustrated and disappointed some people, but local residents had no further reactions.

A review of controversies surrounding the interpretation and preservation of the Sorori site reveals that the voices of both small local groups and activists, and the voices of dominant decision makers, specifically the Cultural Properties Committee (especially of the central government), were articulated. The Cultural Properties Committee *(Munhwajae Wiwonhoe)* is a consultation branch associated with the Cultural Heritage Administration (CHA) of the South Korean government. The committee is composed of approximately 120 scholars who have knowledge and experience in the academic fields related to cultural properties. The committee members have a 2-year term and are selected primarily at the request of the director of the Cultural Heritage Administration. The members typically have doctoral degrees and hold academic positions in universities or museums. On the other hand, many small activist groups that claim that the site should be preserved virtually have no professional archeologists as their members. Nevertheless, the views of these groups' members were expressed regardless of whether or not their opinions were accepted by professional archaeologists.

The site has also been used by those who are not particularly interested in its preservation. In May 2004, 17 local households adjacent to the Sorori site launched a research society. Motivated partly by the possible early date of rice found in the region, members of this society decided to try to produce high-quality organic rice that retains the taste of traditional rice (Kim 2004). The Sorori rice has also been featured in an advertisement for a commercially available brand of local rice (Kim 2005). Both the advertisement and the research society emphasize the high quality of rice from this area, and the Sorori rice adds temporal dimension to their claims.

The commercialization of local rice in this manner closely relates to the situation South Korean farmers are facing: global free trade and the opening of Korean rice markets. Under the global trading regulations of the World Trade Organization (WTO), South Korea is facing the difficult challenge of sustaining its farming sector, especially rice farming. Opening the national rice market to imported rice, which can be sold at much lower prices than domestic rice, will devastate Korean farmers and agricultural markets. As agricultural producers, farmers understand that a drastic opening of the market is inevitable. The claim that Sorori rice is the world's oldest bolsters their efforts to market their local products, because they can present the region as the place where rice agriculture started. The commercial interests of these local fanners and rice distributors may be served by this claim regardless of the scientific credibility of the archaeological findings.

The process described above cannot be described simply as the articulation of marginalized voices. Sorori rice is also featured in nationalist discourses which assume that the Korean people have fixed and securely traceable cultural traits. Such discourses are often implicitly or explicitly related to the claims of ethnic superiority. For example, Hyojin Oh, the district governor of Cheongwon County where the Sorori site is located, says that the purpose of the Sorori Web site is "to let the world know that Cheongwon is the origin of the rice." In a greeting message to the Web site's visitors, he reiterates that the Sorori rice is 3,000 years older than any rice found in China. The importance of the findings is emphasized by implicitly attributing them with the supposed superiority of Koreans over Chinese.

Numerous examples can be found where Sorori rice is featured in nationalist statements. Byung-chan Kwak, an editorial writer for Hankyoreh Newspaper, a major newspaper in South Korea, reflects on the implications of the Sorori rice findings by stating, "Rice was the basis of life in the Korea peninsula over 15,000 years. Sedentary agricultural societies started and became the root of culture that is based on communities. It is hardly deniable that rice is the protoplasm of our bodies and spirit of our culture" (Kwak 2005). Suil Jeong, professor of Dankook University, traces the origin of the Korean culture from time immemorial and argues that the Sorori rice proves that Korea was the original place of so-called Rice Culture in East Asia (Jeong 2005). Sunghun Kim, processor at Chungang University and a representative of the National Trust (NT) of Korea, argues that the Sorori site should be preserved saying, "this is a way, as a suzerain state of rice culture and industry, to announce that rice is indeed Korean people's blood, flesh, and spirit" (Kim 2004). If statements in personal blogs may also be included, we see that many marginalized individuals also raise their voices to relate the Sorori site findings to nationalist discourses. The process described above, therefore, seems to be double-edged: while we witness the burgeoning of small groups that articulate their marginalized voices and benefit from their engagement with the past to challenge the nation-state's message, we also witness nationalist discourses being propagated through the same mechanisms by both powerful societal leaders and individuals, and presumably marginalized citizens. Furthermore, these two processes seem to feed off each other. . . .

42

Decolonizing Methodologies as Strategies of Practice: Operationalizing the Postcolonial Critique in the Archaeology of Rajasthan

Uzma Z. Rizvi

Assuming that all knowledge gathered at the archaeological field site has a specific methodology associated with it, the desire to decolonize a practice creates a discourse in which variables include visibility and artifact density to personal bias based on privilege, scientific and cultural imperialism, and, in some cases, racism (Dibble, Raczek, and McPherron 2005; Wobst 2005). Decolonization integrates methodology with social

Excerpted from Rizvi, Uzma Z. 2008. Decolonizing Methodologies as Strategies of Practice: Operationalizing the Postcolonial Critique in the Archaeology of Rajasthan. In *Archaeology and the Postcolonial Critique*, ed. Matthew Liebmann and Uzma Z. Rizvi, 109–27. Lanham, MD: AltaMira Press.

activism and makes relevant the performed identity of those practicing archaeology and those within whose spaces and locales the practice unfolds. An active acknowledgment of identity allows for an investigation of politics and power, based on new models of interaction, social systems, and codes of conduct, rather than a reliance on imperial and colonial models of interaction based on histories of oppression. Relying on older systems of power reflects the scarcity of time and energy required to negotiate and renegotiate our positions of power and privilege when we enter into the field as researchers, and such economies are symptomatic of complacency. Most decisions to maintain and reify power structures are not maliciously intended, but are the byproducts of prioritizing research over inequality, disenfranchisement and, in a callous sense, of prioritizing our research over the present, past, or future of others. . . .

Methodological Conundrums: Conducting the Ganeshwar-Jodhpura Cultural Complex Survey

I began preliminary survey work in Rajasthan, India, during the summer of 2000 and in 2003 returned to direct a survey project. It was the first step in a larger project that problematizes and reconceptualizes the Ganeshwar-Jodhpura Cultural Complex (GJCC), located in northeastern Rajasthan, as a collection of third-millennium BC settlements bound together by a shared cultural language that includes similarities in material culture, production of copper tools, and geographic proximity to copper mines. Located within the regions of the Aravalli Hill Range, primarily along the Kantli, Sabi, and Sota rivers, the GJCC was the largest copper-producing community in third-millennium BC South Asia. The GJCC is primarily located in present-day Jaipur, Jhunjhunu, and Sikar districts of Rajashtan, India. In geographic and chronological proximity to GJCC is the Harappan culture to the west, the Ahar-Banas Complex to the southwest, the Kayatha Culture to the southeast, and, at a later date, the OCP-Copper Hoard sites mainly to the east. This part of India is known for its farming and pastoral resources, as well as for minerals, the most important of which is copper. Khetri, the largest copper source in Rajasthan, has been exploited since antiquity and continues today as one of the major resources for copper production in India.

Based on collaborative interpretations of field research conducted during this study, the GJCC illustrates an indigenous development that sustains a larger regional economic need for copper products. The underpinnings for such a regional economic organization are resource-specialized complexes, which may have come together through certain variables, such as population increase, technological know-how, or a simple adaptation to a landscape, which most significantly pivot within highly circumscribed natural locales. As key resource centers for the region, the GJCC defines and is defined by its economic interactions and proximity to the Harappan Civilization and the Ahar-Banas Complex.

The survey team consisted of ten members, including doctoral students from the University of Rajasthan, Jaipur, and the New School University, New York. Smaller collaborative projects were formed with participating villages and communities in order to conduct the archaeological survey. These collaborative spaces emerged through discussions about interpretation with individuals who joined us on our surveys, communities who chose to engage in discussions about copper mining, and publics that formed around the discourse of tourism, heritage management, and the use of archaeology in their contemporary world. Our work involved a range of persons including: officers of the Archaeological Survey of India (ASI); the State Government of Rajasthan; Secretary of Tourism, Art and Culture; the Directorate of Archaeology and Museums; the District Magistrate; the Assistant District Magistrate; *tehsildars*; *patwaris*; police officers at the stations where artifacts were stored after a chance find; the *panchayat*; individual *sarpanj*; schoolteachers (particularly history teachers); community leaders; elders; head of households and farmsteads; interested individuals passing by; and, most of all, children. The methods developed through our interactions with these individuals and groups.

Each new survey began with a visit to the village *sarpanj* to discuss the overall project. This would often result in a discussion with other *panchayat* members and interested community leaders, including farmers. Such discussions made each of these individual stakeholders in the overall project, each with a particular point of view and specific interests in collaboration with the survey project. In most cases, local history teachers would also join in the efforts and discussion and their classes would join our surveys. In some instances, these students would actually become part of after-school programs in which the GJCC survey team would teach the students survey techniques and lessons in the general archaeology of South Asia.

These discussions and interactive spaces were crucial for the types of methodological interventions I had in mind. I felt it was important for the village and community to enable and empower us to conduct the survey, rather than our team's demanding their services. Already, the fact that we had come to their village to understand the past shifted privilege to the archaeological team. The only way, in my mind, to reverse that power situation was to draw upon lessons from my own cultural heritage about the student coming to master, thus presenting the village *panchayat* with the analogy that likened the team to eager students, which we were, coming to learn from the land and its inhabitants the history of that place. This was an easily translatable concept for most of the individuals and groups with whom we interacted. However, this constant dialogue complicated each process—and invariably, our workday did not always reflect the "plan" that was established at the start of the day. This was difficult, as it took control out of my hands (as director of a project) and placed decision-making abilities into multiple hands, shaped by others' schedules, moods, and ideas, which *theoretically* is the point of collaborative, interactive (as opposed to reactive) work but is difficult to operationalize *practically*. I realized however, that by giving up control, the survey was open to experiencing and documenting the past in a manner that would not have been possible otherwise (see also Green, Green, and Góes Neves 2003, excerpted in Chapter 32 this volume). One way to dismantle the colonial control of knowledge production was to give up that very control that continued to reiterate itself in my mind based on my own Western pedagogy.

This survey consisted of collaborations among the many levels and scales of "local" and the survey team. The team, cognizant of local involvement, was simultaneously critical of the concept as well. Lynn Meskell has warned of the patronizing tendency archaeologists adopt in using "local" as a trope, which designates the concept of local interaction as a "catchall for the complex and ethically necessary encounters we have with various constituencies in and around archaeological locales" (2005, 82). These locals are not passive receptors existing for our intellectual mining or to hear our grand theories about their histories. Rather, she argues that they are "directly enmeshed in their own critical reformulations, political negotiations, and constitutions of theory and interpretation" (Meskell 2005, 82). Based on the experience of this survey project, I would argue that all archaeologists interacting with locals necessarily change the stakes for those reformulations and political negotiations for both the locals and the archaeologists (for example, see Dural 2007).

The methodology developed for the GJCC survey work was inspired by a desire to decolonize and deconstruct field techniques while keeping in mind the negotiations of a relatively new state (established in 1947) and extant social systems, such as caste. For example, as a Muslim, I operated outside the Hindu caste system but was placed very specifically within the corollary Muslim caste system, expressed most prominently as limits on access to certain spaces and demands to occupy others—although I occasionally chose to subvert such systems, depending on the context. This awareness of religious affiliation was heightened due to the sociopolitical climate causing tension between various religious groups (Brass 2003).

Also during this time, there was increased suspicion of those collecting artifacts due to the arrest and raid on the warehouse of V. N. Ghiya by the Jaipur police, who recovered more than 300 Rajasthan antiques (*Hindustan Times*, Jaipur edition; June 27, 2003). Village residents near the site of Tyonda refused to allow the survey team to conduct work on their land and near their village due to the large-scale looting that had taken place in and around there, which they blamed on Ghiya. The looting was very obvious from a cursory visual inspection. The *panchayat* refused to meet with us and all doors shut upon arrival. Respecting their wishes, we moved our survey elsewhere. In some measure, this shift of focus had no quantifiable effects, as there was more land to cover and the team had already surveyed the surrounding regions. Qualitatively, however, it reassured the various community collaborators from other villages that we, as a team, respected the wishes of the village *panchayat*. The ramifications of looting on the local level escalated the stakes, particularly in issues of global significance such as the U.S. invasion of Iraq, which was a constant question for me at these meetings. Each of these conversations was used to ascertain levels of trust and establish a working relationship and sense of camaraderie, providing the framework for collaborative, community-based work.

These complicated interpersonal negotiations were the most basic of all interactions. At every stage, each member of the team entered into relationships that could potentially have personal, professional, and legal ramifications. Moreover, we began to realize that there was one question that kept resurfacing: everyone wanted to know why we were there. In essence, that query for justification is the basis for the methodological shift that I argue informs, colors, and contextualizes archaeological practice. When they asked *why*, was it curiosity or suspicion? . . .

The experience of the GJCC survey confirms that at each level of interaction, the coexistence of suspicion and curiosity is a traumatic remnant of a colonial past and a reiteration of an unequal present, in which information, power, and prestige continue to be stolen from the caretakers of the land (Nandy 2001). It was only at the highest levels of the Indian bureaucracy, and within the company of internationally recognized senior scholars, usually with some Western training, that such a suspicion was not blatant and there was an expressed interest in my academic qualifications. At this privileged level, the individuals are recognized, legitimized, and authorized as some part of the elite on the national or international stage. In contrast, the vast majority of the middle-class Indian bureaucracy showed less interest in my academic prowess; rather, in order to gain access to locked cabinets, museum records, and information about previous excavations, I had to prove my trustworthiness by locating my spatial practice and performance within their social systems and cultural norms.

Is the suspicion of Western archaeologists working in a contemporary moment in India due to a larger, perhaps, metadistrust of colonial attitudes of knowledge production? Or is it more about the signs of *that* type of colonial privilege apparent in our performative moments, based on our pedagogical training, that might unwittingly link us to a neo-colonial attitude that simultaneously controls all centers of knowledge production and, for the betterment of science, forces a conceptual separation between the overlapping realities of the object excavated from the ground and the object taken from the people?

The shifting nuances between suspicion and curiosity are significant in understanding the ways in which people recognize power and privilege. During our 2003 survey, it became very clear that the power we carried was somewhat transferable. When we were invited to tea in a village household, the cultural capital of that household was enhanced. A connection was made that often seemed to be very intimate on the part of the host and cautious on our part. Indeed, this may link to rules of hospitality, but perhaps more realistically, these levels of intimacy have to do with the ways in which power and privilege operate. Often our caution articulated a fear of not understanding complex village politics and the tacit knowledge that we, as privileged archaeologists, could not give them everything our power might have suggested.

Through our training, we are transformed into vessels of power that signify promise, yet often we cannot live up to that potential. It is a performance of power that we reenact by occupying a specific space that is not local to us, which recalls in collective memory the colonial archaeologists and the power vested in their positions as embodiments of empire. I believe that a shift in methodology—one that accounts for privileged practice, the collective memory of the colonial archaeologist, and the context for any curiosity and suspicion—enables the archaeologist to dismantle the colonial structures upon which she or he stands. . . .

43

Whose Archaeology? Decolonizing Archaeological Perspective in Hokkaido Island

Hirofumi Kato

Indigenous archaeology is one of the most dynamic trends in public archaeology. In many formerly colonized areas, it has forced archaeologists to fundamentally reconsider their aims and methods. In this paper, I explore some possibilities for promoting Indigenous archaeology in Hokkaido Island, the original homeland of the Ainu people that had been colonized by the modern Japanese state.

The relationship between Indigenous peoples and archaeologists in the colonized area has begun to be reconsidered. As pointed out by many commentators (see for example, Smith and Wobst 2005b), the relationship between archaeologists and members of Indigenous groups still continues to be unequal and asymmetrical. Here we also can see the political aspects and influence of archaeology, and archaeologists must become aware of it.

On the other hand, archaeology in the Japanese archipelago has been explained using the monogenesis theory in view of the island environment, and Indigenous people were only recently accorded the status as "the ancient ones" (Fujisawa 2006). Experts and politicians did not recognize as Indigenous peoples in Japan. In this paper, I will explore the possibilities for promoting Indigenous archaeology in Hokkaido, the original homeland of the Ainu people that had been colonized by the modern state. I will discuss this in terms of who has the authority for speaking about the past in Hokkaido.

Excerpted from Kato, Hirofumi. 2009. Whose Archaeology? Decolonizing Archaeological Perspective in Hokkaido Island. *Journal of the Graduate School of Letters, Hokkaido University* 4:47–55.

Who Is the Public of Archaeology?

The argument that archaeology is not the exclusive possession of experts and scholars has emerged in discussions of who is the public for the disciplines. "The public" has two meanings: the state and the people. One concept of "the public" refers to the collective body of all citizens, and has been used since the Roman periods in contrast to the private realm (Milton 2001, 1). In modern archaeology, the word "public" tends to be associated with the state and its institutions. As in the case of the national museum, the archaeology as it is displayed relates to the formation of national identity, and is a result of the era of intensive state formation. Of course, we are aware of the discussion pertaining to public archaeology and Cultural Resource Management (CRM) in the United States (for example, see Merriman 2004). However, this is not the focus of the paper.

A second concept of "the public" refers to the group of individuals who debate issues and consume cultural products, and whose reactions form the "public opinion." Archaeological sites are cultural heritage located in local societies, and are a part of the infrastructure and commons of local societies. This concept of "public" essentially means that "the issue is open to be discussed by all people and should be decided by all citizens through collective discussion." This has led to the recognition of the historical contingency of archaeological work, and the multivalence of archaeological interpretation. Archaeologists have come to realize that the public is interested in archaeology. Thus, for example, Schadla-Hall (1999, 147) has defined public archaeology as "any area of archaeological activity that interacted or had the potential to interact with the public." Public archaeology was expanded from state archaeology to the affected citizens, and empowered the local community. For instance, the discussion of the shared memory of colonial history in local communities has reignited the discussion of colonialism within the archaeological discipline and has re-established the authority of indigenous people on their cultural heritage. As a result, this paradigm shift in archaeology has impelled indigenous archaeology, following the efforts of Indigenous and other minority peoples to have a say in the study and interpretation of their own past.

What Is Indigenous Archaeology?

On 6 June 2008, the Japanese Diet (the 169th Diet, Resolution No.1) unanimously passed a resolution . . . and issued a statement . . . [that] formally recognizes the Ainu as "an indigenous people with a distinct language, religion and culture". In a nation that has until now preferred to perceive itself as ethnically homogenous, this is a highly significant move. It is a political and social change for Japanese archaeology that will be a big problem . . . in the future. However, the virtual absence of a reaction in the academic society shows that it has not fully recognized the importance of this problem. The resolution by the Japanese Diet is related to the U.N. Declaration on "the Rights of Indigenous Peoples" which was adopted on 13 September 2007. This declaration stated that indigenous people clearly have political, legal, economical and social rights. Article 11 and 12 clearly state that Indigenous peoples have the right of management, conservation and repatriation for the archaeological collections and human remains from archaeological sites (www.un.org/esa/socdev/unpfii/documents/DRIPS en.pdf.).

The fact that the Japanese government officially recognized Ainu people as an indigenous people in Japan indicates that this issue has an immediate impact on archaeology in Japan. Are archaeologists really recognizing this problem? Indigenous archaeology is one of the categories in public archaeology. As a result of the increasing publicness of archaeology, many archaeologists have recognized that the past is widely open to the citizens and the local societies. One thus must consider the right of Indigenous people who have owned the past and are directly affected by its historical interpretation.

The question "who has the right to control the past?" is not just an academic question, but a practical reality that must be faced in the many day-to-day interactions between archaeologists and Indigenous peoples (Siller 2005; Smith and Wobst 2005b; Watkins 2000). The debate over "who owns the past" runs particularly hot when it involves the cultural and intellectual property of Indigenous peoples (Hollowell and Nicholas 2008; Nicholas 2004). The core issues include the debate on who benefits from archaeological research. Do archaeologists have a right to control the past of others?

Although the Ainu people are the original inhabitants of Hokkaido Island and have generated most of its archaeological and historical heritage, the Indigenous viewpoint is not sufficiently reflected in museum exhibits nor in the historical interpretation of archeological collections. This is reflected by the avoidance of discussions between the interpretations generated by archaeologists with archaeological information, and the historical sense of Indigenous people.

What historical events occurred to the Ainu after the 13th century and to the *Satsumon* culture that preceded the Ainu? What kinds of continuities or discontinuities can we find there? Should I discuss the history of the formation of the ethnic group called the Ainu along with the past? Should archaeologists classify and discuss the "historical story" and the formation process of the ethnic group? The relationship between traditional archaeology and Indigenous peoples has been pointed out, when we considered the necessity of Indigenous perspectives on archaeology. As Claire Smith and Martin Wobst pointed out "traditionally, archaeology has been done 'on', not 'by', 'for' or 'with' Indigenous peoples" (Smith and Wobst 2005b, 7). This applies to the situation of archaeology in Hokkaido Island.

In the next section, I will discuss the necessity of an Indigenous Archeology perspective in Japan. The case study is a problem concerning the Shiretoko National Park which is listed as a World Natural Heritage Site, and contains archaeological sites and cultural heritage of the Ainu.

Shiretoko as World Heritage Site

The Shiretoko peninsula is located in the East part of Hokkaido Island. On July 14th 2005, the Shiretoko peninsula was declared a UNESCO World Natural Heritage Site. As pointed out by the nomination committee, it provides an outstanding example of the interaction of marine and terrestrial ecosystems (http://whc.unesco.org/en/list/1193/). The name of "Shiretoko" is Japanese, but derived from Ainu. *Sir-etok* means "the end of the earth" or "the place where the earth protrudes." In addition, the park contains many archaeological sites from the *Jomon* to the *Ainu* periods. However, in the nomination process, the voice of Ainu people was not included. The Shiretoko peninsula was only declared to be *natural* heritage.

The Situation of the Ainu around Shiretoko

Despite demands from Ainu People to be recognized as an Indigenous people, the Japanese government designates the Ainu people as an ethnic minority. Most Japanese academics agree that the Ainu are the original inhabitants of Hokkaido Island, but there are serious problems with the position of Ainu in Japanese history. After the Meiji Restoration, the main topic of debate in the anthropological community was the racial origins of people in the Japanese archipelago. Some western researchers thought the Ainu belonged to the "Caucasian" race, and were direct descendants of European Stone Age people. On the other hand, Edward Morse who excavated the Omori shell midden, argued that the Ainu had replaced a pre-Ainu people that had lived in the Neolithic period (Morse 1983 [1977]).

Japanese researchers also joined the debate about the first inhabitants of the Japanese archipelago. Shogoro Tsuboi, the reader of the Anthropological Society of Japan (at that time, the Anthropological Society of Tokyo) argued that the Stone Age inhabitants of Japan were the Koropokkur, which means "dwarfs living under the butterbur leaves" (Tsuboi 1887). On the other hand, Mitsutaro Shirai regarded the Ainu as pit dwellers who made stone tools and pottery (Shirai 1887; Watase 1886). In this historical context, Japanese academics have played the principal role in defining Ainu identity. And in 1899 the Meiji Regime passed the *Act for the Protection of the Former Aborigines*. This act forced the Ainu to change their traditional livelihood and to assimilate into Japanese society.

The Relationship between the Archaeological Record and Indigenous Peoples

. . . The chronological framework of Hokkaido Island has become a part of Japanese history strongly influenced by Japanese archaeologists, and it is pervaded by the specific perspectives of national archaeology. Basically Japanese history could be divided into prehistoric, protohistoric and historic periods. Prehistory is divided into the Paleolithic, Jomon and Yayoi periods. Jomon Culture is the name for the original local Neolithic culture in the Japanese archipelago. This culture covers the entire territory of modern Japan, including Hokkaido Island, but not Sakhalin and Kuril Island. Here we can see a bias in archaeological interpretation. Archaeologists and anthropologists are trying to clarify when the Ainu culture emerged. They place it around the 13th century, on the basis of the replacement of pottery by lacquerware ("Iomante"), and by the appearance of the bear ceremony in the archaeological record (Udagawa 2001; Watanabe 1972).

World Heritage "Shiretoko" and the Ainu

Let us turn to the "Shiretoko" peninsula. Ainu people had not been officially asked to participate in the nominating process. In relation to World Heritage sites, the idea of an Indigenous Peoples Council of Experts was presented to the 24th Session of the World Heritage Committee. This proposal influenced UNESCO's Convention for Safeguarding the Intangible Cultural Heritage. In terms of the nominating process, the Advisory of the International Union for Conservation of Nature (IUCN) noted that "it considered it important that representatives of the Ainu people, such as through the Hokkaido Utari Association (the Hokkaido Ainu Association), have the opportunity to be involved in the future management of the property, including in relation to the development of appropriate ecotourism activities which celebrate the traditional customs and uses of the nominated property" (IUCN World Heritage Evaluation Report 2005, 31).

Actually, there are 114 archaeological sites in the Shiretoko peninsula, including 19 "Chashi-Kotsu" (Ainu for "remains of fort," but its function is not only that of a fort, but as a place for negotiating between groups and a sacred place). Today, the Ainu consider "Chashi-Kotsu" to be sacred sites. Therefore, in the future management of the "Shiretoko" heritage, we have to be concerned with working with the Ainu people and how they can access their heritage.

The New Situation and New Projects

In 1994, Shigeru Kayano, an Ainu, was elected as member to the (national) House of Councilors. In 1997 the Japanese parliament ratified the Act for the Promotion of Ainu Culture and the Dissemination and Advocacy for the Traditions of the Ainu and Ainu Culture. Increasingly, since the adoption of the new act, Ainu research and cultural events have been organized by the Foundation for Research and Promotion of Ainu Culture, an organization created as a result of the Act. Ten years later, in 2007, Hokkaido University founded the new "Center for Ainu and Indigenous Studies" (CAIS). This research center is the first one to focus on Ainu and Indigenous Studies at a Japanese university. An important characteristic of the Center is its interdisciplinary approach. It reflects the strengths of the university as its members include experts not only from cultural anthropology, history, archaeology, linguistics and other humanities but also from other social sciences, such as law, political science, sociology and pedagogy, as well as environmental science and other natural sciences.

The center is working on the following projects (working groups):

1. The restoration of legal rights for the Ainu and Indigenous peoples;
2. The preparation of teaching materials and educational programs;
3. Museum presentations;
4. Social surveys;
5. Ainu language;
6. Indigenous Eco-tourism;
7. Generating a New Ainu history (including Ainu archaeology as Indigenous Archaeology).

Within the project "Generating a New Ainu History", we are turning Ainu archaeology into Indigenous Archaeology. And as a first field project, begun in April 2008, we started working on the World Heritage site "Shiretoko."

The Creation of Indigenous Archaeology in World Heritage "Shiretoko"

Our project "Indigenous Archaeology in Shiretoko" (IAS) has the following aims:

1. collaboration with the Ainu in research activities;
2. collaboration with the local community;
3. using Indigenous ecotourism as cultural resource management.

As an organizing principle, we chose an interdisciplinary approach. The first IAS goal is the most important for us. It is the first attempt at inviting Ainu people to participate in designing the research for the archaeological investigation. We would like to build Ainu views and voices into the research and conservation plan. We believe that it is important to access Indigenous voice at all levels. A more important aspect of this is that Indigenous people are working with non-Indigenous researchers in partnership.

The second aim of IAS is also significant. Any archaeological site is located in the local community. In the World Heritage "Shiretoko," archaeological and historical monuments are also very important spaces and places for the local community. We would like to create a place for exchanging opinions of the conservation model in "Shiretoko" among all of the participants of the projects, including local people and Ainu peoples.

We think that Indigenous ecotourism is an effective method for using archaeological sites to teach tourists and students local history. Here we cooperate with a local NGO that is organizing ecotourism, and support preparing manuals and guide books for Indigenous ecotourism. Project members consist of different experts including archaeology, geology, history, and tourism studies.

In the past three years, we have found many important remains that demonstrated that the roots of the Ainu bear cult and bear ceremony go back to the 11th century AD. There are many multi-layer sites from the prehistoric periods to the Ainu culture. . . . In the 2008 field season, our group carried out archaeological investigations in the top of Shiretoko peninsula. On the edge of the sea terrace near Keikichi Bay, we were successful in finding the remains of a ritual space of the Ainu people, which dates from the 17th and 18th century. This structure contains many fragments of iron items including iron pan and axes, and others. All artifacts were intentionally broken. Also in the same area was a lot of prehistoric pit dwellings which date from the 4th to 11th century AD.

"Shiretoko" is not simply a natural park and but provides great value as complex heritage (natural and cultural). Unfortunately, when "Shiretoko" Natural Park was declared a UNESCO World Natural Heritage Site in 2005, it had not been fully evaluated for its historical and cultural value.

To the Next Stage

There are few archaeologists who study Indigenous archaeology in Hokkaido and I could not find Indigenous archaeologists here. Even while this paper insists on the necessity of an Indigenous archeology perspective, the academy has not taken such a perspective seriously, yet. However, knowledge about the field is increasing rapidly. Thus, we also shall not be indifferent to this movement.

We have to understand the impact on society by the stances taken by archaeologists and by museum representations. The communication and behavior of archaeologists are not non-political action. They should be extremely conscious that their actions are political actions that influence people and their rights. The influence on Indigenous people is especially strong. A serious discussion of the research ethics of archaeology is vital. We have to become conscious of, and understand, our position and the effects of our initiative on the history of other peoples. That is why archaeologists cannot exist without building partnerships with communities. Zimmerman (2005) has noted "not to do so opens the door to uninformed decision-making and an uncertain future for the discipline."

SECTION IX

Europe

European nation-states have long been agents of imperial expansion into Indigenous territories. European scientists have "archaeologized" Indigenous peoples, artifacts, and sites, and European museums still house many Indigenous collections. Repatriation has become an increasingly visible point of contact, as Native American, Aboriginal, African, and other colonized peoples demand access to collections and the return of ancestral remains and cultural patrimony. Europe is more than just a homeland of colonizers, however, since many Indigenous people live within the borders of European nations.

This section focuses on some of the unique venues in which Indigeneity is constructed, communicated, and contested in European contexts. Europe's Indigenous peoples—Basques in France, Frisians in the Netherlands, and Scots in Britain, to name just a few—view themselves as linguistically, culturally, and politically separate from the nation-states that surround them. These groups maintain deep historical attachments to marked ancestral landscapes where they have long resided, but representations of these landscapes and their cultural heritage are not always under their control. Images of Euro-Indigenes are frequently co-opted (even stereotyped) by dominant nations to encourage tourism and market the consumption of uniquely European cultures and histories. Some highly visible and less sedentary ethnic groups, such as the Roma (popularly called Gypsies) and the Irish Travellers of the British Isles, are also subject to stereotyping in popular culture. These marginalized groups have yet to be tracked by archaeologists, in part because their movements transgress territorial bounds, and their campsites often transgress local regulations (Drummond 2007).

This section opens with Angèle Smith's discussion of Anglo-Norman removals of medieval Irish history in "Written Off the Map: Cleared Landscapes of Medieval Ireland." Spatiality is constructed through patterns of inclusion and exclusion and is mapped by physical, social, and cognitive boundaries. Colonialism, she notes, often consists of "the physical removal of a people from their place along with the infilling of outsiders into that same place." Focusing on the politics of public representation, she describes the impact of ideological clearances that justify acts of colonization in the past. Indigenous spatial constructions are somewhat difficult to reclaim, she argues, since the map of Ireland at present is not that of the Irish but is an echo of the colonial landscape created by Anglo-Norman lords.

In "Colonial Constructs: Colonialism and Archaeology in the Mediterranean," Peter van Dommelen illustrates the persistence of colonialist representations and neo-imperialist models in archaeology. "Civilization" has long implied the "subjection and the 'civilizing' of the natives as well as the act of founding colonies" (Morel 1984, 124). Colonial narratives suggest that the Italic peoples were culturally inferior and that exposure to Greek civilization naturally resulted in the emergence of a superior Western culture. Although there have been concerted efforts to decolonize elsewhere, these one-sided representations persist in the Mediterranean. Van Dommelen critiques the routine reproduction of dualistic representations that imply distinct, boundaried, essentialist categories, and he suggests the use of hybrid models that can more accurately reflect the social complexities and mutual influences of disparate cultures in contact.

Mike Parker Pearson and Ramilisonina (Malagasy), authors of "Public Archaeology and Indigenous Communities," grapple with the question of who constitutes the "Indigenous" in the Western Scottish Isles. Many inhabitants are relatively recent newcomers (having migrated in the nineteenth century), yet Hebrideans boast an "utterly distinct and unassailably self-confident regional identity which other Scots often find annoying." "Indigenous," in this region, has little to do with ethnic purity; instead, it is a self-definition that distinguishes insiders from outsiders. Pearson and Ramilisonina note that archaeologists have become key participants in the tourist trade, by providing intriguing archaeological destinations and by joining in community events and social relations. The authors suggest that public archaeologists should emphasize local community involvement and personal relationships, rather than concern themselves with mediating Indigenous identity.

Barbara Bender, writing of England in "Time and Landscape," explores notions of time and memory. Natural landscapes, says Bender, are not passive and static; they are undisciplined, making mock of "oppositions that we create between time (history) and space (geography) or between nature (science) and culture (anthropology)." Although these places constitute time materializing, they are subjectively mediated by human interactions and memories in the moment. Bender identifies filtering processes that shape our experience of the prehistoric embodied landscape while critiquing Western notions that create artificial distances between observer and observed. In a case study at Leskernick Hill in England, for example, she describes Bronze Age stones set in an ancient cultural landscape. Modern observers tend to distinguish between glacial and human agency in the positioning of these megaliths, but she doubts that Indigenous inhabitants made these same distinctions. In a modern context, scientific concentrations on a distinct era may confuse those who see history as a layered palimpsest of human experience. Bender emphasizes the importance of attention to constructions of meaning, cautioning that "official" histories may appear to contradict the lived experiences of locals.

The excerpt from "Indigenous Journeys—Splinterville, Drenthe, Amherst" by Margaret M. Bruchac (Abenaki) describes her fieldwork in the northern Netherlands, where she investigated popular memories of past histories linked to ancient sites in the northern Dutch landscape. She observes that all human expressions (including folklore and invented traditions) constitute observable phenomena that record data concerning the past and that all ancestral remains represent somebody's relatives. Bruchac calls for "restorative methodologies," including examinations of the habits and thought patterns of collectors, as crucial elements of repatriation research. In the global commons, cross-cultural cooperation is increasingly necessary to address situational ethics surrounding the handling of ancestral remains and patrimony. As a case in point, she relates an instance when Dutch archaeologists were compelled to reconsider their own Indigeneity after a collection of "bog bodies" became subject to cultural protocols imposed by Canadian First Nations museum professionals.

Odd Mattis Hætta (Saami) taps the public fascination with ancient rock carvings as an entry point for discussions of politics and ethnicity in "Rock Carvings in a Saami Perspective: Some Comments on Politics and Ethnicity in Archaeology." Norwegian ethnicity is frequently implied back to Mesolithic times, but the Indigenous Saami people are conspicuously overlooked in the archaeology of Fennoskandia. Hætta focuses on this asymmetry and on the general lack of consideration for Saami peoples, while calling for new approaches to research from three angles: archaeological perspectives (ancient markers of ethnicity); historical perspectives (interpretations of motifs and contexts); and political perspectives (how and why Saami and Norwegian communities are positioned vis-à-vis the past).

The closing excerpt, from Janet Levy, is titled "Prehistory, Identity, and Archaeological Representation in Nordic Museums." National and regional museums throughout Europe have been constructed as repositories for "authoritative narratives" intended to evoke and shape representations of prehistory and nationalistic state formations. Levy identifies anthropological and archaeological museums, in particular, as arenas for exerting authority over representations of others. European archaeologists often shy away from drawing overt connections between past ethnic and present national groups, as a reaction to the Nazi use of racialized archaeology to legitimize imperialist ambitions (Arnold 1990, 2002). Linkages between race and nation have nonetheless remained evident in museum discourse and display. Levy examines the "primitivizing" of the Saami in Nordic museums, alongside Saami movements to "culturize" the environment in museums that integrate land, climate, and people over time. Although this excerpt focuses on the Saami, the issues raised—cultural identity, primitivism, museum representation, political voice—and methodology offered are applicable to a range of global contexts where ancient landscapes have been depicted as empty and pristine, ideologically disconnecting them from Indigenous populations past and present.

44

Written Off the Map: Cleared Landscapes of Medieval Ireland

Angèle Smith

Archaeological landscapes are assumed to be those that, while once lively, have since been abandoned. How these lands have been abandoned or cleared of human society varies; abandonment can be the result of a slow and gradual decline of the population, or it can be the result of a forceful and even violent removal of peoples from their lands and homes as a result of pestilence and disease, economic expansion, warfare, or colonization. In this chapter, I will explore the colonial clearance of the Irish landscape in the late twelfth century, not so much by the physical removal of peoples from their land, but by removing them ideologically from the landscape. In doing so, the colonizer is able to justify and authorize their place by portraying Ireland as a barren, empty landscape. This strategy is not uncommon and certainly has been examined elsewhere, for example in the case of colonizing North American lands and the removal of First Nations or indigenous peoples (Axtell 1981; French 2003; Harris 2002). In this study however, I explore how the Anglo-Normans ideologically "cleared" or removed the early medieval Irish society from their lands by writing them off the map of Ireland.

. . . This paper is not so much about the archaeology of this early medieval landscape or about the archaeological evidence of the colonial act of clearance. Rather this chapter aims to explore the complex process of ideologically removing the Irish from their landscape and remaking that landscape—a process that has not been examined through archaeology,

Excerpted from Smith, Angèle. 2008. Written Off the Map: Cleared Landscapes of Medieval Ireland. In *Landscapes of Clearance: Archaeological and Anthropological Perspectives*, ed. A. Smith and A. Gazin-Schwartz, 49–70. Walnut Creek, CA: Left Coast Press.

yet has great implication for understanding the gap in the archaeological record of this period (a gap which further serves to reinforce the notion of an empty Irish landscape). In examining the colonial process through the artifacts of Giraldus Cambrensis's early texts and his single map, which represent the newly colonized Ireland, I seek to illustrate and analyze how the landscape is refashioned cartographically and ideologically. It is clear that a robust archaeological plan to reinvestigate this period of early colonization is necessary. The analysis in this chapter sets the stage for and allows such archaeological inquiry to now be possible.

Ireland's colonial history comprises various periods in which the landscape was literally cleared of its local inhabitants to reshape it as British space (Andrews 1985; Brady and Gillespie 1986; Canny 2001). The late twelfth-century "invasion" by the Anglo-Normans into Ireland is the earliest evidence of colonialism in the island. However, it was not the first time that peoples from Ireland and Britain had interacted: trade, culture, and religious ties forged close links between the two islands. The new political relationship created through the Anglo-Norman intervention required a process of justification. It was a paradoxical process through which the long-standing friendly connections were severed, the sense of "sameness" replaced by "otherness," and the landscape reimagined and re-presented as barren, yet bountiful and profitable for colonization; uninhabited, yet inhabited by wild beast-like people. The fact that clearance was necessary for colonization presupposes that the land had indeed been occupied and used. To legitimize intervention, more than just the people had to be evicted: the landscape itself had to be made barren. This was accomplished in several ways through physical, cartographic, and ideological removal and/or distancing. . . .

Ideological Clearances

Colonialism is in part the physical removal of a people from their place along with the infilling of outsiders into that same place. But colonialism is also an act of the ideological clearance of people from place in order to justify and authorize the physical acts of clearance on the landscape. In the late twelfth century this ideological colonialism was cunning and complex. There were extensive economic, political, and religious relationships already well forged between the two countries, as well as much shared cultural custom. In order to legitimize the invasion and colonization, the image and understanding of Ireland and the Irish people had to be drastically changed.

I examine Giraldus Cambrensis's *Topographia Hibernica* and the accompanying map as acts and artifacts of this process of colonizing the representation of the place and the people of Ireland. The new representation had to create and support a novel relationship between the two countries that justified colonialism; it needed to transform what was sameness between the two into an otherness. But first, it needed to make the landscape appear as an empty, barren wasteland. I particularly focus on the map as the key to painting Ireland in a new light, as "a country so remote from the rest of the world, and lying at its furthest extremity, forming as it were another world" (Giraldus Cambrensis 1982 [1188]). . . .

While other, often ancient classical, accounts might also be cited (including Solinus, Strabo, Tacitus, Julius Caesar, and Hector Boethius, among others), it is Giraldus who provides the principal source of information. The Renaissance period may be crucial for the founding of an English sense of national identity (Helgerson 1992) as well as an Irish identity springing from their united efforts during the Nine Years' War (1594–1603). Much recent interest in Renaissance colonial literature (Bradshaw, Hadfield, and Maley 1993; Morgan 1999; Murphy 1999; Rambo 1994) has focused on the writings of Spenser, Shakespeare, and Geoffrey Keating. However, I argue that emergent national identities had their foundation much earlier, in the twelfth century. Although some have dismissed Giraldus's work as simply royal propagandist literature, close examination illustrates the creation of the ideologies of colonialism in Ireland. Mapping Ireland as the "world beyond" and defining Irish identity as "the other" controlled the image of England's western neighbor and lay the foundation of the long process of colonization in Ireland. . . .

The Spatiality of Map and Text

In looking at this medieval map of Ireland and its place within the wider context of Christian Europe, I have employed the spatial categories used by Andrew Murphy (1999) in his analysis of the two geographical writings of Giraldus Cambrensis. These spatial categories establish the link between place/space on the one hand, and identity and social relations of power on the other. This is not simply a spatial metaphor. Rather, as Soja (1989) and Foucault (1984) have argued, spatial relations and social relations are dynamically linked, such that social relations produce and are simultaneously produced by spatial relations. In this case, spatial proximity is likened to social/cultural sameness and hence familiarity and acceptance. In contrast, spatial distancing is associated with the process of othering, thereby legitimizing power inequalities in the form of colonization and colonial ideologies. Said (1978, 1993) suggests identity is about the discourses of inclusion and exclusion articulated against a hostile other. I argue here that spatiality is also understood in terms of inclusion and exclusion defined by boundaries, whether they be physical (e.g., a body of water), social (e.g., a national border) or cognitive (e.g., ideological differences), or all of these combined. Yet space is, by its very essence, fluid. The sense of boundedness is arbitrary and always in the process of being created, torn down, or recreated. Similarly, identity is fluid and always shifting in the process of being defined, and redefined. Thus in analyzing the spatial artifact of the Giraldus map, it is important to see that the spatial/identity categories that seem to be rigidly defined are actually determined by their borders and boundaries; yet these are permeable and (often) crossed. Boundaries are breached as Ireland-the-place is simultaneously depicted as proximate and distant, and the Irish identity as simultaneously the same and the other. This creates problems for installing the dominant colonial ideologies, for justifying political actions of inequality, and for legitimizing new power structures because such crossing of boundaries (spatial and identity) creates a liminal state which is, in actuality, much more representative of the complexity of the social and spatial relations.

In inventing a colonial Ireland and the colonial Irish, England has a difficult task: it must fashion out of a sense of spatial proximity and cultural sameness, a distant other. Set against this background of geographical proximity and cultural sameness, the writing of Giraldus and the *Topographia* map sought to justify the colonial endeavor of Britain in Ireland. . . .

Written off the Map: Cleared Landscapes of Medieval Ireland

This is a unique act of colonialism, and as a result allows for a critical analysis of the ideological process of clearance and othering that works to justify and authorize colonization. It is unique because it is the *first* colonial episode that initiates and influences the subsequent long history of colonial relations between Ireland and Britain. It is also unique in that unlike most colonial experiences, this invasion and conquest was not the meeting of unfamiliar peoples from different cultures in lands foreign to the colonizer. Rather, Ireland and the Irish were well known to the colonizing Anglo-Normans. Economic and political, as well as cultural and religious ties, had linked the two countries prior to the 1169 invasion. Thus the act of colonialism was much more than the physical act of removing people from their landscape, it was an ideological reimaging of Ireland and the Irish people. While this colonial "invasion" has yet to be extensively examined using an archaeological approach, the implications of the analysis made here of Giraldus Cambrensis's contemporary map and texts are significant for archaeology and the historical reconstruction of the early medieval Irish landscape. As noted by Barry earlier in this chapter, the relative absence of archaeological inquiry into the Anglo-Norman period simply reaffirms the colonial control (still) by assuming this period to be more a part of English rather than Irish history. By examining the spatial and social relations mapped out by Giraldus in the twelfth century, it becomes clear that archaeological investigations of the colonial process and the colonial landscape are necessary to examine and critique the map and texts for their reimaging of Ireland and the Irish people.

The new image of Ireland was that of a barren wasteland, "unoccupied" especially in the sense that the Irish did not live in cities. The depiction of Ireland represented in the map is not of an Irish-inhabited landscape but of the colonial landscape of the Anglo-Norman lords. By mapping Ireland as a "world beyond," at the extreme West of Christian Europe, Ireland and Irish identity becomes the other. This is in contrast to (and ideologically transforms) the previous close relationship and social sameness and proximity between the two countries. Controlling the image of Ireland and its people helped to lay the foundation for an ideology of colonization that cleared the landscape of shared commonness and wrote the Irish off the map of medieval Christian Europe.

45

Colonial Constructs: Colonialism and Archaeology in the Mediterranean

Peter van Dommelen

While the West had to decolonize Africa and Asia after the Second World War, one-sided representations of ancient colonial situations have persisted much longer. In the revised 1980 edition of his often-cited *The Greeks Overseas,* Boardman expressed his philhellenic and colonialist perception of the relationships between colonizing Greeks and colonized Italic peoples perhaps most clearly by concluding that "the natives weighted their new prosperity, brought by the Greeks, against the sites and land they had lost to them, and were generally satisfied" (Boardman 1980, 198). The kernel of this statement is the apparently unsurpassable value and desirable nature ascribed to the "new prosperity," which is the newly acquired colonial Greek culture; the implicit assumptions are that the colonized Italic peoples were uncivilized, or at least culturally inferior, and that they could only benefit from participating in the superior Greek civilization—which would eventually result in Western culture. The equation of "civilization" and "colonization" has even more explicitly been made by Morel, who defined the "two meanings of the word colonization . . . [as] the subjection and the 'civilizing' of the natives as well as the act of founding colonies" (Morel 1984, 124). There evidently is not much difference between such a point of view and the *mission civilisatrice* of nineteenth-century Western colonizers and colonialist archaeologists alike, who attributed a similar attitude to their Roman and Greek predecessors (Sheldon 1982, 103).

Such explicit statements of a colonialist and philhellenic conception of colonial situations in the ancient Mediterranean have become

---

Excerpted from Dommelen, Peter van. 1997. Colonial Constructs: Colonialism and Archaeology in the Mediterranean. *World Archaeology* 28(3):305–23.
Reprinted by permission of Taylor & Francis Ltd., www.informaworld.com.

relatively rare over the last two decades. Since the mid-1980s, an awareness of the partiality of representations of colonial situations in which only colonizing Greeks or Romans played an active role has been growing, as shows the statement that "we are witnessing a change in the long-lived and excessive tendency to consider the natives only as passive and receptive elements"(Morel 1984, 132). Evolutionist assumptions of Greek or Roman superiority which have been a prominent feature of Classical Archaeology since its early days (Shanks 1996, 68–74) are likewise waning, as illustrated by the remark that "'primitive' is not an adjective that I would willingly apply to the Italian Iron Age" (Ridgway 1990, 62). At the same time, however, much work in both Greek and other colonial archaeologies in the Mediterranean has continued to take place in a partial and evolutionist framework: most work on Phoenician colonialism, for instance, hardly considers the colonized at all.

Far more persistent and pervasive, however, is the dualist conception of colonialism, which represents colonial situations as a confrontation between two essentially distinct entities, each of which is internally homogeneous and externally bounded. In this view a profound colonial divide between the two sides constitutes a fundamental determinant of colonial situations (Pels 1993, 9–10). These ideas have not only set the standard for the study of colonialism in (Mediterranean) archaeology but have also remained virtually unquestioned. The roots of the perspective can be traced back to a holistic notion of culture, which treats culture as a well-defined and clear-cut whole and which allows colonial situations to be reduced to a mere clash between two basically independent entities (cf. Stoler 1989, 135–36). These ideas were already inherent in colonialist views, in which it appeared inevitable, indeed natural, that the colonizing side would prevail over its "native" counterpart, and which would thus give rise to the partial, one-sided representations of colonial situations discussed above. The increased attention to the indigenous part in colonial situations has however only reinforced the dualistic nature of colonial representations, as has been demonstrated by the call for "a twofold view of the single reality of Roman Africa" (Bénabou 1976, 18): in a pioneering study of indigenous resistance to Roman rule, the indigenous population was in the end reified as an integrated totality at the expense of ethnic, class and other divisions, resulting in a polarized, that is dualist, representation of the colonial situation (Sheldon 1982, 103–04; Thébert 1978). As a result, the subordinated position of the colonized to the colonizers was effectively reconfirmed, as the unequal relationships between the reified entities on either side of the colonial divide were accepted at face value (Pels 1993, 7–11; cf. van Dommelen 1998). . . .

46

Public Archaeology and Indigenous Communities

Mike Parker Pearson and Ramilisonina

The Western Isles—An Indigenous Community?

"No offence pal but I hate the f**king English" is one of those immortal phrases which summarizes certain Scottish attitudes to the descendants of their conquerors of old. During fieldwork in the Western Isles, university students from England react with hurt puzzlement when their hosts cheer for the opposing side whenever the English football team is playing an international match. For many of the students have never been to Scotland before and, politically naive, are startled to discover that being Scottish is an oppositional national identity—the Scots are vehemently not English.

Identities in the Western Isles are even more complex since the people of the islands have an utterly distinct and unassailably self-confident regional identity which other Scots often find annoying. Scottish Gaelic may be spoken by only 2 per cent of the Scottish population but it is an almost universally spoken first language in the Western Isles. Even lowland Scots culture is thus excluded by language and by traditions. The tiny population of the islands is also subdivided by religious identity—Protestants live in the north and Catholics in the south—which on a day-to-day basis is probably invisible to many outsiders. People also express a local identity, belonging to a particular township (parish or dispersed settlement).

Excerpted from Parker Pearson, Mike, and Ramilisonina. 2004. Public Archaeology and Indigenous Communities. In *Public Archaeology*, ed. N. Merriman, 224–39. London: Routledge.

Hebrideans—the people of the Western Isles—can be considered "an indigenous community" for several reasons. They have been perceived as not just different, but primitive. Until the 1930s archaeologists considered the people of this ethnically distinct community to be "living Ancient Britons," inhabiting drystone longhouses and occupying the lower rungs of the Victorian evolutionary ladder. They are a colonized people with a recent history of exploitation and forced emigration as bitter as that of many of the world's colonized nations. They are a small community with strong ties to their land, and an identity in opposition to that of the rest of the nation. Like other peripheral communities living under the control of a far-away dominant elite and political system, their existence is economically precarious, dependent on global changes outside their control such as EC subsidies, the defence industry and limited tourism.

Yet this community fails to meet one of the apparent criteria for being considered "indigenous," the question of ancestry and long-term ties to the land. Strangely enough, a large number of the people who live in the Western Isles today cannot be described as indigenous in this sense since the ancestors of many families arrived only in the nineteenth century, after the forced migrations of most of the native population to North America. Many descendants of the true indigenes actually live in Nova Scotia, in Canada. To add to the confusion of definitions, the Medieval and Norse period evidence suggests that this deported population may well have had few genetic links to the people who lived on the islands before the area was colonized by the Vikings.

So does this mean that the term "indigenous" is useless and misleading or that only certain groups who fulfill all the criteria may be considered "indigenous"? It is from the perspective of self-definition that "indigenous" has meaning: it serves to distinguish insiders from outsiders. As used by archaeologists, the term always possesses a political dimension, in that "indigenous" exists only in relation to "colonized." People who are indigenous can only be defined as such through their relationship to outsiders or to colonists who have obtained rights over their current and former lands. And yet within the two communities in which we have worked, the Western Isles and Madagascar, this definition is still inadequate since the relationship between the community, the archaeologists and the archaeology contains further subtleties.

Public Archaeology in the Western Isles

From a Malagasy perspective, South Uist is exceptionally cold, with weather so unrelentingly stormy that it seems to presage hurricanes which would destroy our caravan accommodation in an instant. And yet it is an ideal world from many other perspectives. People can remain close to the land, keeping animals and cultivating, whilst at the same time they enjoy running water, electricity, television, telephones and impressive access to education, protected by the copious government and European subsidies which make modern economic life possible and prevent these islands from being instantly depopulated should the jobs and money disappear.

The islands are a tightly knit community free from car theft, robbery and burglary, where misdemeanors are largely drink-related. After some sticky moments ten years ago, the archaeologists—formerly referred to in the bar as "the gynaecologists"—have become a recognized part of annual life. In the early years of the project there was relatively little communication and dissemination of results, generating a degree of mutual suspicion. Since then archaeology has made a big impact in terms of information, economic benefit, community life and prospective development.

People on South Uist are no more or no less interested in archaeology than anyone else in Britain. Some individuals are passionate about it and others cannot see the point at all. It is mainly the men and not the women who take an active interest, coming along to join in the digging, helping with the environmental sample processing, or providing other help in kind. Children are also encouraged through visits with parents or school parties. Archaeology gives them opportunity to learn about their own place's history because otherwise they learn nothing about it in the national curriculum.

The archaeological presence has risen to an annual complement of 120 people from five universities over two summer months. This makes a profound impact on a population of only 2,000 people. The archaeologists not only provide a resource for tourists—albeit modest in the form of archaeological sites under excavation—but they are also themselves part of the tourist trade. Large block bookings of accommodation and heavy use of local shops, garages and bars provide a substantial cash injection to the local economy. The project's staff and students also join in with the life of the community in ways that other tourists do not. They participate fully in the public parts of community life, attending events such as the *ceilidh* dances and building friendships that strengthen over the years. The private life of the inhabitants, dependent on family ties and the Catholic faith, remains fairly closed, since few students are churchgoers and no-one has as yet pursued a romantic liaison as far as marriage and local residence.

In this sense the archaeologists remain outsiders, transient visitors. Indeed, they are ideal tourists because they are predictable, relatively high spenders and are known to the community. South Uist has a relatively embryonic tourist trade, especially when compared to Skye, its neighbour in the Inner Hebrides. No one locally seems to want Uist to become a tourist mecca to the extent that Skye has become. Yet tourism is seen as the growth industry to replace a defunct seaweed industry, the uncertain prospects of the military rocket range and base, the declining building trade and the increasingly lean returns from farming and fishing. Tourism currently revolves around specialized holidays. The upper classes come here to fish and shoot. The middle classes come for birdwatching and cycling holidays. Few come—as yet—for the heritage aspects of Gaelic culture and archaeology, but the recent £ 0.5 million extension of the museum and a growing number of heritage-related activities and sites to be seen are laying the foundations for this new direction.

If visitors come to South Uist to explore their Hebridean roots, are they part of the "indigenous community"? Such tourists are certainly not local, but in terms of self-identity they may well perceive themselves as having a very strong link to the land of their ancestors. The Western Isles have a long history of movement away from the islands, both for emigration and in search of work, before and after the clearances. The population of South Uist has never been static. Today many native-born islanders leave either temporarily or permanently and new residents arrive. People who settle in small communities without pre-existing family ties—"incomers"—always have to negotiate their social position. In a society with an identity as strong as that of South Uist, being an incomer can be a difficult social role. Some non-native residents are deeply interested in the island's history and archaeology and as archaeologists we often have contact with this part of the population—those members of the community who are certainly "local" but who are not "indigenous."

This difference between the "local" and the "indigenous" in practice goes far beyond defining the status of individual community members. Even on an island as small as South Uist—only some 30 km long north to south, with all settlement confined to a strip barely 5 km wide east to west—our contacts with the inhabitants are at two levels. Island-wide contact is made with the indigenous community as a whole (including the incomer members) at a fairly formal, semi-official level. Through leaflets, magazine items, site tours, local radio and television news items, open clays, museum exhibitions and public lectures people have the opportunity to find out that South Uist has some of the rarest and best preserved archaeological remains in Britain.

Yet our most successful presentations of archaeology are at a local level, in the geographically tiny area in the south of the island in the townships where we live and work. Personal relations are crucial: people know who we are and what we are doing and their driving interest in the archaeology is that it is on their doorsteps. With the discovery in 1998 of a 1,500-year-old skeleton in a tomb on the beach—referred to as "Kilpheder Kate"—there has been an explosion of interest in archaeology in the immediate area, leading to packed houses at archaeological talks and presentations arranged not for the island-wide community, nor for tourists, but for the residents of the township. Local community involvement is the key and has been extremely successful on South Uist because of our own efforts at creating personal relationships combined with the overarching sense of identity of the indigenous community. . . .

47

Time and Landscape

Barbara Bender

Embodiment of Place and Time

Deconstruction serves to destabilize and question, but how are we to move towards a more constructive engagement? This is not the time or place for a long theoretical exegesis; I would simply make a plea for

---

Excerpted from Bender, Barbara. 2002. Time and Landscape. *Current Anthropology* 43(supplement):S103–12.

more open-ended theorizing that questions disciplinary boundaries and recognizes the untidiness and contradictoriness of human encounters with time and landscape.

A small example taken from our work at Leskernick Hill on Bodmin Moor in southwestern England (Tilley, Hamilton, and Bender 2001) illustrates the constraints imposed by historically constituted disciplinary boundaries:

Leskernick is a small hill, covered in rivers of moorstone or clitter. These were once great tabular strata that, through peri-glacial action, shattered into smaller and larger pieces and slid down the hillside. In among the stones are the remains of Bronze Age settlements, field-systems, cairns and field-shrines.

It became clear to the anthropologists surveying the hill that these Bronze Age people were, in some sense, communicating with the stones. Perhaps the stones were the ancestors, or the ancestral spirits? The anthropologists then began to notice that in among the moor-stones there were some that had been slightly shifted—a propped stone here, a line or semi-circle there, a circlet of stones around a boulder. The changes were so subtle that it was hard to know where "culture" began and "nature" ended.

Specialist geologists arrived. They had studied peri-glacial action. It had never occurred to them that some of the patterning might be caused by human action. Now they looked again, and confirmed that, yes, there were stones that had been moved.

Oddly enough, in the end, it seemed almost irrelevant whether a stone had been moved by peri-glacial action or by human agency. The distinctions were ours not theirs. A "naturally" upright stone, a "naturally" strangely weathered shape, an overhang or fissure may have been as culturally significant as the stones that had been moved. Indeed, the moved stones may have replicated or responded to ones that were in place.

Geologist and anthropologist moved towards each other, and moved away from the categorisations that each had imposed upon the landscape.

Landscapes refuse to be disciplined; they make a mockery of the oppositions that we create between time (history) and space (geography) or between nature (science) and culture (anthropology). Academics have been slow to accept this and slow, too, to notice the volatility of landscape. A person may, more or less in the same breath, understand a landscape in a dozen different ways (field notes, 1999):

> I'm in Devon, walking with E, who owns the small dairy farm, up a steep, muddy pathway between high hedgerows. She points to a small, triangular field: "That used to be an orchard—cider apples. Dad used to pay the farm workers with cider. A gallon a day. They had to stop

> when mechanisation came in—you couldn't be pissed on a tractor." She grumbles about the steepness of the slope and the north-facing aspect of the farm; worries about whether the new organically grown meadow will be too rich; and, looking over at the cattle, voices her bitterness at government lack of interest in the falling price of livestock following the BSE [Mad-Cow Disease] scare. She glances down towards the farm and is reminded that the National Trust is going to repair the old waterwheel—"That should bring the punters in!" Then she laughs, remembering how her kids used to toboggan down this hill on their tin trays. Towards the top of the hill, she turns round, gestures expansively towards the boundaries of her land, and says—slightly mockingly—"Isn't it picturesque ?"

I leave it to the reader to deconstruct this interlude—there is almost every sort of place and time contained within it.

Different people, differently placed, engage with the world in different ways. Looking at a small portion of a London map—streets, domestic houses, public places (a church), an alleyway—you might think about it as a palimpsest, a historically constituted 'scape. Or you might want to think about how and why, by whom and for whom, the map was drawn. And then you might try and people it: Why are some people hurrying, some loitering? Who has a place to go to, who is barred from going? Who goes with whom? What dictates the different patterns, the different timings of their comings and goings, their partings and assembling? The past is not only etched on the present in the form of architecture and layout but also drawn into the present, invested with meaning, used and reused in any number of different ways. The alleyway ("Angler's Lane": the River Fleet once ran through here) is for some (often women) a fearful place, a place to be avoided; for others it's a shortcut, or an escape route. Perhaps it's a secret place, a place of assignation? Or a place to mark with graffiti? Or a place to dump unwanted things or scavenge for wanted things? A place to be viewed with an eye to setting up a cardboard box for a night's uneasy rest, or a place ripe for development?

This plurality of place is always in the making, and how it is used and perceived depends on the contours of gender, age, status, ethnicity, and so on, and upon the moment. Being Jewish or coloured, being a woman, being young or old, rich or poor, may assume significance in one context but not another. Or perhaps one's political orientation will be relevant. And the moment or context will be both particular—dependent upon the time of day, the company one is in, the memories evoked—and generally dependent upon things happening off-scene. What people feel about that alleyway, what they can do or what might be done to them, may depend upon something happening on the stock market in a distant city or some broad flow of events that washes people up in strange places. The lived particularity of encounter works at many different scales.

The action that takes place—habitual, accidental, subversive—is both "of the moment" and something that extends forward and backward in time and place. And while I have chosen to focus on place, the same is true of time (Munn 1992, 111):

> [The idea of clock time] as "lifeless time," "a chronological series of points on a string" is misleading. Considered in the context of daily activity, clock time is quite alive, embodied in purposeful activity and experience. Coordinately, people are ongoingly articulated through this temporalization into a wider politico-cosmic order, a world time of particular values and times. This articulation may include conflicts over clock time, as well as daily operations carried on in its terms. . . . The clock may be "hated, endured . . . and manipulated."

What I have attempted to sketch is ways of talking about time and landscape that no longer privilege the visual over other senses or the mind over the body but instead work with an embodied phenomenological approach to time and landscape married to a larger political understanding—one that attends not only to how people are socialized through their daily (timed) encounters but to how they negotiate, question, and create those encounters (Bourdieu 1977; Giddens 1985; Pred 1990; Rose 1993, Chap. 2; Tilley 1994), that recognizes not just experiences of time and place rooted in familiar landscapes (Basso 1983; Edmonds 1999; Gow 1995; Ingold 1993) but the dislocated but nonetheless always physically grounded experiences of people on the move (Bender and Winer 2001). People relate to place and time through memory, but the memories may be of other places and other times. Hoffman (1989, 106), in *Lost in Translation*, discusses the thinness of a landscape translated into new and unfamiliar words: "'River' in Polish was a vital sound, energized with the essence of riverhood, of my rivers, of my being immersed in rivers. 'River' in English is cold—a word without aura. It has no accumulated associations for me. . . . It does not evoke." . . .

We are all too aware that our attempts to understand the prehistoric embodied landscape, the engagement of prehistoric people with the world around them, is filtered through our sense of place and landscape, and so we have been concerned to understand how, over the past five years, we have interacted with the moor—how age, gender, social position, and variable context all play into our experience, our changing, dynamic experience of place. And just as we have attempted a more phenomenological approach to a prehistoric engagement with place, so we are concerned with a contemporary embodied negotiation of landscape. How do we move around? How do places get invested with memories? How do we appropriate ancient footpaths and house spaces or make the journey to and from the hill, and how, back at our base—the caravan park—do we move between caravans (our "homes") and the communal spaces of pub and washhouse? Who moves where? With whom? When? How? And how do these intimate spaces of temporary habitation interdigitate with our wider landscapes and networks of social relations?

We have created art installations (Tilley, Hamilton, and Bender 2001), a website, and a travelling exhibition. Our work—like any ethnographic or archaeological undertaking—is an intrusion on local or regional sensibilities, and in this instance there was an added urgency in making contact because among the many local or regional groups were Cornish nationalists who undoubtedly resented our (English) appropriation of their history. We needed not only to explain what we were doing but to make clear that our interpretations were just some among many. We wanted to create spaces for other people to consider and to express their involvement with the moor and with the past. Sitting in on the exhibition, talking to people about what the moor and the prehistoric settlements meant to them and about their reactions to our work and to the exhibition, we came to understand better the heterogeneity—and fluidity and context-dependency—of an engagement with place and past. We saw, for example, how peculiar our myopic concentration on the Bronze Age landscape appeared to most local people, who saw stone row, medieval field systems, 17th-century granite working, and 19th-century peat-cutting either as layered palimpsest or, more simply, as "history." We saw how ignorance of "official" history could go hand-in-hand with a great depth of local knowledge and how the same person who helped create parts of the exhibition could, in a slightly different context, vent his anger at our "invasion." . . .

48

Indigenous Journeys—Splinterville, Drenthe, Amherst

Margaret M. Bruchac

My work as a traditional Abenaki storyteller often dovetails with my efforts as an Indigenous archaeologist. In both roles, I explore and interpret physical and ephemeral locales where memories reside, where Indigenous knowledges are situated, and where histories of past events speak in some way to the present. I am particularly attentive to places where Indigenous stories and understandings have been distorted, threatened, or forgotten. . . . The quixotic, and yet always informative nature of these encounters has trained me to pay close attention to local landscapes and historical memories, phenomenological experiences and collecting processes, and my own situatedness in any particular project or place, at any given time. I believe that the ethics of our profession demand such attentiveness, such reflexiveness. As archaeologists, when we choose to place our hands into the past, we become active agents in shaping that past. We are not just neutral observers; our physical being, thought patterns, and subsequent sorting behaviors interrupt the momentary stasis between what lies above and below, and as we break that barrier, our actions can disrupt and distort the very object of our study . . . unless we are very careful. Storytelling holds much the same dangers. . . .

The collection and display of Native American remains and artifacts in American colleges and museums is inextricably linked to the old "cabinets of curiosity" in elite European and American homes and museums that were once filled with diverse objects to satisfy scientific and aesthetic impulses. Collectors used these collections to construct and situate

---

Excerpted from Bruchac, Margaret M. 2010. Indigenous Journeys—Splinterville, Drenthe, Amherst. In *Being and Becoming Indigenous Archaeologists*, ed. G. P. Nicholas, 66–75. Walnut Creek, CA: Left Coast Press.

themselves vis-à-vis the people who were the subjects of their interest. In the minds of collectors, hypothetical stories about Indigenous pasts took shape, animated and populated by the isolated things stored in collections. These visions were shared and embellished over time until they comprised a sort of museological shadow world, identified as Indigenous, but separate from the real world experienced by Indigenous communities. This imaginative history-making is, to my mind, most problematic when applied to other peoples' remains, when bones that had once walked around inside their own flesh, as parts of individuals who were themselves part of families, are dislocated, disarticulated, reassembled, and conscripted to move in manners not of their own making, regardless of where their spirits might have chosen to travel after death. . . .

Somebody Else's Relatives

The practices of storytelling and archaeology, as I noted at the outset, sometimes dovetail in unexpected places. As a case in point, during the spring of 2000, I set out to conduct field research in Europe, seeking oral traditions indigenous to that place that might illuminate or otherwise intersect with archaeological understandings of past peoples. My project, "Ancient Memory in the Northern Netherlands," explored cultural connections to ancient lived landscapes at significant sites (e.g., standing stones, churches, historical markers). I interviewed folklorists, museum directors, archaeologists, farmers, musicians, and others who served as caretakers of these sites, or who had constructed present identities based on creative understandings of the past. Through ethnographic interviews and site visits, I expected to discover reinvented traditions, and hoped to discover the survival of older stories, thereby illustrating how the physical landscape, and the marking of that landscape, figure as components of group memory and regional identity (similar to Barbara Bender's work at Stonehenge [1998]). . . .

Dutch stereotypes (equating my Native American identity with an almost mystical connection to nature) actually improved my access to information, since many people assumed that the Indian would appreciate the tidbits of folklore their neighbors found tedious. In every interview, I found that folklore of the ancient landscape was common knowledge, almost seamlessly interwoven with the present, yet many informants insisted that stories from the long dead past had no real significance in their lives, since their personal identities (unlike mine, they assumed) were thoroughly modern. . . .

So it is that I was thinking about other peoples' relatives on the day that archaeologist Willem Deetman brought me to the Drents Museum in the nearby town of Assen. One of the ancient bodies found in a local peat bog, the *Meisje van Yde*, a young redhaired girl, was on display, lying beneath a finely woven blanket in a climate-controlled glass case. As I gazed into the case (in ways that I would never have gazed upon the bodies of the Native dead at UMass), I felt like an intruder, and found myself wondering about her relatives. Which neighbors were now asking after *her* well-being? Who was there to claim her, to lay her in a more peaceful place, away from the staring eyes of strangers?

In a corner outside the building, I left a little tobacco offering while asking her to forgive me for invading her rest. I asked the birds to make their songs carry through the glass of that silent case, so that she might hear the sounds that had surrounded her in life. Willem empathized with my distinctly unscientific reactions, and we wondered aloud whether there could be some gesture of respect made for the old ones on display—perhaps prayers, covering them at certain hours, or even returning them to the ground. Willem considered the cause hopeless, since the girl from Yde was being readied for a new exhibition; she was about to embark on a world tour. When I left Drenthe, I tried to forget her.

Three years later, I was buried deep in repatriation research, prowling through the archives at Amherst College and Smith College, when "The Mysterious Bog People" exhibition (including the Meisje van Yde) arrived at the Canadian Museum of Civilization in Gatineau, Quebec. Willem wrote to tell me that all did not go exactly as planned. When the moving van arrived, the Dutch curator, Dr. Vincent van Vilsteren, "was met with five grand gentlemen [all Aboriginal Canadians], who told him that the remains of what they considered to be the ancestors of contemporary [white] Canadians should be given back to the earth, instead of being put in museums. Ergo: no exhibit" (Deetman 2003). Deetman quoted van Vilsteren:

> The Canadians of Indian descent had much difficulty with the European ways of handling human remains. So there was nothing for it but to hold a purification meeting (*reinigingsbijeenkomst*), as composers of the exhibition we had to set right with the upperworld. With much respect I have taken part in this smudging-ceremony. It was very harmonious. (van Vilsteren 2003)

After much negotiation, Dr. Stephen Augustine, a hereditary Mi'kmaq elder and a curator in the Ethnology Services Division, had offered to take responsibility for caring for these Dutch ancestral remains while they were at the museum. They would be displayed during the day and covered every night, as a compromise between Euro-American museum practices and Aboriginal customs. Van Vilsteren, a self-described "scientist and atheist, a non-believer," was so moved by the experience that, on his return to Assen, he wrote an article titled "Holy Smoke and Bad Vibrations." He e-mailed a draft version to Stephen Augustine, who e-mailed it to me; I e-mailed it to Willem Deetman, who then walked around the corner to the Assen Museum to speak to Vincent in person. Van Vilsteren was stunned at having sent a text to Canada, only to have it translated within hours by one of his neighbors. Deetman said that's just how Indians are. At the end of the world tour, van Vilsteren promised, they would arrange a special ceremony to properly welcome the Meisje home to the Drents Museum. It would be very *gezellig*. . . .

Indigenizing Academic Relations to the Indigenous Past

There was a time when I naively imagined that repatriation work was little more than the physical transfer of Indigenous remains and objects from one location to another. While delving into the relations and ideologies that allowed some people to become the "collectors" and some to be the "collected," I have become an advocate for what I call "restorative methodologies." Restorative methodologies attend to more than just repatriating items to their source; they intentionally make visible the social relations and epistemological dimensions of archaeological collecting and history-making, calling attention to the habits and thought patterns that shape the collecting of other peoples' stuff. I use, quite consciously, some of the same strategies I learned as a tracker, to discern how my quarry (in this case, 19th-century archaeologists) thinks and moves, in order to predict where they, and their collections, can be found.

An awareness of the ways in which various forms of knowledge are constructed and situated is crucial to help diverse communities understand themselves and one another, as we reflect on our positions, origins, and responsibilities. Our understanding of various peoples' pasts is improving, as we strive to include, in theory and practice, those who were once among the voiceless, the vanished, the archaeologized. The "past," as I see it, is not an unambiguous collection of data, a point in a historic timeline, or a logical narrative. It is a multilayered assemblage of material and immaterial stuff, held together mostly by physical circumstance, locational happenstance, and human memory. Situations that seem to be temporally and geographically disparate may become linked when we move through them, physically, or metaphysically, generating complex, constructive cross-cultural dances across time. We need not dismiss science, folklore, or reinvention out of hand, since all of these are human expressions, forms of observable data that can encode and convey myriad meanings; all are potentially destructive, all are potentially restorative. When we touch the past or recall a memory, emotional connections may surface that can evoke a sense of kinship and relationship between present-day people and long-dead ancestors—even (at times) in skeptical scientists. . . .

49

Rock Carvings in a Saami Perspective: Some Comments on Politics and Ethnicity in Archaeology

Odd Mattis Hætta

If you talk about "The *Swedish* rock carvings in Østfold (Norway)," some people will think they are not hearing properly and others will react angrily, but if you say "The *Norwegian* rock carvings in Østfold," no one will raise an eyebrow. You will experience more or less the same reaction if you talk about "The *Saami* rock carvings in Alta." Some

Excerpted from Hætta, Odd Mattis. 1995. Rock Carvings in a Saami Perspective: Some Comments on Politics and Ethnicity in Archaeology. In *Perceiving Rock Art: Social and Political Perspectives*, ed. Knut Helskog and Bjørnar Olsen, 348–56. Oslo: Instituttet for Sammenlignende Kulturforskning.

will react aggressively, others will correct you, saying that they are not Saami. If, on the other hand, you ask about "The *Norwegian* rock carvings in Alta," most people will consider this normal.

This is not only the case among the public at large in Norway, but also among many researchers, if one considers their way of presenting the prehistoric period in Fennoscandia. Conclusions and interpretations about prehistoric material are often based on the socialisation, preconceptions and national political platform and ballast of a person, whether a carpenter or a researcher.

I dislike the title "Rock Carvings in a Saami Perspective" because (1) I am not politically engaged by rock carvings, and (2) I have never seen corresponding introductions entitled, for instance, "Rock Carvings in a Norwegian Perspective." But it gives me an opportunity to touch upon something that occupies many Saami researchers to an ever-increasing degree.

There is never any problem in talking about Norwegian ethnicity—or taking it as implied—right from Mesolithic times, whereas Saami ethnicity is often questioned even if one only goes back as far as the Middle Ages. This asymmetry is a characteristic feature throughout northern Fennoscandia when the topic is archaeological or prehistoric. It is typical that a respected Norwegian archaeologist said that "the first Norwegians must have come to this country at least 12,000 years ago" in a discussion about the rock carvings here in Alta.

Very few professional Saami archaeologists or historians are working on the prehistoric period—and none are involved in Saami research groups concerned with archaeology or history. Hence, rock carvings are not viewed in a "Saami perspective" either. . . .

Rock Carvings in an Ethnic and Political Perspective

There are several routes of approach to a contribution about "rock carvings in a Saami perspective"—the archaeological, the historical and the political. The first is concerned with what archaeological research can tell us about ethnicity in association with rock carvings; the second with whether historical research can interpret the motifs and contexts of the rock carvings in the light of history; and the third is the political viewpoint.

The assemblage of motifs represented by the rock carvings is fairly nonspecific in character, comprising reindeer, elk, bears and other mammals, birds and fish. Even carvings depicting boats, skis, snowshoes and perhaps shaman drums are too general to permit broad conclusions to be drawn.

I for my part lack specialist knowledge in the fields of archaeology and history to draw conclusions on the basis of ethnic association as regards prehistoric monuments dating back several thousand years. However, my intuition tells me that Norwegians cannot have carved the figures in the rock. Neither do I have evidence allowing me to place other ethnic designations on people who lived so long ago. But it is just as important for Saami society to emphasise that prehistoric monuments in the area are Saami as it is for contemporary Norwegian researchers and textbook authors to write that the rock carvings in Østfold are Norwegian.

50

Prehistory, Identity, and Archaeological Representation in Nordic Museums

Janet E. Levy

Archaeology and prehistory are contested, both in postcolonial situations in Africa, Australia, and the Americas (e.g., Watkins 2000) and in arenas of nationalist debate as in Europe (e.g., Diaz-Andreu and

Excerpted from Levy, Janet E. 2006. Prehistory, Identity, and Archaeological Representation in Nordic Museums. *American Anthropologist* 108(1):135–47.

Champion 1996; Meskell 1998a). At the same time, indigenism is contested on a variety of levels (Hodgson 2002; Kuper 2003). These include debates about which individuals are indigenous, which groups are indigenous, and whether indigenousness exists at all. Archaeological and anthropological museums are situated within both of these arenas because they are homes to public representations of the past and culture (Krebs 2003). In Europe, the manipulation, suppression, and even destruction of archaeological evidence by, among others, the Nazis has led to an understandable appeal to depoliticize archaeological heritage. But this appeal can be paradoxical. Although the representation of difference or otherness can be (and, indeed, has been) manipulated for destructive purposes, the denial of otherness can also be destructive. These points can be illustrated with a case study of the Saami, one of the rare populations in Europe that participates in the discourse of indigenism.

It is now widely recognized that archaeology and prehistory are contested arenas, and the past is often used to interpret and legitimate the present. Debate occurs in numerous contexts, including land claims, museum exhibitions, textbooks, repatriation, and the daily practice of archaeology. In North America, these debates are based within complex postcolonial relationships among anthropologists, archaeologists, and Native Americans (Watkins 2000). In contrast, in Europe, debates about the politics of archaeology are infrequently framed within a colonial discourse, and more commonly framed as competition between various national ethnic groups. Within the Nordic countries, as elsewhere in Europe, archaeological dialogue with indigenous people is underdeveloped. Although the Nordic countries are often thought of as ethnically homogeneous, they are not and have not been for centuries. The northernmost regions of Norway, Sweden, and Finland are the home of a minority community of Saami (or Sami, Sámi) people, earlier known as Lapps. The Saami conceive of themselves as the indigenous people of the northern region and refer to the region—known to much of Europe as "Lapland"—as "Sápmi." They lay claim to a cultural and historical distinctiveness in relationship to the majority populations. Yet within the current national borders, Norwegians, Swedes, and Finns might well consider themselves indigenous as well. This ambiguous situation provides a distinctive case study in the politics of archaeological representation. . . .

Visiting Museums

During academic year 1998–1999 and again in summer, 2002, I had the opportunity to visit a variety of museums in Finland, Sweden, and

Norway, all of which had exhibitions, some large and some small, about archaeology and prehistory. These included national and regional museums and those run by Saami communities. I also spoke with a variety of people in the museum and archaeology worlds in the Nordic countries, although these data are limited. Here, I focus on seven museums in particular (the date of my visit is in parentheses):

National or regional ("majority") museums found in major cities:

The National Museum of Finland, Helsinki (2002)

Museum of Northern Ostrobothnia, Oulu, Finland (1998–1999)

The National Museum of Antiquities, Stockholm (1999)

The Nordic Museum, Stockholm (1999)

Museums run by the Saami community:

Siidá, Inari, Finland (1999)

Ájtte, Jokkmokk, Sweden (2002)

Sámiid Vuorka-Dávvirat (The Sami Museum), Karasjok, Norway (1999)

Let me start with the exterior of the museums. The national and regional museums not only display "authoritative narratives," following Hooper-Greenhill, they also present themselves in "authoritative" architecture. They are massive stone structures often with architectural details that evoke medieval or Renaissance periods. The museum brochures for the Nordic Museum in Stockholm and the National Museum in Helsinki tell us that the structures were specifically built to evoke heroic periods in the national narrative. However, these styles and this narrative exclude the far north and its more modest indigenous architecture.

If we go inside to the prehistory halls, especially in Stockholm and Helsinki, we see a striking example of what Hooper-Greenhill (2000, 129–30) describes as "carefully spaced and ordered identical display cases, each with its own group of objects systematically placed in their proper places." The two national museums are laid out in long corridors that lead the visitor on a predetermined path. Consciously or not, the national museums are physically laid out to present an authoritative view of prehistory and history, each emphasizing a singular path toward the nation as it is known in the modern world. In a variety of ways, we see the Saami separated from the central narrative.

For example, in both Helsinki and Oulu in northern Finland, the prehistory exhibitions either do not mention Saami (as in Oulu) or mention them in very peripheral ways (as in Helsinki). Exhibitions about Saami culture are found in different galleries and even on different floors than exhibitions about prehistory. Thus, the Saami are excluded from the antiquity of the nation. In Oulu, the archaeology exhibition is explicitly described as stressing the "prehistory of Northern Finland and its special features," yet there is no mention of Saami at all. The path of the prehistory exhibition leads into displays about Finnish peasant life. The Saami exhibition is two floors away.

In Helsinki, the prehistory exhibition is housed in a dramatic space resembling a medieval castle. The word Saami appears in one case only, in the Iron Age section where the visitor is told that the Early Saami Iron Age (C.E. 300–1300) is very poorly known and the Later Saami Iron Age is somewhat better known; no details are given and no artifacts are explicitly affiliated with the Saami. There is a separate case about the widespread pitfall systems used in the north for hunting reindeer, but no statement is made about who was doing the hunting, although this technique was used by the Saami at the time of first written documentation. One long corridor of cases leads toward two dramatically lit cases with life-sized, realistic mannequins dressed in early medieval costume. The visual message is clear: All of this prehistory leads to the people of the Finnish nation. In fact, there are very fine Saami costumes in this museum, but they are exhibited on another floor so they are not integrated into Finnish history. These Saami costumes are represented as barely part of any living community, displayed on faceless metal armatures, not on mannequins. So, the Saami are in the National Museum, but not of the nation. In both Oulu and Helsinki, the Saami galleries emphasize a limited time period, approximately the 18th to early 20th centuries; they are ethnological rather than historical presentations. The Saami are a classic example of "people without history" (Wolf 1982).

In the Iron Age gallery of the archaeology exhibition in the National Museum of Antiquities in Stockholm, in 1999, a case about the Saami Iron Age was labeled "under development." The text of this case says in Swedish: "The Saami have since time of earliest memory lived in the northern parts of Sweden, Norway, and Finland. Archaeological finds show connections back in time to the Stone Age" (my translation). Yet the Stone and Bronze Age galleries, which are older installations than the Iron Age gallery, make no acknowledgement of the Saami. Whereas in 1999, this museum continued the story of Sweden from late prehistory on the ground floor into lavish medieval galleries on the second floor, again the Saami were not mentioned; the later historical material about the Saami is found about a mile away in the Nordic Museum, the ethnology and folklore museum. So, although by 1999 concern about exclusion of the Saami had led to some inclusion in the national archaeology exhibition, they were not integrated into the full story of the development of Sweden; their antiquity is ambiguous. The antiquity of Swedes is not explicitly stated; however, it is implicit through the layout of the galleries that the most ancient finds lead eventually to the Swedish nation. The new prehistory exhibition, opening in November, 2005, may provide a different impression.

There are distinctive contrasts with the Saami community museums, of which there is one each in Finland, Sweden, and Norway. The Saami museums are smaller, lower to the ground, rural, and built of wood or stucco. All have outdoor walking trails and reconstructed domestic structures and facilities. Each exhibition contains a prominent map that illustrates a Saami "nation" that cuts across the modern nation-state boundaries.

The exhibitions are less linear than those in the majority museums. At Ájtte on the Arctic Circle in Jokkmokk, Sweden, the layout of the museum is modeled after a reindeer corral: Wedge-shaped galleries open in a circle from a central point. In Finland and Norway, the exhibitions are laid out in open rectangles, with displays both along the walls and in the center. The design of the exhibition is most traditional in Norway, which is the oldest of these three museums. Here, individual glass cases with traditional artifact displays line the four walls of the rectangular space; however, the entire space is visible from any point. At Siidá and Ájtte, there are cases dispersed across the open space in a nonlinear fashion, and there are more objects outside of cases, sometimes in full-size reconstructions of rooms or structures. In fact, there is nothing particularly cutting-edge about these exhibition techniques, but they are strikingly absent from the prehistory exhibitions in Stockholm, Helsinki, and Oulu.

In the Saami community museums, especially the two newer ones in Finland and Sweden, Saami history and culture are closely tied to the natural setting and climate of Lapland. This is done through text and visuals (including life-sized panoramic photographs and reconstructed natural scenes) and even through sounds such as rushing water. Although in the wrong hands, this might be a strategy for "primitivizing" the Saami by connecting them with nature rather than with history, in fact this strategy fits well with Saami contemporary politics. The goal is not to "naturalize" the Saami but to "culturize" the environment: that is, claim it as Saami heritage. Some related processes are occurring among those claiming indigenous status in tropical South America (Conklin 2002). The northern landscape, as it is organized into national parks and preserves, is often discussed in tourist and national literature as empty and pristine, despite millennia of human occupation (Mulk 1997; Mulk and Bayliss-Smith 1999). The Saami museums contest this view by integrating the land, climate, and Saami adaptation into single exhibitions. This strategy is an example of the importance of understanding local motivations in uses of the past, as Helaine Silverman (2002) has suggested. Yet, there is also ambiguity and risk in this strategy of linking culture and nature, as will be discussed below.

Finally, all three Saami museums emphasize the time depth of Saami occupation through visuals, layout, and text. At each, the earliest Mesolithic settlements are claimed unproblematically as ancestral to Saami culture. For example, one enters the main exhibition at Ájtte by walking down a corridor lined with cardboard cutouts of humans doing something typical of the northern regions; the first figure is a Mesolithic fisherperson and the figures then continue in chronological order through medieval periods and on to a modern Saami.

Shared Icons

Despite the differences in approach to Saami history and prehistory between majority museums, on the one hand, and Saami community museums, on the other hand, both types of museum actually share key visual icons: repeated striking and familiar images, as described by Moser (1998, 17–19). One visual icon represents Saami in the present: the snowmobile. Two visual icons that represent Saami in the past are the shaman's drum and the *kota* (or *kåta* or *goatte*), the skin tent used during part of the annual cycle of reindeer herding.

The kota is more visually obvious in exhibits than the drums (besides being bigger, the kota is often displayed in brightly lit galleries, whereas the drums are under much dimmer light, for conservation purposes). All of the Saami community museums and majority museums in Oulu and Stockholm and a temporary exhibit in Helsinki exhibit kotas. The presence of the kota visually represents a common dilemma of these exhibits. Although the texts may give a somewhat more nuanced view, this visual icon says one key thing: The Saami are migratory reindeer herders. Yet both the use of the kota and the practice of transhumant reindeer herding are only true of a segment of the Saami population and then only true for only limited periods of their history. Both majority and community museums rely on this link between Saami and reindeer herding in their exhibitions, although the background reasoning is probably different. For the majority institutions, the kota fits into the common presentation of Saami as timelessly frozen in about the 18th–19th centuries, without an ancient past and, indeed, without a future (this is particularly striking in Helsinki and Oulu).

In contrast, for the Saami community museums, the kota emphasizes Saami distinctiveness and lays claim to the landscape and to certain territorial usufruct rights that are tied to reindeer herding. In the larger political arena, for better or worse, Saami identity and legitimacy are often closely tied to reindeer. This is why Saami political activists raised a kota outside the Norwegian parliament in Oslo during the protests in the 1980s against damming the Alta-Kautokeino River to create hydroelectric power for southern regions. However, this emphasis potentially raises problems for a history of the Saami community because, in fact, the majority of Saami today are not herders and were not for long periods in the past. So, it is understandable why the image of the kota may dominate Saami museum exhibitions, but, like the explicit link to nature, the image is a double-edged sword.

Discussion

There is a temptingly easy critique to be made of these contrasting museums: The national and regional museums diminish or even deny a Saami role in the antiquity of the nation. In contrast, the Saami institutions grant the Saami the same ancientness as the other Nordic populations, the ones that eventually become the national majorities. Yet it is only fair to note that there are pragmatic constraints on the exhibitions. The majority museums, to start with, are confined to buildings with their own heritage significance that has to be respected, to say nothing of structural constraints that have to be worked around. Their funding has been restricted in recent years, so revising older exhibitions is not an easy task and there are demands throughout the collections. New wall texts can be added fairly easily, but major change to the visual appearance of an exhibit is a much more expensive proposition. Indeed, the prehistory exhibit in Helsinki does have a relatively new wall text that explicitly discusses Finnish and Saami origins. However, none of the information is reflected in the displays, and the text itself is ambiguous at best.

In addition, museum exhibitions may be influenced by administrative requirements out of the control of curators. For example, after recent renovations (not including the prehistory exhibition) at the Finnish National Museum, I was told by one curator of the Saami materials that the architect's design requirements—which gave the new Saami display less space than before and demanded that no photos be included—were given priority over the curator's plans for the exhibition.

In contrast, Ájtte in Sweden and Siidá in Finland are newer facilities. They have the luxury of focusing their exhibitions in a way that the national and regional museums cannot. They are in rural areas, so open-air trails and exhibits are more feasible than in the national museums. They may have better access to EU funding because they are in poorer rural areas to which economic development funds have been directed. Thus, there are a range of factors that impinge on how museums represent the Saami past, and it is overly simplistic to attribute the differences to ideological factors alone.

Nevertheless, the exhibitions ultimately are ideological statements. The lack of information about the prehistory of the Saami at the National Museum in Helsinki is highlighted by the presence of two cases in the prehistory exhibit explicitly about the Iron Age in the Åland Islands, off the southwest coast of Finland. It is almost too easy to see here the difference in contemporary political power reflected in an interpretation of the past: Within the Finnish state, the Åland Islands have special political, land tenure, and (Swedish) language rights, whereas the Saami have almost no communal political clout. The distinctive ethnicity of the islanders is made clear in the exhibition while the Saami are ignored.

A key ideological factor derives from the history of archaeology in Europe, in particular the use of archaeology by the Nazis to legitimate their racialist views and imperialistic ambitions (Arnold 1990, 2002). Following World War II, many European archaeologists became sensitive to this misuse of archaeological information, in general, and ideas about ethnic identity in the past, in particular (Jones 1997). The response was to turn away from concepts of ethnicity, race, and nation. Thus, out of sensitivity to misuse of archaeology on the subject of ethnicity, the topic largely disappeared from explicit discussion. For majority populations, this is not a problem: For example, in the National Museum of Finland or the National Museum of Antiquities in Stockholm, it will be assumed that the subject is Finns or Swedes, particularly as in both places the prehistory exhibitions physically lead into exhibitions of historic periods. But for minority populations, the issue is more complicated. Sensitivity can mean silence: the result of sensitivity is the virtual disappearance of minority populations from the past, particularly the ancient past.

Identity, Power, and the Past

Hooper-Greenhill (2000, 19) notes another paradox about museums: They have the power both to present narrow authoritative images of the past and to raise new questions and make visible what had been invisible. The museums examined here reveal a range of ways to approach the complexities of identity and the past in the far north of Europe. At one extreme, there are the National Museum of Finland and the Museum of Northern Ostrobothnia, both of which physically separate the Saami from the story of Finland—the latter museum even excludes Saami from the story of northern Finland—providing them virtually no space within the national discourse. At the National Museum of Antiquities in Stockholm, a similar model apparently once existed. But by 1999, there was concern to include the Saami to some degree in the story of the nation's past, focusing on the later Iron Age and early medieval period, for which scholars can turn to a combination of archaeological and documentary sources to identify ethnic groups in the far north. So, one well-designed case was devoted to the "Saami Iron Age" within the Viking period gallery. In late 2005, redesigned prehistory galleries may integrate the Saami further into the national prehistory.

The Saami have a greater presence in the Nordic Museum, the ethnology museum in Stockholm. The first part of the Saami exhibition is made of miniature dioramas and, again, focuses on Saami and reindeer, placing the Saami in an unchanging ethnographic present rather as is done in Oulu and Helsinki. The dioramas tend to visibly "miniaturize" Saami culture. However, the museum has added new wall text to explain that these display cases represent an old-fashioned view. In addition, there have been added new display cases with life-sized reconstructions of recent Saami houses and activities (including the ubiquitous snowmobile) as well as a photographic exhibition of the modern Saami parliament. The visuals and text of the exhibition are testimony to changing attitudes and to a commitment to bring into view the diversity of modern developments among the Saami, once made invisible by the older exhibition.

The Saami community museums, in contrast, foreground the environmental setting, annual cycle, and modern politics of the Saami. They present the occupations of the north, from the earliest onward, as directly ancestral to the historically documented Saami communities. In recognition of the complexity of ethnicity, there may be textual statements that a specifically recognizable Saami culture appeared in the later Iron Age, but the visual message of the exhibitions is always of continuity back in time to deep antiquity, indeed to the first occupants after the melting of the Pleistocene ice cap. A common phrase in wall text and publications tells the visitor that the Saami have lived in the area "since time immemorial" (e.g., Mulk 1997, 10).

Ultimately, there are pragmatic implications of public understandings of the antiquity of occupation of a region. In Norway, the rights of Saami to claim heritage interest and usufruct right in large areas of land were challenged in the early 1980s by plans to dam the Alta-Kautokeino River, which the Saami protested in alliance with environmental groups (Eidheim 1997; Paine 1994, 153). In 1995, archaeologists testified (on both sides) in a legal case about Saami usufruct rights in north-central Sweden (Beach 2001, 229–33; Svensson 1997). It is notable that during these legal proceedings, there was intensive discussion of how one could identify a Saami archaeological site but no debate about how to identify a Scandinavian one (Gustafson 1998), demonstrating the reality of Hætta's complaint above. The Saami ultimately lost both cases, but they gained political savvy. In addition, archaeology for the first time became part of the public debate about identity, antiquity, and power in the north.

In this context, the paradoxes and ambiguities inherent in the representation of Saami ethnicity are more obvious. The use of symbolic capital from the past is a sensitive operation for anyone, including those who claim indigenous status. The visual focus on the kota and on links to surrounding nature may run the risk of an oppressive, primitivizing essentialism (Kuper 2003); among other things, such essentialism may aggravate internal Saami tensions over the role of reindeer and reindeer herders in self-representation and politics. Alternatively, Saami control and presentation of certain images can be seen as an example of "strategic essentialism" (Hodgson 2002, 1040, 1046, see n.10) that allows the community to "intentionally manipulate, project, and homogenize their public images and identities to accord with 'Western' stereotypes in order to seek recognition and demand rights" (Hodgson 2002, 1040).

Unlike Native American and Native Australians, Saami have few legal claims to land and resources. However, they do have significant control of their own self-representation through Saami educational institutions and media and through museums. Thus, the Saami use the tools of the state—radio, museums, and colleges—to lay claim to autonomy and to resist the state. They do this, in part, by laying claim jointly to the environment and to the past through media and museum images.

Unifying Europe

The dilemma of representation for the Saami has been how to maintain distinctiveness in the face of hegemonic nationalism. Now, continuing Saami control of both representation and heritage is influenced by even larger homogenizing institutional developments: the European Union and related institutions. Despite recognition of national interests in culture and heritage, the cultural apparatus of the European Union is strongly focused on analyzing, defining, and strengthening a nonnational "European identity" (Gröhn 2004, 144–87; Shore 1995). A well-known archaeological example of this ideological stance is the lavish traveling exhibition, in the late 1990s, on Bronze Age Europe (Council of Europe 1999). The Bronze Age was explicitly chosen as the first truly "European" period. Yet such an approach has potential negative implications for the far north, which only peripherally participated in what are conceived of as truly European cultural developments of prehistory and early history: the Neolithic Revolution, the Bronze Age, the spread of Celtic cultures, and the Roman Empire (Council of Europe 1999, ix; Gröhn 2004; Zvelebil 1995). In the new pan-European economy and culture, claims of indigenousness—or, for that matter, any kind of "otherness"—may well be stigmatized as much as, or more than, claims of national interest. The Saami lack the economic and political clout that nation-states can and do use to contest EU directives with which they disagree. Paradoxically, although the Saami past may be conceived of as "non-European" and thus possibly stigmatized, the European Union also provides funding that has benefited a variety of museums in rural areas far from the national capitals (although not in Norway, which is not a member of the European Union).

Summary

Until recently, Saami prehistory has been ignored or marginalized in the Nordic archaeological community. Within the Saami community, although history is considered important, archaeology has only recently and intermittently been a focus of interest. A Finnish Saami student of archaeology told me in 1998 that she felt alienated from the Saami community by her interest in archaeology. A non-Saami archaeology student who worked in far northern Finland found the same indifference. To some Saami intellectuals (e.g., Hætta 1996), much archaeology would be seen as unnecessary if Saami oral tradition were granted the respect it is due. Other Saami scholars (Aikio and Aikio 1989) argue that excavation of Saami sites should be limited until there are Saami archaeologists to control the research agenda. These positions resemble positions held by some Native American activists regarding archaeology. Yet, as Saami continue the struggle for economic and cultural autonomy, I predict that the practice of archaeology will grow in significance within their communities. Among other things, Saami participate in the World Congress of Indigenous People and come into contact there with Native Americans and Native Australians, for some of whom archaeology has become a salient arena of contestation with the majority society.

As noted before, reputable scholars have put forward calls both to take archaeology out of the political arena and to take indigenousness out of the discourse of difference. Ultimately, these recommendations themselves have political implications. For several hundred years, scientific and popular understandings of the Saami (or Lapp) past were the basis for discrimination and forced assimilation. It is bitterly ironic that just as the legitimacy of Saami identity is being acknowledged in the Nordic region, archaeologists put forth arguments, however well-intentioned, to stop use of the past for clarifying and strengthening that identity. As tourism, forestry, mining, and power generation expand in the far northern region, rights to land and heritage will become more and more salient and contested. Museums are influential in creating public understandings of past identities, which in turn influence public ideas about who holds legitimate rights to land and resources in the region. One way that the Saami lay claim to identity and rights in the far north is through representations of the deep and recent past in community museums. Over time, there will be increasing pressures on metropolitan museums to acknowledge these identities and rights.

There is a deep desire within archaeology to be safe from politics because we know of the misuse of the past for a range of political causes. But representations of the past are inevitably political because they are fundamentally about connections of people to place. Where claims to land, resources, and identity are contested, where land and resources are being exploited by distant metropolises, and where identity is challenged by globalizing forces, archaeological representation will be political. It is far better to accept this and grapple with the complexities with our eyes open than to propose the goal of a depoliticized archaeological heritage.

Section X

Futures

Students in the Simon Fraser University Indigenous Archaeology Field School on Kamloops Indian Reserve, Kamloops, British Columbia: Murray Jules, Eunice Ned, Kim Christensen, and Achinie Wijesinghe (photo courtesy of George Nicholas)

51

Imagining the Future of Indigenous Archaeologies

Margaret M. Bruchac

Archaeologists have been increasingly compelled to consider not only who owns the past but also who constructs the past. The future of Indigenous archaeologies may be glimpsed, therefore, in at least three distinct ways. By reflecting backward, we can examine the relationships that produced certain kinds of evidence and knowledge, and the stories archaeologists have been telling themselves and us about the Indigenous past. By examining where we stand at this moment, setting aside colonial ideologies and listening to what Indigenous peoples have to say about archaeology (as the authors in this volume have done), we can consider a more holistic range of evidence and interpretation. Looking forward, with the intent of incorporating the Indigenous as full partners in the archaeological project, we can imagine how new relationships and increasingly multicultural and multivalent discursive exchanges might reveal and shape other knowledges, other stories.

The Past Is Not Yet Past

In extrapolating from past and present trends, one might observe that archaeology, as a discipline, has been slow to incorporate Indigenous perspectives (Zimmerman 2006) and to practice habits of reflexivity, perhaps because archaeologists imagine their informant populations to be dead and therefore inaccessible. Part of the problem lies in disciplinary divisions: studies of living Indigenous peoples have often been relegated to the "soft" sciences of ethnography and ethnohistory; "hard" relics of the ancient Indigenous past have often landed in the hands of archaeologists, who have historically exercised imperfect and unequal relations with Indigenous populations. Interpretations of Indigenous materiality have thus been inferred, rather than ethnographically collected, based on studies of only those materials that appear to be both visible and significant to non-Indigenous researchers.

How might an archaeologist understand the phenomenological experiences of peoples from another time or retroactively grasp the beliefs that guided depositions in the ground? Are there universal signifiers in certain kinds of material objects? How have Indigenous peoples charted their relations to human and nonhuman entities and to the land itself across space and time? Are there coherent linkages and continuities from the deep past to the present, or have processes of modernization and globalization made us all into "moderns"? Vastly different answers to these and other questions are emerging from the thinking of Indigenous archaeologists.

Until recently, archaeology, as a global movement, has largely avoided these questions by assuming inherent rights to excavate for the common good, with or without the permission of Indigenous communities. Much of the history of archaeology has been inextricably tangled with processes of searching for human origins—biological, cultural, political. Scientists have constructed temporal, geographical, and ideological boundaries to encompass specific sites, specific cultures, and specific research territories. Knowledge gleaned from Indigenous archaeological sites has, as a result, been shaped by outsiders' imaginings as much as by scientific theories. Generations of non-Indigenous professional and amateur collectors have destroyed sites and removed materials to satisfy scientific, capitalistic, or fetishistic desires of the moment. The physical and philosophical interferences created by routine archaeological explorations and curatorial habits, even those imagined to be processes of "recovery," may therefore be difficult, if not impossible, to repair. Some might argue that the intellectual ruptures and power differentials among archaeologists and archaeologized, colonizers and colonized, have produced deeply flawed "empirical" knowledge and left profound damages in their wake (Carter 1997; Smith 1999).

The Social Worlds and Thought Patterns of Indigenous Archaeologies

The use of the label "Indigenous," as noted by Wobst at the outset, has become a signifier of common cause among peoples once oppressed by colonization. The label of "Indigenous archaeologist," similarly, signals common cause among archaeologists who hope to resist colonizing ideologies (Wobst 2005), encourage collaboration (Silliman 2008), and otherwise promote Indigenous control over physical and metaphysical aspects of the past (Nicholas 2010). The politicization of the term "Indigenous" is also, of course, linked to the efforts by the United Nations to honor and to highlight the human rights concerns of multiple world communities (United Nations 2007).

Expressions of Indigeneity—as personal experience, political identity, global movement—have long been rooted in intricate, lived connections with unique landscapes, flora and fauna, human and nonhuman entities. Unique methods of encoding and transmitting, enacting and reenacting these connections are preserved in oral traditions, seasonal practices, and situated knowledges of distinct landscapes (for example, Anyon et al. 1997; Echo-Hawk 2000). It is also pertinent to note, when one reflects on the experiences of modern communities in diaspora, that Indigenous identity is frequently quite portable, although linked to a particular landscape (for example, Drummond 2007). For many Indigenous peoples, good relations in the present are inextricably linked to good relations with the past; reciprocal relations with the ancestors are crucial to preserving unique cultural practices and ensuring the stability of the ecosystem (for example, Julien, Bernard, and Rosenmeier 2008 [excerpted in Chapter 19 this volume]; Million 2005 [excerpted in Chapter 24 this volume]; Stewart, Keith, and Scottie 2004 [excerpted in Chapter 20 this volume]). "Indigenous archaeologies" emerge from all of these experiences, thought streams, and relationships.

Many Indigenous peoples around the world have chosen to work with archaeologists, whether exerting their traditional roles as keepers, controlling resource extraction and development, reshaping public understandings of the Indigenous, or adapting the tools of the scientists to their own ends. Some have become practicing archaeologists (for example, Colwell-Chanthaphonh 2009; Nicholas 2010; Watkins 2000). With their growing participation in scientific endeavors, as the excerpts in this volume illustrate, these people have become increasingly vocal about the uses, abuses, and interpretations of the Indigenous past (for example, Tsosie 1997; Wobst and Smith 2003). Self-identified Indigenous archaeologists (including those of both Indigenous and non-Indigenous ethnic origins) share membership in professional organizations (the World Archaeological Congress and the Society for American Archaeology, among others) that offer venues for wide-ranging discussion of these concerns. Together, these individuals are expanding the discourse around archaeology, Indigeneity, materiality, and reciprocity. They are also complicating the entire profession by drawing (often unwanted) attention to human rights issues in local and global venues, by collaborating in restructuring or restricting archaeological access to sites, by insisting on adherence to traditional Indigenous protocols, and by otherwise forcing both theoretical and practical shifts in the discipline.

Archaeologists and Indigenous peoples have been thrust together, not as a result of their natural willingness to articulate relations with one another but as a direct result of colonial legacies and contesting claims to the land that stands between them (for instance, Smith 1999; Wolfe 1999). Legislation is now in place in many locales that protects Indigenous concerns and that threatens penalties for the alienation of Indigenous ownership. New legislation in Oceania explicitly identifies Aboriginal communities as primary stakeholders (Anderson 2005; Wolfe 1999). With the passage of the 1993 Native Title Act, Australia revoked the *terra nullius* doctrine, through which lands inhabited by the Indigenous were deemed to be legally vacant. Aboriginal peoples are now acknowledged "by laws of customs" to "have a connection to the land or waters," and their rights are "recognized by the common laws of Australia" (Native Title Act 1993, S.208, i).

In North American contexts, protections for Indigenous lands remain couched in terms that protect the state's interest and custodianship. The Archaeological Resources Protection Act (ARPA), for example, identifies Native archaeological sites as "an accessible and irreplaceable part of the Nation's heritage" and urges that artifacts and data "be preserved by a suitable university, museum, or other scientific or educational institution" (ARPA 1979). Even the legislation that guides acts of repatriation—the Native American Graves Protection and Repatriation Act (NAGPRA 1990), and the American Indian Religious Freedom Act (AIRFA 1978)—allows museums to retain a great deal of choice and control over determinations of cultural affiliation (Brown and Bruchac 2006). Repatriation legislation cannot fully restore the physical materiality and sacred context of disrupted sites, remains, and objects. Nor can it be assumed that legislative and restorative efforts will protect Indigenous interests in the future.

Despite the passage of NAGPRA in the United States, hundreds of thousands of Indigenous remains, funerary objects, sacred objects, and items of cultural patrimony remain in the control of museums and federal institutions. Many scientists and Indigenous peoples remain at odds over the definitions and protocols governing the identification and repatriation of so-called culturally unidentifiable remains. In addition, unknown thousands of Indigenous remains and objects from America and elsewhere are still circulating in private collections and antiquities markets that are neither subject to nor compliant with NAGPRA. Efforts at repatriating privately owned Indigenous collections and sites have met with a surprising degree of resistance from mainstream archaeologists and the general public (Bruchac 2010).

Protocols that guide practices in one region are not necessarily transportable. Many American archaeologists work in areas abroad (Europe,

Africa, South America, and so on), where the human rights and intellectual property of Indigenous populations continue to be trampled in the pursuit of archaeology, in ways that are no longer legal in North American or Oceanic contexts. Consideration of these issues in a worldwide context illustrates the great advances made by Australia and New Zealand in enforcing protection of, and collaboration with, the Indigenous, as well as the great distances that some archaeologists have yet to travel in respecting Indigenous rights and patrimony.

The Future of Indigenous Archaeologies

To illustrate the present state of Indigenous archaeologies for this volume, we composed geographic groupings to strategically highlight particular issues. Yet, in considering Indigenous archaeologies as a whole, we must admit that physical and geographic boundaries do not always accurately map or define Indigenous relations. Some Indigenous nations share commonalities across space and time that cannot be easily circumscribed on a map. Some resolutions that appear to be perfectly suited to one locale might prove disastrous in another. There is no single "Indigenous" approach, since all archaeology, and all Indigeneity, is locally situated and shaped. There is no single future to predict.

A larger toolbox of theory and method should expand the range of possible approaches and enrich the discipline of archaeology, but Indigenous archaeologies are more than just a new addition to the menu. How will issues of imbalance and inequity (for example, power dynamics, colonial legacies, political and human rights struggles) be weighed in the process of vetting precisely which Indigenous perspectives would be considered for inclusion? Who will hold in check future authoritarian actions or research agendas that threaten Indigenous continuity? If archaeological practices are to be deconstructed on a worldwide scale, can they be equitably reconstructed, or will new unbalanced power dynamics emerge? Can we build on a foundation of imperialist theories and methods, or must we also dismantle the thought worlds and political landscapes that have been constructed (and are constantly being reconstructed) by imperialist ideologies? What are we to do if antiquated practices remain in play, or if similarly totalizing theories of already subjugated peoples emerge?

If, as Franz Fanon has suggested, "colonization and decolonization are simply a question of relative strength" (Fanon 1967, 47), then we have not yet entered the era of postcolonization, since colonial theories still dominate the practice of archaeology in many venues. How, then, might we imagine Indigenous archaeologies taking shape in the future?

The increased involvement of Indigenous peoples in recent decades has forced confrontations and encouraged collaborations that have reshaped the discipline of archaeology (as we've demonstrated in this volume)—but how will this reshaping continue? Is legislative action the most appropriate means of redress for past disturbances? Have archaeologists appropriately responded to the material concerns of the Indigenous, or will archaeological sites and finds continue to be routinely handled as private/scientific/public property? Could the influence of Indigenous knowledges and philosophies shift the epistemologies and ideologies of archaeological practice? How might a worldwide approach to these questions be useful in grappling with shifting relationships that are guaranteed to continue shifting?

This much is certain: configurations of the future of Indigenous archaeologies will continue to evolve, with an increasingly diverse body of participants in the field. Ethnographic approaches and research protocols will exert more influence on archaeological digs as more archaeologists attend to the political nuances, human rights, and ancestral relations of Indigenous peoples. Conceptions of social geography will shift as more Indigenous people share insights into their complex relations with Indigenous flora, fauna, and landscapes over time. As Indigenous descendants become increasingly engaged in Indigenous research, they will become increasingly vocal about their concerns and increasingly active in crafting solutions. Demands for the protection of intellectual and physical property and human rights are likely to shape legislation and protocols that will clarify and codify obligations to the Indigenous. Indigenous people who fill cross-cultural roles as archaeologists, curators, educators, administrators, and resource custodians will wield increasing levels of authority in issues of heritage, patrimony, land preservation, and political representation.

In the past, archaeology's practitioners and audiences—scientists and dominant societies—have been the primary beneficiaries of research, often at the expense of the Indigenous. It is hoped that in the future, archaeology's historic subjects—Indigenous peoples and their descendants—will experience far less harm, far more control, and far greater benefits when scientific research is conducted in their homelands.

References

Aboriginal and Torres Strait Islander Commission. 1998. *The Aboriginal and Torres Strait Islander Heritage Protection Bill.* www.aph.gov.au/library/Pubs/BD/1997-98/98bd226.htm (accessed March 20, 2010).

Abu El-Haj, N. 1998. Translating truths: Nationalism, the practice of archaeology, and the remaking of contemporary Jerusalem. *American Ethnologist* 25: 166–88.

Abu-Lughod, J. 1989. On the remaking of history: How to reinvent the past. In *Remaking history*, eds. B. Kruger and P. Morland, 111–30. Seattle: Dia Art Foundation, Bay Press.

Abu-Rabia, A. 2000. Bury my heart at wounded tree. Paper presented at the Conference on the Transmission and Assimilation of Culture in the Near East, Council for British Research in the Levant, Jerusalem.

Academy of Social Science. 1977. *Chosun gogohak gaeyo (Introduction to Chosun Archaeology).* Pyongyang: Gwahak Baekgwasajeon Chulpansa (Science Encyclopedia Press).

———. 1991. *Chosun jeonsa (A History of Chosun).* Pyongyang: Gwahak Baekgwasajeon Chulpansa (Science Encyclopedia Press).

Adas, M. 1989. *Machines as the measure of man: Science, technology and ideologies of Western dominance.* Ithaca, NY: Cornell University Press.

Ahmed, A., and C. Shore, eds. 1995. *The future of anthropology: Its relevance to the contemporary world.* London: Athlone.

Aikio, M., and P. Aikio. 1989. A chapter in the history of the colonization of Sámi lands: The forced migration of Norwegian Reindeer Sámi in Finland in the 1800s. In *Conflict in the archaeology of living traditions,* ed. R. Layton, 116–30. London: Unwin Hyman.

AIRFA. 1978. American Indian Religious Freedom Act of 1978. www.nps.gov/history/local-law/fhpl_IndianRelFreAct.pdf (accessed February 10, 2010).

Alfonso Martínez, M. 1999. *Study on treaties, agreements, and other constructive arrangements between states and Indigenous populations.* Commission on Human Rights. U.N. doc. E/CN.4/Sub.2/1999/20.

Allen, C. 1870. *Report on the Stockbridge Indians to the Legislature, Massachusetts: House document no. 13.* Boston: Wright and Porter.

Allen, H., D. Johns, C. Phillips, K. Day, T. O'Brien, and Ngāti Mutunga. 2002. Wāhi Ngaro (The lost portion): Strengthening relationships between people and wetlands in North Taranaki, New Zealand. *World Archaeology* 34(2): 315–29.

Allen, J. 1987. *The politics of the past.* Professorial Inaugural Address Series. Bundoora: La Trobe University Press.

Allen, T. 1997. *The invention of the white race: The origin of racial oppression in Anglo-America.* New York: Verso.

Alonso, A. M. 1995. *Thread of blood: Colonialism, revolution and gender on Mexico's northern frontier.* Tucson: University of Arizona Press.

Anaya, J. 1996. *Indigenous peoples in international law.* Oxford: Oxford University Press.

Andah, B. W. 1987. Foundations of civilizations in tropical Africa. *West African Journal of Archaeology* 17: vii–x.

———. 1990. Prologue to cultural resource management: An African dimension. *West African Journal of Archaeology* 20: 2–8.

Anderson, B. 1991. *Imagined communities.* London: Verso.

Anderson, I. 1995. Re-claiming TRU_GAN_NAN_NER: Decolonising the symbol. In *Speaking positions, Aboriginality, gender and ethnicity in Australian cultural studies,* eds. P. van Toorn and D. English, 31–42. Melbourne: Victoria University of Technology.

———. 1997. I, the "hybrid" Aborigine: Film and representation. *Australian Aboriginal Studies* 1: 4–14.

Anderson, J. 2005. The making of Indigenous knowledge in intellectual property law in Australia. *International Journal of Cultural Property* 12(3): 347–73.

Andrews, J. H. 1985. *Plantation acres: An historical study of the Irish land surveyors and his maps.* Omagh, Co. Tyrone: Ulster Historical Foundation.

Andrews, T. D., and J. B. Zoe. 1997. The *Idaà* trail: Archaeology and the Dogrib cultural landscape, Northwest Territories, Canada. In *At a crossroads: Archaeologists and First Peoples in Canada,* eds. G. P. Nicholas and T. D. Andrews, 160–77. Burnaby, B.C.: Archaeology Press.

Ang, I. 2001. *On not speaking Chinese: Living between Asia and the West.* New York: Routledge.

Anyon, R., and T. J. Ferguson. 1995. Cultural resources management at the pueblo of Zuni. *Antiquity* 69: 919–30.

Anyon, R., T. J. Ferguson, L. Jackson, and L. Lane. 1996. Native American oral traditions and archaeology. *SAA Bulletin* 14(2): 14–16.

Anyon, R., T. J. Ferguson, L. Jackson, L. Lane, and P. Vicenti. 1997. Native American oral tradition and archaeology: Issues of structure, relevance, and respect. In *Native Americans and archaeologists: Stepping stones to a common ground,* eds. N. Swidler, K. E. Dongoske, R. Anyon, and A. S. Downer, 77–87. Walnut Creek, CA: AltaMira Press.

Anyon, R., T. J. Ferguson, and J. R. Welch. 2000. Heritage management by American Indian tribes in the southwestern United States. In *Cultural resource management in contemporary society: Perspectives on managing and presenting the past,* eds. F. P. McManamon and A. Hatton, 120–41. London: Routledge.

Anzaldúa, G. 1990. Haciendo caras, una entrada. In *Making face, making soul/ hacienda caras: Creative and critical perspectives by women of color,* ed. G. Anzaldúa, xv–xxvii. San Francisco: Aunt Lute Books.

Appiah, K. A. 1994. Identity, authenticity, survival: Multicultural societies and social reproduction. In *Multiculturalism: Examining the politics of recognition,* ed. A. Gutmann, 149–63. Princeton, NJ: Princeton University Press.

Ardren, T. 2004. Where are the Maya in ancient Maya archaeological tourism? Advertising and appropriation of culture. In *Marketing heritage: Archaeology and the consumption of the past,* eds. Y. Rowan and U. Baram, 103–13. Walnut Creek, CA: AltaMira Press.

Arimitsu, K. 1996. 1945–1946 nyeon-e iteotdeon na-ui gyeongheomdam (Archaeology and museum in Korea between 1945–1946: a personal account). *Hanguk gogohakbo (Journal of Korean Archaeological Society)* 34: 7–27.

Ariss, R. 1988. Writing black: The construction of an Aboriginal discourse. In *Past and present: The construction of Aboriginality,* ed. J. R. Beckett, 131–46. Canberra: Aboriginal Studies Press.

Arnold, B. 1990. The past as propaganda: Totalitarian archaeology in Nazi Germany. *Antiquity* 64(244): 464–78.

———. 2002. Justifying genocide: Archaeology and the construction of difference. In *Annihilating difference: The anthropology of genocide,* ed. A. L. Hinton, 95–116. Berkeley and Los Angeles: University of California Press.

ARPA. 1979. Archaeological Resources Protection Act of 1979. October 31, 1979. Public Law 96-95; 16 U.S.C. 470aa-mm, www.nps.gov/history/local-law/fhpl_ArchRsrcsProt.pdf.

Atalay, S. 2006. Indigenous archaeology as decolonizing practice. *American Indian Quarterly* 30(3&4): 280–310.

Attwood, B., and J. Arnold, eds. 1992. *Power, knowledge and Aborigines.* Melbourne: La Trobe University Press in association with National Centre for Australian Studies, Monash University.

Australian Archaeological Association. 1994. Code of ethics. *Australian Archaeology* 39: 129.

———. 2004. Code of ethics, www.australianarchaeologicalassociation.com.au/ ethics (accessed March 30, 2010).

Australian Bureau of Statistics. 2002. *National Aboriginal and Torres Strait Islander social survey 2002* (ABS Cat. No. 4714.0). Canberra: Commonwealth of Australia.

———. 2003. *Population characteristics, Aboriginal and Torres Strait Islander Australians, 2001* (ABS Cat. No. 4713.0). Canberra: Commonwealth of Australia.

Australian Government, Attorney-General's Department. 1994. Stopping the rip offs, www.ag.gov.au/agd/WWW/securitylawHome.nsf/Page/Publications_

Intellectual_Property_Stopping_the_Rip_Offs_Report (accessed March 30, 2010).

Awatere, D. 1983. Awatere on intellectuals: Academic fragmentation or visionary unity. *Craccum* (Auckland University Students' Association) May 3: 6–7.

Axtell, J. 1981. *The European and the Indian: Essays in the ethnohistory of colonial North America.* Oxford: Oxford University Press.

Bahrani, Z. 1998. Conjuring Mesopotamia: Imaginative geography and a world past. In *Archaeology under fire: Nationalism, politics, and heritage in the eastern Mediterranean and Middle East,* ed. L. Meskell, 159–74. London: Routledge.

Bannerji, H. 1992. But who speaks for us? Experience and agency in conventional feminist paradigms. In *Unsettling relations: The university as a site of feminist struggles,* eds. H. Bannerji, L. Carty, K. Dehli, S. Heald, and K. McKenna, 67–108. Boston: South End Press.

Bannister, K. 2000. Chemistry rooted in cultural knowledge: Unearthing the links between antimicrobial properties and traditional knowledge in food and medicinal plant resources of the Secwepemc (Shuswap) Aboriginal Nation. PhD. Diss, University of British Columbia, Vancouver, B.C., Canada.

Bannister, K., and K. Barrett. 2001. Challenging the status quo in ethnobotany: A new paradigm for publication may protect cultural knowledge and traditional resources. *Cultural Survival Quarterly* 24(4): 10–13.

Basso, K. 1983. Stalking with stories: Names, places and moral narratives among the Western Apache. In *Text, play, and story,* ed. E. Brunner, 19–55. Prospect Heights, IL: Waveland Press.

Battiste, M., and J. Youngblood Henderson. 2000. *Protecting Indigenous knowledge and heritage: A global challenge.* Saskatoon: Purich.

Bazin, M. 1993. Our sciences, their science. *Race and Class* 34(2): 35–36.

Beach, H. 2001. *A year in Lapland: Guest of the reindeer herders.* Seattle: University of Washington Press.

Beck, W., C. Brown, D. Murphy, T. Perkins, A. Smith, and M. Somerville. 2002. *Yarrawarra places: Making stories.* Armidale, N.S.W.: University of New England Press.

Becker, H., and B. Geer. 1986. Participant observation: The analysis of qualitative field data. In *Field research: A sourcebook and field manual,* ed. R. G. Burgess, 239–50. London: Allen and Unwin.

Begay, R. 1997. The role of archaeology on Indian lands: The Navajo Nation. In *Native Americans and archaeologists: Stepping stones to common ground,* eds. N. Swindler, K. E. Dongoske, R. Anyon, and A. S. Downer, 161–66. Walnut Creek, CA: AltaMira Press.

———. 2001. Doo dilzin da: Abuse of the natural world. *American Indian Quarterly* 25(1): 21–27.

———. 2003. Exploring Navajo—Anaasazi relationships using traditional (oral) histories. Master's thesis, Northern Arizona University.

Belknap, J., and J. Morse. 1796. Report on the Oneida, Stockbridge and Brotherton Indians. Originally published in *Collections of the Massachusetts*

Historical Society, first series, 5: 12–32. Reprinted 1955 in *Indian Notes and Monographs,* no. 54. New York: Museum of the American Indian, Heye Foundation.

Ben-Haim, E., and Z. Margalit. 2000. Masada. Paper presented at the Getty Conservation Institute workshop on archaeological site management in the eastern Mediterranean, Corinth, Greece.

Bénabou, M. 1976. *La résistance africaine à la romanisation.* Paris: Maspéro.

Bender, B. 1998. *Stonehenge: Making space.* Oxford and New York: Berg.

———. 2002. Time and landscape. *Current Anthropology* 43(supplement): S103–12.

Bender, B., and M. Winer, eds. 2001. *Contested landscapes: Movement, exile, and place.* Oxford: Berg.

Bentley, P. A., H. D. G. Maschner, and C. Chippindale, eds. 2008. *Handbook of archaeological theories.* Lanham, MD: AltaMira Press.

Berg, B. L. 1998. *Qualitative research methods for the social sciences.* Boston: Allyn & Bacon.

Berggren, Å., and I. Hodder. 2003. Social practice, method, and some problems of field archaeology. *American Antiquity* 68(3): 421–34.

Berkes, F. 1993. Traditional ecological knowledge in perspective. In *Traditional ecological knowledge: Concepts and cases,* ed. J. T. Inglis, 1–10. Ottawa: Canadian Museum of Nature.

Bernard, H. R. 1988. *Research methods in cultural anthropology.* Newbury Park, CA: Sage Publications.

Bernardini, W. 2005. Reconsidering spatial and temporal aspects of prehistoric cultural identity: A case study from the American Southwest. *American Antiquity* 70: 31–54.

Berte, S. 2001. Indigenous perception of cultural heritage and its management: A cursory blueprint among the Senufo in the Sikasso region of Mali. *Papers from the Institute of Archaeology* 12: 105–09.

Blakeney, M. 1999. Intellectual property in the Dreamtime—Protecting the cultural creativity of Indigenous people. *Oxford Intellectual Property Research Center Electronic Journal of Intellectual Property Rights,* www.oiprc.ox.ac.uk/EJWP1199.html.

Boardman, J. 1980. *The Greeks overseas: Their early colonies and trade.* London: Thames & Hudson.

Bodenhorn, B. 1993. Gendered spaces, public places: Public and private revisited on the North Slope of Alaska. In *Landscape: Politics and perspectives,* ed. B. Bender, 169–203. Oxford: Berg.

Boladeras, J. 2002. "It's easier to be Black if you're black": Issues of Aboriginality for fair-complexioned Nyungar people. Master's thesis, Centre for Aboriginal Studies, Curtin University of Technology, Perth, Western Australia.

Bond, G., and A. Gilliam. 1994. Power/knowledge. In *Social construction of the past: Representation as power,* eds. G. Bond and A. Gilliam, 78–109. London: Routledge.

Bonfil Batalla, G. 1972. El concepto de indio en América. Una categoriá de la situación colonial. In *Anales de Antropología,* volume 9, 105–24. México, D.F.: Universidad Nacional Autónoma de México.

Bourbon, F. 2000. *The lost cities of the Mayas: The life, art and discoveries of Frederick Catherwood.* New York: Abbeville Press.

Bourdieu, P. 1977. *Towards a theory of practice.* Cambridge: Cambridge University Press.

———. 1984. Delegation and political fetishism. *Thesis Eleven* 10(11): 56–69.

Bowdler, S. 1992. Unquiet slumbers: The return of the Kow Swamp burials. *Antiquity* 66: 103–06.

Bradley, B., and D. Stanford. 2004. The North Atlantic ice-edge corridor: A possible Paleolithic route to the New World. *World Archaeology* 36(4): 459–78.

———. 2006. The Solutrean-Clovis connection: Reply to Straus, Meltzer and Goebel. *World Archaeology* 38(4): 704–14.

Bradley, R. 2002. Fieldwork and its discontents: Confessions from the Clavia Cairns. Paper presented at the Annual Meeting of the Society for American Archaeology, Denver, Colorado.

Bradshaw, B., A. Hadfield, and W. Maley, eds. 1993. *Representing Ireland: Literature and the origins of conflict, 1534–1660.* Cambridge: Cambridge University Press.

Brady, C., and R. Gillespie. 1986. *Natives and newcomers: Essays on the making of the Irish colonial society, 1534–1641.* Dublin: Irish Academic Press.

Braniff, B., and R. S. Felger. 1976. *Sonora: Antropología del desierto, noroeste de México I.* Hermosillo: Centro INAH Sonora.

Brass, P. 2003. *The production of Hindu–Muslim violence in contemporary India.* Seattle: Jackson School Publications in International Studies at the University of Washington Press.

Brasser, T. J. 1978. Mahican. In *Handbook of North American Indians,* vol. 15: Northeast, ed. B. Trigger, 198–212. Washington, D.C.: Smithsonian Institution Press.

Bray, T. L., ed. 2001. *The future of the past: Archaeologists, Native Americans, and repatriation.* New York: Garland.

Brewster, G. R. 2006. Soils at the Debert-Belmont archaeological site. Report on file at the Confederacy of Mainland Mi'kmaq, Truro, Nova Scotia.

Brothwell, D. R., and E. Higgs, eds. 1963. *Science in archaeology: A comprehensive survey.* New York: Basic Books.

Brough, M. A. 1999. A lost cause? Representations of Aboriginal and Torres Strait Islander health in Australian newspapers. *Australian Journal of Communication* 26(2): 89–98.

———. 2003. *Who owns Native culture?* Cambridge: Harvard University Press.

Brown, M. F. 1998. Can culture be copyrighted? *Current Anthropology* 39: 193–222.

Brown, M. F., and M. M. Bruchac. 2006. NAGPRA from the middle distance: Legal puzzles and unintended consequences. In *Imperialism, art, and restitution,* ed. J. H. Merryman, 193–217. Cambridge: Cambridge University Press.

Brubaker, R., and F. Cooper. 2000. Beyond identity. *Theory and Society* 29: 1–47.

Bruchac, M. 2010. Constructing Indigenous associations: Protocols of recognition and NAGPRA compliance. *Anthropology News* 51(3): 5, 8.

Brumfiel, E. 1998. A role for archaeology in feminist and gender studies. Paper presented at Doing Archaeology as a Feminist Advanced Seminar, organized by M. Conkey and A. Wylie. School of American Research, Santa Fe, New Mexico.

Brydon, D. 1995. The white Inuit speaks: Contamination as literary strategy. In *The post-colonial studies reader,* eds. B. Ashcroft, G. Griffiths, and H. Tiffin, 136–42. London: Routledge.

Burgess, R. G. 1986. *Field research: A sourcebook and field manual.* London: Allen and Unwin.

Burke, H., C. Smith, D. Lippert, J. Watkins, and L. Zimmerman, eds. 2008. *Kennewick Man: Perspectives on the Ancient One.* Walnut Creek, CA: Left Coast Press.

Butler, E. 1946. The brush or stone memorial heaps of southern New England. *Bulletin of the Archaeological Society of Connecticut* 19: 2–11.

Butler, J. 1990. *Gender trouble: Feminism and the subversion of identity.* New York: Routledge.

Byrne, D. 1996. Deep nation: Australia's acquisition of an Indigenous past. *Aboriginal History* 20: 82–107.

———. 2003a. Nervous landscapes: Race and space in Australia. *Journal of Social Archaeology* 3(2): 169–93.

———. 2003b. The ethos of return: Erasure and reinstatement of Aboriginal visibility in the Australian historical landscape. *Historical Archaeology* 37(1): 73–86.

———. 2004. Archaeology in reverse. In *Public archaeology,* ed. N. Merriman, 240–54. London: Routledge.

Cajete, G. 1994. Look to the mountain. Skyland, NC: Kivaki Press.

Canny, N. 2001. *Making Ireland British, 1580–1650.* Oxford: Oxford University Press.

Capiberibe, A. 2001. *Os Palikur e os Cristianismo.* Master's diss., Universidade Estadual de Campinas. Campinas Brazil.

Carby, H. 1987. *Reconstructing womanhood: The emergence of the Afro-American woman novelist.* New York: Oxford University Press.

Carmichael, D. L., J. Hubert, B. Reeves, and A. Schanche, eds. 1994. *Sacred sites, sacred places.* New York: Routledge.

Carter, C. E. 1997. Straight talk and trust. In *Native Americans and archaeologists: Stepping stones to common ground,* eds. N. Swidler, K. E. Dongoske, R. Anyon, and A. S. Downer, 151–55. Walnut Creek, CA: AltaMira Press.

Casella, E. C. 2000. Bulldaggers and gentle ladies: Archaeological approaches to female homosexuality in convict-era Australia. In *Archaeologies of sexuality,* eds. R. A. Schmidt and B. L. Voss, 143–59. London: Routledge.

Castañeda, Q. E., and C. N. Matthews, eds. 2008. *Ethnographic archaeologies: Reflections on stakeholders and archaeological practices.* Lanham, MD: AltaMira Press.

Cavander Wilson, A. 2004. Reclaiming our humanity: Decolonization and the recovery of Indigenous knowledge. In *Indiginizing the academy,* eds. D. A. Mihesuah and A. C. Wilson, 69–87. Lincoln: University of Nebraska Press.

Chaloupka, G. 1986. *Burrunguy, Nourlangie Rock.* Darwin: Northart.

Chamberlin, J. E. 1999. Doing things with words: Putting performance on the page. In *Talking on the page: Editing Aboriginal oral texts,* eds. L. J. Murray and K. Rice, 69–90. Toronto: University of Toronto Press.

Chase, A. K. 1989. Perceptions of the past among North Queensland Aboriginal people: The intrusion of Europeans and consequent social change. In *Who needs the past? Indigenous values and archaeology,* ed. R. Layton, 169–79. London: Unwin Hyman.

Chato, G., and C. Conte. 1988. The legal rights of American Indian women. In *Western women: Their land, their lives,* eds. L. Schlissel, V. Ruiz, and J. Monk, 229–46. Albuquerque: University of New Mexico Press.

Chatters, J. C. 2000. The recovery and first analysis of an early Holocene human skeleton from Kennewick, Washington. *American Antiquity* 65(2): 291–316.

Chatwin, B. 1987. *The songlines.* New York: Penguin Books.

Childs, S. T. 1995. Technological history and culture in western Tanzania. In *The culture and technology of African iron production,* ed. P. Schmidt, 277–320. Gainesville: University Press of Florida.

Chittick, H. N. 1974. *Kilwa: An Islamic trading city on the East African coast.* Memoir 5. Nairobi: British Institute in Eastern Africa.

———. 1984. *Manda: Excavations at an island port on the Kenya coast.* Memoir 9. Nairobi: British Institute in Eastern Africa.

Chungcheong Province. 2004. *Bodojaryo: Chungbukdo jijeongmunhwajae simui gyeolgwa (News report summary: The selection of provincial cultural properties).* Munhwa yesulgwa, Munhwajaedamdang (The Office of Culture and Arts, Deparmment of Cultural Resource Management) November 16, 2004.

Clancy, M. 1999. Tourism and development: Evidence from Mexico. *Annals of Tourism Research* 26(1): 1–20.

Clark, A., and U. Frederick. 2005. Closing the distance: Interpreting cross-cultural engagements through Indigenous rock-art. In *Archaeology in Oceania: Australia and the Pacific Islands,* ed. I. Lilley, 116–33. Oxford: Blackwell.

Cleere, H., ed. 1989. *Archaeological heritage management in the modern world.* London: Routledge.

Clifford, J. 1988. *The predicament of culture, twentieth century ethnography, literature and art.* Cambridge: Harvard University Press.

———. 1994. Diasporas. *Cultural Anthropology* 9: 302–38.

Cojti Cuxil, D. 1995. *Configuracion del pensamiento politico del Pueblo Maya: (2da. Parte).* Quetzaltenango, Guatemala: Asociación de Escritores Mayances de Guatemala.

Cojti Cuxil, D. 1997. *El movimiento Maya. Editorial Cholsamaj*. Iximulew, Guatemala.

Cojti Ren, A. 2006. Maya archaeology and the political and cultural identity of contemporary Maya in Guatemala. *Archaeologies: Journal of the World Archaeological Congress* 2(1): 8–19.

Colley, S. 2002. *Uncovering Australia: Archaeology, Indigenous peoples and the public*. Crows Nest, N.S.W.: Allen & Unwin.

Colley, S., and A. Bickford. 1997. "Real" Aborigines and "real" archaeology: Aboriginal places and Australian historical archaeology. *World Archaeological Bulletin* 7: 5–21.

Collins, P. H. 1990. *Black feminist thought: Knowledge, consciousness, and the politics of empowerment*. New York: Chapman and Hall, Routledge.

Colwell-Chanthaphonh, C. 2009. *Inheriting the past: The making of Arthur C. Parker and Indigenous archaeology*. Tucson: University of Arizona Press.

Colwell-Chanthaphonh, C., and T. J. Ferguson, eds. 2008. *Collaboration in archaeological practice: Engaging descendant communities*. Lanham, MD: AltaMira Press.

Conkey, M. W. 1993. Making the connections: Feminist theory and archaeologies of gender. In *Women in archaeology: A feminist critique*, eds. H. DuCros and L. Smith, 3–15. Department of Prehistory Monographs No. 23. Canberra: Australian National University.

———. 2005. Dwelling at the margins, action at the intersection? Feminist and Indigenous archaeologies, 2005. *Archaeologies: Journal of the World Archaeological Congress* 1(1): 9–59.

Conklin, B. A. 2002. Shamans versus pirates in the Amazonian treasure chest. *American Anthropologist* 104(4): 1050–61.

Council of Europe. 1999. *Gods and heroes of the Bronze Age*. London: Thames and Hudson.

Cowlishaw, G. 1988. *Black, white or brindle: Race in rural Australia*. Cambridge: Cambridge University Press.

———. 2004a. *Blackfellas, whitefellas and the hidden injuries of race*. Carlton, Vic.: Blackwell Publishing.

———. 2004b. Racial positioning, privilege and public debate. In *Whitening race: Essays in social and cultural criticism*, ed. A. Moreton-Robinson, 59–74. Canberra: Aboriginal Studies Press.

Crown, P. L., ed. 2000. *Women and men in the prehispanic Southwest*. Santa Fe, NM: School of American Research Press.

Cunningham, J. L. 1997. Colored existence: Racial identity formation in light skin blacks. *Smith College Studies in Social Work* 67(3): 375–400.

Cunningham, R. 2005. *Archaeology, relics and the law* (2nd edition). Durham, NC: Carolina Academic Press.

Curran, M. L. 1999. Exploration, colonization and settling in: The Bull Brook phase, antecedents, and descendants. In *The Archaeological Northeast*, eds. M. A. Levine, K. E. Sassaman, and M. S. Nassaney, 3–24. Westport, CT: Bergin and Garvey.

Curran, M. L., and J. R. Grimes. 1989. Ecological implications for Paleoindian lithic procurement economy in New England. In *Eastern Paleoindian lithic resources use,* eds. C. J. Ellis and J. C. Lothrop, 41–74. Boulder, CO: Westview Press.

Currie, G., and C. Rothenberg, eds. 2001. *Feminist (re)visions of the subject: Landscapes, ethnoscapes, and theoryscapes.* Lanham, MD: Lexington Books.

Dagua, A., M. Aranda, and L. G. Vasco. 1998. *Guambianos: Hijos del arioris y del agua.* Bogotá: CEREC.

Dauenhauer, N. M., and R. Dauenhauer. 1999. The paradox of talking on the page: Some aspects of the Tlingit and Haida experience. In *Talking on the page: Editing Aboriginal oral texts,* eds. L. J. Murray and K. Rice, 3–41. Toronto: University of Toronto Press.

David, B., and I. McNiven. 2004. Western Torres Strait cultural history project: Research design and initial results. In *Torres Strait archaeology and material culture,* eds. I. McNiven and M. Quinnell, 199–208. Memoirs of the Queensland Museum Cultural Heritage Series 3(1). Brisbane: Queensland Museum.

Davidson, I. 1991. Notes for a code of ethics for Australian Archaeologists working with Aboriginal and Torres Strait Islander heritage. *Australian Archaeology* 32: 61–64.

Davidson, I., C. Lovell-Jones, and R. Bancroft, eds. 1995. *Archaeologists and Aborigines working together.* Armidale, N.S.W.: University of New England Press.

Davis, H. 2003. Creating and implementing a code and standards. In *Ethical issues in archaeology,* eds. L. J. Zimmerman, K. D. Vitelli, and J. Hollowell-Zimmer, 251–60. Walnut Creek, CA: AltaMira Press.

Day, K. 2001. *Måaori wood carving of the Taranaki region.* Auckland: Reed Publishing.

de Zayas, A. M. 2006. *Die deutschen Vertriebenen.* Graz: Ares Verlag.

Deetman, W. 2003. Translation from the *Ochtendblad Trouw.* January 7, 2003.

Delle, J. 1999. Extending Europe's grasp: An archaeological comparison of colonial spatial process in Ireland and Jamaica. In *Old and New Worlds,* eds. R. L. Michael and G. Egan, 106–16. Oxford: Oxbow Press.

Deloria, V., Jr. 1969. *Custer died for our sins: An Indian manifesto.* New York: The Macmillan Company.

———. 1992. Indians, archaeologists, and the future. *American Antiquity* 57(4): 595–98.

———. 1995. *Red earth, white lies: Native Americans and the myth of scientific fact.* New York: Scribner.

———. 1997. *Indians, anthros, and planetary reality. In Indians and anthropologists: Vine Deloria, Jr., and the critique of anthropology,* eds. T. Biolsi and L. Zimmerman, 209–21. Tucson: University of Arizona Press.

Denetdale, J. N. 2004. Planting seeds of ideas and raising doubts about what we believe: An interview with Vine Deloria, Jr. *Journal of Social Archaeology* 4(2): 131–46.

Derry, L. 1997. Pre-emancipation archaeology: Does it play a role in Selma, Alabama? In *In the realm of politics: Prospects for public participation in African-American and plantation archaeology*, eds. C. McDavid and D. W. Babson. *Historical Archaeology* 31(3): 18–26.

Dever, W. 1999. Can "biblical archaeology" be an academic and professional discipline? In *Archaeology, history and culture in Palestine and the Near East: Essays in memory of Albert E. Glock*, ed. T. Kapitan, 11–22. Atlanta: Scholars Press.

Diaby, B. H., and K. Sanogo. 2000. Sauvegarde du patrimoine archéologique du Mali. In *L'archéologie en Afrique de l'ouest: Sahara et Sahel*, ed. R. Vernet, 79–83. Saint-Maur: Editions Sepia.

Diaz-Andreu, M., and T. Champion, eds. 1996. *Nationalism and archaeology in Europe*. Boulder, CO: Westview Press.

Dibble, H., T. Raczek, and S. McPherron. 2005. Excavator bias at the site of Pech de l'Azé IV, France. *Journal of Field Archaeology* 30: 317–28.

Discovery Channel. 2003. World's "oldest" rice found in South Korea. http://dsc.discovery.com/news/afp/20031020/rice.html.

Dixon, J., T. Heaton, and T. Fifield. 1997. Early Holocene human remains and the paleoenvironment of Prince of Wales Island, Southeast Alaska. Paper presented at the 24th Annual Meeting of the Alaska Anthropological Association, Whitehorse, Yukon.

Do, Y. 1994 (1960). *Chosun wonsi gogohak (Prehistoric Archaeology of Chosun)*. Pyongyang (Seoul): Gwahakwon chulpansa (reprinted by Balsan).

Dodson, M. 1994. The Wentworth lecture: The end in the beginning: Re(de)fining Aboriginality. *Australian Aboriginal Studies* 1: 2–13.

Dolf-Bonekämper, G. 2002. Sites of hurtful memory. *Conservation* 17(2) www.getty.edu/conservation/publications/newsletters/17_2/feature.html.

Dongoske, K. E., M. Aldenderfer, and K. Doehner, eds. 2000. *Working together: Native Americans and archaeologists*. Washington, D.C.: Society for American Archaeology.

Doyel, D. E. 1982. Medicine men, ethnic significance, and cultural resource management. *American Antiquity* 47: 634–42.

Drummond, A. 2007. The construction of Irish travelers (and Gypsies) as a problem. In *Migrants and memory: The forgotten "postcolonials,"* ed. Micheál Ô hAodha, 2–42. London: Cambridge Scholars Publishing.

Duara, P. 1995. *Rescuing history from the nation: Questioning narratives of modern China*. Chicago: University of Chicago Press.

Dudgeon, P., and D. Oxenham. 1989. The complexity of Aboriginal diversity: Identity and kindredness. *Black Voices* 5(1): 22–38.

Dunn, K. M., J. Forrest, I. Burnley, and A. McDonald. 2005. Constructing racism in Australia. *Australian Journal of Social Issues* 39(4): 409–30.

Dural, S. 2007. *Protecting Çatalhöyük: Memoir of an archaeological site guard*, with contributions by I. Hodder. Translated by D. C. Cleere. Walnut Creek, CA: Left Coast Press.

Ebert, J. I., A. Thoma, M. C. Ebert, R. K. Hitchcock, and M. Oabile. 1976. Report and recommendations for land allocation and Basarwa development in the Sandveld region of Central District, Botswana. Serowe, Botswana: Central District Council and Ngwato Land Board.

Echo-Hawk, R. 1993. Exploring ancient worlds. *SAA Bulletin* 11: 5–6.

———. 1997. Forging a new ancient history for Native America. In *Native Americans and archaeologists: Stepping stones to a common ground,* eds. N. Swidler, K. E. Dongoske, R. Anyon, and A. S. Downer, 88–102. Walnut Creek, CA: AltaMira Press.

———. 2000. Ancient history in the New World: Integrating oral traditions and the archaeological record in seep time. *American Antiquity* 62(2): 267–90.

Echo-Hawk, R., and L. J. Zimmerman. 2006. Beyond racism: Some opinions about racialism and American archaeology. *American Indian Quarterly* 30(3): 461–85.

Edmonds, M. R. 1999. *Ancestral geographies of the Neolithic.* Oxford: Berg.

Egan, T. 1998. Old skull gets white looks stirring dispute. *The New York Times* 147(511–15): A12.

Eidheim, H. 1997. Ethno-political development among the Sami after World War II: The invention of selfhood. In *Sami culture in a new era: The Norwegian Sami experience,* ed. G. Harald, 29–61. Karasjok: Davvi Girji OS (distributed in North America by University of Washington Press).

English, A. 2002a. More than archaeology: Developing comprehensive approaches to Aboriginal heritage management in NSW. *Australian Journal of Environmental Management* 9(4): 218–27.

———. 2002b. *The sea and the rock gives us a feed.* Hurstville: N.S.W. National Parks and Wildlife Service.

Everett, J. 1990. Significance to Tasmanian Aborigines. Paper presented at the Tasmanian Wilderness World Heritage Symposium, Hobart.

Fabian, J. 1983. *Time and the other: How anthropology makes its object.* New York: Columbia University Press.

Falk, J. H., and L. D. Dierking. 2000. *Learning from museums: Visitor experiences and the making of meaning.* Walnut Creek, CA: AltaMira Press.

Fanon, F. 1967. *Black skin, white masks.* New York: Grove Press.

Faust, A. 2000. A commodity or a threat?: Imported pottery in the Iron Age II. Paper presented at the Conference on the Transmission and Assimilation of Culture in the Near East, Council for British Research in the Levant, Jerusalem.

Feder, K. 1984. Pots, plants, and people: The Late Woodland period of Connecticut. *Bulletin of the Archaeological Society of Connecticut* 47: 99–111.

———. 1994. *A village of outcasts: Historical archaeology and documentary research at the Lighthouse site.* Mountain View, CA: Mayfield Publishing Company.

Fedje, D., and T. Christiansen. 1999. Modeling paleoshorelines and locating early holocene coastal sites in Haida Gwaii. *American Antiquity* 64: 635–52.

Fedje, D., and H. Josenhans. 1999. A prehistoric stone tool recovered from a deeply drowned fluvial fan in Hecate Strait, British Columbia, Canada. Unpublished manuscript, Parks Canada, Victoria.

Ferguson, K. 1993. *The man question: Visions of subjectivity in feminist theory.* Berkeley and Los Angeles: University of California Press.

Ferguson, T. J. 2000. NHPA: Changing the role of Native Americans in the archaeological study of the past. In *Working together: Native Americans and archaeologists,* eds. K. E. Dongoske, M. Aldenderfer, and K. Doehner, 25–36. Washington, D.C.: Society for American Archaeology.

Fiedel, S. J. 2004. The Kennewick follies: "New" theories about the peopling of the Americas. *Journal of Anthropological Research* 60(1): 74–110.

Field, J., J. Barker, R. Barker, E. Coffey, L. Coffey, E. Crawford, L. Darcy, T. Fields, G. Lord, B. Steadman, and S. Colley. 2000. "Coming back": Aborigines and archaeologists at Cuddie Springs. *Public Archaeology* 1: 35–48.

Fienup-Riordan, A. 1999. Collaboration on display: A Yup'ik Eskimo exhibit at three national museums. *American Anthropologist* 101(2): 339–58.

Fienup-Riordan, A., W. Tyson, P. John, M. Meade, and J. Active. 2000. *Hunting tradition in a changing world: Yup'ik lives in Alaska today.* New Brunswick: Rutgers University Press.

Findji, M. T. 1993. Tras las Huellas de los Paeces. In *Encrucijadas de Colombia Amerindia,* ed. F. Correa, 49–69. Bogotá: Instituto Colombiano de Antropología.

Flyvbjerg, B. 2001. *Making social science matter: Why social inquiry fails and how it can succeed again.* Cambridge: Cambridge University Press.

Foley, D. 2000. Too white to be black, too black to be white. *Social Alternatives* 19(4): 44–49.

Forsman, L. 2004. Cultural resource management and Indian tribes: Who owns the past? Paper presented at the Annual Meeting of the Society for American Archaeology, Montreal.

Foster, R., and D. R. Croes. 2002. Tribal archaeological cooperative agreement: A holistic cultural resource management approach. *Journal of Wetland Archaeology* 2: 25–38.

Foucault, M. 1984. Space, knowledge, and power. In *The Foucault reader,* ed. P. Rabinow, 239–56. New York: Pantheon Books.

Fraser, N. 1997. *Justice interruptus: Critical reflections on the "post-socialist" condition.* New York: Routledge.

French, L. 2003. *Native American justice.* Chicago: Burnham.

Friends of America's Past. 2003. www.friendsofpast.org. (accessed February 18, 2003).

Friesen, T. M. 1998. *Qikiqtaruk-Inuvialuit archaeology on Herschel Island.* Toronto: University of Toronto.

Frisbie, C. J., and D. P. McAllister, eds. 1978. *Navajo blessingway singer: The autobiography of Frank Mitchell, 1881–1967.* Tucson: University of Arizona Press.

Fujisawa, A. 2006. Minzoku-no-Monogatari-toshiteno-Sengo Nihon Koukogak (Japanese archaeology of the post-war as the story of Japanese Nation). *Nihonshi no Houhou (Method of Japanese History)* 4:125–32.

García, S., and D. Rolandi, eds. 2004. *¿Quiénes somos? Entretejiendo identidades en la puna catamarqueña.* Buenos Arias: Asociación Amigos del Instituto Nacional de Antropología and Ediciones Del Tridente.

Gardiner, D., B. D. Compton, and S. Peacock. 1999. Tk'emlúpsesmc (Kamloops Indian Band) traditional use study. Report prepared for the Kamloops Indian Band, Kamloops, BC, and the Ministry of Forests.

Gazin-Schwartz, A., and C. Holtorf, eds. 1999. *Archaeology and folklore.* London: Routledge.

Geingos, V., and M. Ngakaeaja. 2002. Traditional knowledge of the San in southern Africa: Hoodia gordonia. Paper presented at Biopiracy: Ten years post Rio, 2nd South-South Biopiracy Summit, Johannesburg, August 2002.

Gero, J. M. 1989. Producing prehistory, controlling the past: The case of the New England beehives. In *Critical traditions in contemporary archaeology,* eds. V. Pinsky and A. Wylie, 96–103. Cambridge: Cambridge University Press.

———. 1995. Railroading epistemology: Paleoindians and women. In *Interpreting archaeology: Finding meaning in the past,* eds. I. Hodder, M. Shanks, A. Alexandri, V. Buchli, J. Carman, J. Lastland, and G. Lucas, 175–80. London: Routledge.

Gibb, J. G. 1997. Necessary but insufficient: Plantation archaeology reports and community action. In *In the realm of politics: Prospects for public participation in African-American and plantation archaeology,* eds. C. McDavid and D. W. Babson. Historical Archaeology 31(3): 51–64.

Giddens, A. 1985. Time, space, and regionalization. In *Social relations and spatial structures,* eds. D. Gregory and J. Urry, 265–95. London: Macmillan.

Gill, N., A. Paterson, and M. Japanangka Kennedy. 2004. Murphy, do you want to delete this? In *Hidden histories and hidden landscapes in the Murchison and Davenport Ranges, Northern Territory, Australia.* Darwin, Northern Territory: Northern Australia Research Unit.

Gilroy, P. 1993. *Small acts: Thoughts on the politics of Black cultures.* London: Serpent's Tail.

———. 2000. *Against race: Imagining political culture beyond the color line.* Cambridge: Harvard University Press.

Giraldus Cambrensis. 1982 [1188]. *The history and topography of Ireland* (Topographica Hibernica). London: Penguin Books.

Glazier, D. 1999. *The ancient port of Myos Hormos at Quseir al-Qadim.* Plain language report of the 1999 field season, Department of Archaeology, University of Southampton and Quseir Heritage Preservation Society.

———. 2001. Archaeological communities? A socio-political analysis of archaeological investigation at Quseir al-Qadim. Ph.D. upgrade document, Department of Archaeology, University of Southampton.

Gloade, G. 2007. Cultural memory timeline imbedded in the Mi'kmaw legends of Kluskap. Paper presented at the 40th Annual Meeting of the Canadian Archaeological Association, St. John's, Newfoundland, May 19.

Glock, A. 1999. Archaeology as cultural survival: The future of the Palestinian past. In *Archaeology, history and culture in Palestine and the Near East: Essays in memory of Albert E. Glock,* ed. T. Kapitan, 343–65. Atlanta: Scholars Press.

Gnecco, C. 2006. A three-takes tale: The meaning of WAC for a pluralistic archaeology. *Archaeologies* 2(2): 80–86.

Gnecco, C., and C. Hernández. 2008. History and its discontents: Stone statues, Native histories, and archaeologists. *Current Anthropology* 49(3): 439–66.

Goddard, P. E. 1933. Navajo texts. *American Museum of Natural History* 34(1).

Golding, F. N. 1989. Stonehenge—past and future. In *Archaeological heritage management in the modern world,* ed. H. F. Cleere, 256–64. London: Unwin Hyman.

Goldstein, L., and K. Kintigh. 1990. Ethics and the reburial controversy. *American Antiquity* 55: 585–91.

Gómez, H., and C. A. Ruíz. 1997. *Los Paeces: Gente territorio.* Popayán: FUNCOP-Universidad del Cauca.

Goonatilake, S. 1982. Colonies: Scientific expansion (and contraction). *Review* 5(3): 413–36.

Gordimer, N. 1988. *The essential gesture. In The essential gesture: Writing, politics and places,* ed. Stephen Clingman, 285–300. New York: Alfred A. Knopf.

Gosden, C. 1994. *Social being and time.* Oxford: Oxford University Press.

Gosden, C., and Y. Marshall. 1999. The cultural biography of objects. *World Archaeology* 31(2):169–78.

Gotthardt, R., and G. Hare. 1994. *Lu Zil Man: Fish Lake.* Whitehorse: Yukon Heritage Branch.

Gow, P. 1995. Land, people and paper in western Amazon. In *The anthropology of landscape,* eds. E. Hirsch and M. O'Hanlon, 43–62. Oxford: Oxford University Press.

Grant, S. 2002. *The tears of a stranger: A memoir.* Pymble, N.S.W.: HarperCollins.

Green, L. F., D. R. Green, and E. Góes Neves. 2003. Indigenous knowledge and archaeological science: The challenges of public archaeology in the Reserva Uaçá. *Journal of Social Archaeology* 3(3): 366–98.

Greer, G. 2003. Whitefella jump up: The shortest way to nationhood. *Quarterly Essay* 11: 1–78.

Greer, S. 1997. Traditional knowledge in site recognition. In *At a crossroads: Archaeologists and First Peoples in Canada,* eds. G. P. Nicholas and T. D. Andrews, 145–59. Burnaby, B.C.: Archaeology Press.

Griffiths, G. 1995. The myth of authenticity. In *The post-colonial studies reader,* eds. B. Ashcroft, G. Griffiths, and H. Tiffin, 237–41. London: Routledge.

Griswold del Castillo, R. 1990. *The treaty of Guadalupe Hidalgo: A legacy of conflict.* Norman: University of Oklahoma Press.

Gröhn, A. 2004. *Positioning the Bronze Age in social theory and research context.* Acta Archaeologica Lundensia Series. Stockholm: Almqvist and Wiksell.

Gustafson, B. 1998. Arkeologerirättegång. *Populär Arkeologi* 1998(4): 29.

Haber, A. F. 1999. Uywaña, the house and its indoor landscape: Oblique approaches to, and beyond, domestication. In *The prehistory of food: Appetites for change,* eds. C. Gosden and J. Hather, 57–82. London: Routledge.

———. 2007a. This is not an answer to the question "who is Indigenous?" *Archaeologies: Journal of the World Archaeological Congress* 3(3): 213–29.

———. 2007b. Reframing social equality within an intercultural archaeology. *World Archaeology* 39(2): 281–97.

Haber, A. F., and C. Lema. 2006. Dime cómo escribes y te diré quién eres: Representaciones textuales del campesinado Indígena de la Puna de Atacama. *Memoria Americana* 14.

Hætta, O. M. 1995. Rock carvings in a Saami perspective: Some comments on politics and ethnicity in archaeology. In *Perceiving rock art: Social and political perspectives,* eds. Knut Helskog and Bjørnar Olsen, 348–56. Oslo: Instituttet for Sammenlignende Kulturforskning.

———. 1996. *The Sami: An Indigenous people of the Arctic.* Ole Petter Gurholt, trans. Karasjok, Norway: Davvi Girji OS.

Hage, G. 2003. *Against paranoid nationalism: Searching for hope in a shrinking society.* Annandale, N.S.W.: Pluto Press.

Haile, Fr. Berard. 1938a. Origin legend of the Navaho enemy way: Text and translation. *Yale University Publication in Anthropology* 17.

———. 1938b. Navajo chantways and ceremonials. *American Anthropologist* 40(4): 639–52.

Hall, M. 1996. *Archaeology Africa.* Cape Town: David Phillip.

———. 2005. Situational ethics and engaged practice: The case of archaeology in Africa. In *Embedding ethics,* eds. L. Meskell and P. Pels, 169–96. Oxford: Berg.

Hall, S. 1992. The west and the rest: Discourse and power. In *Formations of modernity,* eds. S. Hall and B. Gielben, 276–320. Cambridge: Polity Press and Open University.

Hallam, E., and B. V. Street. 2000. Introduction. In *Cultural encounters: Representing "otherness,"* eds. E. Hallam and B. V. Street, 1–10. London: Routledge.

Hamilakis, Y. 1999. La trahison des archeologues? Archaeological practice as intellectual activity in postmodernity. *Journal of Mediterranean Archaeology* 12(1): 60–79.

———. 2004. Archaeology and the politics of pedagogy. *World Archaeology* 36(2): 287–309.

Hammersley, M., and P. Atkinson. 1983. *Ethnography: Principles in practice.* London: Tavistock.

Hampton, E., and S. Henderson. 2000. Discussion paper on Indigenous knowledge and intellectual property: Scoping the definitions and issues (executive summary). In *Protecting knowledge: Traditional resource rights in the new millennium,* i–vi. Vancouver, B.C., Canada.

Han, C. G., and G. E. Son. 2000. Cheongwon sorori guseokgi yujeok (B jigu)-ui jicheung-gwa chulto yumul (The layers and artifacts of the Sorori Paleolithic site [Area B] in Cheongwon). *Silhak Sasang Yeongu* 14: 635–53.

Han, Y. H. 1996. The origin of Korean ethnicity. In *Hanguk minjok-ui giwon-gwa hyeongseong (The origin of Korean ethnicity and its formation),* 73–117. Seoul: Sohwa.

Handsman, R. 1989. Algonkian wigwams: An invisible presence, political spaces. *Artifacts* 17(4): 19–21.

———. 1991. What happened to the heritage of the Weantinock people? *Artifacts* 19(1): 3–9.

Handsman, R., and T. L. Richmond. 1995. Confronting colonialism: The Mahican and Schaghticoke peoples and us. In *Making alternate histories: The practice of archaeology and history in non-Western settings,* eds. P. R. Schmidt and T. C. Patterson, 87–117. Santa Fe, NM: School of American Research Press.

Hanks, C. C. 1997. Ancient knowledge of ancient sites: Tracing Dene identity from the Late Pleistocene and Holocene. In *At a crossroads: Archaeology and First Peoples in Canada,* eds. G. P. Nicholas and T. D. Andrews, 178–89. Burnaby, B.C.: Archaeology Press.

Hanna, M. 1997. We can go a long way together, hand-in-hand. In *At crossroads: Archaeology and First Peoples in Canada,* eds. G. P. Nicholas and T. D. Andrews, 69–84. Burnaby, B.C.: Archaeology Press, Simon Fraser University.

Haraway, D. 1991. *Simians, cyborgs, and women: The reinvention of nature.* London: Free Association Press.

Harding, S. 2003. A world of sciences. In *Science and other cultures: Issues in philosophies of science and technology,* eds. R. Figueroa and S. Harding, 49–69. New York: Routledge.

Hardt, M. and A. Negri. 2000. *Empire.* Cambridge, MA: Harvard University Press.

Hare, G., and S. Greer. 1994. *Desdele mene: The archaeology of Annie Lake.* Whitehorse: Yukon Heritage Branch.

Harmsworth, G. 1995. *Maori values for land-use planning: Discussion document.* Palmerston North: Manaaki Landcare Research New Zealand.

Harris, H. 2002. Remembering 12,000 years of history: Oral history, Indigenous knowledge and ways of knowing in northwestern North America. Unpublished Ph.D. thesis, University of Alberta, Department of Anthropology, Edmonton.

———. 2005. Indigenous worldviews and ways of knowing as theoretical and methodological foundations behind archaeological theory and method. In *Indigenous archaeologies: Decolonizing theory and practice,* eds. C. Smith and H. M. Wobst, 33–41. London: Routledge.

Harris, R. 2002. *Making Native space: Colonialism, resistance, and reserves in British Columbia.* Vancouver: University of British Columbia Press.

Hartley, S. H. 1997. Is shared leadership an oxymoron? *CRM: Cultural Resource Management* 20(4): 6–8.

Harvey, D. 2000. Cosmopolitanism and the banality of geographical evils. *Public Culture* 12: 529–64.

Hasenstab, R. 1989. Workshop on field sampling methods and modeling, held at the CNEA annual meeting, April 9, 1988, Sturbridge, Massachusetts. *Newsletter of the Conference on New England Archaeology* 8(1): 3–6.

Hassan, F. 1998. Memorabilia: Archaeological materiality and national identity in Egypt. In *Archaeology under fire: Nationalism, politics, and heritage in the eastern Mediterranean and Middle East,* ed. L. Meskell, 200–16. London: Routledge.

Heaton, T., and F. Grady. 1993. Fossil grizzly bears (*Ursus arctos*) from Prince of Wales Island, Alaska, offer new insights into animal dispersal, interspecific competition, and age of deglaciation. *Current Research in the Pleistocene* 10: 98–100.

Heaton, T., S. Talbot, and G. Shields. 1996. An Ice Age refugium for large mammals in the Alexander Archipelago, Southeast Alaska. *Quaternary Research* 46: 186–92.

Hein, G. 1998. *Learning in the museum.* London: Routledge.

Helgerson, R. 1992. *Forms of nationhood: The Elizabethan writing of England.* Chicago: University of Chicago Press.

Hemming, S. J. 1993. Camp Coorong: Combining race relations and cultural education. *Social Alternatives* 12(1): 37–40.

———. 2002. The problem with Aboriginal heritage. Paper presented at Sharing the Space Conference hosted by Flinders University Australian Studies Program and Yunggorendi First Nations Centre in association with International Australian Studies Association, Flinders University, Adelaide.

Hemming, S., and T. Trevorrow. 2005. Kungun Ngarrindjeri Yunnan: Archaeology, colonialism and reclaiming the future. In *Indigenous archaeologies: Decolonizing theory and practice,* eds. C. Smith and H. M. Wobst, 243–61. London: Routledge.

Henriksen, G. 1993. *Hunters in the barrens: The Naskapi on the edge of the white man's world.* St. John's, Newfoundland: Institute of Social and Economic Research.

Hervik, P. 1998. The mysterious Maya of National Geographic. *Journal of Latin American Anthropology* 4(1): 166–97.

Herzfeld, M. 1992. Metapatterns: Archaeology and the uses of evidential scarcity. In *Representations in archaeology,* eds. J. C. Gardin and C. S. Peebles, 66–86. Bloomington: Indiana University Press.

Hetherington, R., V. Barrie, R. Reid, R. MacLeod, and R. Kung. 2001. The search for an hospitable home for early peoples in Queen Charlotte Islands between 9,750 and 14,000 C14 YBP. Paper presented at the Canadian Archaeological Association meeting, Banff, Alberta.

Hidalgo, J., and N. Castro. 1999. Rebelión y Carnaval en Ingaguasi (San Pedro de Atacama) 1775–1777. *Estudios Atacameños* 17: 61–90.

Hidalgo, L. J. 1978. Incidencias de los patrones de poblamiento en el Cálculo de la población del partido de Atacama desde 1752 a 1804: Las revisitas inéditas de 1787–1792 y 1804. *Estudios Atacameños* 6: 53–111.

———. 1982. Fases de la rebelión Indígena de 1781 en el corregimeiento de Atacama y Esquema de la inestabilidad política que la precede, 1749–1781. Anexo: Dos Documentos Inéditos Contemporáneos. *Chungará* 9: 192–246.

———. 1987. Tierras, exacciones fiscales y mercado en las scoiedades Andinas de Arica, Tarapacá y Atacama, 1750–1790. In *La participación social, Siglos IVI a XX,* eds. O. Harris, B. Larson, and E. Tandeter, 193–231. La Paz: CERES/SSRC.

Higham, C., and T. Lu. 1998. The origins and dispersal of rice cultivation. *Antiquity* 72: 867–77.

Higounet, C. 1986. *Die deutsche Ostsiedlung im Mittelalter.* Translated from French. Berlin: Siedler Verlag.

Hitchcock, R. K. 2003. Keynote address. Paper presented at the Khoe and San Conference, University of Botswana, Gaborone, Botswana, September 9–12.

———. 2004a. The roles of applied and development anthropology and archaeology among the San of Botswana. *Botswana Notes and Records* 36: 125–35.

———. 2004b. Human rights and anthropological activism among the San. In *Human rights: The scholar as activist,* eds. C. Nagengast and C. G. Velez-Ibanes, 169–91. Norman: Society for Applied Anthropology.

Hodder, I. 1999. The *archaeological process: An introduction.* Oxford: Blackwell.

———. 2004. Archaeology beyond dialogue. Salt Lake City: University of Utah Press.

Hodgson, D. L. 2002. Introduction: Comparative perspectives on the Indigenous rights movement in Africa and the Americas. *American Anthropologist* 104(4): 1037–49.

Hoffman, E. 1989. *Lost in translation.* London: Vintage.

Hollowell, J., and G. Nicholas. 2008. Intellectual property issues in archaeological publication: Some questions to consider. *Archaeologies: Journal of the World Archaeological Congress* 4(2): 208–17.

Holtorf, C., and Q. Drew. 2009. *Archaeology is a brand! The meaning of archaeology in contemporary popular culture.* Oxford: Archaeopress.

Holtorf, C., and A. Piccini, eds. 2009. *Contemporary archaeologies.* Frankfurt: Lang Verlag.

Hooper-Greenhill, E. 2000. *Museums and the interpretation of visual culture.* London: Routledge.

Hopkins, S. 1753. *Historical memoirs, relating to the Housatunnuck Indians.* Boston: S. Kneeland.

Howells, C. 1999. *Derrida: Deconstruction from phenomenology to ethics.* Malden, MA: Blackwell Publishers.

Huggins, J. 2003. Always was always will be. In *Blacklines: Contemporary critical writing by Indigenous Australians,* ed. M. Grossman, 60–65. Carlton, Vic.: Melbourne University Press.

ICOMOS New Zealand. 1995. *ICOMOS New Zealand charter for the conservation of places of cultural heritage value.* Auckland: ICOMOS New Zealand.

Im, H. 1996. New discoveries in the Korean Neolithic archaeology. In *Interdisciplinary perspectives on the origins of the Japanese,* ed. K. Omoto, 155–68. Tokyo: International Research Center for Japanese Studies.

Ingold, T. 1993. The temporality of landscape. *World Archaeology* 35: 152–74.

———. 2000. *The perception of the environment: Essays in livelihood, dwelling and skill.* London: Routledge.

Irele, A. 1991. The African scholar: Is Black Africa entering the Dark Ages of scholarship? *Transition* 51: 56–69.

IUCN World Heritage Evaluation Report. 2005.World Heritage Nomination—IUCN Technical Evaluation Shiretoko (Japan) ID no. 1193.

Jackson, G., and C. Smith. 2005. Living and learning on Aboriginal lands: Decolonising archaeology in practice. In *Indigenous archaeologies: Decolonizing theory and practice,* eds. C. Smith and H. M. Wobst, 326–49. London: Routledge.

Jacobs, M. D. 1999. *Engendered encounters: Feminism and Pueblo cultures.* Lincoln: University of Nebraska Press.

Jaggar, A. 1983. *Feminist politics and human mature.* Sussex: Harvester Press.

Janke, T. 1998. *Our culture. Our future. Report on Australian indigenous cultural and intellectual property rights.* Surrey Hills, N.S.W.: Australian Institute of Aboriginal and Torres Strait Islander Commission/Michael Frankel.

———. 1999. *Our culture, our future: Proposals for the recognition of Indigenous cultural and intellectual property.* Canberra: Australian Institute of Aboriginal Studies and the Aboriginal and Torres Strait Islander Commission.

———. 2003. *Minding culture: Case studies on intellectual property and traditional cultural expressions.* Washington, D.C.: World Intellectual Property Organization.

Jay, M. 2005. *Songs of experience: Modern American and European variations on a universal theme.* Berkeley and Los Angeles: University of California Press.

Jenkins, R. 1994. Rethinking ethnicity: Identity, categorization and power. In *Ethnic and racial studies* 17(2): 197–223.

Jeong, S. I. 2005. Mummyeong gyoryu gihaeng (47) (Traveler's journal of cultural interactions [47]). *Hankyoreh Sinmun* May 10:16.

Johnson, M. 1999. *Archaeological theory: An introduction.* Oxford: Blackwell Publishers.

Johnson, V. 1996. *Copyrites: Aboriginal art in the age of reproductive technologies.* Sydney: National Indigenous Arts Advocacy Association and Macquarie University.

Jones, E. 1854. *Stockbridge, past and present, or records of an old mission station.* Springfield, MA: Samuel Bowles and Company.

Jones, S. 1997. *The archaeology of ethnicity: Constructing identities in the past and present.* New York: Routledge.

Julien, D. M., T. Bernard, and L. M. Rosenmeier, with review by the Mi'kmawey Debert Elders' Advisory Council. 2008. Paleo is not our word: Protecting and growing a Mi'kmaw place. In *Archaeologies of placemaking: Monuments, memories, and engagement in Native North America,* ed. P. E. Rubertone, 35–57. Walnut Creek, CA: Left Coast Press.

Kahn, M. 1995. Heterotopic dissonance in the museum representations of Pacific Island cultures. *American Anthropologist* 97(2): 324–38.

Kato, H. 2009. Whose archaeology? Decolonizing archaeological perspective in Hokkaido Island. *Journal of the Graduate School of Letters, Hokkaido University* 4: 47–55.

Kawharu, I. H. 1989. *Waitangi: Maori and Pakeha perspectives of the Treaty of Waitangi.* Auckland: Oxford University Press.

Kawharu, M. 2000. Kaitiakitanga: A Maori anthropological perspective of the Maori socio-environmental ethic of resource management. *Journal of the Polynesian Society* 110: 349–70.

Kehoe, A. 1998. *The land of prehistory.* New York: Routledge.

Kelley, K. B., and H. Francis. 1994. *Navajo sacred places.* Bloomington: Indiana University Press.

Kerber, J. E., ed. 2006. *Cross-cultural collaboration: Native peoples and archaeology in the northeastern United States.* Lincoln: University of Nebraska Press.

Kim, H. 2005. "Cheongwon saengmyeong ssal" Internet shopping mall gaejang ("Cheongwon organic rice" Internet shopping mall open). *Daejon llbo* April 26: 13.

Kim, J. H. 2004. Segye choego byeopssi chulto-doen cheongwon sorari jumin choego ssal saengsan-wihae yeonguhoe baljok (People at Sorori, where the oldest rice was found, launched a research society), http://news.naver.comfnewslread.php?mode=LSD&office_id=OO3&article_id=OOOOOS844I&section_id=I02&menu_id=I02.

Kim, M. 2008. Multivocality, multifaceted voices and Korean archaeology. In *Evaluating multiple narratives: Beyond nationalist, colonialist, and imperialist archaeologies,* eds. J. Habu, C. Fawett, and J. M. Matsunaga, 118–37. New York: Springer.

Kim, S. H. 2004. Ssal-eun minjok-ui hon (Rice is ethnic spirit). *Segye llbo* June 7: 27.

Kim, W. Y. 1986. *Hanguk gogohak gaeseol (Introduction to Korean archaeology).* Seoul: Iljisa.

Kim, Y. E. 2004. Sorori byeopssi bakmulgwan 6wol-ui gwonjang site (The Sorori rice museum: The recommended site for June). *Kyunghyang Sinmun* June 24.

King, T. S. 1998. *Cultural resource laws and practice, an introductory guide.* Walnut Creek, CA: AltaMira Press.

Kintigh, K. W. 1996. SAA principles of archaeological ethics. *SAA Bulletin* 14(3): 5, 17.

Kirkman, J. 1963. *Gedi: The palace.* The Hague: Mouton.

Ki-Zerbo, J., ed. 1981. *General history of Africa I: Methodology and African prehistory.* Berkeley and Los Angeles: University of California Press.

Klesert, A. L. 1990. Contracting federal historic preservation functions under the Indian Self-Determination Act. In *Preservation on the reservation: Native Americans, Native American lands, and archaeology,* eds. Anthony L. Klesert and A. S. Downer, 113–21. Window Rock, AZ: Navajo Nation Archaeology Department and the Navajo Nation Historic Preservation Department.

Klesert, A. L., and S. Powell. 1993. A perspective on ethics and the reburial controversy. *American Antiquity* 58: 348–54.

Kluger, J., and D. Cray. 2006. Who should own the bones. *Time* 167(11): 50–51.

Kohl, P. 1995. The material culture of the modern era in the ancient Orient: Suggestions for future work. In *Domination and resistance,* One World Archaeology Series, eds. D. Miller, M. Rowlands, and C. Tilley, 240–45. London: Routledge.

Kowal, E., and Y. Paradies. 2005. Ambivalent helpers and unhealthy choices: Public health practitioners' narratives of Indigenous ill-health. *Social Science & Medicine* 60(6): 1347–57.

Krebs, C. F. 2003. *Liberating culture: Cross-cultural perspectives on museum curation and heritage preservation.* London: Routledge.

Kritsch, I. D., and A. M. Andre. 1997. Gwich'in traditional knowledge and heritage studies in the Gwich'in settlement area. In *At a crossroads: Archaeologists and First Peoples in Canada,* eds. G. P. Nicholas and T. D. Andrews, 125–44. Burnaby, B.C.: Archaeology Press.

Krupat, A. 1992. *Ethnocriticism: Ethnography, history, literature.* Berkeley and Los Angeles: University of California Press.

Kuper, A. 1988. *The invention of primitive society.* London: Routledge.

———. 2003. The return of the native. *Current Anthropology* 44(3): 389–402.

Kus, S. 2002. An archaeologist's imagination: Sympathetic magic or studied audacity? Between materiality and interpretation: Archaeological confessions. Paper presented at the Annual Meeting of the Society for American Archaeology, Denver, Colorado.

Kwak, B. C. 2005. Sorori byeopssi (Sorori rice). *Hankyoreh Sinmun* December 9: 26.

Laird, S. A., M. N. Alexiandes, K. P. Bannister, and D. A. Posey. 2002. Publication of biodiversity research results and the flow of knowledge. In *Biodiversity and traditional knowledge: Equitable partnerships in practice,* ed. S. A. Laird, 77–101. London: Earthscan.

Lâm, M. C. 1994. Feeling foreign in feminism. *SIGNS: Journal of Women in Culture and Society* 19(4): 865–93.

Lambert, R., and G. Henry. 2000. *Taranaki: An illustrated history.* Auckland: Reed.

Land, C., and E. Vincent. 2005. Thinking for ourselves. *New Matilda* 29 June.

Lane, K., and A. Herrera. 2005. Archaeology, landscapes and dreams: Science, sacred offerings, and the practice of archaeology. *Archaeological Review from Cambridge* 20(1): 111–29.

Langford, R. 1983. Our heritage—Your playground. *Australian Archaeology* 16: 1–6.

Langton, M. 1981. Urbanizing Aborigines: The social scientists' great deception. *Social Alternatives* 2(2): 16–22.

———. 1993. *Well I heard it on the radio and I saw it on the television.* Sydney: Australian Film Commission.

Latour, B. 1999. *Pandora's hope: Essays on the reality of science studies.* Cambridge, MA: Harvard University Press.

Lattas, A. 2001. Redneck thought: Racism, guilt and Aborigines. *UTS Review* 7(1): 106–24.

Lavin, L. 1988. Coastal adaptations in southern New England and southern New York. *Archaeology of Eastern North America* 16: 101–20.

Lawry, S., and A. Thoma. 1978. *A spatial development plan for remote settlements in northern Kgalagadi.* Tsabong and Gaborone, Botswana: Kgalagadi District Council and Ministry of Local Government and Lands.

Layton, R., ed. 1989. *Conflict in the archaeology of living traditions.* London: Unwin.

Layton, R., and P. J. Ucko. 1999. Introduction: Gazing on the landscape and encountering the environment. In *The archaeology and anthropology of landscape: Shaping your landscape,* eds. P. J. Ucko and R. Layton, 1–20. London: Routledge.

Lee, K. P. 2000. Segye choego byeopssi guknae balgul hwakin (The world's oldest rice excavated in Korea). *Donga Ilbo* August 2.

Lee, R. B., and M. Biesele. 2002. Local cultures and global systems: The Ju/'hoansi-!Kung and their ethnographers fifty years on. In *Chronicling cultures: Long-term field research in anthropology,* eds. R. V. Kemper and A. Peterson Royce, 160–90. Walnut Creek, CA: AltaMira Press.

Lee, R. B., M. Biesele, and R. K. Hitchcock. 1996. Three decades of ethnographic research among the Ju/'hoansi of northwestern Botswana: 1963–1996. *Botswana Notes and Records* 28: 107–20.

Lee, Y. J., and I. Y. Woo. 2000. *Cheongwon sorori guseokgi yujeok (The Sorori Paleolithic Site in Cheongwon County).* Cheongju: Chungbuk National University Museum and Korea Land Corporation.

———. 2002. Sorori byeopssi-ui balgul-gwa gwaje (The excavation of the Paleolithic Sorori rice and its important problems). In *First International Conference of Cheongwon County—Prehistoric Agriculture in Asia and Sorori Rice,* 17–24. Cheongju: Chungbuk National University Museum and Korea Land Corporation.

Lehman, G. 2004. Authentic and essential: A review of Anita M. Heiss' "DhuuluuYala (to talk straight): Publishing Indigenous literature." *Australian Humanities Review* 33.

Lemonick, M. D., and D. Cray. 1996. Bones of contention. *Time* 148(18): 81.

Lemonick, M. D., A. Dorfman, and D. Cray. 2006. Who were the first Americans? *Time* 167(11): 44–55.

Lertrit, S. 1997. Who owns the past? A perspective from Chiang Saen, Thailand. *Conservation and Management of Archaeological Sites* 2(2): 81–92.

Levy, J. 2006. Prehistory, identity and archaeological representation in Nordic Museums. *American Anthropologist* 108(1): 135–47.

Lewis, D., and D. Bird Rose. 1985. Some ethical issues in archaeology: A methodology of consultation in northern Australia. *Australian Aboriginal Studies* 1: 37–44.

Lewis, R. 2006. Mi'kmaq rights and title claim: A review of pre-contact archaeological factors. *Mi'kmaq Maliseet Nation News* June 2006: 16–17.

Liddle, K. 2002. Alexandrina Council and Ngarrindjeri people sign historic agreement. *Aboriginal Way* 16: 1.

Lightfoot, K., O. Parrish, R. Jewett, E. Parkman, and D. Murley. 2001. The Metini Village project: Collaborative research in the Fort Ross State Historic Park. *Society for California Newsletter* 35(2): 23–26.

Lilley, I. 2006. Archaeology, diaspora and decolonization. *Journal of Social Archaeology* 6(1): 28–47.

Lippert, D. 2006. Building a bridge to cross a thousand years. *American Indian Quarterly* 30(3&4): 431–40.

Little Bear, L. 2000. Jagged worldviews colliding. In *Reclaiming Indigenous voice and vision,* ed. M. Battiste, 77–85. Vancouver: UBC Press.

Livingstone, D. 1992. *The geographical tradition.* Oxford: Blackwell.

Longino, H. 1994. In search of feminist epistemology. *The Monist* 77(4): 472–85.

Lorde, A. 1984. *Sister outsider: Essays and speeches.* Trumansburg, NY: Crossing Press.

Loring, S. 1997. On the trail to the Caribou House: Some reflections on Innu caribou hunters in northern Ntessinan (Labrador). In *Caribou and reindeer hunters of the Northern Hemisphere,* eds. L. J. Jackson and P. T. Thacker, 185–220. Avebury: Aldershot.

———. 2001. Repatriation and community anthropology: The Smithsonian Institution's Arctic Studies Center. In *The future of the past: Archaeologists, Native Americans, and repatriation,* ed. T. Bray, 185–200. New York: Garland Press.

Loring, S., and D. Ashini. 2000. Past and future pathways: Innu cultural heritage in the twenty-first century. In *Indigenous cultures in an interconnected world,* eds. C. Smith and G. K. Ward, 167–89. Sydney: Allen and Unwin.

Lovgren, S. 2004. Masks and other finds suggest early Maya flourished. *National Geographic News Online.* Electronic document, May 2, 2004, http://news.nationalgeographic.com/news/2004/05/0504_040505_mayamasks.html (accessed February 22, 2006).

Lowenthal, D. 1985. *The past is a foreign country.* Cambridge: Cambridge University Press.

Luckert, K. W. 1977. *Navajo Mountain and Rainbow Bridge religion.* Flagstaff: Museum of Northern Arizona Press.

———. 1981. *The Navajo hunter traditions.* Tucson: University of Arizona Press.

Lundholm Associates Architects. 2007. Mi'kmawey Debert Cultural Centre plan for visitor experiences. Manuscript on file at the Confederate of Mainland Mi'kmaq, Truro, Nova Scotia.

Macintosh, N. G. W. 1977. Beswick Creek Cave two decades later: A reappraisal. In *Form in Indigenous art,* ed. P. J. Ucko, 191–97. Canberra: Australian Institute of Aboriginal Studies.

Macleod, F. 2005. Give us back our treasures. *Mail & Guardian* 8 July 2005.

Maffi, L. 2000. Language preservation vs. language maintenance and revitalization: Assessing concepts, approaches, and implications for the language sciences. *International Journal of the Sociology of Language* 142: 175–90.

Mamani Condori, C. 1989. History and prehistory in Bolivia: What about the Indians? In *Conflict in the archaeology of living traditions,* ed. R. Layton, 46–59. London: Unwin Hyman.

———.1996. History and prehistory in Bolivia: What about the Indians? In *Contemporary archaeology in theory: A reader,* eds. R. W. Preucel and I. Hodder. Oxford: Blackwell Publishers.

Mannik, H., ed. 1993. Oral histories, Baker Lake, Northwest Territories, 1992–1993. Report on File, Inuit Heritage Centre, Baker Lake, Nunavut Territory.

———, ed. 1998. *Inuit Nunamiut: Inland Inuit.* Baker Lake, Nunavut Territory: Inuit Heritage Centre.

Markey, N. M. 2001. "Gathering dust": An analysis of traditional use studies conducted within Aboriginal communities in British Columbia. Master's thesis, Department of Sociology and Anthropology, Simon Fraser University, Burnaby, B.C.

Marquardt, W. 1994. The role of archaeology in raising environmental consciousness. In *Historical ecology: Cultural knowledge and changing landscapes,* ed. C. Crumley, 203–21. Santa Fe, NM: School of American Research Press.

Marshall, J., and C. Ritchie. 1984. Where are the Ju/Wasi of Nyae Nyae: Changes in Bushman society 1958–1981. Cape Town: Centre for African Studies. University of Cape Town.

Marshall, L. 1976. *The !Kung of Nyae Nyae.* Cambridge, MA: Harvard University Press.

———. 1999. *Nyae Nyae !Kung beliefs and rites.* Cambridge: Peabody Museum Monographs.

Martin, R. 1997. How traditional Navajos view historic preservation: A question of interpretation. In *Native Americans and archaeologists: Stepping stones to common ground,* eds. N. Swindler, K. E. Dongoske, R. Anyon, and A. S. Downer, 128–34. Walnut Creek, CA: AltaMira Press.

Martinez, D. R. 2006. Overcoming hindrances to our enduring responsibility to the ancestors: Protecting traditional cultural places. *American Indian Quarterly* 30(3&4): 486–505.

Martínez, G. 1989. *Espacio y pensamiento: I. Andes meridionales*. La Paz: Hisbol.

Martínez Cobo, J. R. 1987. *Study of the problem of discrimination against Indigenous populations*. Vol. 5. U.N. doc. E/CN.4/Sub.2/1986/7/Add.4.

Maschner, H. D. G., and C. Chippindale, eds. 2005. *Handbook of archaeological methods*. Lanham, MD: AltaMira Press.

Massey, D. 1994. *Space, place, and gender*. Minneapolis: University of Minnesota Press.

Matthews, W. 1994 [1897]. *Navaho legends*. Salt Lake City: University of Utah Press.

May, S. K., D. Gumurdul, J. Manakgu, G. Maralngurra, and W. Nawirridj. 2005. You write it down and bring it back: Revisiting the 1948 removal of human remains from Kungalanya (Oenpelli), Australia. In *Indigenous archaeologies: Decolonizing theory and practice,* eds. C. Smith and H. M. Wobst, 110–29. London: Routledge.

Maybury-Lewis, D. 1997. *Indigenous peoples, ethnic groups, and the state*. Boston: Allyn & Bacon.

McBride, K. A. 1995. CRM and Native Americans, an example from Mashantucket Pequot Reservation. *CRM: Cultural Resource Management* 18(3): 15–17.

McBride, K. A., and N. F. Bellantoni. 1982. The utility of ethnohistoric models for understanding Late Woodland—Contact culture change in southern New England. *Bulletin of the Archaeological Society of Connecticut* 45: 51–64.

McBryde, I. 1986. *Who owns the past?* Melbourne: Oxford University Press.

———. 1987. Goods from another country. In *Australians to 1788*, eds. D. J. Mulvaney and J. P. White, 206–73. Sydney: Fairfax, Syme, and Weldon.

McDowell, L., and J. P. Sharp, eds. 1997. *Space, gender, knowledge: Feminist readings*. London: J. Wiley.

McGuire, R. H. 1994. Decolonializing archaeology. Paper presented at the Annual Meeting of the Society of American Archaeology, Anaheim, California.

———. 2002. The meaning and limits of the Southwest/Northwest. In *Boundaries and territories: Prehistory of the U.S. Southwest and Northern Mexico,* ed. M. E. Villalpando, 173–83. Tempe: Arizona State University.

———. 2008a. *Archaeology as political action*. Berkeley and Los Angeles: University of California Press.

———. 2008b. Chapter 4: México. In *Archaeology as political action,* 140–87. Berkeley and Los Angeles: University of California Press.

McKinlay, J. 1973. *Archaeology and legislation*. Monograph 5. Wellington: New Zealand Archaeological Association.

———. 1976. The New Zealand historic places trust and the new legislation. *New Zealand Archaeological Association Newsletter* 19: 38–65.

McLoughlin, M. 1999. *Museums and representation of Native Canadians: Negotiating the borders of culture*. New York: Garland.

Mead, S. M., ed. 1984. *Te Maori: Maori art from New Zealand collections*. Auckland: Heinemann.

Meehan, B. 1995. Aboriginal views of the management of rock art sites in Australia. In *Perceiving rock art: Social and political perspectives,* eds. K. Helskog and B. Olsen, 295–315. Oslo: Institute for Sammenlignade Kulturforskning.

Meighan, C. W. 1992. Some scholars' views on reburial. *American Antiquity* 57: 704–10.

Mellor, D. 2003. Contemporary racism in Australia: The experiences of Aborigines. *Personality and Social Psychology Bulletin* 29(4): 474–86.

Memmi, A. 1967. *The colonizer and the colonized.* Boston: Beacon Press.

Merrell, J. H. 1989. Some thoughts on colonial historians and American Indians. *William and Mary Quarterly* 46(1): 94–119.

Merrill, W. L., E. J. Ladd, and T. J. Ferguson. 1992. The return of the ahayu:da: Lessons for repatriation from Zuni Pueblo and the Smithsonian Institution. *Current Anthropology* 34: 523–67.

Merriman, N. 2004. Introduction: Diversity and dissonance in public archaeology. In *Public archaeology,* ed. N. Merriman, 1–17. London: Routledge.

Meskell, L. M., ed. 1998a. *Archaeology under fire: Nationalism, politics and heritage in the Eastern Mediterranean and Middle East.* London: Routledge.

———. 1998b. Introduction: Archaeology matters. In *Archaeology under fire: Nationalism, politics, and heritage in the Eastern Mediterranean and Middle East,* ed. L. Meskell, 1–12. London and New York: Routledge.

———. 2001a. Archaeologies of identity. In *Archaeological theory today,* ed. I. Hodder, 187–213. Oxford and Malden: Polity Press and Blackwell.

———. 2001b. The practice and politics of archaeology in Egypt. In *Ethics and anthropology: Facing future issues in human biology, globalism and cultural property,* eds. A. M. Cantwell, E. Friedlander and M. L. Tram, 149–69. New York: Annals of the New York Academy of Sciences.

———. 2005. Archaeological ethnography: Conversations around Kruger National Park. *Archaeologies* 1(1): 81–100.

Mihesuah, D. A. 1998. Preface. In *Natives and academics: Researching and writing about American Indians,* ed. D. A. Mihesuah, ix–xi. Lincoln: University of Nebraska Press.

———. 1999. *American Indians: Stereotypes and realities.* Atlanta: Clarity Press.

———. 2003. *Indigenous American women: Decolonization, empowerment, activism.* Lincoln: University of Nebraska Press.

Miller, D., ed. 2005. *Materiality.* Durham, NC: Duke University Press.

Million, T. 2002. Using circular paradigms within an archaeological framework: Receiving gifts from White Buffalo Calf Woman. Unpublished Master's thesis, University of Alberta, Canada.

———. 2005. Developing an Aboriginal archaeology: Receiving gifts from White Buffalo Calf Woman. In *Indigenous archaeologies: Decolonizing theory and practice,* eds. C. Smith and H. M. Wobst, 44–55. London: Routledge.

Mills, B. J., and T. J. Ferguson. 1998. Preservation and research of sacred sites by the Zuni Indian Tribe of New Mexico. *Human Organization* 57: 30–42.

Milton, J. H. V. 2001. *The rise of the public in enlightenment Europe.* Cambridge: Cambridge University Press.

Minh-ha, T. T. 1989. *Woman, Native, other.* Bloomington: Indiana University Press.

Mitchell, T. 2000. Making the nation: The politics of heritage in Egypt. In *Consuming tradition, manufacturing heritage: Global norms and urban forms in the age of tourism,* ed. N. A. Sayyad. London: Routledge.

Mohanty, C. T. 1987. Feminist encounters: Locating the politics of experience. *Feminist Review* 30: 61–88.

Montejo, V. D. 1999. Becoming Maya? Appropriation of the White Shaman. Electronic document, http://nativeamericas.aip.cornell.edu/spr99pe.html (accessed February 22, 2006).

Moore, H. 1986. *Space, text, and gender: An anthropological study of the Marakwet of Kenya.* Cambridge: Cambridge University Press.

———. 2001. Afterword: A "masterclass" in subjectivity. In *Feminist (re)visions of the subject: Landscapes, ethnoscapes, and theoryscapes,* eds. G. Currie and C. Rothenberg, 261–66. Lanham, MD: Lexington Books.

Moore, K. 1997. *Museums and popular culture.* London: Cassell.

Moore, T. 2005. Problematising identity: Governance, politics and the "making of the Aborigines". *Journal of Australian Studies* 80: 177–88.

Morel, J. P. 1984. Greek colonization in Italy and in the West (problems of evidence and interpretation). In *Crossroads of the Mediterranean,* eds. T. Hackens, and R. Holloway, 123–61. Louvain-la-Neuve and Providence: Institut Supérieur d'Archéologie et d'Histoire de l'Art, Collège Erasme and Brown University.

Moreton-Robinson, A. 2003. I still call Australia home: Indigenous belonging and place in a white postcolonizing society. In *Uprootings/regroundings: Questions of home and migration,* eds. S. Ahmed, C. A. Cantaneda, A. M. Fortier, and M. Sheller, 23–40. New York: Oxford University Press.

Moreton-Robinson, E. 2000. *Talkin' up to the white woman: Aboriginal women and feminism.* St. Lucia: University of Queensland Press.

Morgan, H., ed. 1999. *Political ideology in Ireland, 1541–1641.* Dublin: Four Courts Press.

Morrissey, P. 2003. Moving, remembering, singing our place. In *Blacklines: Contemporary critical writing by Indigenous Australians,* ed. M. Grossman, 189–93. Carlton, Vic.: Melbourne University Press.

Morse, E. 1983 [1877]. *Omori kaizuka (Omori shell midden).* Tokyo: Iwanami Shoten.

Moser, S. 1996. Science, stratigraphy, and the deep sequence: Excavations vs. regional survey and the question of gendered practice in archaeology. *Antiquity* 70: 813–23.

———. 1998. *Ancestral images: The iconography of human origins.* Ithaca, NY: Cornell University Press.

———. 2001. The Quseir Heritage Centre: An exhibition plan. Report for Quseir Heritage Preservation Society.

Moser, S., D. Glazier, J. E. Phillips, L. Nasser el Nemr, M. Saleh Mousa, R. Nasr Aiesh, S. Richardson, A. Conner, and M. Seymour. 2002. Transforming archaeology through practice: The community archaeology project at Quseir, Egypt. *World Archaeology* 34(2): 220–48.

Mountford, C. 1976. *Nomads of the Western Desert*. Adelaide: Rigby.

Mudimbe, V. Y. 1988. *The invention of Africa. Gnosis, philosophy, and the order of knowledge*. Bloomington: Indiana University Press.

Muecke, S. 1992. Lonely representations: Aboriginality and cultural studies. *Journal of Australian Studies* 35: 32–44.

Mulk, I. 1997. *Sámi cultural heritage in the Laponian world heritage area*. Jokkmokk, Sweden: Ájtte, Swedish Mountain and S'ami Museum.

Mulk, I., and T. Bayliss-Smith. 1999. The representation of Sámi cultural identity in the cultural landscapes of Northern Sweden: The use and misuse of archaeological knowledge. In *The archaeology and anthropology of landscape: Shaping your landscape*, eds. P. J. Ucko and R. Layton, 358–96. London: Routledge.

Mulvaney, D. J. 1991. Past regained, future lost: The Kow Swamp pleistocene burials. *Antiquity* 65(246): 12–21.

Munn, N. 1992. The cultural anthropology of time: A critical essay. *Annual Review of Anthropology* 21: 93–123.

Murphy, A. 1999. *But the Irish Sea betwixt us: Ireland, colonialism, and Renaissance literature*. Lexington: University Press of Kentucky.

Murr, A. 1999. Who got here first? *Newsweek* 134(20): 71.

———. 2005. A 9,000-year old secret. *Newsweek* 146(4): 52.

Myers, F. R. 1986. *Pintupi country, Pintupi self: Sentiment, place, and politics among Western Desert Aborigines*. Washington, D.C.: Smithsonian Institution Press.

NAGPRA. 1990. Native American Graves Protection and Repatriation Act. Public Law 101-601—NOV. 16, 1990. www.nps.gov/history/nagpra/MANDATES/25USC3001etseq.htm (accessed February 10, 2010).

Nakata, M. 2003. Better. In *Blacklines: Contemporary critical writing by Indigenous Australians*, ed. M. Grossman, 132–44. Carlton, Vic.: Melbourne University Press.

Nandy, A. 2001. *Time warps: The insistent politics of silent and evasive pasts*. Delhi: Permanent Black.

Naranjo, T. 1995. Thoughts on migration by Santa Clara Pueblo. *Journal of Anthropological Research* 14: 247–50.

———. 2000. Archaeology, education, and the Secwapemc. In *Working together: Native Americans and archaeologists*, eds. K. E. Dongoske, M. Aldenderfer, and K. Doehner, 155–63. Washington, D.C.: Society for American Archaeology.

National Park Service (NPS). 1906. Antiquities Act of 1906. 16 U.S.C. 431-433. www.cr.nps.gov/local-law/anti1906.htm (accessed March 30, 2007).

Native Title Act. 1993. Native Title Act 1993 (Cth). January 1, 1994. Australia Commonwealth Consolidated Acts. www.austlii.edu.au/au/legis/cth/consol_act/nta1993147 (accessed March 30, 2010).

Nelson, S. M. 1995. The politics of ethnicity in prehistoric Korea. In *Nationalism, politics, and the practice of archaeology,* eds. P. L. Kohl and C. P. Fawcett, 218–31. Cambridge: Cambridge University Press.

NHPA. 1966. National Historic Preservation Act. October 15, 1966. United States Public Law 89-665; 16 U.S.C. 470 et seq. www.achp.gov/nhpa.html (accessed March 31, 2010).

Nicholas, G. P. 1997. Education and empowerment: Archaeology with, for, and by the Shuswap Nation, British Columbia. In *At a crossroads: Archaeology and First Peoples in Canada,* eds. G. P. Nicholas and T. D. Andrews, 85–104. Burnaby, B.C.: Archaeology Press.

———. 2000. Archaeology, education and the Secwepemc. In *Forging respect: Archaeologists and Native Americans working together,* eds. K. E. Dongoske, M. Aldenderfer, and K. Doehner, 153–63. Washington, D.C.: Society for American Archaeology.

———. 2003. Understanding the present, honoring the past. In *Indigenous peoples and archaeology,* eds. T. Peck, E. Siegfried, and G. Oetelaar. Calgary: University of Calgary Archaeological Association.

———. 2004. Copyrighting the past? *Current Anthropology* 45(3): 327–50.

———. 2006. Decolonizing the archaeological landscape: The practice and politics of archaeology in British Columbia. *American Indian Quarterly* 30(3–4): 350–80.

———. 2008. Native peoples and archaeology (Indigenous Archaeology). In *The Encyclopedia of Archaeology*, ed. D. Pearsall, vol. 3, 1660–69. Oxford: Elsevier.

———, ed. 2010. *Being and becoming Indigenous archaeologists.* Walnut Creek, CA: Left Coast Press.

Nicholas, G. P., and T. D. Andrews, eds. 1997. *At a crossroads: Archaeology and First Peoples in Canada.* Burnaby, B.C.: Archaeology Press.

Nicholas, G. P., and K. P. Bannister. 2004. Copyrighting the past? Emerging intellectual property rights issues in archaeology. *Current Anthropology* 45(3): 327–50.

Nicholas, G. P., J. Jules, and C. Dan. 2008. Moving beyond Kennewick: Other Native American perspectives on bioarchaeological data and intellectual property rights. In *Kennewick Man: Perspectives on the Ancient One,* eds. H. Burke, C. Smith, D. Lippert, J. Watkins, and L. Zimmerman, 233–43. Walnut Creek, CA: Left Coast Press.

Niezen, R. 2003. *The origins of indigenism: Human rights and the politics of identity.* Berkeley and Los Angeles: University of California Press.

Nomura, G. 1994. Native leaders address the United Nations: Giichi Nomura, Executive Director, Ainu Association of Hokkaido (Northeast Asia). In *Voice of Indigenous peoples: Native people address the United Nations,* ed. A. Ewen, for the Native American Council of New York City, 68–71. Santa Fe, NM: Clear Light Publishers.

Norder, J. W. 2007. Iktomi in the land of the Maymaygwayshi: Understanding lived experience in the practice of archaeology among American Indians/First Nations. *Archaeologies* 3(3): 230–48.

Nur el-Din, H. 2000. Domestic architecture as a reflection of the inter-relationships between different groups. Paper presented at the Conference on the Transmission and Assimilation of Culture in the Near East, Council for British Research in the Levant, Jerusalem.

O'Bryan, A. 1956. The Dine: Origin myths of the Navaho Indians. *Bureau of American Ethnology Bulletin* 163.

O'Connor, M. M. 1995. *Lost cities of the ancient Southeast.* Gainesville: University Press of Florida.

O'Donoghue, L. 1994. Native leaders address the United Nations: Lois O'Donoghue, Chairperson, Aboriginal and Torres Strait Islander Commission (Pacific Islands). In *Voice of Indigenous peoples: Native people address the United Nations,* ed. A. Ewen, for the Native American Council of New York City, 72–76. Santa Fe, NM: Clear Light Publishers.

Okpoko, A. I. 1991. Review article: A history of African archaeology. *African Archaeological Review* 9: 111–18.

O'Neill, G. 1994. Cemetery reveals complex aboriginal society. *Science* 264: 1403.

O'Regan, H. 1999. If it's good enough for you it's good enough for me: The hypocrisy of assimilation. In *Indigeneity: Construction and re/presentation,* eds. J. Brown and P. Sant, 193–208. New York: Nova Science.

Ouzman, S. 2005. Another world: Archaeology and intellectual property. *The Digging Stick* 22(2): 16–17.

Owsley, D. W., and R. L. Jantz. 2001. Archaeological politics and public interest in Paleoamerican studies: Lessons from Gordon Creek Woman and Kennewick Man. *American Antiquity* 66(4): 565–75.

Oxenham, D., K. Collard, P. Dudgeon, D. Garvey, M. Kickett, and T. Kickett. 1999. *A dialogue in Indigenous identity: Warts 'n' all.* Perth: Curtin University of Technology, Centre for Aboriginal Studies.

Ôzdogan, M. 1998. Ideology and archaeology in Turkey. In *Archaeology under fire: Nationalism, politics, and heritage in the Eastern Mediterranean and Middle East,* ed. L. Meskell, 111–23. London: Routledge.

Pai, H. I. 1994. The politics of Korea's past: The legacy of Japanese colonial archaeology in the Korean peninsula. *East Asian History* 7: 25–48.

———. 1998. The colonial origins of Korea's collected past. In *Nationalism and the construction of Korean identity,* eds. H. I. Pai and T. R. Tangherlini, 13–32. Berkeley and Los Angeles: Institute of East Asian Studies, University of California.

———. 2000. *Constructing "Korean" origins: A critical review of archaeology, historiography, and racial myth in Korean state-formation theories.* Cambridge, MA: Harvard University Press.

Paine, R. 1994. *Herds of the tundra: A portrait of Saami reindeer pastoralism.* Washington, D.C.: Smithsonian Institution Press.

Palmer, D., and D. Groves. 2000. A Dialogue on identity, intersubjectivity and ambivalence. *Balayi: Culture, Law and Colonisation* 1(2): 19–38.

Paradies, Y. C. 2005. Affirmative action and equity in Aboriginal and Torres Strait Islander health. *Medical Journal of Australia* 183(5): 269–70.

Paradies, Y. C. 2006a. Whitening race: Essays in social and cultural criticism (book review). *Anthropological Forum* 16(2): 197–99.

———. 2006b. Beyond black and white: Essentialism, hybridity, and indigeneity. *Journal of Sociology* 42(4): 355–67.

Pardo, J. 2000. The development of Empuries, Spain, as a visitor-friendly archaeological site. In *Archaeological displays and the public,* ed. P. M. McManus, 13–27. London: University College London.

Pardoe, C. 1990. Sharing the past: Aboriginal influence on archaeological practice, a case study from New South Wales. *Aboriginal History* 14: 208–23.

Parker Pearson, M., and Ramilisonina. 2004. Public archaeology and Indigenous communities. In *Public archaeology,* ed. N. Merriman, 224–39. London: Routledge.

Parkipuny, M. L. 1994. Native leaders address the United Nations: Moringe L. Parkipuny, KIPOC (Africa). In *Voice of Indigenous peoples: Native people address the United Nations,* ed. A. Ewen, for the Native American Council of New York City, 77–81. Santa Fe, NM: Clear Light Publishers.

Parks Canada. 2010. *Unearthing the law: Archaeological legislation on lands in Canada.* www.pc.gc.ca/eng/docs/r/pfa-fap/index.aspx (accessed March 31, 2010).

Parry, M. L., O. F. Canziani, J. P. Palutikof, P. J. van der Linden, and C. E. Hanson, eds. 2007. *Contribution of Working Group II to the fourth assessment report of the Intergovernmental Panel on Climate Change: Impacts, adaptation, vulnerability,* www.ipcc.ch/publications_and_data/ar4/wg2/en/contents.html (accessed February 11, 2010).

Passes, A. 1998. The hearer, the hunter and the Agouti head: Aspects of intercommunication and conviviality among the Pa'ikwene (Palikur) of French Guiana. Ph.D. diss., Department of Anthropology, University of St. Andrews, U.K.

Patten, L. H., and Associates. 2006. Mi'kmawey Debert Cultural Centre feasibility study. Manuscript on file at the Confederacy of Mainland Mi'kmaq, Truro, Nova Scotia.

Paul, C. 2007. The science of a Mi'kmaq legend. *Mi'kmaq-Maliseet Nation News* May 2007: 24.

Peacock, S. 1998. Putting down roots: The emergence of wild food production on the Canadian Plateau. Ph.D. diss., University of Victoria, Victoria, B.C., Canada.

Pearson, M. D. 2000. Give me back my people's bones: Repatriation and reburial of American Indian skeletal remains in Iowa. In *Perspectives on American Indians in Iowa: An expanded edition,* eds. G. Bataille, D. M. Gradwohl, and C. L. P. Silet, 131–41. Iowa City: University of Iowa Press.

Pels, P. 1993. Critical matters. Interactions between missionaries and Waluguru in colonial Tanganyika, 1930–1961. Ph.D. diss., University of Amsterdam.

Perkins, M. 2004. False whiteness: "Passing" and the stolen generations. In *Whitening race: Essays in social and cultural criticism,* ed. A. Moreton-Robinson, 164–75. Canberra: Aboriginal Studies Press.

Perry, J. E. 2004. Authentic learning in field schools: Preparing future members of the archaeological community. *World Archaeology* 36(2): 236–60.

Phillips, J. E. 2000. *Myos Hormos, Quseir al-Qadim: A plain language report of the 2000 field season.* Department of Archaeology, University of Southampton and Quseir Heritage Preservation Society.

———. 2001a. *Quseir al-Qadim: A short introduction to the ancient trading port of the Red Sea.* Department of Archaeology, University of Southampton and Quseir Heritage Preservation Society.

———. 2001b. Object lifeways: "Archaeological" objects, collaborative field methods and strategies for presenting the past at Quseir, Egypt. Master's diss., Department of Archaeology, University of Southampton.

———. forthcoming. *Quseir al-Qadim: A guide.* Department of Archaeology, University of Southampton and Quseir Heritage Preservation Society.

Pi-Sunyer, O., R. B. Thomas, and M. Daltabuit. 1999. *Tourism and Maya society in Quintana Roo, Mexico.* Latin American Studies Consortium of New England Occasional Paper No. 17. Storrs: Center for Latin American and Caribbean Studies, University of Connecticut.

Portes, A. 1998. Social capital: Its origins and applications in modern sociology. *Annual Review of Sociology* 24: 1–24.

Powell, S., C. E. Garza, and A. Hendricks. 1993. Ethics and ownership of the past: The reburial and repatriation controversy. *Archaeological Method and Theory* 5:1–42.

Pred, A. 1990. *Making histories and constructing human geographies.* Boulder, CO: Westview Press.

Preston, D. 1997. The lost man. *New Yorker* 73(16): 70–81.

———. 1998. Skin and bones. *New Yorker* 73(46): 53.

Preston, S. 1954. The clans. In *Navajo historical selections,* eds. R. Young and W. Morgan, 23–29, 98–102. Phoenix: Bureau of Indian Affairs, Phoenix Indian School Print Shop.

Price, R. 1983. *First time: The historical vision of an Afro-American people.* Baltimore: Johns Hopkins University Press.

Prickett, N. 1990. *Historic Taranaki: An archaeological guide.* Wellington, N.Z.: GP Books.

Purcell, L. 2002. *Black chicks talking.* Sydney: Hodder Headline Australia.

Purdie, N., P. Tripcony, G. Boulton-Lewis, J. Fanshawe, and A. Gunston. 2000. *Positive self-identity for Indigenous students and its relationship to school outcomes.* Brisbane: Commonwealth of Australia.

Pwiti, G. 1996. Let the ancestor rest in peace? New challenges for cultural heritage management in Zimbabwe. *Conservation and Management of Archaeological Sites* 1: 151–60.

Pyburn, K. A. 1999. Native American religion versus archaeological science: A pernicious dichotomy revisited. *Journal of Science and Engineering Ethics* 5: 355–66.

Raimbault, M., and K. Sanogo, eds. 1991. *Recherches archéologiques au Mali.* Paris: ACCT Karthala.

Rambo, E. 1994. *Colonial Ireland in Medieval English literature.* Selinsgrove, PA: Susquehanna University Press.

Rand, S. T. 1917 [1893]. *Legends of the Micmacs*. New York: Johnson Reprint Corporation.

Rappaport, J. 1981. Mesianismo y las transformaciones de símbolos Mesiánicos en Tierrandentro. *Revista Colombiana de Antropología* 23: 365–413.

———. 1989. Geography and historical understanding in indigenous Columbia. In *Who needs the past? Indigenous values and archaeology,* ed. R. Layton, 84–94. London: Unwin Hyman.

———. 1990. *The politics of memory: Native historical interpretation in the Colombian Andes*. Cambridge: Cambridge University Press.

Ravesloot, J. C. 1990. On the treatment and reburial of human remains: The San Xavier Project, Tucson, Arizona. *American Indian Quarterly* 14(1): 35–50.

Register of Professional Archaeologists. 2002. www.rpanet.org/about.htm (accessed April 2002).

Reid, D. M. 1985. Indigenous Egyptology: The decolonisation of a profession? *Journal of the American Oriental Society* 105(2): 233–46.

———. 1997. Nationalizing the Pharaonic past: Egyptology, imperialism, and Egyptian nationalism 1922–1952. In *Rethinking nationalism in the Arab Middle East,* eds. I. Gershoni and J. Jankowski, 127–35. New York: Columbia University Press.

———. 2001. *Whose pharaohs? Museums, archaeology, and Egyptian national identity from Napoleon to World War I*. Berkeley and Los Angeles: University of California Press.

Reid, J. J. 1992. Editor's corner: Recent findings on North American prehistory. *American Antiquity* 57: 195.

Reimer, R. 2001. Extreme archaeology: The results of investigations at high elevations in the Northwest. Master's thesis, Department of Archaeology, Simon Fraser University, Burnaby, B.C.

Reissner, R. A. 1983. *El indio en los diccionarios. Exégesis léxzica de un estereritipo*. México, D.F.: Instituto Nacional Indigenista.

Ridgway, D. 1990. The first western Greeks and their neighbours 1935–1985. In *Greek colonists and native populations,* ed. J. P. Descoeudres, 61–72. Canberra: Clarendon Press (Proceedings of the first Australian congress of Classical Archaeology held in honour of Emeritus Professor A.D. Trendall, Sydney, 9–14 July 1985).

Riley, M., ed. 2004. *Indigenous intellectual property rights*. Walnut Creek, CA: AltaMira Press.

Riley-Mundine, L. 1998. An Aboriginal perspective to Australian archaeology. Paper presented to the Department of Archaeology, University of New England.

Ritchie, D. 1993. Principles and practice of site protection laws in Australia. In *Sacred sites, sacred places,* eds. D. L. Carmichael, J. Hubert, B. Reeves, and A. Schanche, 227–44. London: Routledge.

Rizvi, U. Z. 2008. Decolonizing methodologies as strategies of practice: Operationalizing the postcolonial critique in the archaeology of Rajasthan. In

Archaeology and the postcolonial critique, eds. M. Liebmann and U. Z. Rizvi, 109–27. Lanham, MD: AltaMira Press.

Roberts, A. 2003. Knowledge, power and voice: An investigation of indigenous South Australian perspectives of archaeology. Ph.D. diss., Flinders University, Adelaide, Australia.

Roberts, A., S. Hemming, T. Trevorrow, G. Trevorrow, M. Rigney, G. Rigney, L. Agius, and R. Agius. 2005. Nukun and kungun Ngarrindjeri Ruwe (Look and Listen to Ngarrindjeri Country): An investigation of Ngarrindjeri perspectives of archaeology in relation to native title and heritage matters. *Australian Aboriginal Studies* 1: 45–53.

Roberts, L. 1997. *From knowledge to narrative: Educators and the changing museum.* Washington, D.C.: Smithsonian Institute.

Roberts, R. M., and P. Wills. 1998. Understanding Maori epistemology: A scientific perspective. In *Tribal epistemologies,* ed. H. Wautischer, 43–77. Sydney: Ashgate.

Robertshaw, P. 1990. The development of archaeology in East Africa. In *A history of African archaeology,* P. Robertshaw, ed. 78–94. London: James Currey.

Robinson, M. P. 1996. Shampoo archaeology: Towards a participatory action research approach in civil society. *The Canadian Journal of Native Studies* 16(1): 125–38.

Roh, H. J. 1996. The Bronze Age. In *Hanguk minjok-ui giwon-gwa hyeongseong (The origin of Korean ethnicity and its formation),* 119–83. Seoul: Sohwa.

Roman, Y. 2000. The young men of Gibeon. *Eretz* 70: 47.

Roosevelt, A. 1991. *Moundbuilders of the Amazon: Geophysical archaeology on Marajó Island, Brazil.* San Diego: Academic Press.

Rose, D. B. 2001. The silence and power of women. In *Words and silences: Aboriginal women, politics and land,* ed. P. Brock, 92–116. Sydney: Allen and Unwin.

Rose, D. B., and A. Clarke, eds. 1997. *Tracking knowledge in North Australian landscapes: Studies in indigenous and settler ecological knowledge systems.* Darwin, Northern Territory: North Australia Research Unit.

Rose, G. 1993. *Feminist geography.* Cambridge: Polity Press.

Rose, J. C., T. J. Green, and V. D. Green. 1996. NAGPRA is forever: Osteology and the repatriation of skeletons. *Annual Review of Anthropology* 25: 81–103.

Rosenmeier, L. M., R. Stea, G. Brewster, and G. Gloade. 2006. Recent work at the Debert Belmont sites. Paper presented at the 39th Annual Meeting of the Canadian Archaeological Association, Toronto, Ontario.

Ross, K. 1999. *Population issues, Indigenous Australians.* Canberra: Commonwealth of Australia.

Rostain, S. 1994. *L'occupation Amerindienne ancienne du littoral de Guyane.* Ph.D. diss., Center de Recherche en Archaeologie Precolombienne, Université de Paris I, Paris, France.

Rothschild, N. 2003. *Colonial encounters in a Native American landscape: The Spanish and Dutch in North America.* Washington, D.C.: Smithsonian Institution Press.

Rubertone, P. E. 2001. *Grave undertakings: An archaeology of Roger Williams and the Naragansett Indians.* Washington, D.C.: Smithsonian Institute Press.

Russell, L. 2001. *Savage imaginings: Historical and contemporary constructions of Australian Aboriginalities.* Melbourne: Australian Scholarly Publishing.

———. 2002. *A little bird told me.* St. Leonards, N.S.W.: Allen and Unwin.

Russo, A. 1991. We cannot live without our lives. In *Third world women and the politics of feminism,* ed. C. T. Mohanty, A. Russo, and L. Torres, 297–313. Bloomington and Indianapolis: Indiana University Press.

Ryser, R. 1998. Observations on "self" and "knowing." In *Tribal epistemologies,* ed. H. Wautischer, 17–30. Sydney: Ashgate.

SA (South Australian) Murray-Darling Basin Integrated Natural Resource Management Group. 2002. *Integrated natural resource management plan for the Lower Murray Region.* Adelaide, South Australia.

Sabbioni, J., K. Schaffer, and S. Smith. 1998. *Indigenous Australian voices.* New Brunswick, NJ: Rutgers University Press.

Sable, T. 2010. Legends as maps. In *Ta'n Wetapeksi'k: Understanding from where we come,* ed. T. Bernard. Truro, Nova Scotia: Eastern Woodland Publishing.

Sahlins, M. 1999. What is anthropological enlightenment? Some lessons of the twentieth century. *Annual Reviews in Anthropology* 29: i–xxiii.

Said, E. W. 1978. *Orientalism.* New York: Vintage Books.

———. 1985. Opponents, audiences, constituencies, and community. In *Postmodern culture,* ed. H. Foster, 135–59. London: Pluto Press.

———. 1989. Representing the colonised: Anthropology's interlocutors. *Critical Inquiry,* 15: 205–25.

———. 1993. *Culture and imperialism.* New York: Knopf.

———. 1994. *Culture and imperialism.* New York: Vintage Books.

———. 1999. Palestine: Memory, invention, and space. In *The landscape of Palestine: Equivocal poetry,* eds. I. Abu-Lughod, R. Heacock, and K. Nashef, 3–30. Birzeit-Palestine: Birzeit University Publications.

Salama, A. M. 1997. Proposed action plan for Quseir. Final draft. The Promotion of Environmentally Sustainable Tourism Project and the United States Agency for International Development.

Salem, H. 2000. Pottery traditions and cultural tradition: A case from traditional Palestinian pottery. Paper presented at the Conference on the Transmission and Assimilation of Culture in the Near East, Council for British Research in the Levant, Jerusalem.

Sanders, E. 2004. An 8-year fight ends over a 9,200 year old man. *The New York Times* 153(52196): F2.

Sanogo, K. 2000. Le cadre chronologique. In *L'archéologie en Afrique de l'ouest: Sahara et Sahel,* ed. R. Vernet, 84–85. Saint-Maur: Editions Sepia.

Saugestad, S. 2001. *The inconvenient indigenous: Remote area development in Botswana, donor assistance, and the first peoples of the Kalahari.* Uppsala, Sweden: Nordic Africa Institute.

Scatamacchia, M. C. M., and C. Baretto. 2000. *Arqueologia.* São Paolo: Fundação Bienal de São Paolo.

Schaap, A. 2005. Reconciliation through a struggle for recognition. Working Paper 2003/12. Centre for Applied Philosophy and Public Ethics, University of Melbourne.

Schadla-Hall, T. 1999. Editorial: Public archaeology. *European Journal of Archaeology* 2(2): 147–58.

Scham, S. 2001. The archaeology of the disenfranchised. *Journal of Archaeological Method and Theory* 8: 183–213.

Scheinin, M. 2000. The right to enjoy a distinct culture: Indigenous and competing uses of land. In *The jurisprudence of human rights law: A comparative interpretive approach,* eds. T. Orlin, A. Rosas, and M. Scheinin. Turku, Finland: Institute for Human Rights, Åbo Akademi University.

Scheper-Hughes, N. 1995. The primacy of the ethical: Propositions for a militant anthropology. *Current Anthropology* 36: 409–20.

Schmidt, P. R. 1978. *Historical archaeology: A structural approach in an African culture.* Westport, CT: Greenwood Press.

———. 1983. An alternative to a strictly materialist perspective: A review of historical archaeology, ethnoarchaeology, and symbolic approaches in African archaeology. *American Antiquity* 48: 62–79.

———. 1988. Eastern expressions of the "Mwitu" tradition: Early Iron Age industry in the Usambara Mountains of Tanzania. *Nyame Akuma* 30: 36–37.

———. 1994. Historical ecology and landscape transformations in eastern equatorial Africa. In *Historical ecology: Cultural knowledge and changing landscapes,* ed. C. Crumley, 99–125. Santa Fe: School of American Research Press.

———. 1995. Using archaeology to remake history in Africa. In *Making alterative histories: The practice of archaeology and history in non-Western settings,* eds. P. R. Schmidt and T. C. Patterson, 119–48. Santa Fe, NM: School of American Research Press.

Schmidt, P. R., and D. H. Avery. 1978. Complex iron smelting and prehistoric culture in Tanzania. *Science* 201: 85–99.

Schmidt, P. R., and S. T. Childs. 1995. Ancient African iron production. *American Scientist* 83: 524–33.

Schmidt, P. R., and N. J. Karoma. 1987. Preliminary report: Archaeological survey of the western Usambara Mountains, west and southwest of Lushoto, Tanga region, and Kilwa, Kilwa coastal zone, Lindi region. Archaeology Unit, University of Dar es Salaam, Tanzania.

Schmidt, P. R., and R. J. McIntosh. 1996. *Plundering Africa's past.* Bloomington: Indiana University Press.

Schmidt, P. R., and T. C. Patterson, eds. 1995. *Making alterative histories: The practice of archaeology and history in non-Western settings.* Santa Fe, NM: School of American Research Press.

Schrire, C. 1995. *Digging through darkness: Chronicles of an archaeologist.* Charlottesville: University of Virginia Press.

Schwab, J. 1994. Ambiguity, style and kinship in Adelaide Aboriginal identity. In *Being Black: Aboriginal cultures in "settled" Australia,* ed. I. Keen, 77–95. Canberra: Aboriginal Studies Press.

Scott, J. W. 1991. The evidence of experience. *Critical Inquiry* 17: 773–97.

———. 1992a. Experience. In *Feminists theorize the political,* eds. J. Butler and J. W. Scott, 22–40. New York: Routledge.

———. 1992b. Multiculturalism and the politics of identity. *October* 61: 12–19.

Shackley, M. 1997. Tourism and the management of cultural resources in the Pays Dogon, Mali. *International Journal of Heritage Studies* 3(1): 17–27.

Shankland, D. 1996. Çatalhöyük: The anthropology of an archaeological presence. In *On the surface: Çatalhöyük 1993–1985,* ed. I. Hodder, 349–58. Cambridge: McDonald Institute for Archaeological Research and the British Institute of Archaeology at Ankara.

———. 1999. Integrating the past: Folklore, mounds and people at Çatalhöyük. In *Archaeology and folklore,* eds. A. Gazin-Schwartz and C. Holtorf, 139–57. London: Routledge.

Shanks, M. 1996. *Classical archaeology of Greece. Experiences of the discipline.* London: Routledge.

———. 2009. *The archaeological imagination.* Walnut Creek, CA: Left Coast Press.

Sharp, A. 1991. *Justice and the Maori: Maori claims in New Zealand political argument in the 1980s.* Auckland: Oxford University Press.

Shaw, L. C., E. Savulis, M. T. Mulholland, and G. P. Nicholas. 1987. *Archaeological locational survey in the central Berkshires, Pittsfield, Massachusetts.* Report no. 18. Amherst, MA: University of Massachusetts Archaeological Services.

Sheldon, R. 1982. Romanizzazione, acculturazione e resistenza: Problemi concettuali nella storia del Nordafrica. *Dialoghi di Archeologia* 4: 102–06.

Shennan, S., ed. 1989. *Archaeological approaches to cultural identity.* London: Unwin Hyman.

Shepherd, N. 2002. The politics of archaeology in Africa. *Annual Review of Anthropology* 31: 189–209.

———. 2005. From "one world archaeology" to one world, many archaeologies. *Archaeologies* 1(1): 1–6.

Shin, H. 1998. 10 mannyeonjeon byeo balgul (Rice 100,000 years old excavated). *Chosun llbo* March 17: 17.

Shirai, S. 1887. Korobokkur hatashite Hokkaido ni sumishiya (Have Korobokkru ever inhabited Hokkaido). *Jinruigak-kai Houkoku (The Bulletin of the Tokyo Anthropological Society)* 2(11): 70–82.

Shore, C. 1995. Imagining the new Europe: Identity and heritage in European community discourse. In *Cultural identity and archaeology: The construction of European communities,* eds. P. Graves-Brown, S. Jones, and C. Gamble, 96–115. London: Routledge.

Shostak, M. 1981. *Nisa: The life and words of a !Kung woman.* Cambridge, MA: Harvard University Press.

———. 2000. *Return to Nisa.* Cambridge, MA: Harvard University Press.

Shotridge, L. 1920. Ghost of courageous adventurer. *The Museum Journal, University of Pennsylvania Museum* 11(1): 11–26.

Silberman, N. A. 1998. Whose game is it anyway? The political and social transformations of American biblical archaeology. In *Archaeology under fire: Nationalism, politics, and heritage in the Eastern Mediterranean and Middle East,* ed. L. Meskell, 175–88. London: Routledge.

Siller, B. 2005. Who's indigenous? Whose archaeology? *Public Archaeology* 4: 71–94.

Silliman, S. W., ed. 2008. *Collaborating at the trowel's edge: Teaching and learning in Indigenous archaeology.* Amerind Studies in Archaeology 2. University of Arizona Press: Tucson.

Silliman, S. W., and K. H. Sebastian Dring. 2008. Working on pasts for futures: Eastern Pequot field school archaeology in Connecticut. In *Collaborating at the trowel's edge: Teaching and learning in Indigenous archaeology,* ed. S. W. Silliman, 67–76. Tucson: University of Arizona Press.

Silverman, H. 2002. Touring ancient times: The present and the presented past in contemporary Peru. *American Anthropologist* 104(3): 881–902.

Simpson, L. R. 1999. The construction of traditional ecological knowledge: Issues, implications and insights. Ph.D. diss., University of Manitoba, Winnepeg, Manitoba, Canada.

Smallcombe, S. 2000. On display for its aesthetic beauty: How Western institutions fabricate knowledge about Aboriginal cultural heritage. In *Political theory and the rights of Indigenous peoples,* eds. D. Ivison, P. Patton, W. Sanders, 152–62. Cambridge: Cambridge University Press.

Smith, A. 1998. Landscapes of power: The archaeology of 19th-century Irish ordnance survey maps. *Archaeological Dialogues* 5(1): 69–84.

———. 2008. Written off the map: Cleared landscapes of Medieval Ireland. In *Landscapes of clearance: Archaeological and anthropological perspectives,* eds. A. Smith and A. Gazin-Schwartz, 49–70. Walnut Creek, CA: Left Coast Press.

Smith, C., and H. Burke. 2003. In the spirit of the code. In *Ethical issues in archaeology,* eds. L. J. Zimmerman, K. D. Vitelli, and J. Hollowell-Zimmer, 177–97. Walnut Creek, CA: AltaMira Press.

Smith, C., and G. Jackson. 2006. Decolonizing Indigenous archaeology: Developments from down under. *American Indian Quarterly* 30(3&4): 311–49.

Smith, C., and G. K. Ward, eds. 2000. *Indigenous cultures in an interconnected world.* Sydney: Allen and Unwin.

Smith, C., and H. M. Wobst, eds. 2005a. *Indigenous archaeologies: Decolonizing theory and practice.* London: Routledge.

———. 2005b. Archaeology for social justice. In *Indigenous archaeologies: Decolonizing theory and practice,* eds. C. Smith and H. M. Wobst, 390–92. London: Routledge.

Smith, L. T. 1999. *Decolonizing methodologies: Research and Indigenous peoples.* London: Zed Books.

Smith, S. P. 1910. *History and traditions of the Maoris of the West Coast North Island of New Zealand.* New Plymouth: Thomas Avery.

Snead, J. 2002. Time and the Tano: Archaeology, history and interpretation in New Mexico's Galisteo. Between materiality and interpretation: Archaeological confessions. Paper presented at the annual meeting of the Society for American Archaeology, Denver, Colorado.

Snow, D. 1980. *The archaeology of New England.* New York: Academic Press.

Soja, E. W. 1989. *Postmodern geographies.* London: Verso.

Specht, J., and C. MacLulich. 2000. Changes and challenges: The Australian Museum and indigenous communities. In *Archaeological displays and the public,* ed. P. M. McManus, 39–63. London: University College London.

Spector, J. 1993. *What this awl means: Feminist archaeology in a Wahpeton Dakota village.* Minneapolis: Minnesota Historical Society Press.

Speiss, A. 1984. Arctic garbage and New England Paleo-Indians: The single occupation option. *Archaeology of Eastern North America* 12: 280–85.

Stanley, L., and S. Wise. 1993. *Breaking out again: Feminist ontology and epistemology.* London: Routledge.

Stannar, W. H. H. 1998. The dreaming. In *Traditional Aboriginal society* (2nd edition), ed. W. H. Edwards, 227–38. South Yarra: Macmillan Australia.

Starn, O. 1994. Rethinking the politics of anthropology: The case of the Andes. *Current Anthropology* 35(1): 13–38.

Stea, R. R. 2006. Geology and the paleoenvironmental reconstruction of the Debert/Belmont site. Report on file at the Confederacy of Mainland Mi'kmaq, Truro, Nova Scotia.

Stea, R. R., and R. J. Mott. 1989. Deglaciation environments and evidence for glaciers of Younger Dryas age in Nova Scotia, Canada. *Boreas* 18(2): 169–87.

———. 1998. Deglaciation of Nova Scotia: Stratigraphy and chronology of lake sediment cores and buried organic sections. *Géographie physique et Quaternaire* 51(1): 3–21.

Stewart, A. 1994. Report of a preliminary investigation through archaeology and oral history of the site of Piqqiq (150X), a caribou water-crossing on the Kazan River, District of Keewatin, Northwest Territories. Report on file, Federal Archaeology Office, Parks Canada, Hull, Quebec.

Stewart, A., D. Keith, and J. Scottie. 2004. Caribou crossings and cultural meanings: Placing traditional knowledge and archaeology in context in an Inuit landscape. *Journal of Archaeological Method and Theory* 11(2): 183–211.

Stewart, A., T. M. Friesen, D. Keith, and L. Henderson. 2000. Archaeology and oral history of Inuit land use on the Kazan River, Nunavut: A feature-based approach. *Arctic* 53: 260–78.

Stocking, G., Jr. 1987. *Victorian anthropology.* London: The Free Press.

Stoler, A. 1989. Rethinking colonial categories: European communities and the boundaries of rule. *Comparative Studies in Society and History* 31: 134–61.

Straus, L. G. 2000. Solutrean settlement of North America? A review of reality. *American Antiquity* 65(2): 219–26.

Straus, L. G., D. J. Meltzer, and T. Goebel. 2005. Ice Age Atlantis? Exploring the Solutrean-Clovis "Connection." *World Archaeology* 37(4): 507–32.

Strickland, R. 1997. *Tonto's revenge.* Albuquerque: University of New Mexico.

Sutton, P. 1994 [1988]. Myth as history, history as myth. In *Being Black: Aboriginal cultures in "settled" Australia,* ed. I. Keen, 251–68. Canberra: Aboriginal Studies Press.

Svensson, T. G. 1997. *The Sámi and their land.* Instituttet for Sammenlignende Kulturforskning, Serie B, 96. Oslo: Novus Forlag.

Swedlund, A., and D. Anderson. 1999. Gordon Creek Woman meets Kennewick Man: New interpretations and protocols regarding the peopling of the Americas. *American Antiquity* 64(4): 569–76.

———. 2003. Gordon Creek Woman meets Spirit Cave Man: A response to comment by Owsley and Jantz. *American Antiquity* 68(1): 161–67.

Swidler, N., K. E. Dongoske, R. Anyon, and A. S. Downer, eds. 1997. *Native Americans and archaeologists: Stepping stones to common ground.* Walnut Creek, CA: AltaMira Press.

Syms, E. L. 1997. Increasing awareness and involvement of Aboriginal people in their heritage preservation: Recent developments at the Manitoba Museum of Man and Nature. In *At a crossroads: Archaeology and the first peoples in Canada,* eds. G. P. Nicholas and T. Andrews, 53–68. Burnaby: Archaeology Press.

Tapsell, P. 1997. The flight of Pareraututu: An investigation of Taonga from a tribal perspective. *Journal of the Polynesian Society* 106: 323–74.

Taranaki Regional Council. 1998. *Proposed regional fresh water plan for Taranaki.* Stratford: Taranaki Regional Council.

Taussig, M. 1987. *Shamanism, colonialism, and the wild man.* Chicago: University of Chicago Press.

Taylor, C. J. 1882. *History of Great Barrington, Massachusetts.* Great Barrington, MA: Clark W. Bryan.

Te Hennepe, S. 1993. Issues of respect: Reflections of First Nations students' experiences in postsecondary anthropology classrooms. *Canadian Journal of Native Education (Researching with Mutual Respect)* 20(2): 193–259.

Temm, P. 1990. *The Waitangi Tribunal: The conscience of the nation.* Auckland: Random Century.

Thébert, Y. 1978. Romanisation et déromanisation en Afrique: Histoire décolonisée ou histoire inversée? *Annales ESC* 33: 65–82.

Thomas, D. H. 2000. *Skull wars, Kennewick Man, archaeology, and the battle for Native American identity.* New York: Basic Books.

Thomas, N. 1994. *Colonialism's culture: Anthropology, travel and government.* Princeton, NJ: Princeton University Press.

Thomas, P. A. 1976. Contrasting subsistence strategies and land use as factors for understanding Indian-White relations in New England. *Ethnohistory* 23(1): 1–18.

Thorbahn, P. F. 1988. Where are the Late Woodland villages in southern New England? *Bulletin of the Massachusetts Archaeological Society* 49(2): 46–57.

Tilley, C. 1994. *The phenomenology of landscape.* Oxford: Berg.

Tilley, C., S. Hamilton, and B. Bender. 2001. Art and the re-presentation of the past. *Journal of the Royal Anthropological Institute* 6: 35–62.

Tindale, N. B. 1974. *Aboriginal tribes of Australia: Their terrain, environmental controls, distribution, limits, and proper names.* Canberra: Australian National University Press.

Todorov, T. 1987. *La conquista de América: El problema del otro.* Buenos Aires: Siglo XXI.

Torrence, R., and A. Clarke. 2000. *The archaeology of difference: Negotiating cross-cultural engagements in Oceania.* London: Routledge.

Toumey, Christopher P. 1996. *Conjuring science: Scientific symbols and cultural meanings in American life.* New Brunswick, NJ: Rutgers University.

Trask, H. K. 1993. *From a Native daughter: Colonialism and sovereignty in Hawai'i. Monroe,* ME: Common Courage Press.

Trigger, B. G. 1984. Alternative archaeologies: Nationalist, colonialist, imperialist. *Man* 19: 355–70.

———. 1990. The history of African archaeology in world perspective. In *A history of African archaeology,* ed. P. Robertshaw, 309–19. London: James Currey.

Tringham, R. 1991. Households with faces: The challenge of gender in prehistoric architectural remains. In *Engendering archaeology: Women and prehistory,* eds. J. Gero and M. Conkey, 93–131. Oxford: Basil Blackwell.

Trope, J. F., and W. R. Echo-Hawk. 2000 [1992]. The Native American Grave Protection and Repatriation Act: Background and legislative history. In *Repatriation reader: Who owns American Indian remains?,* ed. D. A. Mihesuah, 123–68. Lincoln: University of Nebraska Press.

Tsosie, R. 1997. Indigenous rights and archaeology. In *Native Americans and archaeologists: Stepping stones to common ground,* eds. N. Swidler, K. E. Dongoske, R. Anyon, and A. S. Downer, 64–76. Walnut Creek, CA: AltaMira Press.

Tsuboi, S. 1887. Korobokkur Hokkaido ni sumishinarubeshi (Koropokgru seems to have inhabited in Hokkaido). *Jinruigak-kai Houkoku (The Bulletin of the Tokyo Anthropological Society)* 2(12): 93–97.

Two Bears, D. 2000. A Navajo student's perception: Anthropology and the Navajo Nation Archaeology Department Student Training Program. In *Working together: Native Americans and archaeologists,* eds. K. E. Dongoske, M. Aldenderfer, and K. Doehner, 15–22. Washington, D.C.: Society for American Archaeology.

———. 2006. Navajo archaeologist is not an oxymoron: A tribal archaeologist's experience. *American Indian Quarterly* 30(3&4): 381–87.

Ucko, P. J. 2000. Enlivening a "dead" past. *Conservation and Management of Archaeological Sites* 4: 69–92.

Udagawa, H. 2001. *Ainu Koukogaku Kenkyu Jyoron (Introduction to Ainu archaeological studies).* Sapporo: Shuppan Hokkaido Kikaku Center.

Ulm, S. 2006. *Coastal themes: Archaeology of the southern Curtis Coast, Queensland.* Terra Australis 24. Canberra: Australian National University.

United Nations. 2007. Declaration on the Rights of Indigenous Peoples, adopted by the General Assembly September 13, 2007, www.un.org/esa/socdev/unpfii/en/declaration.html (accessed January 30, 2010).

United Nations Secretariat of the Permanent Forum on Indigenous Issues. 2004. The concept of Indigenous Peoples. PFII/2004/WS.1/3. Background Paper Prepared for Workshop on Data Collection and Disaggregation for Indigenous Peoples, January 19–21, New York.

Urud, A. M.1994. Native leaders address the United Nations: Anderson Muutang Urud, Sarawak Indigenous Peoples' Alliance (Southeast Asia). In *Voice of Indigenous peoples: Native people address the United Nations,* ed. A. Ewen, for the Native American Council of New York City, 103–07. Santa Fe, NM: Clear Light Publishers.

U.S. Department of the Interior National Park Service Rocky Mountain Region. 1995. Final climbing management plan: Finding of no significant impact, February 1995 Devils Tower National Monument Crook Country, Wyoming.

Van Dommelen, Peter. 1997. Colonial constructs: Colonialism and archaeology in the Mediterranean. *World Archaeology* 28(3): 305–23.

———. 1998. Punic persistence: Colonialism and cultural identity in Roman Sardinia. In *Cultural identity in the Roman Empire,* eds. J. Berry and R. Laurence, 25–48. London: Routledge.

van Vilsteren, V. 2003. Holy smoke and bad vibrations. Draft article for *Museumkrant*. Netherlands.

Van Willigen, J. 2002. *Applied anthropology: An introduction* (3rd edition). Westport, CT: Bergin and Garvey.

Vansina, J. 1985. *Oral tradition as history.* London: James Curry and Heinemann.

Vasco, L. G. 1992. Arquelogía e identidad: El caso Guambiano. In *Arquelogía en América Latina Hoy,* ed. G. Politis, 176–91. Bogotá: Fondo de Promoción de la Cultura.

Vasco, L. G., A. Dagua, and M. Aranda. 1993. En el segundo día la gente grande (numisak) sembró la aytridad y las plantas con su jugo, bebió el sentido. In *Encrucijadas de Colombia Amerindia,* ed. F. Correa, 9–48. Bogotá: Instituto Colombiano de Antropología.

Villalobos, C. A. 2004. La diversidad emergente: Complejidad y metáforas textuales en la investigación arqueológica de Sonora, México. Tesis de maestro en antropología, Universidad Nacional Autónoma de México, Ciudad de México.

Vizenor, G. R. 1984. *The people named the Chippewa: Narrative histories.* Minneapolis: University of Minnesota Press.

Voss, B. L. 2000. Colonial sex: Archaeology, structured space and sexuality in Alta California's Spanish-colonial missions. In *Archaeologies of sexuality,* eds. R. A. Schmidt and B. L. Voss, 35–61. London: Routledge.

Waitangi Tribunal. 1996. The *Taranaki Report: Kaupapa Tuatahi.* Waitangi Tribunal Report WAI 143. Wellington: GP Publications.

Wallis, L., S. Hemming, and C. Wilson. 2006. *The Warnung (Hack's Point) Old People's Place Project: A collaborative approach to archaeological survey, research management and planning*. Confidential Report Prepared for the Ngarrindjeri Heritage Committee (NHC), Ngarrindjeri Native Title and Management Committee (NNTMC) and Ngarrindjeri Tendi (NT).

Watanabe, H. 1972. *The Ainu ecosystem: Environment and group structure.* Tokyo: University of Tokyo Press.

Watase, S. 1886. Sapporo kinkou pitto sonohoka koseki no koto (The remains of pit dwelling and other archaeological sites around Sapporo). *Jinruigakkai Houkoku (The Bulletin of the Tokyo Anthropological Society)*1: 8–14.

Watkins, J. 2000. *Indigenous archaeology: American Indian values and scientific practice.* Walnut Creek, CA: AltaMira Press.

———. 2003. Beyond the margin: American Indians, First Nations, and archaeology in North America. *American Antiquity* 68(2): 273–85.

———. 2005. Through wary eyes: Indigenous perspectives on archaeology. *Annual Review of Anthropology* 34: 429–49.

Watkins, J., L. Goldstein, K. Vitelli, and L. Jenkins. 1995. Accountability: Responsibilities of archaeologists to other interest groups. In *Ethics in American archaeology: Challenges for the 1990s,* eds. M. Lynott and A. Wylie, 33–37. Washington, D.C.: Society for American Archaeology.

Watkins, J., A. K. Pyburn, and P. Cressey. 2000. Community relations: What the practicing archaeologist needs to know to work effectively with local and/or descendant communities. In *Teaching archaeology in the twenty-first century,* eds. S. J. Bender and G. Smith, 73–81. Washington, D.C.: Society for American Archaeology.

Watson, I. 2002. *Looking at you looking at me: Aboriginal culture and history of the Southeast of South Australia,* Vol. 1. History Trust of South Australia, SA.

Webb, S. 1987. Reburying Australian skeletons. *Antiquity* 61: 292–96.

Werbner, P., and T. Modood, eds. 1997. *Debating cultural hybridity: Multicultural identities and the politics of anti-racism.* London: Zed Books.

Wetherbee, M., and N. Taylor. 1986. *Legend of the bushwacker basket.* Sanbornton, NH: Martha Wetherbee Basket Shop.

Whitehouse, D. 2003. World's "oldest" rice found. *BBC News Online* October 21, 2003. http://news.bbc.co.ukf2Jhi/science/nature/3207552.stm.

Whitley, P. M. 2002. Archaeology and oral tradition: The scientific importance of dialogue. *American Antiquity* 67: 405–15.

Whyte, W. F. 1986. Interviewing in field research. In *Field research: A sourcebook and field manual,* ed. R. G. Burgess, 111–22. London: Allen and Unwin.

Wilford, J. N. 1999. New answers to an old question: Who got here first? *The New York Times* 149(51701): F1.

Wilk, R. R. 1985. The ancient Maya and the political present. *Journal of Anthropological Research* 41(3): 307–26.

Will, D. 1978. Opinion in re: Common-law leases of tribal land, Attorney General's Chambers, January 23. Gabarone, Botswana: Land Development Committee.

Williams, D. V. 1989. Te Tiriti o Waitangi: Unique relationship between Crown and Tangaga Wehnua? In *Waitangi: Maori and Pakeha perspectives on the*

Treaty of Waitangi, ed. I. H. Kawharu, 4–91. Auckland: Oxford University Press.

Williams, R. 1983. *Keywords.* New York: Oxford University Press.

Williams, R. A. 1989–1990. Gendered checks and balances: Understanding the legacy of white patriarchy in an American Indian cultural context. *Georgia Law Review* 1989–1990: 1019–44.

Williamson, C., and R. Harrison. 2002. Introduction: "Too many Captain Cooks?" An archaeology of Aboriginal Australia after 1788. In *After Captain Cook: The archaeology of the recent Indigenous past in Australia,* ed. R. Harrison and C. Williamson, 1–13. Sydney: Archaeological Computing Laboratory, University of Sydney.

Willmot, E. 1986. The dragon principle. In *Who owns the past,* ed. I. McBryde, 41–48. Oxford: Oxford University Press.

Wilson, C. 2005. Return of the Ngarrindjeri: Repatriating Old People back to country. Unpublished B.Arch. (Hons.) Thesis, Department of Archaeology, Flinders University.

———. 2007. Indigenous research and archaeology: Transformative practice in/with/for the Ngarrindjeri community. *Archaeologies: Journal of the World Archaeological Congress* 3(3): 320–34.

Wilson, R. 1984. A case for the re-evaluation of Maori art. *Art Galleries and Museums Association of New Zealand Journal* 15(4): 18–19.

Wobst, H. M. 1983. We can't see the forest for the trees: Sampling and the shapes of archaeological distributions. In *Archaeological hammers and theories,* eds. J. A. Moore and A. S. Keene, 37–85. New York: Academic Press.

———. 1991. The invention of Europe, prehistory, and the utility of Columbus. Paper presented in Symposium on Anthropological Interlocutors—Martin Bernal at 90th Annual Meeting of the American Anthropological Association, Chicago, IL.

———. 2004. Indigenous archaeologies in world-wide perspective: Who is in charge and who benefits? Paper presented at Eleventh Annual Deerfield—Wellesley Symposium, Historic Deerfield, Deerfield, MA.

———. 2005. Power to the (Indigenous) past and present! Or: The theory and method behind archaeological theory and method. In *Indigenous archaeologies: Decolonizing theory and practice,* eds. C. Smith and H. M. Wobst, 17–32. London: Routledge.

———. 2006. Artifacts as social interference: The politics of spatial scale. In *Confronting scale in archaeology: Issues of theory and practice,* eds. G. Lock and B. Molyneaux, 55–64. Springer Verlag: New York City.

Wobst, H. M., and C. Smith. 1999. Unothering theory and practice in archaeology. Paper presented at the 31st Chacmool Conference on Indigenous People and Archaeology, University of Calgary, Alberta.

———. 2003. "Unothering": Theory and practice in archaeology. In *Indigenous people and archaeology: Proceedings of the 29th annual Chacmool Conference,* eds. T. Peck and E. Siegfried, 211–25. Calgary: Archaeological Association of the University of Calgary.

Wolf, E. R. 1982. *Europe and the people without history.* Berkeley and Los Angeles: University of California Press.

Wolfe, P. 1999. *Settler colonialism and the transformation of anthropology: The politics and poetics of an ethnographic event.* London: Cassell.

Woody, A. 2000. The power of the past in the present: Historic uses of rock art in Nevada. Paper presented at the 64th annual meeting of the Society for American Archaeology, in Philadelphia, Pennsylvania.

Working Group of Indigenous Minorities in Southern Africa (WIMSA). 2001. *Media and research contract of the San of Southern Africa.* Windhoek.

World Archaeological Congress. 1989. Vermillion accord on human remains. www.worldarchaeologicalcongress.org/site/about_ethi.php (accessed March 30, 2010).

———. 1991. First code of ethics. www.worldarchaeologicalcongress.org/site/about_ethi.php#code1 (accessed March 30, 2010).

Wylie, A. 1995. Alternative histories: Epistemic disunity and political integrity. In *Making alternative histories: The practice of archaeology and history in non-Western settings,* eds. P. R. Schmidt and T. C. Patterson, 255–72. Santa Fe, NM: School of American Research Press.

———. 2000. Foreword. In *Working together: Native Americans and archaeologists,* eds. K. E. Dongoske, M. Aldenderfer, and K. Doehner, v–x. Washington, D.C.: Society for American Archaeology.

Wyman, L. 1970. *Blessingway.* Tucson: University of Arizona Press.

Yellowhorn, E. 1996. Indians, archaeology and the changing world. *Native Studies Review* 11(2): 23–50.

———. 2002. Awakening internalist archaeology in the Aboriginal world. Ph.D. diss., Department of Anthropology, McGill University, Montreal.

Yi, S. 1992. Bukhan gogohaksa siron (A preliminary discussion on North Korean archaeology). *Dongbanghakji* 74: 1–74.

———. 2001. Noebugo (On the thunder-axe). *Hanguk gogohakbo (Journal of Korean Archaeological Society)* 44: 151–88.

Yoo, T. J. 2004. Sorori byeopssi chultoji gukga munhwajae jijeong musan (Proposal to register the Sorori site as a national cultural property rejected). *Chosun Ilbo* November 3: A14.

York, A., R. Daly, and C. Arnett. 1993. *They write their dreams on the rock forever: Rock writings in the Stein River valley of British Columbia.* Vancouver: Talonbooks.

Young, M. E. 1980. Women, civilization and the Indian question. In *Clio was a woman: Studies in the history of American women,* eds. M. E. Deutrich and V. C. Purdy, 98–110. Washington, D.C.: Howard University Press.

Zimmerman, L. J. 1989. Made radical by my own. In *Conflicts in the archaeology of living traditions,* ed. R. Layton, 60–67. London: Unwin.

———. 1997. Remythologizing the relationship between Indians and archaeologists. In *Native Americans and archaeologists: Stepping stones to a common ground,* eds. N. Swidler, K. E. Dongoske, R. Anyon, and A. S. Downer, 44–56. Walnut Creek, CA: AltaMira Press.

Zimmerman, L. J. 2001. Usurping Native American voice. In *The future of the past: Archaeologists, Native Americans, and repatriation,* ed. T. L. Bray, 169–84. New York: Garland Publishing.

———. 2005. First, be humble: Working with Indigenous peoples and other descendant communities. In *Indigenous archaeologies: Decolonizing theory and practice,* eds. C. Smith and H. M. Wobst, 284–96. London: Routledge.

———. 2006. Liberating archaeology, liberation archaeologies, and WAC. *Archaeologies* 2(1): 85–95.

Zimmerman, L. J., and R. Echo-Hawk. 1990. Ancient history of the Pawnee Nation: A summary of archaeological and traditional evidence for Pawnee ancestry in the Great Plains. Manuscript on file, Native American Rights Fund, Boulder, Colorado, and Tribal Office of the Pawnee Tribe of Oklahoma, Pawnee, Oklahoma.

Zubrick, S. R., D. M. Lawrence, S. R. Silburn, E. Blair, H. Milroy, and T. Wilkes. 2004. *Western Australian Aboriginal child health survey: The health of Aboriginal children and young people.* Perth: Telethon Institute for Child Health Research.

Zvelebil, M. 1995. Farmers: Our ancestors and the identity of Europe. In *Cultural identity and archaeology: The construction of European communities,* eds. P. Graves-Brown, S. Jones, and C. Gamble, 145–66. London: Routledge.

INDEX

B

D

E

F

G

T

X

Y

Z

About the Editors

Margaret M. Bruchac, of Abenaki descent, is Assistant Professor of Anthropology and Coordinator of Native American and Indigenous Studies at the University of Connecticut. Her research engages with historical landscapes, museum representations, popular memory, and the circulation and repatriation of cultural patrimony. She is also a cultural performer, rooted in Algonkian Indian oral traditions.

Siobhan M. Hart is Visiting Assistant Professor of Anthropology at Binghamton University. Her research focuses on Native American history and archaeology in Northeastern North America with an emphasis on the intersections of heritage work and social justice efforts, particularly confronting historical erasures through archaeological research and community collaborations.

H. Martin Wobst is Professor of Anthropology at the University of Massachusetts, Amherst, where he has taught for almost forty years. His interests include the social articulations of material culture in the past and present, Indigenous Archaeologies, and the theory between archaeological method and archaeology in the interest of historically underprivileged societies and social groups.